MW01025894

BEYOND NATIONS

UT

EVOLVING HOMELANDS IN THE
NORTH ATLANTIC WORLD, 1400–2000

Beyond Nations traces the evolution of "peripheral" ethnic homelands around the North Atlantic, from before transoceanic contact to their current standing in the world political system. For example, "Megumaage," homeland of the Micmac is transformed into the French colony of Acadia, then into the British colony of Nova Scotia, and subsequently into the present Canadian province. John R. Chávez tracks the role of colonialism in the transformation of such lands, but especially the part played by federalism in moving beyond the national, ethnic, and racial conflicts resulting from imperialism.

Significantly, Chávez gives attention to the effects of these processes on the individual mind, arguing that historically federalism has permitted the individual to sustain and balance varying ethnic loyalties regionally, nationally, and globally. *Beyond Nations* concludes with a discussion of an evolving global imagination that takes into account migrations, borderlands, and transnational communities in an increasingly postcolonial and postnational world.

John R. Chávez is currently Professor of History at Southern Methodist University. He is the author of *The Lost Land: The Chicano Image of the Southwest* (1984), which earned him a Pulitzer Prize nomination. Among his other works are *Memories and Migrations: Mapping Boricua and Chicana Histories* (2008), which he coedited with Vicki Ruiz, and *Eastside Landmark: A History of the East Los Angeles Community Union* (1998).

BEYOND NATIONS

EVOLVING HOMELANDS
IN THE NORTH ATLANTIC
WORLD, 1400–2000

JOHN R. CHÁVEZ
Southern Methodist University

CAMBRIDGE
UNIVERSITY PRESS

CAMBRIDGE UNIVERSITY PRESS

Cambridge, New York, Melbourne, Madrid, Cape Town, Singapore, São Paulo, Delhi

Cambridge University Press
32 Avenue of the Americas, New York, NY 10013-2473, USA

www.cambridge.org
Information on this title: www.cambridge.org/9780521736336

First published 2009

Printed in the United States of America

A catalog record for this publication is available from the British Library.

Library of Congress Cataloging in Publication Data

Chávez, John R., 1949–
Beyond nations : evolving homelands in the North Alantic world,
1400–2000 / John R. Chávez.
p. cm.
Includes bibliographical references and index.
ISBN 978-0-521-51667-9 (hardback) – ISBN 978-0-521-73633-6 (pbk.)
1. North Atlantic Region – Ethnic relations. 2. Europe – Colonies – History.
3. North Atlantic Region – Colonial influence. 4. America – Colonial influence.
5. Africa – Colonial influence. 6. Ethnicity – History. 7. Community life – History.
8. Imperialism – Social aspects – History. 9. Federal government – History.
10. Globalization – Social aspects – History. I. Title.
D210.C523 2009
305.80091821–dc22   2008045479

ISBN 978-0-521-51667-9 hardback
ISBN 978-0-521-73633-6 paperback

A Lori, mi querida esposa,
La madre de nuestra familia cósmica

Los primeros . . . de esta provincia de Tlaxcala . . .porblaron sin defensa ni resistencia alguna, porque hallaron estas tierras inhabitadas y despobladas.

Y estando . . . en su quieta paz . . . llegaron los Chichimecas sediciosos y crueles con la sedienta ambición, últimos pobladores y conquistadores de esta provincia.

– Muñoz Camargo

Contents

LIST OF ILLUSTRATIONS

Figures

Maps

Acknowledgments

I extend my deep thanks for the institutional support that has allowed *Beyond Nations* to come to fruition. Southern Methodist University, particularly Dedman College, supplied several grants and leaves, including funds for a trip to England, to pursue the research and do the writing for the book. SMU's William P. Clements Department of History and Center for Southwest Studies made travel to different regions of North America possible through such funds as well. Despite the Southwest Center's regional focus, this book should inform readers that the institution is by no means provincial. SMU's John Goodwin Tower Center for Political Studies generously offered two grants for study in Mexico though circumstances only allowed me to use one. Gratitude is owed, moreover, to the J. William Fulbright Scholar Program that funded a lectureship in Spain permitting me more extensive experience of homelands on the eastern side of the Atlantic.

As a synthesis based on secondary and published primary sources, *Beyond Nations* rests heavily on the works of many authors from whom I have borrowed. My deepest hope is that my words will do them justice and spread their ideas ever more widely. My book also rests on information provided by national and international repositories, information now more readily accessible than ever; thus, for their assistance my thanks go out to the anonymous staffs of the many libraries I used online and through interlibrary loan. Of course, I still spent time between bookshelves at many public and private collections in the United States and abroad, but especially in California and Texas, states at opposite ends of my ethnic region, the Mexican American borderlands. Almost every summer I return to California State University, Los Angeles, my alma mater, whose John F. Kennedy Memorial Library has remained a wealth of information for me since my undergraduate years. Needless to say, for about two decades now, SMU's collections have also supplied invaluable intellectual support for this project, particularly the Edwin J. Foscue Map Library, whose staff, namely Scott Cassingham and Robert Foxworth, provided the cartography essential for this study.

Many colleagues, both near and far, have assisted my work over the years. For their hospitality and help at the University of Granada, Jorge Fernández Barrientos Martín and Luis Quereda Rodríguez Navarro have my deep gratitude. At SMU David J. Weber, Sherry L. Smith, Sarah K. Schneewind, and especially Dennis D. Cordell offered written comments on portions of the manuscript. Many of my colleagues at a departmental colloquium also read and offered useful oral comments. Particularly helpful were those of John A. Mears, David H. Price, Thomas J. Knock, Glenn M. Linden, Alexis M. McCrossen, James K. Hopkins, and Kathleen A. Wellman. The editors and anonymous readers at Cambridge University Press patiently assisted with the revising process and consequently deserve my recognition as well; special thanks go to Eric Crahan for his faith in the project.

Finally and most importantly, I thank my family, both immediate and extended, too many relatives to list. My mother, Andrea Chávez, and my in-laws, Gerry and Robby Poirier, have provided hospitality during long summers in California, where curiously much of this work was written – far from the Atlantic. My sisters Carmela and Linda, and my brother Manny, have provided companionship since birth. Of course, my wife Lori and my children Monica and David have been at the heart of my family – the ultimate source of my inspiration.

PREFACE

Born of an "Anglo" mother of Scotch-Irish-Cajun descent and a "Chicano" father of Indian-Spanish-African ancestry, my children are citizens of the United States, which clearly defines their legal status as "Americans." But what are they ethnically? Mexican Americans? Hispanics? Euro-Americans? And where do they belong? Born in California and Texas, they seem to belong to the Southwest, but with roots running to Mexico, Spain, and Africa by way of myself, and to Canada, France, and Britain by way of their mother, my wife. Are they then more deeply children of the North Atlantic World? The answers to these questions might be reached objectively, through social science, but ultimately the questions are human, more readily answered subjectively. Within the broad margins of their history and culture, my son and daughter must discover and ultimately decide who they are and where they belong.

Naturally, being a father, I would like to offer some guidance. The present book, *Beyond Nations: Evolving Homelands in the North Atlantic World, 1400–2000*, should help my children find and construct their identities within local homelands and global communities, within distinct ethnicities, yet within a common humanity. For example, they might want to follow their maternal grandfather's French ancestry, by way of the Acadians to Canada's Atlantic Coast. Obligingly, this book traces Megumaage, homeland of the Micmac nation, transformed into the French colony of Acadia, then to the British colony of Nova Scotia, and finally to the Canadian province of the latter name. But the book also tracks the evolution of other homelands and communities that made the North Atlantic World coherent historically; it tracks them from their sociopolitical positions prior to transoceanic contact to their current standing among the nations in which my children and the rest of us live.

Besides my family reasons for taking on this project, there were of course academic reasons as well. Along with other Chicano historians, I have consistently maintained that Mexican Americans deserved a history of themselves more comprehensive than traditional immigrant narratives. In my previous work, I have thus argued for recognition of their native ties to the southwestern United States, Mexico's lost northern borderlands – ties bound and severed through colonialism and empire. But these themes were clearly not unique to the Southwest, and I was interested in applying the lessons of Chicano historiography to a larger stage. I wished to examine certain theories and methods used in that field, particularly colonial thought, by illustrating them in narrative form to see how they applied on a global scale. According to this thought, colonialism (often conflated with "imperialism") is the process through which many if not most peoples have confronted each other around the world. Colonial theorists argue that, through this process, one people for its own benefit dominates another, usually including the latter's land. Formal colonialism is the acknowledged governing system utilized by empires in the provinces, but it has deeper economic, cultural, and social processes. Because colonialism has played such an historic role in the evolution of the Atlantic World, *Beyond Nations* traces the role of imperialism in the development of homelands, but especially the part played by federalism in resolving the ethnic and national conflicts created by centuries of migration, conquest, and settlement. In the broadest sense federalism is a system in which autonomous units, usually local, regional, and national, share power. Historically, federalism has generally permitted individuals and ethnic groups to sustain and balance varying loyalties regionally, nationally, and even globally.

In terms of method, I attempt to tell history from the geographical fringes to reveal more about lesser known peoples and places on the edges of the mainstream. (See Figure 1.) My chapters highlight the homelands on the margins of central states (e.g., Ireland rather than England, Tlaxcala rather than the Aztec Empire). By comparing ethnic regions rather than national states, I further deemphasize the major countries of Europe and North America in the narrative in an effort to show that peoples have often had tighter emotional ties to such regions than to such states. Methodologically, I also attempt to clarify

Figure 1. A View of Bassa Cove in Liberia, Mid-Nineteenth Century. Lithography by Lehman and Duval. Courtesy of the Library of Congress, Washington, D.C.

and elaborate colonial theory by illustrating it in narrative form, setting the stage geographically and following the processes and events chronologically.

Because of my personal Chicano perspective, *Beyond Nations* does touch on my ethnic group and its region, to examine how Mexican Americans fit among others in a larger world. However, my ultimate reason for writing this book is for my readers to recognize that even as we appreciate our diversity, we should value the ideas that have peacefully united peoples and places over time. After all, this is a book for future generations.

IMAGES OF CONCENTRIC COMMUNITY

THE WORLD ORDER

At the beginning of the twenty-first century, globalization was the vision of the future to many people. It seemed that loyalty to local communities, regions, and even nations would soon disappear as consumers embraced international commerce. Multinational corporations straddled the globe, making sovereign states appear anachronistic. Global financial bodies, such as the World Bank and the International Monetary Fund, dictated economic policy – at least to underdeveloped countries. The United States, the remaining superpower, increasingly worked through the G-8 Nations and the World Trade Organization in financial matters. Regional trading blocks, such as the North American Free Trade Agreement, appeared ready to replace independent states in the economic sphere. Not only did particular nations seem less and less relevant, nationality itself appeared threatened, as Germans seemed more inclined to give their loyalties to the European Union than to the fatherland. And Europe, despite apprehensions about immigrants from such countries as Algeria and Turkey, continued to receive economic refugees from beyond its borders. Significantly, many people seemed more interested in economic mobility than in country or nationality, let alone region or ethnicity.[1]

---

[1] Benjamin R. Barber, *Jihad vs. McWorld* (New York: Random House, Time Books, 1995; Ballantine Books, 2001), 3–20; and Saskia Sassen, "U.S. Immigration Policy toward Mexico in a Global Economy," in *Between Two Worlds: Mexican Immigrants in the United States*, ed. David G. Gutiérrez, Jaguar Books on Latin America, no. 15 (Wilmington, Del.: Scholarly Resources, SR Books, 1996), 217–21.

On the other hand, ethnicity and nationalism surged again in regions and countries around the world. From the collapsed Soviet empire, old nations arose again and new states appeared – Estonia, Belarus, Kazakhstan. Despite their own notions of global economic integration, nationalists called for political independence. Even in well-established nations, such as Australia, aboriginal peoples demanded self-determination and regional autonomy. Major international organizations, such as the United Nations and the North Atlantic Treaty Organization, scrambled to deal with the political and military repercussions of nationalist demands. While globalization seemed to promise integration and centralization, the renewed nationalism and regionalism suggested provincialism, separatism, and even anarchy. Facing a bewildering array of new choices in the world market of goods and ideas, the individual often longed for a familiar group and place – the nation, the homeland. Indeed, opposing centripetal and centrifugal forces pulled at the individual, a process beginning with the modern era.[2]

From about 1400 dramatic changes had occurred in the global order, many originating in the lands about the North Atlantic, changes altering the relations between people and their communities. (See Map I.1.) In this Atlantic World commercial and imperial expansion had led to ethnic and racial conflict on a massive scale, causing the disruption of countless aboriginal bonds between people, their social groups, and homelands, especially in the sixteenth century. Born of these violent clashes new peoples, such as the mestizos of New Spain and the Creoles of Louisiana, developed over the following two hundred years. In the nineteenth and twentieth centuries, many new nations and states arose from the empires on both sides of the Atlantic – Haiti, Liberia, Canada, and Ireland, to name only a few. Indeed, regenerative elements appeared again and again, leading to greater multiethnic community by the turn of the twenty-first century. Identifying with various ethnic groups and homelands, from bands to nations, individuals had often been drawn into aggression or violent resistance by their associations, but had also found cooperative characteristics in such groups. The latter elements were increasingly evident in the Atlantic World as it moved

[2] E[ric] J. Hobsbawm, *Nations and Nationalism since 1780: Programme, Myth, Reality*, 2nd ed. (Cambridge: Cambridge Univ. Press, 1992), 163; and Peter L. Berger, "Introduction: The Cultural Dynamics of Globalization," in *Many Globalizations: Cultural Diversity in the Contemporary World*, ed. Berger and Samuel P. Huntington (New York: Oxford Univ. Press, 2002), 16.

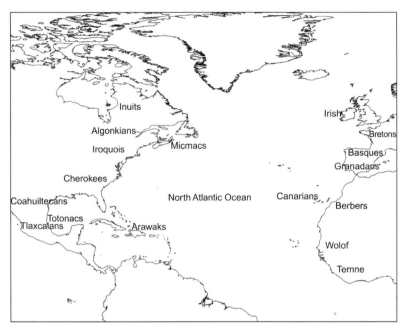

Map I.1. Some Peoples around the North Atlantic. Adapted from Meinig, *The Shaping of America*, vol. 1, *Atlantic America 1492–1800*, front cover. Cartography by Cassingham and Foxworth, courtesy of the Edwin J. Foscue Map Library, SMU.

toward the third millennium. Whether such cooperative characteristics could effectively tie men and women, their homelands, and nations to the world through federalism is the general question of this book.[3]

[3] Benedict Anderson, *Imagined Communities: Reflections on the Origin and Spread of Nationalism*, rev. ed. (New York: Verso, 1991), 190–1; Bernard Bailyn, *Atlantic History: Concept and Contours* (Cambridge, Mass.: Harvard Univ. Press, 2005), 61–2; and "Chronology of Events," in *The Atlantic World in the Age of Empire*, ed. Thomas Benjamin, Timothy Hall, and David Rutherford, *Problems in World History* (Boston: Houghton Mifflin, 2001), xi–xiv. Even though the Atlantic World of the colonial era extended as far down as South America and South Africa and at least as deep as New Mexico in the west and the Baltic in the east, I have generally limited my study to the shores of the North Atlantic to keep the project manageable, to anchor the work in natural geography, but more importantly to focus on local cultural homelands, rather than on the socioeconomic world systems incorporating them especially after transoceanic contact. However, I am discussing the ethnic and geopolitical evolution of these homelands into the twenty-first century.

MIGRATION

Naturally, migration played a major role in the evolving order of the
Atlantic World. While contact across the Atlantic was sporadic before 1500, migration within each continent had a long history. Prior to
sustained contact across the sea, many distinct peoples traversed and
occupied multiple regions along its shores and hinterlands. To utilize
the land, men and women organized societies, including bands in
places now called Munster and Ontario, kingdoms in Mississippi
and Tlaxcala, and chiefdoms in Sierra Leone and Granada. In all of
these places, varied peoples made diverse social connections – economic, political, and other – between themselves and the lands they
moved over and occupied. Economically, some societies, such as the
Pueblo, bequeathed land through matrilineal inheritance, whereas
others, including the English, bequeathed it through primogeniture,
the size of private estates usually manifesting differences in class.
Politically, understanding how distinct migrating peoples established
homelands, nations, and empires helps us understand the world order
at the beginning of the modern era.[4]

Of course, there were always migrants of many kinds transforming
whole countries and regions, usually moving into the space of earlier
inhabitants. Obviously, migrants were initially less anchored to land or
region, but within a generation as individuals, they were born natives
and could thus claim the homeland if they desired. "Africans" in
sixteenth-century Puerto Rico, "Scots" in seventeenth-century Ulster,
"French" in eighteenth-century Quebec, and "African Americans" in
nineteenth-century Liberia were only a few examples. Twentieth-
century migration complicated the picture further because of its even
more diverse origins – Vietnamese and Asian Indians, for example,
entered the countries of the Atlantic World in greater numbers. The
assimilation of subsequent generations often strengthened the receiving

---

[4]   Janet L. Abu-Lughod, *Before European Hegemony: The World System* A.D. *1250–
1350* (New York: Oxford Univ. Press, 1989), 3–8, 12; and D[onald] W[illiam]
Meinig, *The Shaping of America: A Geographical Perspective on 500 Years of History*, vol. 1, *Atlantic America, 1492–1800* (New Haven, Conn.: Yale Univ. Press,
1986), 19, 44; throughout my chapters I am most indebted to Meinig's monu-
mental, multivolume work. In contradistinction, my work does not focus on the
national development of the United States, but on the impact of imperialism
and federalism on ethnic regions around the North Atlantic, homelands as
important to their peoples as their encompassing national states.

country's dominant culture if the latter's population was sufficiently numerous. On the other hand, only rarely did migration reinvigorate regional culture. Relying on local traditions for survival, often without support from the dominant culture, regional ethnic groups usually gained only if migrants similar to themselves arrived. In general migration contributed to globalization because the movement increased cultural cross-pollination.[5]

As twentieth-century states experienced the immigration of culturally different peoples, citizenship became less defined by lineage or even residency, and nations feared loss of coherence. Even though Americans of European and African descent had long comprised the citizenry of the United States, French and British nationals of African or Asian background, respectively, have resided in Europe in significant numbers only since 1900. Yet by 2000 residency, given the mobile populations of globalization, no longer seemed permanent enough to provide migrants with the loyalties associated with nationality. According to historian David Gutiérrez: "it may well be that the most logical decision for transmigrants and even permanent immigrants is one that actively . . . disavows allegiance to a single national entity." Recognizing this phenomenon, several members of the European Union instituted open border policies, which the Mexican government prodded the United States to imitate in North America, despite the misgivings of ethnic majorities in all these countries who felt themselves becoming decreasingly homogeneous. In fact, most people continued to have an almost primordial need to attach themselves to place, including the globe's migrants, who while looking for a living, always seemed to be searching for a home.[6]

[5] John H. Elliott, "Introduction," in *Colonial Identity in the Atlantic World, 1500–1800,* ed. Nicholas Canny and Anthony Pagden (Princeton, N.J.: Princeton Univ. Press, 1987), 3–13. Arguing that multiethnic countries have always been more typical than the idealized nation-state is William H. McNeill, *Polyethnicity and National Unity in World History,* Donald G. Creighton Lectures, 1985 (Toronto: Univ. of Toronto Press, 1986), 6–7, 84–5.

[6] David G. Gutiérrez, "Ethnic Mexicans and the Transformation of 'American' Social Space: Reflections on Recent History," in *Crossings: Mexican Immigration in Interdisciplinary Perspectives,* ed. Marcelo M. Suárez-Orozco (Cambridge, Mass.: Harvard Univ. Press, David Rockefeller Center for Latin American Studies, 1998), 327. A critique of the importance of primordial ideas to modern ethnicity appears in Thomas D. Hall, "The Effects of Incorporation into World Systems on Ethnic Processes: Lessons from the Ancient World for the Contemporary World," *International Political Science Review,* 19 (no. 3, 1998): 261–2.

HOMELANDS

Imagining the homelands of native peoples about the Atlantic prior
to the modern era requires a vocabulary often unavailable to us.
With images of contemporary maps in mind, we are often at a loss
to perceive the earlier geography. For example, an Algonkian people, known as Micmacs, inhabited a place they called Megumaage
(or Migmagi) – impossible to locate today without reference to Nova
Scotia in Canada. Kajoor draws a blank in the contemporary imagination without reference to Senegal in modern West Africa. Yet
these two place names represent homelands, not empty spaces –
territories identified with distinct ethnic groups, territories culturally dominated by these groups at some time. These peoples had
migrated to and occupied these lands long enough to become native
and develop deep loyalties to their birthplace. Such attachments
often led to resistance to newcomers and conflicts during the
modern era. These same attachments to the homeland often transferred to the immigrants, especially their children, and interethnic
accommodation, if not equality, also often resulted. Commonly,
a homeland sat at the core of a wider ethnic region whose margins
were shared more fully with immigrants and surrounding peoples.
Historically, overwhelming migration transformed many a region
from the homeland of one ethnic group to another, as in the case
of Megumaage, which became French Acadia and then British Nova
Scotia by 1800. Thus, regions evolved along with the larger world
order.[7]

Indeed, a definitive ethnic map of the "Atlantic World" in 1400
would contain many names unfamiliar to all concerned, given that
this global region was inconceivable to human beings who had
scarcely crossed it yet. There were hundreds of bands, clans, tribes,
fiefdoms, chiefdoms, and kingdoms on the continents bordering the
northern sea. The Micmacs were only one of the native peoples of
present northeastern Canada. In addition to other Algonkians, such
as the Montagnais and Naskapis, bands of Inuits extended far into
the Arctic north. To the southwest of the Micmacs resided the
Mohawks and Oneidas, member tribes of the Iroquois Confederacy.

---

[7] Olive Patricia Dickason, *Canada's First Nations: A History of Founding Peoples
from Earliest Times*, Civilization of the American Indian Series (Norman: Univ.
of Oklahoma Press, 1992), 71–4.

Linguistically related to the latter, the Cherokees occupied extensive areas of the present southeastern United States. Despite their varied sociopolitical organizations, these peoples similarly considered their respective regions home.[8]

To the west of the Cherokees and the Atlantic, though linked to it by the Gulf of Mexico, lived the Chickasaws, Choctaws, and the Natchez tied through tradition to Texas and Mexico. These peoples represented complex cultures rooted in riverine homelands, distantly related to the sophisticated cities of Mesoamerica. From the latter the Aztec Empire influenced a multitude of peoples within and beyond its borders – the Yaquis to the northwest and the Mayas to the southeast, to name only a few. Through direct and indirect trade Aztec goods crossed beyond the modern borders of Mexico. Indeed, indirect contact had existed for at least two thousand years before 1400 as the cultivation of maize, originating in central Mexico, had extended well into Canada and out into the Caribbean, establishing a common element of material culture among the diverse ethnic homelands on the western side of the Atlantic.[9]

In the fifteenth century on the eastern shore of the great ocean also stretched a Babel of peoples whose homelands ranged politically from fiefdoms to kingdoms. Norman fiefs dotted the landscape of what we now know as Wales. Celts in Brittany and Basques in the Pyrenees organized themselves in lineages, allied to this or that larger power. Royal dynasties struggled for dominance over the French homeland. On the Iberian Peninsula, Christian Castile and Aragon challenged the Muslim Kingdom of Granada, as Portuguese mariners launched voyages to the south. Beyond the lands of the Moors, along the West African coast, lay the kingdoms of the Temne, a land the Portuguese named Sierra Leone.[10]

On both sides of the Atlantic, the political units were both small and large, varying from family-centered bands to bureaucratic states.

[8] Ibid.; for a definition of native peoples, stressing "nonstate societies," see Thomas D. Hall and Joane Nagel, "Indigenous Peoples," in *Encyclopedia of Sociology*, vol. 5, *He-Le*, ed. George Ritzer (Oxford: Blackwell, 2006), 2281.

[9] Alice Beck Kehoe, *North American Indians: A Comprehensive Account*, Prentice-Hall Series in Anthropology (Englewood Cliffs, N.J.: Prentice-Hall, 1981), 175–6.

[10] Anthony D. Smith, *The Ethnic Origins of Nations* (New York: Basil Blackwell, 1987), 139.

But in all cases they were human communities related to place – to water holes or hunting grounds, to farms or grazing lands, to towns or cities. Regardless of the economy or political organization, cultures took hold of geography, making and remaking homelands for their peoples as the global order evolved. By the end of the fifteenth century, that order underwent revolutionary change as the Atlantic World came together through commerce and conquest. The era of transatlantic empires began.[11]

IMPERIALISM

Worldwide, competition over land among the various bands, chiefdoms, and kingdoms had often led to conflict. Chiefs, local lords, and petty kings extended their domains, usually their homelands, by conquering their neighbors. Victory in war led to the growth of empires – extended societies found on both sides of the Atlantic well before sustained contact across the ocean. Empires based on conquest, such as the Aztec in Mesoamerica, the Moorish in North Africa, the English in Western Europe, sometimes developed into nation-states by integrating the conquered; at other times empires formed loose associations of peoples, but associations always resting on a substantial amount of force. Empires, vast collections of varied lands and peoples, generally benefited one people or ethnic group, particularly its elite. The elite acquired the wealth that came from the conquered; nevertheless, the wealth, power, and prestige of empire trickled down to the masses of the conquering ethnicity. In the sixteenth century, empires spanned the Atlantic.[12]

The order of the new trans-Atlantic World rested on imperialism, a relationship of dominance and subordination between peoples founded on conquest. Leading the way across the ocean

[11] Ibid.; and James F. Searing, *West African Slavery and Atlantic Commerce: The Senegal River Valley, 1700–1860*, African Studies Series, 77 (New York: Cambridge Univ. Press, 1993), 10–12.

[12] Jurgen Osterhammel, *Colonialism: A Theoretical Overview*, trans. Shelley L. Frisch (1995; Princeton, N.J.: Markus Weiner Publishers, 1997), 8–9; for one major empire in two phases, see Xavier Yacono, *Histoire de la colonization française, Que sais-je?* Le point des connaissances actuelles, no. 452, 2nd rev. ed. (Paris: Presses universitaires de France, 1973).

was, needless to say, the Spanish Empire, followed in North America principally by the English and French. Whatever formal or informal empire we examine, military, political, economic, cultural, and general social power rested in the hands of the conquering ethnic group even as it co-opted local leadership. Imperialism, synonymous with colonialism for our purposes, naturally had a geographical dimension. The dominant ethnic group had a historic homeland at the core of the empire, populated densely by that group – Spain, England, France. Radiating from that core were the provinces or colonies, generally less integrated as one moved farther from the center. In the case of imperial Spain, the Canaries, Mexico, and Texas exemplified this pattern. In the provinces resided ethnic groups usually unrelated to the dominant group, often conquered and restive – the Guanches, Aztecs, and Coahuiltecans.[13]

THE NATION

On both sides of the Atlantic, early nations had generally formed from bands, clans, and tribes that had a common heritage, often lineal and linguistic – the Tlaxcalans in the Western Hemisphere or the Moroccans in the Eastern. A nation was usually an ethnic group that had established a sovereign state in its homeland, as had Tlaxcala and Morocco. As we have seen, a people expanding at the expense of other ethnic groups often became an empire. To the degree that the national core integrated the provinces politically, and especially culturally, imperialism became national expansion. That process, however, was long and uncertain, with a product liable to disintegration, for on the periphery were other nationalities,

---

[13] Mario Barrera, *Race and Class in the Southwest: A Theory of Racial Inequality* (Notre Dame, Ind.: Univ. of Notre Dame Press, 1979), 193; Amy Kaplan, *The Anarchy of Empire in the Making of U.S. Culture* (Cambridge, Mass.: Harvard Univ. Press, 2002), 26–7; and Thomas D. Hall, "Ethnic Conflict as a Global Social Problem," in *Handbook of Social Problems: A Comparative International Perspective*, ed. George Ritzer (Thousand Oaks, Calif.: Sage Publications, 2004), 141–2. Although colonialism has materialistic motives at its base, the role of ethnicity receives greater attention in colonial theory than in the world systems paradigm into which the theory is sometimes embedded (e.g., Meinig, vol.1, 258–67).

subordinate ethnic groups, located in competing homelands within ethnic regions.[14]

European nations came to dominate the Atlantic World at the beginning of the modern era as they unified their homelands and launched expansion overseas. England sought more effective control over the Celtic Fringe – Wales, Scotland, and Ireland – after losing its foothold on the continent at the end of the Hundred Years War. On the other hand, France secured its unity with the defeat of the English, followed by incorporation of peripheral ethnic regions, such as Brittany and the Basque Country north of the Pyrenees. Modern Spain formed after its victory over the Moors at Granada in 1492, followed by the conquest of Navarre two decades later. This national development, or nation building, occurred in conjunction with the imperial thrust down and across the Atlantic.[15]

---

[14] What I call "early nations," McNeil, 17, describes as "close analogues to the nation state of modern times"; cf. Anderson, 36–7; for much of my understanding of domestic colonialism beyond the United States, I owe Michael Hechter, *Internal Colonialism: The Celtic Fringe in British National Development, 1536–1966* (Berkeley and Los Angeles: Univ. of California Press, 1975), 4–5. In the 1960s "internal colonialism" became an important theory advanced to explain the historical development of ethnic and racial inequality in modern national states. The concept gained wide applicability among historians and others in Latin America, Europe, and the United States, especially as regards ethnic Mexicans in the latter. Though by the 1980s the theory had been dismissed as inadequate by many scholars, its influence resurged, especially as postcolonial theory evolved. In *Beyond Nations*, I accept the validity of internal colonialism for the historical interpretation of ethnic regions – see Pablo González-Casanova, "Sociedad plural, colonialismo interno y desarrollo," *América Latina* 6 (no. 3, 1963): 16, 18, the seminal article on the theory; Barrera, 193, the major study of internal colonialism and Chicanos; Robert J. Hind, "The Internal Colonial Concept," *Comparative Studies in Society and History* 26 (July 1984): 548, 552–3, 558, 561; and Emma Pérez, *The Decolonial Imaginary: Writing Chicanas into History, Theories of Representation and Difference* (Bloomington: Indiana Univ. Press, 1999), 6, 131 n.16, a postcolonial work that supports internal colonialism.

[15] Walker Connor, *Ethnonationalism: The Quest for Understanding* (Princeton, N.J.: Princeton Univ. Press, 1994), 211–24; Immanuel Wallerstein, *The Modern World-System*, Studies in Social Discontinuity, vol. 1, *Capitalist Agriculture and the Origins of the European World Economy in the Sixteenth Century* (New York: Harcourt Brace Jovanovich, Academic Press, 1974), 146–7; and Paul Kennedy, *The Rise and Fall of the Great Powers: Economic Change and Military Conflict from 1500 to 2000* (New York: Random House, 1987), 16–30.

Federalism

Although nations frequently developed through imperialism, federalism – a system of power shared among autonomous units, usually, local regional, and national – and its variant confederatism, offered another option for global order. In contrast to the imperial process, there were instances of "voluntary" mergers of nations – Castile and Aragon, the Iroquois Confederacy, England and Scotland – in the first half of the modern era. These unions, though sometimes the result of subtle coercion if not force, early suggested the possibilities of federalism as opposed to imperialism. Federalism allowed for the centralization and integration of power, wealth, and even culture, but with substantial autonomy remaining in regions, though achieving an acceptable balance could be a long and arduous task. Confederatism left more power to regions than to the center in a looser union of states. The utility of federalism gradually became more evident as the modern era unfolded down to our own time. According to sociologist Michael Hechter, "Although federation is an organizational form that has medieval roots, modern technology gives it new life by allowing local decision-making to coexist with legal universalism. This permits individual rights and cultural autonomy to be safeguarded at the same time."[16]

In the late 1700s the United States established a large-scale federation with a system built around Anglo-American nationalism; in the 1800s Canada established a federal system built on dual ethnicity, English and French Canadian. In the twentieth century the latter was extended to native peoples, notably the Inuits in the Arctic, though Quebec grew increasingly restive. In the United States ethnically defined regions were not admitted to statehood basically because Anglo-American culture remained a defining feature of American nationalism. Indian reservations and the Commonwealth of Puerto Rico remained outside the states, remnants of empire, stubbornly ethnic, consequently denied full membership in the federal union. Born of empire, both the United States and Canada sought to avoid the

---

[16] Michael Hechter, *Containing Nationalism* (Oxford: Oxford Univ. Press, 2000), 157–8; for an overview of federal ideas, especially definitions, from the Enlightenment to the present, see Dimitrios Karmis and Wayne Norman, eds., *Theories of Federalism: A Reader* (New York: St. Martin's Press, Palgrave Macmillan, 2005), 5–7.

coercive features of imperialism but also perpetuated that process in many ways.[17]

Other sovereign states imitated these federal models as the world sought a more cooperative order. In the nineteenth-century North Atlantic World, Mexico and Liberia followed the U.S. system, but with no more success in absorbing ethnic regions into the body politic; in the next century Mexico's native peoples in places like Chiapas continued to experience the harsh effects of imperialism as did indigenous groups in Liberia's interior. The national states that confederated in the European Common Market, first economically in the 1950s, then politically, followed a pattern more similar to that of Canada than that of the United States. While building international institutions for its members, the states of the European Union nevertheless maintained their national cultures. Moreover, they extended greater autonomy to ethnic regions within their boundaries, such as Catalonia in Spain and Scotland in Great Britain. Ultimately, as a vast developing federation of multiethnic nation-states, the EU went well beyond the United States and Canada in offering a voluntary and cooperative model of world order.[18]

COMMUNITIES WITHIN COMMUNITIES

By the twenty-first century the global order appeared to rest increasingly on the recognition that a person belonged to multiple groups arranged in a concentric pattern. One could see oneself as a loyal member of an ethnic group, a province, a nation, and a world, all at the same time, just as one could join a credit union, a national insurance system, and an international mutual fund without conflicting allegiances. How to minimize potential conflict between such overlapping loyalties was at the core of the conundrum involving individualism, ethnicity, nationalism, and globalization.[19]

---

[17] For seminal work on internal colonialism in the United States, see Robert Blauner, *Racial Oppression in America* (New York: Harper & Row, 1972), 54–5.

[18] Geir Lundestad, *"Empire" by Integration: The United States and European Integration, 1945–1997* (New York: Oxford Univ. Press, 1998), 42–3; and Jürgen Habermas, *The Postnational Constellation: Political Essays*, trans. and ed., with an introduction by Max Pensky, Studies in Contemporary German Social Thought (1998; reprint, Cambridge, Mass.: MIT Press, Polity Press, 2001), xix.

[19] Meinig, vol.1, 452–3.

To minimize this conflict, some people frequently imagined community exclusively at the global level – beyond the local, the ethnic, the regional, and even the national. They saw themselves as citizens of the world, or more often as global consumers. To them the development of a common international culture, most often imagined as Euro-American popular culture, seemed a solution to the conundrum. But local, ethnic, regional, and national visions persisted. Despite the wonders of modern communications, people still had to live life at the local level, a circumstance that often sustained minority ethnic communities. At the regional level, however, individuals struggled to preserve their homelands because there they often lacked political control, without which a subordinate ethnic group could disappear. Though ordinary citizens also saw challenges in globalization to their visions of the nation, nationalism tended to regenerate itself through the assimilative powers of the state. In fact, members of subordinate ethnic groups often disappeared into dominant national cultures. On the other hand, some men and women rediscovered regional ethnicity and strengthened it with the knowledge they had gained from the larger nation and world. In this sense they transcended both nationalism and globalization.[20]

Indeed, a person could move beyond region and nation, through the world and back through a voluntary, cooperative, multiethnic federalism. Even as human communities increasingly meshed through economic globalization, ethnicity and nationalism often played a creative role in resisting homogenization as different cultures, in preserving traditional points of views, regenerated material for new visions. Cooperatively structured, federalism could permit the individual to sustain and balance varying ethnic, geographic, political, and economic loyalties. At the beginning of the twenty-first century, such trends about the Atlantic suggested greater community around the globe.[21]

[20] Ibid.; Anderson, 46; James Davison Hunter and Joshua Yates, "In the Vanguard of Globalization: The World of American Globalizers," in *Many Globalizations*, 324–5; and Mario Barrera, *Beyond Aztlán: Ethnic Autonomy in Comparative Perspective* (New York: Praeger, 1988), 175–6.

[21] Meinig, vol.1, 452–3; Habermas, 108–9; and Jean Meyer, "Historia, nación y región," keynote address presented at the 25th Coloquio de antropología e historia regionales, Colegio de Michoacán, Mexico, 22 October 2003, pp. 9–10; my thanks to David J. Weber for providing me with a copy of this paper.

CHAPTER ONE

NATIVE AMERICAN IMAGES OF COMMUNITY

EVOLVING HOMELANDS

At the beginning of the fifteenth century, individuals moved from region to region less than they would in the centuries to come. On both sides of what we call the Atlantic Ocean, peoples had more or less established themselves in certain lands. Even those ethnic groups considered nomadic roamed within and between specific hunting and gathering areas. While humans had migrated great distances throughout history, the tendency was for this process to occur across generations, though more sudden movements obviously occurred as well. Given this limited mobility, many peoples on both sides of the ocean had lived long enough in their respective regions to consider themselves native, though ethnic identities were rarely fixed. Precedence or length of residence in a particular place clearly had an important effect on an ethnic group's image of its relationship to the land. While a "homeland" might be claimed in as little as a generation, generally such a claim had more time behind it.[1]

The territorial configuration of Atlantic communities around 1400 A.D. varied and overlapped; homelands could include many different

---

[1] See Walter D. Mignolo, *Local Histories/Global Designs: Coloniality, Subaltern Knowledges, and Border Thinking*, Princeton Studies in Culture/Power/History (Princeton, N.J.: Princeton Univ. Press, 2000), 26–9, 64–5, 270, 272; and Immanuel Wallerstein, *World-Systems Analysis: An Introduction* (Durham, N.C.: Duke Univ. Press, 2005), 20–1. In keeping with a holistic colonial approach, my work agrees with postcolonialists, such as Mignolo, in stressing local cultural perspectives; it nonetheless accepts the necessity of a socioeconomic context, such as Wallerstein's.

natural landscapes and built environments, occupied by a wide variety of societies and states. These were, of course, comprised of individuals whose images of their people and land formed the loyalties at the base of ethnic group and nation. Indeed, in North and Middle America during the fifteenth century a man or woman belonged to a band, a tribe, a city, a nation, a kingdom, an empire, or a federation, as all these forms of political community existed in the Western Hemisphere prior to contact with the Eastern. From the Arctic to Yucatan, Native Americans envisioned themselves as members of such communities, both large and small, and those images included their homelands.[2]

ALGONKIAN BANDS AND THE MICMAC NATION

According to one tradition of the Algonkian-speaking Micmacs of eastern Canada, "Our people were on a journey from a distant land across the Great Waters of the East, but they moved in darkness." That the Micmacs' ancestors launched into the unknown and sailed in "darkness" implies that exploration and migration played an epic role in their origins. The narrative suggests that in ancient times these ancestors voyaged across the Atlantic Ocean to what became their homeland in the Maritime Provinces. (See Map 1.1.) Given the small size of hunting and gathering bands, transportation by canoe would more likely make the place of origin one of the many islands and peninsulas lying to the northeast of the region's core. The narrators do not specify the precise point of departure, nor do they seem concerned with exactly when this occurred. Given that this legend has been repeated across generations, such details doubtless disappeared in the retelling, if they were ever deemed important. Regardless, the voyage of the Micmac ancestors led to discovery of a new world.[3]

The Micmacs established themselves in Migmagi, a cold but promising region, including Prince Edward Island, southern Newfoundland, the shores of the gulf of New Brunswick, as well as Nova

[2]   Raymond D. Fogelson, "Perspectives on Native American Identity," in *Studying Native America: Problems and Prospects*, ed. Russell Thorton (Madison: Univ. of Wisconsin Press, 1998), 43–4.

[3]   Michael B. Running Wolf and Patricia Clark Smith, *On the Trail of Elder Brother: Glous'gap Stories of the Micmac Indians*, Karen and Michael Braziller Books (New York: Persea Books, 2000), 128; cf. Chrestien le Clercq, "Nouvelle relation de la Gaspesie," in *Le Clercq: New Relation of Gaspesia*, facsimile ed. (1691; reprint, New York: Greenwood Press, 1968), 85, 338.

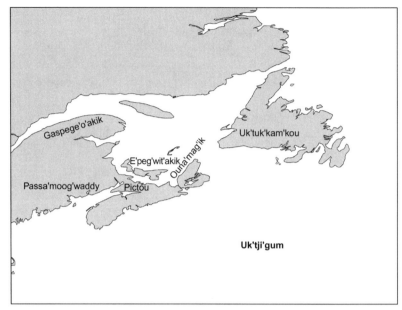

Map 1.1. Megumaage or Migmagi, Homeland of the Micmac. Adapted from Running Wolf and Smith, *On the Trail of Elder Brother*, 132. Cartography by Cassingham and Foxworth, courtesy of the Edwin J. Foscue Map Library, SMU.

Scotia. Their ancestral hero, Gluskap, led the tribe "to this northland of lakes and forests, where the sea teems with fish and deer walk quietly in the woods, this land" that he "helped the Creator to prepare." The story accurately, if generally, describes the flora and fauna, as well as the topography of the bountiful coastal region. Significantly, the region is a gift from God, a holy land, readied for the occupation of its people. As with other nations, the ethnic identity of the Micmacs rested heavily on their place of residence even when migration formed part of their collective memory. They imagined themselves entering the homeland together as a community.[4]

Archeologists and linguists seem to agree that the Micmacs' ancestors migrated to their Maritime homeland over long stretches of time in the past. Perhaps as early as forty thousand years ago, these ancestors followed the general dispersal of early peoples from the Bering

4   Philip K. Bock, "Micmac," *Handbook of North American Indians*, gen. ed. William G. Sturtevant, vol. 15, *Northeast*, ed. Bruce G. Trigger (Washington, D.C.: Smithsonian Institution, 1978), 110, 121; and Running Wolf and Smith, 128.

Strait down through the Americas. Algonkian speakers, including the ancestral Micmacs, probably moved south along the eastern side of the Rocky Mountains into the Great Plains that extend through the middle of North America. Then some groups swung east under the Great Lakes, through the Ohio Valley, north into the regions surrounding the St. Lawrence. By the time of their arrival there, they had diversified, a process that would naturally continue. The exact route of that migration is in dispute, and the precise dating of that migration varies by thousands of years. Exactly where the Micmacs broke off from the migrant stream and became that people cannot be pinpointed in these accounts, nor can their precise point of entry into the Maritime Provinces.[5]

Besides migrating to the East Coast, the Micmacs' Algonkian relatives went as far up as the Subarctic and as far down as the Carolinas, with some remaining west on the Great Plains. However, other language families also dispersed across this vast expanse of the continent and subdivided the Algonkians. For example, Iroquoian speakers resided in New York, as well as North Carolina. Besides the Micmacs, other Algonkian speakers in eastern Canada included the Maliseet of New Brunswick, the Montagnais and Naskapis of Quebec and Labrador, the Abenakis south of the St. Lawrence River, and a particular group named simply the Algonkians at the Ottawa River north of the Great Lakes. Given their linguistic connections, it should be little surprise that these groups had a similar history. Though present in the eastern woodlands for centuries, certainly long enough to claim them as native lands, the ancestral Algonkians were immigrants, linguists tell us.[6]

Migration, however, did not play a role in all Micmac narratives of origin. Alternatively, "the Dawnland," where the sun rose first from the sea, was their "founding home . . . the place where, they had lived since the dawn of time. It was the place where Gluskap . . . had brought them

[5] Francis Jennings, *The Founders of America: How Indians Discovered the Land, Pioneered in It, and Created Great Classical Civilizations; How They Were Plunged into a Dark Age by Invasion and Conquest; and How They Are Reviving* (New York: W. W. Norton & Co., 1993), 28–30, 33, 70–1; and Kenneth R. Shepherd, "Micmac," in *Gale Encyclopedia of Native American Tribes*, ed. Sharon Malinowski et al., vol. 1, *Northeast, Southeast, Caribbean* (Detroit, Mich.: Gale Publishing, 1998), 134.

[6] Jennings, *Founders in America*, 70–1; and Ives Goddard, "Introduction," *Handbook*, vol. 17, *Languages*, ed. Goddard (1996), 4–6 – also see accompanying map.

out of the earth and taught them how to survive in Canada's lands by the Atlantic." In this legend the Micmacs sprang from the earth itself; the land gave birth to the tribe. Consequently, the identity of the people derived from the soil as it might from their parents. Memories of migration tended to recede as occupation of one place for generations encouraged the development of a sociopsychological bonding between people and land.[7]

Over time the Micmacs occupied their homeland and organized their communities around a foraging economy, but in a pattern different from that of their neighbors. Other Algonkians, including the Naskapis of northern Quebec and Labrador, formed bands based on kinship and held land in a totemic system. Individuals who had both technical and ritual knowledge of the animals of a particular territory "owned" that area because they could organize hunts with that knowledge and pass that information on to their descendants. A family consequently became identified with the animals of the hunting ground and could provide leadership on that basis across generations. Outsiders apparently honored the borders of the hunting area, not because they deferred to its mortal caretakers, but more for fear of offending the spiritual owners of the land, the lords of the game. Thus, both outsiders and insiders envisioned land and inhabitants as extensions of the spirit world. Through this system a Naskapi individual or family could hold "property," and a band, depending on size, could hold its hunting territories and consequently its homeland.[8]

The Micmacs also hunted, gathered, and fished, but compared with their neighbors, they imagined their homeland more broadly and consequently organized it and themselves in a more complex economic and political structure, as a nation. According to present Micmac belief and a seventeenth-century missionary, it was "the right of the head of the nation . . . to distribute the places of hunting to each individual." No one was allowed "to overstep the bounds and limits of the region . . . assigned him in the assemblies of the elders." Before every fall and spring this chief and his peers would allot exclusive hunting territories to families, territories with obviously clear boundaries. There was apparently little recognition of land as private property, even in the totemic sense practiced by other Algonkians. Micmac political economy

[7] Shepherd, 134.
[8] Fogelson, 48–9; see also Charles A. Bishop, "Territoriality among Northeastern Algonquians," *Anthropologica*, 28, (spec. issue, nos. 1–2, 1986): 37–63.

was basically collective, based on community, rather than individual needs.[9]

Apparently, the pre-contact Micmacs also had an image of themselves as a loosely unified nation with a clearly delineated homeland. Given their residence in a region of islands and peninsulas, the Micmacs readily subdivided that homeland topographically. Despite the disagreement of some scholars, anthropologist Harald E. L. Prins notes that

> Many Mi'kmaqs today accept the idea that Mi'kmaq country was originally divided into seven districts. Because the grand chief of Cape Breton ranked above his peers, his district, called Unama'kik, was recognized as the head district. The remaining six districts were geographically grouped into a "right hand" . . . and a "left hand" . . .. Each of these districts once had its own chief, who had a measure of influence over local band chiefs and whose settlement served as a district meeting place.

Thus, the Micmacs perceived their land and government as a human body, an extension of themselves, functioning with coordination. Moreover, the name "Micmacs," probably derived from an Algonkian term for "allies," tends to support the view that this nation was perceived as confederated.[10]

"Allies" does seem to describe a loose union, rather than a centralized state, such as a kingdom or empire. Though there was seemingly a hierarchy of district and band chiefs, the "grand chief" had to govern by consensus, rather than command, in what amounted to an informal democracy. According to one seventeenth-century source, all the grand chief's "power and authority are based only on the goodwill of those in his nation, who execute his orders just in so far as it pleases them." At least among men Micmac society was relatively egalitarian with no class structure; however, the division of labor relied on gender. Women did much of the community's heavy work, beyond hunting and warfare and preparation for those activities. Significantly, in

[9] Le Clercq, 237, 403–4; and Harald E. L. Prins, *The Mi'kmaq: Resistance, Accommodation, and Cultural Survival*, Case Studies in Cultural Anthropology (Fort Worth, Tex.: Harcourt Brace College Publishers, 1996), 34–5, 177.

[10] Pierre Biard, "Relation de la Novvelle France," in *Jesuit Relations and Allied Documents: Travels and Explorations of the Jesuit Missionaries in New France, 1610–1791*, ed. Reuben Gold Thwaites, vol. 1, *Acadia: 1610–1613* (New York: Pageant Book Co., 1959), 88–90; Prins, 177; and Shepherd, 134.

terms of landscape, they constructed both the conical wigwams used
by families and the long A-frame houses used for larger gatherings,
thus providing the built-environment of the Micmacs' semipermanent
villages. As mates, both men and women provided the mortar that
unified the Micmac nation, as they had to select spouses from outside
their own bands. These family relationships strengthened mutual aid
in times of war and peace.[11]

Despite cultural similarities, the Micmacs were often hostile to their
neighbors, both Algonkian and other; warfare occurred frequently.
However, early warfare did not involve struggles over territory or even
natural resources, elements integral to imperialism. More often disputes
had the quality of long-term feuds for purposes of vengeance, martial
prestige, or the taking of prisoners for ritual torture or to augment the
Micmac population. Apparently, Algonkian occupation of vast lands
with copious resources made territory less cause for conflict. Sparse
populations allowed Algonkian tribes to operate independently in
their own ethnic regions with flexible boundaries. Significantly, these
accounts of the Micmacs' origins do not mention any earlier inhabitants
of their region. They did not conquer or dispossess another people in
claiming their homeland; though the ancestral Micmacs may have
migrated to the region, they were its first occupants – they were
natives.[12]

The geographical location of the Micmacs gave them an important
role in making the Atlantic World. On the northeastern edges of North
America, they lay exposed to the migrations that would surge across
that ocean. Indeed, they probably encountered the first confirmed
settlers from the Eastern Hemisphere. In one of the few known pre-
Columbian, transtlantic contacts, Icelandic sagas and modern archeology agree that Native Americans met the Norse when the latter
attempted to colonize Newfoundland. In 1001 A.D. the Vikings established a settlement on the island. Unfortunately, skirmishes between
them and some natives, probably Micmacs from the saga's description of
canoes, led to deaths on both sides. Though nearly five hundred years
would pass before much more contact between the hemispheres, the
creation of the Atlantic World seemed destined for violence.[13]

[11] Le Clercq, 234–7, 402–4; and Prins, 34, 32.
[12] Dean R. Snow, "Late Prehistory of the East Coast," Handbook, 15: 58, 60.
[13] "Grænlendinga Saga," in The Vinland Sagas: The Norse Discovery of America
      (New York: New York Univ. Press, 1966), 56–61; and Shepherd, 135.

Before the making of that transoceanic world, the Micmacs, as we have seen, viewed themselves as a nation of loosely unified bands who subdivided their homeland into political districts. Despite the existence of gender inequality and warfare, a subsistence economy, which still permitted families to provide much for themselves, encouraged certain communal and democratic attitudes among the Micmacs that permitted their society to remain relatively egalitarian for centuries. Their decentralized alliance, moreover, caused them to perceive themselves in a context larger than their families and bands and to give their loyalties to the Micmac nation. Other Native American peoples developed this political form and its accompanying self-image to the larger scale of a formal confederation. We find the best example of this in a southwesterly direction, in present New York State, where the Iroquois united a homeland, not of one nation but many.[14]

THE IROQUOIS CONFEDERACY

"After the lapse of ages . . . Sky Holder, resolved upon a special creation of a race which should surpass all others in beauty, strength, and bravery; so from the bosom of the great island, . . . [the creator] brought out the six pairs, which were destined to become the greatest of all people." This narrative goes on to place the parents of the five original Iroquois nations – Senecas, Cayugas, Onondagas, Oneidas, and Mohawks – throughout New York State, with the Tuscaroras in North Carolina. The details of this story of Iroquois origin vary; the Onondagas, for example, add that "they were made of red clay." In any case, as this account has this people arising from the land itself, the Iroquois obviously saw themselves as natives of their homeland. Though conflicting with theories regarding migration across the Bering Strait and North America, this Iroquois account supports archeological opinions that this culture developed in place over at least two thousand years.[15]

[14] Prins, 32–3.

[15] Erminnie Smith, "Myths of the Iroquois," in *Second Annual Report of the Bureau of Ethnology to the Secretary of the Smithsonian Institution, 1880–81,* dir. J. W. Powell (Washington, D.C.: Government Printing Office, 1883), 76; William M. Beauchamp, *Iroquois Folk Lore: Gathered from the Six Nations of New York,* Empire State Historical Publication 31 (1922; reprint, Port Washington, N.Y.: Ira J. Friedman, 1965), 167; and James A. Tuck, "Northern Iroquoian Prehistory," *Handbook,* 15: 322.

While social scientists overwhelmingly accept the Bering Strait thesis, as we have seen, they disagree dramatically on the dates of the migrations over that route, ranging from forty thousand to thirteen thousand years ago. Again, scholars agree on a general southeastward swing of peoples across the continent, but not on the timing. Some archeologists believe Algonkian cultures developed in place as long as ten thousand to twenty thousand years ago. Some linguists accept that the Iroquoian language developed in the New York area at least four thousand to five thousand years ago, and spread elsewhere. But others, while not necessarily refuting these estimates, argue that many migrations followed that from the Bering Strait, and in many directions, especially considering the vast amount of time in question.[16]

Francis Jennings has the earliest Iroquoian language, with proto-Sioux and Caddoan, developing in East Texas and Arkansas, about four thousand years ago, with one branch of speakers moving up the Mississippi River to the Illinois area, then pushing on to the Northeast, in several migrations over the centuries. In the process, the Iroquoians split earlier Algonkian-speaking communities, as the former wedged themselves through the Ohio Valley, to the northeastern Atlantic states, and the St. Lawrence River. This scholar has the last wave of Iroquoians entering New York about 1300 A.D. (after the first signs of confederacy) and transforming local agriculture with advanced techniques introduced from the southwest. This theory at least correlates loosely with the Mohawk account of migration in northern America, as well as other narratives of migration left by the Cayugas and the Algonkian Delawares.[17]

Inhabiting woodlands similar to those of the Micmacs, the Iroquois enjoyed similar advantages in hunting and gathering though relative distance from the sea made fishing less important, and a more temperate climate made farming significant. Like other foragers, the early Iroquois

[16] Shepherd, 134; Floyd G. Lounsbury, "Iroquoian Languages," *Handbook*, 15: 336; Jennings, *Founders in America*, 70; for conservative estimates regarding migration across the Bering Strait, see Dan O'Neil, *The Last Giant of Berengia: The Mystery of the Bering Land Bridge* (Boulder, Colo.: Westview Press, 2004), 174, 181, 183; for a readily accessible discussion of genetic information on migration, see Charles C. Mann, *1491: New Revelations of the Americas before Columbus* (New York: Alfred A. Knopf, 2005), 165–7.

[17] Jennings, *Founders in America*, 72–5, 70; and Barbara Alice Mann, *Iroquoian Women: The Gantowisas*, American Indian Studies, vol. 4 (New York: Peter Lang, 2000), 35.

identified with the principal game in their areas. As extended families evolved, they became clans named Bear, Beaver, Snipe, Deer, Wolf, Tortoise, and other. Though archeologists tell us that about the sixth century A.D., agriculture spread into the Northeast from a southwesterly direction; Iroquois tradition says the Three Sisters – corn, beans, and squash – derived from the sky. In any case, the crops, as well as the game, came to define the Iroquois way of life, a community identified with its natural habitat.[18]

Agriculture allowed for a more settled way of life than seen among exclusive foragers and produced a landscape reflective of the community's image of itself. The Iroquois usually built their towns, which could reach two thousand in population, on hills fortified by palisades as high as twenty feet, sometimes with additional earthworks for defense. As many as sixty structures, in the form of long houses, covered several acres of land. Each of these communal buildings could shelter as many as twenty-four families, typically of the same clan, presided over by the Clan Mother, generally the most respected woman of the lineage. However, clan members did not all live in the same long house, town, or even nation, clans having disbursed across the Iroquois population through an out-marriage system that united the entire people. Clans, moreover, were parts of moieties, larger exogamous groups that cemented the individual in another layer of loyalty between the family and the Iroquois as a whole. Indeed, agriculture and this social system permitted the political organization of the Iroquois nations across a great homeland, which they likened to a long house.[19]

The communal households and intricate social ties among the Iroquois reflected an egalitarian society in economic terms. While status based on clan membership and individual achievement existed, class based on wealth did not. Furthermore, women enjoyed higher status in Iroquois society than in most cultures because they controlled the economy of the tribe. Iroquois women controlled not only land, but tools and seeds as well. Though men cleared the land, elected female leaders organized agricultural activities that yielded dependable harvests. Women retained the right of food distribution, even of products acquired by men in the hunt or through trade, a significant power since

[18] Smith, 76; William Engelbrecht, *Iroquoia: The Development of a Native World*, Iroquois and Their Neighbors (Syracuse, N.Y.: Syracuse Univ. Press, 2003), 23; and Mann, 34.

[19] Engelbrecht, 35, 68, 88–9, 107–8.

family and communal food stores were a major form of tribal wealth. Those stores could be denied households, councils, or even war parties that did not have the approval of powerful matrons. Though families only "owned" plots as long as these were farmed, women controlled the land to such an extent that their eighteenth-century descendents would assert: "we [women] are the owners of the land and it is ours." In a fundamentally agricultural society, such control constituted real power that carried over into areas beyond the economic, into the social and political realms.[20]

Iroquois society was matrilineal – rights, titles, and property passed through the female line; it was also matrilocal – men moved to their wives' households at marriage, which was arranged by their mothers and could easily be dissolved by the wife. But the state was not matriarchal; for example, men only, could sit on the Council of Elders, the most important governing body of the historical Iroquois, where male speakers represented women. Nevertheless, hereditary eligibility for that body passed through women, and they also nominated and could veto candidates for any empty elective positions. In addition, women could veto a declaration of war, dispose of prisoners of war, and effect the restoration of peace. Indeed, the political power of women probably increased with the creation of the famed League of the Iroquois.[21]

Concerning events before the League, native informants tell us, "Those were evil days, for the five Iroquois peoples were all at war with one another, and made themselves an easy prey to their Algonquin enemies." Hiawatha, a chief whose wife and daughters had died in the violence, was filled with anger and despair until he was visited by the Peacemaker, a spirit in human form. Convincing the chief that conciliation must occur among the Iroquois, Peacemaker and Hiawatha set out to spread the word, but first Peacemaker "sought the house of a certain woman who lived by the warriors' path between east and west." Since she had supplied the war parties that crisscrossed the lands of the feuding Iroquois, her conversion to the peace process was

[20] Engelbrecht, 32, 108; Daniel K. Richter, *The Ordeal of the Longhouse: The Peoples of the Iroquois League in the Era of European Colonization* (Chapel Hill: Univ. of North Carolina Press for the Institute of Early American History and Culture, 1992), 22–3; and Red Jacket, "speaker for the women," quoted in Judith K. Brown, "Economic Organization and the Position of Women among the Iroquois, *Ethnohistory* 17(Summer–Fall 1970): 160, 156, 164.
[21] Brown, 154–6.

geopolitically essential. Her assistance secured, the three proceeded to convince the warring nations to settle their differences.[22]

By some accounts Peacemaker's successful prediction of a total eclipse of the sun in 1142 A.D. persuaded the nations to form an early version of the Iroquois League under the Great and Binding Law of Peace. Essentially, the law required the five nations to cease their brutal vindictive wars through the implementation of justice, peace, and power. They were to unite under the authority of the Council of Elders, a democratic body enforcing the rule of law by consensus. Though the nations would engage in their own foreign policies and even their own wars against outsiders, they would remain peaceful toward each other. The confederacy thus formed was called, "the Longhouse, the League. . . . Men shall live together in one community, as in the longhouse, and they shall live in peace because they live under one law." Given that women controlled the real longhouses, their power was also enhanced by the figurative longhouse, extending across the Iroquois homeland from the Hudson River in the east to the Great Lakes in the west. In fact, the Iroquois called themselves, Hodenosaunee, the Longhouse People. Clearly, their men and women long ago imagined themselves, not only as members of families, clans, and phratries, but as members of nations in a great geographical and political confederation. Peacemaker, moreover, suggested the broader socioeconomic possibilities of such a tranquil and cooperative union "among the peoples of the whole earth."[23]

In the eastern woodlands of North America, such confederations historically existed among many other peoples, including the Iroquoian Hurons of Ontario, the Algonkian Powhatans of Virginia, and the Muskogean Creeks of Alabama. Such similar political ideas probably stemmed from the long contacts among these peoples over the centuries, including patterns of migration. Despite Iroquois accounts of local origin, the Mohawks retell at least one story "that they wandered a long time under the conduct of a woman named Gaihonariosk: this woman

---

[22] Quoted in Paul A. W. Wallace, *The White Roots of Peace* (1946; reprint, Port Washington, N.Y.: Ira J. Friedman, 1968), 12–13.

[23] Mann, *Iroquoian Women*, 38–9; Wallace, 13, 16, 41; Engelbrecht, 129–30; for the debate over the date of the eclipse, cf. Barbara A. Mann and Jerry L. Fields, "A Sign in the Sky: Dating the League of the Haudenosaune," *American Indian Culture and Research Journal*, 21(no. 2, 1997): 105–63, and David Henige, "Can a Myth Be Astronomically Dated?" *American Indian Culture and Research Journal*, 23(no. 4, 1999): 127–57.

led them about through all the north of America." Unfortunately, this narrative specifies no place of origin, leaving us with the basic fact of migration. In this, anthropological speculation is no more definite than Indian oral tradition.[24]

CHEROKEE TOWNS

Rejecting theories that Iroquoians dispersed south from a cultural hearth in New York, Jennings's account has the Cherokees separating from other Iroquoians at the lower Mississippi or even Texas and spreading eastward toward the Atlantic Coast. In the wooded Appalachian mountains of North Carolina, Georgia, and Alabama, the Cherokees established their homeland. Cherokee legends of migration, on the other hand, support movement from the north, from either the Virginia or Great Lakes areas, which backs linguists positing a northern Iroquoian hearth. Nevertheless, like the Micmacs and the Iroquois, the Cherokees relate narratives that also support archeological theories that have them developing their culture in place over centuries.[25]

One oral tradition tells that the ancestral Cherokees came out of the ground, and that, despite denying migration, their homeland had once extended to the Great Lakes. Of course, this tradition supports the tribe's long persistence in the country and stresses its deep attachment and extensive claim to the land. Like other American Indians, the Cherokees also recount the creation of their homeland along with the creation of the natural world. Seeking a place for the first humans to live,

> the Great Buzzard . . . flew all over the earth, low down near the ground, and it was still soft. When he reached the Cherokee country, . . . his wings began to flap and strike the ground, and wherever they struck the earth there was a valley, and where they turned up again there was a mountain. When the animals above saw this, they were afraid that the whole world would be mountains, so they called him back, but the Cherokee country remains full of mountains to this day.

[24] Lafitau quoted in Beauchamp, 167; and Mann, *Iroquoian Women*, 35.
[25] Jennings, *Founders in America*, 72; Stanley W. Hoig, *The Cherokees and Their Chiefs in the Wake of Empire* (Fayetteville: Univ. of Arkansas Press, 1998), 8–9; and Loretta Hall, "Cherokee," in *Gale Encyclopedia*, 1: 134.

Apparently, some Cherokees viewed the southern Appalachian range as their place of origin, the core of their homeland, and unsurprisingly as a potential model for the rest of the earth.[26]

By the fifteenth century the Cherokees, like the Iroquois, lived in a sedentary society based primarily on agriculture, in decentralized towns surrounded by palisades. In other respects, however, they developed a culture more similar to that of the Muskogean Chickasaws, Choctaws, and Creeks of the southeastern United States. Public buildings set on terraces demonstrated the importance of civic life and reflected a complex political system. The towns were built around an open public square, formed by four hangar-like wooden structures, which contained a sacred, communal fire, in honor of their dead leaders: "Some say this everlasting fire was only in the larger mounds . . . and a few other towns, and that . . . it was distributed from them to the other settlements." One tall conical building, the "hot house," provided space for official meetings in the winter, and a sunken rectangular yard surrounded by earthen banks served as a venue for spectator sports and dances. Such urban planning and architecture not only indicated a high degree of civic organization, but a strong desire for the regulation of geographical space. This desire found further expression in the dwellings of the populace, which aligned side streets that radiated from the town square. Dwellings could include as many as four buildings – sleeping quarters, kitchen, granary, and winter lodging – also forming a square, with a garden plot nearby. Construction and the organization of space did not reflect haphazard individualized perspectives, but the vision of a nation of autonomous town states united as keepers of the sacred fire.[27]

The Cherokee economy reflected this communal society. Although agricultural fields were divided into family plots, the population of an entire town cultivated the plots. While each family stored its own harvest, it also made voluntary contributions to the common granary. Although agriculture formed the economic base of this society, the population also collected wild fruit, and hunting and fishing provided protein for a community that lacked livestock and had few

[26] Hoig, 8; James Mooney, *Myths of the Cherokee*, Landmarks in Anthropology (1900; reprint, New York: Johnson Reprint Corporation, 1970), 239; see also Barbara R. Duncan, ed., *Living Stories of the Cherokee* (Chapel Hill: Univ. of North Carolina Press, 1998), 40–3.

[27] Mooney, 396; and Angie Debo, *A History of the Indians of the United States*, Civilization of the American Indians Series (Norman: Univ. of Oklahoma Press, 1970), 13–14.

domesticated animals. While the manufacture of baskets, pots, and other material necessities occupied the residents, trade for unusual items thrived. Residing in a vast region of extensive waterways, the Cherokees fashioned dugout canoes and rafts that allowed rather extensive travel to obtain goods not produced in their immediate homeland. These items were also shared within the community.[28]

Given the importance of agriculture, it should be no surprise that religious belief rested on the cultivation of corn, the staple crop of virtually all sedentary North American peoples. According to Cherokee theology, the grain derived from the body of the goddess, appropriately named Corn Woman. The significance of water to an agricultural people appears in the belief that the overall creator was initially a goddess of river foam. The fact that females played such an important role in Cherokee theology suggests that gender functioned in a rather egalitarian fashion in this society, as did class, which was based on personal martial prestige, as well as on matrilineal inheritance.[29]

The relationship between class, gender, ethnicity, and space found expression in the loose political organization of early Cherokee society. This society organized itself and its homeland into clans, with capitals at "mother towns," in a decentralized pattern: "the Cherokees by no means operated a consolidated government presided over by a single chieftain system. . . . But there was a formulated governance, accepted leaders, a format for decision making, and an established place where chiefs and other officials could meet and discuss matters." While towns elected men chiefs from certain families by matrilineal descent, women were among the clan leaders. All leaders ruled by consent, rather than coercion. An assembly, much later called the Women's Council, deliberated and decided on matters as serious as declarations of war. Heading this body was the Beloved Woman of the Nation, a title reflective of real power in this society. On occasion a local leader might gain power over a subregion, but the early Cherokees never formed a confederacy like that of their relatives the Iroquois or their neighbors the Muskogean Creeks.[30]

---

[28] Ibid.; and Theda Perdue, *Cherokee Women: Gender and Culture Change, 1700–1835*, Indians of the Southeast (Lincoln: Univ. of Nebraska Press, 1998), 27.

[29] Debo, 13–14; Paula Gunn Allen, *The Sacred Hoop: Recovering the Feminine in American Indian Traditions* (Boston: Beacon Press, 1986), 25, 41; Hoig, 10–11; and Perdue, 9, 14, 26.

[30] Hoig, 11; Allen, 32, 36; and Perdue, 42.

Though warfare broke out periodically between the Cherokees and their neighbors, all southeastern peoples formed loose political structures rather than empires, despite continual cultural influences from Mesoamerica. Indeed, whether or not the Cherokees migrated from Texas, as suggested by Jennings, they and other southeastern peoples certainly received influences from a southwesterly direction, especially through their mound building Mississippian predecessors, extending from A.D. 700. In fact, archeologists have traced indigenous ceremonial mound building as far as 1400 B.C. in Louisiana, a practice found throughout the Mississippi and Ohio Valleys, as well as the Southeast. According to anthropologist Alice Kehoe,

> the resemblances between the Southeast and Mexico are tantalizing. The layout of towns, the presence of both platform and conical mounds and central plazas, the frequency of square houses and the tendency toward rectangular household compounds around courtyards, the importance of ball games, . . . the symbols of rank, . . . rekindling of fire . . . and, of course, maize, beans, and squashes – all seem generalized Mesoamerican patterns, yet none are identical in detail to any Mexican culture. The relationships across the Gulf of Mexico may never be unraveled.[31]

Be that as it may, the Chickasaws, the Choctaws, and the Natchez, distant Cherokee neighbors on the lower Mississippi, all have migratory traditions linking them to the Southwest and Mexico. According to a Choctaw account recorded in 1820, they and the Chickasaw in ancient times "dwelt in a country far distant toward the setting sun [Texas, part of New Spain (Mexico) in 1820, lay directly west]; and being conquered and greatly oppressed by a more powerful people resolved to seek a country far removed." After "passing over wide extended plains and through forests," they crossed the Mississippi River to their new homes. "Then, as commemorative of this great event in their national history, they threw up a large mound embracing three acres of land and rising forty feet in conical form." Even more suggestive of Mexican origins is a Natchez narrative recorded in 1758 directly from a priest at the tribal temple:

[31] *First Americans*, The American Indians (Alexandria, Va.: Time-Life Books, 1992), 120, 116, 102, 99; Jennings, *Founders in America*, 73; Hoig, 10; and Alice Beck Kehoe, *North American Indians: A Comprehensive Account*, Prentice-Hall Series in Anthropology (Englewood Cliffs, N.J.: Prentice-Hall, 1981), 175–6.

Before we came into this land we lived yonder under the sun (pointing with his finger nearly south-west, by which I [the French recorder] understood that he meant Mexico). . . . Our nation extended itself along the great water [the Gulf of Mexico] . . . where this large river [the Mississippi] loses itself; but as our enemies were become very numerous . . . the Great Sun . . . ordered all his subjects to remove into this land, here to build a temple.[32]

Jennings argues that a colony from Teotihuacan or Tula in central Mexico migrated north and helped spur native civilization during the Mississippian period. As we have seen, the Choctaws recount a journey by land, probably through Texas; the Natchez's account leaves open the possibility of a voyage by canoe or raft along the Gulf Coast. In neither case, however, did the Mesoamericans leave any impression on the Coahuiltecan or Karankawan bands whose Texan territories they presumably crossed, suggesting no long-term stay there. On the other hand, in East Texas and Louisiana the agricultural Caddos had a mound-building tradition. Even scholars who doubt a direct Mexican connection recognize the indirect spread of Mesoamerican culture along the Gulf, and as far as the Atlantic.[33]

IMPERIAL AZTECS AND SUBJECT TOTONACS

While the Mississippians and prior mound building cultures established complex hierarchical societies over an immense expanse of territory, they remained decentralized, matrilineal city-states, unlike the empires of Mesoamerica. In 1400 indirect trade routes undoubtedly connected various North American peoples to the Aztecs (Mexica) of the Valley of Mexico. They were the most recent of a series of sophisticated civilizations and empires that had appeared and disappeared in that area over two millenia, after earlier migrations south from the Bering Strait. Surrounding them were cultures organized in every geopolitical way, from bands, to city-states, to federations. Indeed, their own history reflected these various patterns at different periods of their development. While earlier observers argued that the Aztecs were finally

---

[32] H. B. Cushman, *History of the Choctaw, Chickasaw, and Natchez Indians* (1899; reprint, Norman: Univ. of Oklahoma Press, 1999), 19–21; and Jennings, *Founders in America*, 45.

[33] Ibid., 45–6, 72–3; William B. Griffen, "Southern Periphery: East," *Handbook*, vol. 10, *Southwest*, ed. Alfonso Ortiz (1983), 330–1; and Hoig, 9–10.

organized as a tribute state, a collection of protectorates, today's scholars consider their state an empire, the best example of that form of geopolitical unit in Middle or North America.[34]

Because we have greater knowledge of the Aztecs' origins in the precontact era, we can arrive at more accurate conclusions regarding the connections between their ethnic identity and the land that they occupied. Fortunately, we have a distinct chronicle of migration to examine in this case. According to the Aztecs, their ancestors migrated to the area of later Mexico City from a place to the northwest, which researchers have reliably placed along the Pacific Coast of the modern Mexican state of Nayarit. Embedded in this story, additionally, is a universal Mesoamerican theme that at the time of creation, the people sprang from caves in mother earth, thus claiming native status in central Mexico, as well as corroborating archeological evidence for their long presence in the region. In any case, in the early twelfth century A.D. the Aztecs began a long convoluted migration that by either 1325 or 1345 led them to an island in a lake in the Valley of Mexico. There they encountered a divine sign indicating that they should establish themselves permanently: "Near the rocks they joyfully sighted/An eagle perched proudly on a cactus." On this sacred spot they founded Tenochtitlan, the place of the cactus rock, now Mexico City. On that spot the Aztecs built their temple, their homeland, their nation, and their empire.[35]

At the time of their migration, the Aztecs were a nomadic tribe of hunters and gatherers, but by the year 1400 they had established a city-state. Having migrated into the central valley, they were at first violently rejected by their civilized neighbors, but finally learned the latter's urban ways. Indeed, they eventually built a city of three hundred thousand, the rival of any other in the world. At the center were the Great Pyramid, lesser temples, the royal palaces, and administrative buildings; four major roads radiated from the center, three becoming causeways that crossed the lake waters to the mainland beyond the city.

[34] Victor Wolfgang von Hagen, *The Aztec: Man and Tribe*, rev. ed. (New York: New American Library, Times Mirror, Mentor Books, 1961), 175; and Pedro Carrasco, *The Tenochca Empire of Ancient Mexico: The Triple Alliance of Tenochtitlan, Tetzcoco, and Tlacopan*, Civilization of the American Indian Series, vol. 234 (Norman: Univ. of Oklahoma Press, 1999), 3.

[35] Richard F. Townsend, *The Aztecs*, Ancient Peoples and Places, rev. ed. (London: Thames & Hudson, 2000), 57–58, 65; and Miguel León Portilla, *Los antiguos mexicanos a través de sus crónicas y cantares*, Lecturas mexicanas (Mexico City: Fondo de Cultura Económica, Cultura SEP, 1983), 42, my translation.

Canals and walkways, laid in a grid, subdivided the manufacturing, commercial, residential, and smaller ritual quarters. The residences of the elite lay close to these ritual districts, while the thatched huts of the lower classes extended to the outskirts. Since much of the city was built on land reclaimed from the lake, intensive agriculture was still practiced in some areas on the civic edges. The architecture reflected a highly stratified, male dominated, martial society. Nevertheless, according to art historian, Richard Townsend,

> The city's plan . . . and its place in the natural setting, were visible expressions of religious and aesthetic forces that flowed through the life of the people. In great measure the Aztec state drew its power from . . . seasonal rites . . . . [that] celebrated individual achievements and specific historical events, but more importantly they brought the community into direct contact with the elemental life of the land – the mountains, clouds, rain and thunder, the wind, the lakes, and the sun.

According to Aztec cosmogony, the survival of this world depended on sustaining the Sun with human sacrifice, and the empire had to provide the victims.[36]

Like the Iroquois and Cherokees, the Aztecs relied on the clan as a basic unit of economic and territorial organization, with moieties carrying out social functions that crossed territorial boundaries. On the founding of Tenochtitlan, each clan had received a zone within the city where it built a temple and held land communally. By democratic consensus individual peasant families then received hereditary rights to plots for farming, rights that could be reassigned by the clan for negligence or other serious cause. The peasants paid tribute for use of the land. As the Aztec state expanded, private property, independent of the clans, came into the hands of Mexica leaders as they intermarried with the elite of surrounding towns or acquired land through warfare. Imperialism thus contributed to further social stratification.[37]

After achieving the status of a free city-state, Tenochtitlan formed a federation in 1428 with two neighboring cities, Tetzcoco and

[36] Alfredo Mirandé and Evangelina Enríquez, La Chicana: The Mexican–American Woman (Chicago: Univ. of Chicago Press, 1979), 15–23; Townsend, 26–34; Mann, 1491, 120–1, calculates that proportionally deaths by execution in Western Europe probably exceeded those from human sacrifice in Mexico.
[37] Townsend, 68, 69–70; Von Hagen, 55.

Tlacopan, which the Mexicas dominated from the onset. As a militaristic culture, the Mexicas soon expanded at the expense of surrounding peoples well beyond the Valley of Mexico. As commander of the alliance's armies and distributor of tribute from conquered areas, the king of Tenochtitlan controlled the key military and economic functions of the federation, effectively making him emperor and it an empire. Tetzcoco and Tlacopan also received tribute as they participated in conquest, but they were secondary and tertiary members, respectively, of the imperial core. Nevertheless, through a complex system of territorial segmentation where each city-state occupied lands in conquered areas, the federation maintained a certain level of cooperation, while the empire to a certain degree integrated its factions.[38]

Though lacking clearly defined borders, the Aztec Empire eventually extended from the Pacific Coast to the Gulf of Mexico, from Chiapas in the south to Querétaro in the north. (See Map 1.2.) In distant regions the empire varied in the control it exercised. When states submitted voluntarily to Aztec hegemony or resisted little, they might be accepted as allies with only occasional tribute and military support expected. The Aztecs usually permitted conquered provinces to maintain local governance as long as they paid tribute to Tenochtitlan. But in other areas the empire might introduce an administrative bureaucracy or keep standing armies at strategic locations with settlers from the imperial core as military colonists. Such settlement was the ultimate step in imperial occupation. Thus the empire consisted of a federated core with Tenochtitlan at the center; the core's domain largely comprised the Valley of Mexico, with the periphery composed of allies, protectorates, and conquered provinces beyond the mountains. However, the generally loose system of control confined the actual Aztec homeland to the environs of the capital as acculturation of surrounding peoples proceeded rather slowly.[39]

Though loosely structured, the Aztec state nevertheless had the key elements of empire. The Mexica people, or nation, conquered and dominated vast territories comprised of various cultures primarily for the benefit of its elite. One of the most important regions of the empire was along the Gulf Coast, a region of formerly independent city-states called Cuextlan, with inhabitants known as Totonacs, speaking a language related to Mayan. Archeology has placed this people in the Vera

[38] Carrasco, 3–5, 9, 424.
[39] Ibid., 8, 432–3; and Townsend, 8–9.

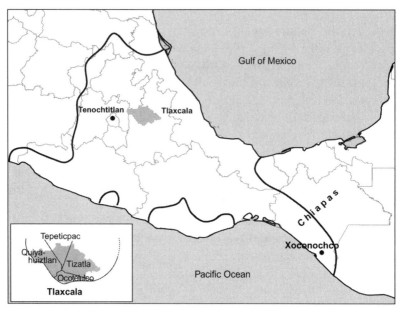

Map 1.2. The Aztec Empire with Present Mexican State Lines in the Background, and Inset of Early Tlaxcala. Adapted from Carrasco, *The Tenochca Empire of Ancient Mexico*, 391; inset adapted from Lockhart, Berdan, and Anderson, *The Tlaxcalan Actas*, xiii. Cartography by Cassingham and Foxworth, courtesy of the Edwin J. Foscue Map Library, SMU.

Cruz region at least since 500 B.C., reflecting indigenous accounts of local origin. The region's civilization was as elaborate as that of the Valley of Mexico: "Cempoala. The temple-city alone . . . had a population estimated at about thirty thousand; the walled plaza . . . had an over-all measurement of . . . nearly 689,000 square feet. The general aspect revealed by research was that it was stone laid with soaring temples . . . surrounded by one-storied houses, gaily painted and grass-thatched." However, its grandeur and that of the other Totonac city-states were no match for Aztec arms.[40]

In 1458 the Aztecs conquered Cuextlan in response to the murder of envoys sent to negotiate for the region's products. The Aztecs then divided the region into several geopolitical entities – the tributary province of Cuetlaxtlan, which it governed directly, and Cempoala, which it ruled through the local leadership, both placed under the surveillance of a broader military district. Shortly after, Cuetlaxtlan

[40] Carrasco, 3, 356; and Von Hagen, 37–8, 190, 148.

rebelled and killed the governor and other Aztec officials, drawing a predictable response from Tenochtitlan. By 1463 the Aztecs had subdued the region, executed the local lords whom the commoners had abandoned, and required the latter to elect new leadership. Significantly, thousands of Mexica families were then transferred to the coast as a military colony to secure continuation of the province's tribute. These events clearly illustrate the role of colonists in holding empire.[41]

As in the Totonac region, distinctions between conquerer and conquered in the Aztec Empire were often based on ethnicity, though the conquered neighbors closest to Tenochtitlan spoke Nahuatl and had very similar cultures. The Aztecs, however, had a distinct history as "barbaric" migrants who had initially been disparaged by the more established peoples of the Valley of Mexico. This history and its subsequent vindication, rather than language or other cultural elements, defined them as a people. Consequently, groups subordinate to them were not necessarily different culturally, except in terms of historical legacy. In any case the empire's loose structure did not permit its rapid development into an extensive national state, though the beginnings of that had occurred in the valley itself as the federated city-states identified increasingly with Tenochtitlan. In the fifteenth century no people on either side of the Atlantic had yet developed the wide-reaching cultural and administrative centralization of the complex modern national state.[42]

The Kingdom of Tlaxcala

Surrounded by the Aztec Empire, in the mountains between the Valley and the Gulf of Mexico, Tlaxcala nevertheless maintained its independence. Curiously, this Nahuatl-speaking nation also had a history of migration similar to that of other Mesoamerican peoples; the Tlaxcalans had originated in the womb of a mountain and arrived in central Mexico somewhat earlier than the Aztecs. On their arrival they encountered two earlier ethnically and linguistically distinct groups, the Pinomes and Otomis. Apparently, clashing with these peoples, the newcomers subdued them in an act of imperial conquest. Some intermixing occurred among these groups, particularly with the Otomis, but this process had not assimilated the earlier groups by the early 1500s. The Otomis, for example, provided servants and soldiers to the

[41] Carrasco, 354–5, 390, 357.
[42] Townsend, 54, 63.

Tlaxcalan state, which marked them as a subordinate group. Moreover, Otomis occupied border areas between the Aztecs and Tlaxcalans, consequently serving as a buffer for the latter. Despite this, the relatively small territory controlled by Tlaxcala, coupled with the hostility of the surrounding Aztec empire, created a relatively cohesive kingdom, with only the remnants of empire at the homeland's edges.[43]

Though fiercely independent, the Tlaxcalans shared many cultural features with the Aztecs and the entire complex of civilizations in central Mexico. The Tlaxcalans lived in populous, permanent towns built of large stone structures including central squares with temple pyramids of stone. Although these towns were not as elaborate as those of the Aztecs, they included many of the same spatial elements, such as vast markets. As an urbanized people with early extensive trading networks, the Tlaxcalans, like the Aztecs, developed class differentiation. Living in a stratified society, the wealthy underwent elaborate initiation rituals to confirm their status. Naturally, clothing marked class difference as well; the wealthy dressed in cotton, while the poor wore skins or grass clothing. The military reflected these differences as well with warrior societies separating elite troops from common soldiers. Constant warfare with the Aztecs, nevertheless, tended to act as a social leveler as the economy suffered.[44]

Despite this constant warfare, the Tlaxcalans and Aztecs shared many religious beliefs. Their religion was polytheistic, including a hierarchy of deities. Though females were represented in this pantheon, militarism tended to produce greater reverence for male gods. The sun god predominated as the cosmos itself depended on his journey across the firmament. Like the Aztecs, Tlaxcalans believed this god and others required human sacrifice for sustenance and continuation of the existence of the universe. Consequently, Tlaxcalans practiced such sacrifice, as did most other Mesoamerican cultures. It was considered an honor to be sacrificed, particularly after capture in battle. Indeed, the Aztecs preferred to allow Tlaxcalan independence in order for continual warfare to provide captives for sacrifice.[45]

---

[43] Ibid., 60, 62; and Charles Gibson, *Tlaxcala in the Sixteenth Century*, Yale Historical Publications, miscellany 56 (New Haven, Conn.: Yale Univ. Press, 1952), 1–15; cf. Carrasco, 356, 388, regarding the status of the Pinomes and Otomis.

[44] Von Hagen, 89–90; and *Hernando Cortés: Five Letters, 1519–1526*, trans. J. Bayard Morris (New York: W. W. Norton, 1969), 50–1.

[45] Gibson, 14.

Apparently, Tlaxcala enjoyed its greatest prosperity between 1300 and 1400, before the expanding Aztecs limited the mountain state's activities. Previously, Tlaxcalans had engaged in extensive coast-to-coast trade and amassed wealth as intermediaries. Because their homeland lacked natural resources and extensive farmland, commerce had become necessary. Trade items included salt, cotton, gold, silver, precious stones, and feathers; however, such items became scarce after 1400 with the stragglehold of the Aztecs. The resulting resentment against the Aztecs played a key role in the warfare between the two peoples, regardless of the need for sacrificial victims. Prior to Aztec expansion, Tlaxcalan relations with surrounding peoples had apparently been amicable, particularly with Nahuatl-speaking neighbors. As Tlaxcala lost its Totonac allies to Aztec conquest, self-defense necessitated an even more militant mentality. Despite the fact that battles basically involved capture, constant warfare and sacrifice was a drain on both the populace and its resources. As an increasingly isolated mountainous enclave, Tlaxcalan culture tended to diminish.[46]

Although the Tlaxcalan nation remained relatively decentralized, the constant state of military preparedness reinforced unity, to a degree unfelt by the distant Cherokees, Iroquois, or Micmacs to the northeast. Four major Tlaxcalan towns served as headquarters for surrounding lesser communities, each of which had its own hereditary lord, but one of these was regarded as the principal leader. The Spanish would later speak of their dealings with the most powerful king named Maxixcatzin, who was descended from a dynasty two hundred years long. Tlaxcala thus had all the elements of a monarchy and would function as such in its encounter with the intruders from across the Atlantic.[47]

VISIONS OF HOMELAND AND COMMUNITY

The ways Native Americans organized their homelands reflected their visions of the land, their people, and themselves as individuals. A Naskapi man perceived himself and his band as caretakers embodying the animal spirits of their hunting territories. A Micmac woman saw herself as part of a nation with a collective, demarcated body of territory, subject to seasonal, individual family distribution. An Iroquois boy viewed himself as one of the People of the Longhouse, a matrilineal

[46] Townsend, 100; and Gibson, 10–12.
[47] Ibid.

confederation of nations stretching across a lengthy homeland. A Cherokee girl saw herself as a member of a Mother Town, surrounded by fields blessed by the feminine deities of corn and water. The Aztec thought of himself as potentially one of the "kings of all that is in the world," reflecting a nation and homeland expanding into empire. While a Totonac male viewed himself and his people as restive vassals in a tropical land, the Tlaxcalan female saw herself and her nation as fierce defenders of a mountainous kingdom. In all these Native American visions, both scenes of migration and native origin helped to describe the establishment of the community and the organization of the homeland. Such was also the case east of the Atlantic.[48]

[48] Engelbrecht, 129; and Townsend, 59.

CHAPTER TWO

VISIONS OF HOMELAND IN
EUROPE AND AFRICA

CHANGING COMMUNITIES

At the beginning of the fifteenth century, as we have seen, humans in the Americas had more or less established themselves in specific lands after long migrations from other places, often distant in both space and time. Given even a brief length of residence, peoples came to envision themselves as native to what they had come to see as their homelands. This process was similar in the many lands bordering the eastern shores of the North Atlantic Ocean, even though ethnic identities were always in flux. As in the Americas prior to transoceanic contact, communities in Western Europe and West Africa varied and overlapped in physical and social geography. Here too, individuals perceived images of their people and land, images sustaining ethnic and national loyalties. From Ireland and Brittany, through the Basque Country, to the Maghreb, Senegambia, and Sierra Leone, a person belonged to a tribe, a city, a nation, a kingdom, an empire, a confederation, and usually more than one. From the British Isles to the Temne country, people viewed themselves as members of such political communities, though especially as natives of homelands. By the end of the fifteenth century, however, empire would become the most powerful vision of community on the eastern shores of the Atlantic, as well as the western.[1]

---

[1] Robert Bartlett, *The Making of Europe: Conquest, Colonization, and Cultural Change, 950–1350* (Princeton, N.J.: Princeton Univ. Press, 1993), 3, 200–1; for one typology of societies, see Jared Diamond, *Guns, Germs, and Steel: The Fates of Human Societies* (New York: W. W. Norton, 1997), 268–9; for a discussion of the politically loaded nature of societal terms, such as tribe and nation, chiefdom and kingdom, see Alice Beck Kehoe, *America before the European Invasions*, Longman History of United States (London: Longman, Pearson Education, 2002), 244–5.

The Irish Earldoms

By 1400 A.D. Ireland had experienced many migrations and invasions and was still in an eight-hundred-year process of dealing with English imperialism. Archeologists tell us the first humans in Ireland probably migrated via a land bridge from Britain around 6000 B.C.; Celtic legends say Partholan, his wife Dalny, and companion deities, came from the west beyond the Atlantic, from "the land of the Happy Dead." Despite these major disagreements, both archeologists and storytellers believe this occurred a long time ago and that other migrations followed. For example, archeologists have discovered prehistoric artifacts from the Baltic and Scandinavian countries and have found human remains suggesting residents of Mediterranean, possibly Spanish heritage, people later called Picts. The legends speak of four migrations after Partholan's, culminating in the invasion of the fully human Milesians, coincidentally from "Spain," the "Land of the Dead." According to folklorists, these Milesians were probably the Celts who invaded Ireland from Britain during the fourth century B.C. There they conquered and acculturated the Picts to become the Irish, who over the next two millenia experienced historic invasions by Vikings, Normans, and then English.[2]

Despite their long residence in Ireland, the Celts had no equivalent to Native American stories of origin in the homeland. The ethnic roots nevertheless ran deep in the soil, as indicated in the folklore. When the goddess Eriu of the third legendary migration married the child of the Sun, they united the sky and earth since she represented the latter. For a pastoral and agricultural people such a vision was natural given the essential connection between sunlight and grasses for the community's survival and prosperity. Various other forms of her name, Erin and Eire, applied to Ireland, one variant known to the Greeks as early as the sixth century B.C.[3]

Geopolitically, the early Celts contributed significantly to the image of Ireland. After their arrival, the country traditionally comprised five

---

[2]   T[homas] W[illiam] Rolleston, *Myths and Legends of the Celtic Race* (London: G. G. Harrap & Co., 1911), 96, 130–1.

[3]   Magnus MacLean, *The Literature of the Celts*, Kennikat Series in Irish History and Culture (1902;reprint, Port Washington, N.Y.: Kennikat Press, 1970), 1–3; Rolleston, 132; and Donnchadh Ó Corráin, "Prehistoric and Early Christian Ireland, in *The Oxford Illustrated History of Ireland*, ed. R[obert] F[itzroy] Foster (New York: Oxford Univ. Press, 1989), 1.

major provinces: Ulster, Connacht, Leinster, Munster, and a floating fifth at various times subdivided from the others or forming the middle known as Meath with a capital at Tara. (See Map 2.1.) The alternative patterns of the fifth province reflected a conflict between a desire for centralization and actual disunity. The provinces were based on the ancient Celtic kingdoms that competed with one another for hundreds of years for hegemony in a united kingship, which was usually more symbolic than operative. From A.D. 500 to 1000 the five provinces became seven major kingdoms, but with outlines following the early patterns. Despite the decentralized states, the idea of a united kingdom went back at least as far as the seventh century A.D. when one commentator spoke of "a great king, fierce and pagan, and emperor of non-Romans, with his royal seat at Tara, which was then the capital of the realm of the Irish." The vision of a larger nation, however, always gave way to local loyalties.[4]

The autonomy of the Irish kings unfortunately left them vulnerable to foreign attack, as when the Norse repeatedly raided the island from the 790s to 1100. Relatively soon thereafter, Pope Adrian IV granted Ireland to Henry II of England, a grant the latter confirmed in 1171 by appearing in Ireland with an impressive army. Most of the Irish kings accepted Henry's suzerainty, but not all. Subsequently, Anglo-Norman lords received vast grants of land and even replaced local rulers, as English law was imposed on the people, including the county geopolitical system and eventually a parliament, representing only the new colonizing "Anglo-Irish." Conquered thus, Ireland would nevertheless remain restive as an incipient English empire sought to absorb it.[5]

In the century following Henry's conquest, colonization secured his holdings and those of the Anglo-Norman lords. In a period of over-population in England and France, the originally military lords readily found colonists to make their new estates remunerative, especially in eastern Ireland. In doing so, the English replaced the old Celtic social organization that included a primarily pastoral economy, open fields and wastes, small hamlets and farms, familism, partible inheritance, and low class stratification. The English imported the continental

---

[4] Alwyn Rees and Brinley Rees, *Celtic Heritage: Ancient Tradition in Ireland and Wales* (New York: Grove Press, 1961), 18–21; and Muirchú quoted in Ó Corráin, 27–8.

[5] Ibid., 31, 34; and Katharine Simms, "The Norman Invasion and the Gaelic Recovery," in Foster, 56–7, 60, 67–8.

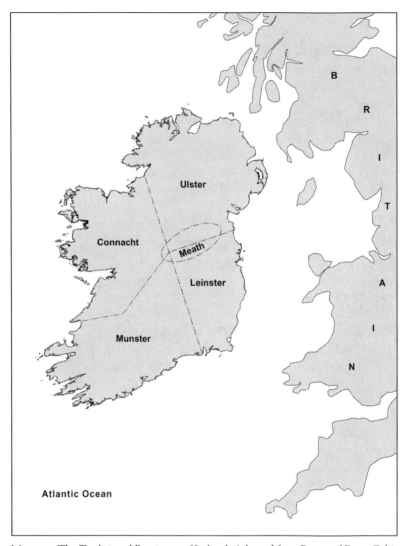

Map 2.1. The Traditional Provinces of Ireland. Adapted from Rees and Rees, *Celtic Heritage*, 121. Cartography by Cassingham and Foxworth, courtesy of the Edwin J. Foscue Map Library, SMU.

feudal system involving a cereal-based agricultural economy, common fields farmed in rotation, nucleated villages, manorial control, primogeniture, and high stratification. In this process the native Irish, even their nobility, became mere tenants on the lands of the Anglo-Norman lords, lands administered, in the opinion of one observer, by "men who . . . spent all their time in the greedy pursuit of wealth."[6]

The landscape itself changed with the coming of the English. In rural areas the conquerors early constructed "mottes," mounds capped with towers of wood, or "ringwork castles" with wooden palisades generally near an established population center with economic possibilities. Later these were built of stone for stronger defense against rebellious Irish or competitive Anglo-Irish. Urban planning changed as the English introduced the grid pattern in place of the older winding streets set to the shape of the natural site. Architecturally, buildings of heavy lumber replaced wattle-work structures; Early English Gothic replaced Irish Romanesque churches. All of this rested on an economy changed from subsistence to trade as the large estates collected the surplus of their tenants for shipment to local or overseas markets. The great stone castles of the thirteenth century reflected the prosperity of the Anglo-Irish colony, not only in their visible military grandeur, but in their function as financial centers.[7]

The English conquest had its sociocultural impact particularly in the fertile river valleys and lowlands of eastern and southeastern Ireland. In the towns and even among the peasants, the English language gained ground while Norman French secured its place within the colonial upper classes. The Irish nobles, now tenants themselves, found their remaining estates confined to the uplands, usually in woods and bogs. The Irish peasants were reduced to the status of serfs, bound to the land, in contrast to the free English husbandmen. Speaking Gaelic and wearing a moustache marked one audibly and visibly as a member of a colonized ethnic group. This of course led to constant armed resistance by

---

[6]   Michael Hechter, *Internal Colonialism: The Celtic Fringe in British National Development, 1536–1966* (Berkeley and Los Angeles: Univ. of California Press, 1975), 58; Gerald of Wales quoted in Simms, 60; and David Armitage, *The Ideological Origins of the British Empire*, Ideas in Context 59 (Cambridge: Cambridge Univ. Press, 2000), 6, 25. Armitage considers internal colonialism too general and deterministic; he prefers "the paradigm of composite monarchy. Ireland thereby appears as a province, comparable to Bohemia or Naples, for example, rather than a colony of an emergent hemispheric empire." Though his analysis is more nuanced in terms of specific time and place, it does not negate Hechter's comparison in terms of conquest, land transfer, settlement, economic change, ethnic inequality, and the other characteristics of colonial domination.

[7]   Simms, 60–4; for a brief overview of the various British empires, see Armitage, 27–9.

Irish nobles or peasant bands even at a peak of English control around 1300.[8]

During the fourteenth and fifteenth centuries, however, the English empire experienced dramatic setbacks. English wars in Wales, Scotland, and France shifted attention away from Ireland and drained it of resources. Conflict and disease, both in Ireland and overseas, lessened immigration and population with a consequent drop in production, trade, and investment. Such problems led to an ethnic Gaelic resurgence, celebrated in song: "Ireland is a woman risen again/ from the horrors of reproach." As some English actually returned to Britain because of declining conditions, those remaining in the colony by the fourteenth century became more Gaelic. After several generations in Ireland, the Anglo-Irish or Old English intermarried with some of the natives and thus began to see themselves as indigenous, even acquiring the Gaelic language and local customs. This acculturation had always been active in the west where English settlement had been least, but it gradually extended to other areas as well.[9]

Politically, the decline in English imperial power led to changes visible on a map during the fifteenth century. In 1460 the Anglo-Irish declared that, while loyal to the king of England (to a pretender in this case), only the laws of their parliament in Dublin applied on their own island. Despite various attempts to restore English control before and after this declaration, including a personal military campaign by Richard II, the area directly under royal control by 1500 remained a fortified enclave around Dublin known as the Pale. This, however, did not mean that the Gaelic Irish had recovered the rest of the map, for the rest was divided into autonomous earldoms in Anglo-Irish hands. While Ireland largely acknowledged English suzerainty, power remained effectively decentralized in the provinces. England had not yet mastered the processes of imperialism, nor had Ireland those of national community. Panoramic visions of homeland, nation, and

---

[8] Nicholas Canny, "Early Modern Ireland, c. 1500–1700," in Foster, 104; Simms, 63; and Art Cosgrove, "The Gaelic Resurgence and the Geraldine Supremacy (c. 1400–1534)," in *The Course of Irish History*, ed. T. W. Moody and F. X. Martin, rev. ed. (Niwot, Colo.: Roberts Rinehart Publishers, 1995), 169.

[9] "Ode for Niall Mór O'Neill" quoted in Simms, 89, 83, 86, 88; James Muldoon, *Identity on the Medieval Irish Frontier: Degenerate Englishmen, Wild Irishmen, Middle Nations* (Gainesville, Fla.: Univ. Press of Florida, 2003), 38–46.

empire required greater breadth and depth of imagination on the part of individuals and peoples to achieve fulfillment.[10]

THE ENGLISH KINGDOM AND THE CELTIC FRINGE

Fronting the Atlantic with Ireland, Britain also shared an early history with its neighbor as a homeland for Picts and Celts, sharing elements of folklore as well. Britain, however, experienced more migration, including Roman invasion and conquest in the first century A.D., beginning a process that would move it away from the Celtic heritage. Later, around 450 A.D., Germanic tribes invaded and defeated the Romanized Celts known as Britons. Migration and conquest thus played a central role in the national development of England, with the English identity deriving primarily from the Teutonic Angles, Saxons, and Jutes. *Beowulf*, the seventh-century epic, recounts that an ancient Anglo-Saxon hero "was born in Noah's ark," Christianizing the migratory origins of these tribes. This same hero, Sceaf, in another account, is, as a child, stranded on an island named Scandza, which some historians place in lower Scandinavia. Afterward, he rules a German town in "Old Anglia being situated between the Saxons and the Goths. From this area the Angles came to Britain."[11]

Significantly, King Arthur, a chieftain of Roman-Briton extraction, resists these Anglo-Saxon invasions during the decline of Roman Britain. Though he is successful during his lifetime, in the long-term the "barbaric" Germanic tribes thoroughly colonize his homeland. Ironically, later English identity, though fundamentally Germanic, draws on the victorious Arthur for his civilized stature, rather than on his ultimately defeated Celtic people. Thus, conflicting Anglo-Saxon and Celtic myths, histories, and peoples reconcile, but in a centuries-long process of amalgamation. For as the chronicler Bede noted in 731: "This island at present . . . contains five nations, the English, Britons, Scots, Picts and Latins, each in his own peculiar dialect." Of these ethnic

---

[10] "Declaration of Independence of the Irish Parliament, 1460," in *Irish Historical Documents, 1172–1922*, ed. Edmund Curtis and R. B. McDowell (1943; reprint, New York: Barnes & Noble, 1968), 72–6; and Simms, 93.

[11] Quoted in Brian Branston, *The Lost Gods of England* (New York: Oxford Univ. Press, 1974), 18–19; for the Roman Empire as a geopolitical model of expansion through "unequal confederations," as well as conquest, see Armitage, 29–31, 129.

groups, obviously the English would eventually dominate in the formation of the later state of England.[12]

After their arrival in Britain, the Angles and Saxons formed independent kingdoms that warred against one another despite being culturally, linguistically, and religiously similar. Indeed, all the royal
families claimed descent from the same Nordic god, Woden, suggesting
that they were all related dynasties. Though the lowland Britons were
gradually assimilated through conquest, acculturation, and interbreed-
ing, unity among the Anglo-Saxons took centuries. In this process one
state achieved dominance in the long run – the Kingdom of Wessex.
Founded in approximately A.D. 494–5 by settlers from the continent,
this state expanded mostly through conquest of its neighbors. While
dominance alternated among the various kingdoms, by 886 only King
Alfred of Wessex could claim direct descent from the kings of the time
of the migrations. Though his grandfather, Egbert, had gained his
dynasty's overlordship over most of the competing kingdoms, Alfred
successfully resisted conquest by another wave of invaders, the Vikings.
He thus assured that what was by then called England remained the
homeland of the English.[13]

Despite Alfred's successes, the unity of England remained shaky,
even with the incorporation of the Danish colonies that the Vikings
had successfully established in Britain. Nevertheless, by the standards of
the early Middle Ages, the Old English state achieved some centralization. Walled towns surrounded by shires, geopolitcal administrative
units, allowed for protection from attack, but also for collection of
a national tax, certainly a sign of state power. Despite another Danish
invasion in 1013, the English state survived as the brief Danish rule
followed English traditions until restoration of the West Saxon dynasty
from 1042 to 1066. At this point England was comprised of two major
ethnic groups, the English of Teutonic heritage and the Danes of Viking
ancestry.[14]

In 1066 England fell to a far more thorough conqueror, William of
Normandy. The subordination of the Saxon and Danish peoples who

---

[12] Quoted in Hugh A. MacDougall, *Racial Myth in English History: Trojans, Teutons, and Anglo-Saxons* (Hanover, N.H.: Univ. Press of New England, 1982), 31.

[13] Hechter, 54; and R. R. Davies, *The First English Empire: Power and Identities in the
British Isles, 1093–1343*, Ford Lectures Delivered in the University of Oxford in
Hilary Term 1998 (Oxford: Oxford Univ. Press, 2000), 50–1.

[14] Ibid., despite these continuing ethnic differences, Davies argues that England
"was becoming a powerfully imagined community, a nation-state"; Hechter, 54.

comprised England to the Norman French further exemplifies the role of imperialism in nation building, even as it exemplifies the role of dynastic struggle in the same process. The Normans, despite their descent from the same ancient Scandinavian roots as the Saxons and the Danes, had adopted a Latin culture that marked them as ethnically distinct. The Normans introduced a new French language and culture that made the conquest bitter and transformational. According to historian Hugh Kearney, "Normans behaved as conquerers and remained conscious of the origins of their power for long after 1066. Late in the thirteenth century William de Warenne spoke of 'how his ancestors came with William the Bastard and conquered their lands by the sword.'" Not until the plague forced the intermingling of Norman and Saxon in the mid-fourteenth century did the English people significantly merge again. Indeed, the ramifications of that conquest continued even to 1400, as the heirs to Norman royalty ironically sought to conquer France, the land from which their ancestors came. Their failure to do so during the Hundred Years War would permanently separate England and France, creating two major national communities in Western Europe.[15]

While national development proceeded gradually in what is now England, this often imperial process would founder in Celtic Wales, Scotland, and – as we have seen – Ireland. For example, after William the Conqueror invaded Britain, various Norman lords independently established their rule over the Welsh. While the Anglo-Norman kings sought to control these nobles, the latter retained much of their autonomy. Despite increasing royal ownership of Welsh estates, Wales remained effectively out of the control of the English monarchy for hundreds of years. It was not until the sixteenth century that the English would impose a greater degree of centralization on the Welsh and the descendants of the Norman lords, who had acculturated to Celtic ways.[16]

The situations of Scotland and Ireland were somewhat similar. From the thirteenth century English cultural influence had penetrated the lowlands to the point where the Scots there became anglicized. On the other hand, the Gaelic-speaking highlanders and Viking colonists in the distant north retained their traditional ways. Despite the

---

[15] Hugh Kearney, *The British Isles: A History of Four Nations* (Cambridge: Cambridge Univ. Press, 1989), 65–6.
[16] Davies, *First English Empire*, 5–6; and Hechter, 56.

dominance of anglicized lowlanders, Scotland developed into a kingdom independent of England and remained so in the fifteenth century.
As such, Scotland often allied itself with France to forestall English
imperialism, thus developing into a distinct dynastic state, in foreign as
well as domestic affairs. As we have seen, Ireland had also stalled
English imperial ambitions, and consequently British national development. In the face of repeated invasions, various Celtic peoples and
homelands, even Cornwall in England, retained their identities as ethnic regions with varying degrees of political autonomy. The man or
woman in the Celtic Fringe still identified more with locale, local lords,
and region, than with distant king or state. In this these people differed
little from others in the lands around the North Atlantic.[17]

THE BRETON DUCHY AND THE FRENCH KINGDOM

As in the case of the British Isles, Celts of Central European origin
migrated to the Atlantic peninsula, now known as Brittany about 400
B.C., apparently merging with their little known predecessors in the
region. According to a Celtic legend recorded in A.D. 120, on the
northern shores of Gaul (now France) existed a people whose occupation as mariners was to ferry souls on their ultimate migration to the
"Land of the Dead," which lay in Cornwall at Britain's western extreme.
Brittany, then called Armorica, was thus on the edge of the world of the
living, an image reflective of a maritime people, historically isolated on
a homeland thrust into the Atlantic. Despite being conquered by Julius
Caesar in 56 B.C., these Celts retained their language and culture after
the rest of Gaul became thoroughly Latinized.[18]

    This Celtic community survived and indeed increased with the
decline of the Roman Empire. In the fifth century Celts fleeing the
Anglo-Saxon invasions of Britain joined their kin in Armorica in such
numbers that the region eventually came to be called Brittany. However, Welsh and Breton traditions describe this migration of Celtic
relatives as a brutal invasion. Awarded the region for service to a Roman
emperor named Maximus (one of three possibilities in the fourth and
fifth centuries), a Briton army under Conan occupied Armorica. To

---

[17] Ibid., 71; cf. Davies, *First English Empire*, 154–7, 200.
[18] Rolleston, 131; and Julius Caesar, C. *Iuli Caesaris Commentarii rerum in Gallia
gestarum VII; A. Hirti Commentarius VIII*, ed. T. Rice Holmes (Oxford: Clarendon Press, 1914), 99, 105–19, 222–3.

assure the preservation of the Celtic language, Conan ordered that the women of the province have their tongues removed. Possibly, Latin or Teutonic elements had undermined the local Celtic dialect to Conan's disapproval. Though illustrating the brutal subordination of women, as well as the local population, this legend also demonstrates the strong desire for Breton ethnic preservation in their new homeland.[19]

The next major challenge to Breton ethnicity arose from the Franks, Germanic migrants who after Romanization would evolve into the modern French. Conquering most of Gaul, including Brittany, their King Clovis temporarily established a unified Frankish state in 481. Paying the isolated region little attention, the following weak and divided Frankish kings allowed quarrelsome tribal leaders to predominate in Brittany: "At that time . . . certain other dukes . . . refused to obey the dukes of the Franks, because they were no longer able to serve the Merovingian Kings." But in 753 Pepin the Short re-conquered these tribes, placing them in a military district, the March de Bretagne, which Charlemagne secured under the Frankish Empire in 790. Curiously, Brittany thus acquired geopolitical form from incorporation into an outside empire, rather than from within. After the death of Charlemagne, the empire itself would lose its geopolitical shape with its division among his grandsons in 843.[20]

One of these descendents, Charles the Bald, beaten in battle, lost all but formal title to the province in 848. Brittany thus gained independence from the Franks and unity as a kingdom under Nominoe, a former governor of Breton descent. His kingdom lasted only fifty years before being overrun by the Normans, another group of marauding Vikings. Reunited and freed from the Norse in 937 by Alain Barbetorte, Brittany thenceforth comprised a duchy with allegiance to the Frankish kings. As vassals of the monarchy, the dukes retained much political autonomy, but also faced constant challenges from local feudal lords over the next two centuries. The aristocracy gradually adopted the more prestigious hierarchical culture of the developing French monarchy. The

---

[19] Ibid., 347; and James MacKillop, *Dictionary of Celtic Mythology* (New York: Oxford Univ. Press, 1998), 52–3.

[20] Throughout my chapters, my discussion of Brittany rests heavily on Jack E. Reece, *The Bretons against France: Ethnic Minority Nationalism in Twentieth-Century Brittany* (Chapel Hill: Univ. of North Carolina Press, 1977), 7–9; *Erchantberti Brevarium* quoted in Patrick J. Geary, *Before France and Germany: The Creation and Transformation of the Merovingian World* (New York: Oxford Univ. Press, 1988), 200.

common folk, on the other hand, continued the Celtic customs of their
ancient ethnic region, customs that allowed greater freedom to women
and better distribution of property among peasant families.[21]

The ducal history of Brittany from 1154 to the end of the fifteenth
century found the region caught between France and England. Henry
II of England extended his imperial rule over the province, causing
the region subsequently to swing between these two major states for
the next three hundred years. Henry's grandson in the next century
allied himself and Brittany, first with one nation then the other,
whichever allowed his own branch of the family to retain its dynastic
rights, and the region, its autonomy. Later the ducal succession became part of the Hundred Years War, in the earlier part of which the
Breton dukes sided with the English. For example, in 1373 one duke
brazenly warned the French king: "you should be in no way surprised if
I order reprisals upon your supporters so as to avenge myself." All this
reversed itself between 1430 and 1453 when the dukes allied themselves with the French monarchy in its struggle for independence
from England.[22]

In spite of the difficulties inherent in the balancing act between two
powerful kingdoms, Brittany managed to remain autonomous within
France between 1453 and 1488; indeed, the dukes maintained this
position through the mere suggestion of an alliance with England.
France conclusively asserted its dominion over Brittany in 1488 when
the Duke Francois II lost his rights in battle. Conquest thus assured
French title to the province. Shortly thereafter, the Duchess Anne
surrendered her personal ducal rights when she became the Queen of
France. Despite this, the ducal crown was not yet merged with the
monarchy, a fact that permitted the region's autonomy to continue.
Any taxes levied on the province had to be approved by the parliamentary Etats de Bretagne, and revenues had to be spent in the region. The
province continued to appoint its own judges, and even after the crown
of Brittany merged with that of France in 1524, the provincial Etats
kept the power to pass laws. This allowed the individual to continue to

---

[21] Reece, 7–9; and Wendy Davies, *Small Worlds: The Village Community in Early
Medieval Brittany* (Berkeley and Los Angeles: Univ. of California Press, 1988),
72–9.

[22] Reece, 11–14; John IV to Charles V, in *Society at War: The Experience of
England and France during the Hundred Years War*, ed. C. T. Allmand, Evidence
and Commentary (New York: Harper & Row Publishers, Barnes & Noble,
1973), 20.

see Brittany, both people and region, as an isolated homeland thrust into the Atlantic.[23]

THE BASQUE COUNTRY

Probably the oldest ethnic group in Atlantic Europe, the Basques have a legend regarding their early presence; according to a Basque bard, "'The men of my race,' . . . 'populated Hispana covered with parasite vegetation; and that virgin soil was cleared.'" The legend says nothing about migration or even ethnic origin, but does claim that the Basques had no predecessors in Spain, apparently an untouched land. Specialists do not agree on the origins of this people because their non-Indo-European language has no clear connection to any other tongue. Some linguists believe they migrated with Indo-Europeans beginning about 2500 B.C.; others argue they are descended from an early obscure Iberian people, possibly of North African descent. Archeology suggests Basque descent from the neolithic inhabitants of the Pyrenees about four to five thousand years ago. Straddling the mountainous frontier between modern France and Spain, the Basque region now comprises three departments of the former state and three provinces of the latter, with 90 percent of the people residing in Spain. The Basques once extended well beyond their present territory, but migrations of Celts, Romans, Visigoths, Normans, and others over the centuries restricted their space.[24]

Only once was the Basque Country united and politically independent. From 1004 to 1035 the Kingdom of Navarre formed to resist encroachment by the French to the north and the Moors to the south. (See Map 2.2.) Although the king was Basque, loyalty to a Basque nationality was neither present among the aristocracy nor the masses. As was the case in other countries about the Atlantic, the idea of an extensive nation was vague. While men and women identified with

---

[23] Michael Jones, *The Creation of Brittany: A Late Medieval State* (London: Hambledon Press, 1988), 304; for more context, see Roger Price, *A Concise History of France*, 2nd ed. Cambridge Concise Histories (Cambridge: Cambridge Univ. Press, 2005), 30–56.

[24] Mariana Monteiro, *Legends and Popular Tales of the Basque People* (1887; reprint, New York: Benjamin Blom, 1971), 242; Roger Collins, *The Basques*, The Peoples of Europe (New York: Basil Blackwell, 1987), 2, 9–11, 13, 15, 30, 181; and Philippe Veyrin, *Les Basques de Labourd, de Soule et de Basse Navarre: Leur histoire et leurs traditions*, new ed. (n.p.: Arthaud, 1955), 90.

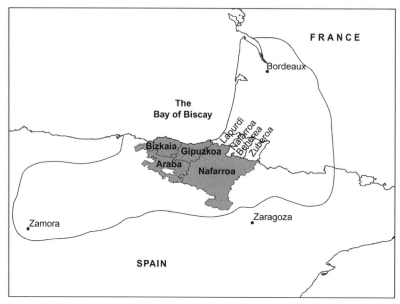

Map 2.2. The Core of the Basque Country with Sancho the Great's Kingdom, c. 1032–3, in the Background. Adapted from Collins, *The Basques*, 181 and en.wikipedia.org/wiki/Image:Mapa_provincias_Euskal_Herria.svg, accessed 21 January 2008. Cartography by Cassingham and Foxworth, courtesy of the Edwin J. Foscue Map Library, SMU.

their ethnic groups, locales, regions, and rulers, poor education, communications, and transportation limited a larger image of nation and homeland. For example, the elite among the Basques and other Europeans used Latin rather than the native language for formal business. The aristocracy considered the "homeland" as a proprietary estate to be divided according to the dynastic needs of royal and noble families. The Basque lower classes were also organized by family, and in a pastoral economy they valued local grazing lands, but not a larger "homeland." This lack of a national self-image led to subdivision of the kingdom in short order, despite strong traditions of Basque ethnic pride and freedom.[25]

In the long history of Spanish national development, Navarre would lose out to Castile, one of its own counties, as the core of the modern nation-state. In 1035 at the death of Sancho III, the most powerful Christian monarchy in Iberia was divided among his sons. Aragon and

[25] Collins, *Basques*, 181; and Monteiro, 242–3.

Castile broke off as separate kingdoms, and the Basque Country's chance to determine the fate of the peninsula disappeared. Interestingly, in 1512 King Ferdinand of Aragon, who together with Queen Isabella of Castile merged modern Spain, would conquer Navarre, the Basque Country's last remaining independent state. Eighteen years later Spain would cede Basse Navarre, north of the Pyrenees, to France, leaving the ethnic region further divided. By then Castilian had become Iberia's dominant language with Basque left a provincial tongue.[26]

Moreover, by then the provinces that remain most thoroughly Basque today, had already been incorporated into Spain and France, one by one in varied fashion. Labourd and Soule found their way into French hands after centuries under the rule of Plantagenet England, which had apparently appointed administrators to the Basques "of their tongue." Guipuzcoa moved from the control of an assembly of lineage heads in the eleventh century, through the hands of Navarre under an appointed lord, to peaceful annexation by Castile in 1200 when fishermen apparently preferred Castile's more liberal regime. With the decline of Navarre after 1035, the elected office of Vizcaya's lordship became inheritable and its allegiance switched to Castile; by 1379 the lordship had become one of the titles of the Castilian monarch. In 1331 the nobility of Avala found it expedient to merge "voluntarily" with Castile after decades of political and economic competition between their fraternal organizations and towns founded in the area by immigrating Castilians. Thus, we see a varied early pattern of incorporation into Spain of a potential national core that was eclipsed by Aragon and ultimately Castile. Nevertheless, the Basque Country, especially along the Bay of Biscay, retained its autonomy for centuries after formal incorporation into the larger neighboring national communities.[27]

[26] Veyrin, 136; Armitage, 22, 60, argues "that England like France was a composite monarchy, just as Britain, like the Spanish Monarchy, was a multiple kingdom. In the former a diversity of territories, peoples, institutions and legal jurisdictions is cemented under a single recognized sovereign authority; in the latter, various kingdoms were ruled by a single sovereign, while they maintained varying degrees of autonomy." The former had "integrated features," the latter, "federative characteristics."

[27] *Calendar of Patent Rolls* quoted in Collins, *Basques*, 246; Veyrin, 116; and Marianne Heiberg, *The Making of the Basque Nation*, Cambridge Studies in Social Anthroplogy, 66 (New York: Cambridge Univ. Press, 1989), 14–20; see also M.G.A. Vale, *English Gascony, 1399–1453: A Study of War, Government, and Politics during the Later Stages of the Hundred Years War*, Oxford Historical Monographs (London: Oxford Univ. Press, Ely House, 1970), 14–15.

Hispanic Kingdoms

Though Spain's origins may lie among the Basques, that modern nation developed over thousands of years from a variety of ethnic groups and regions with many different languages extending from the Atlantic to the Mediterranean. As we have seen, the Basques probably descended from the Iberians, the first known people of the peninsula with which they share a name. Following these people were migrations of Celts, Phoenicians, Greeks, Carthaginians, and Romans who, more or less in sequence, occupied, in whole or in part, the land now shared by Spain and Portugal. Ruling for over five centuries, the Romans stamped their civilization indelibly on all "Hispania" as they called it, including the northern regions of Catalonia and Celtic Galicia, which later developed Romance languages alongside Castilian. Only the Basque Country retained its earlier tongue. After the Romans came several Germanic invasions with the Visigoths establishing a kingdom from 414–711. Already Latinized and Christianized on their arrival, the Visigoths modified but did not destroy the fundamentally Roman culture of the majority of Hispania's inhabitants. However, the Moorish invasion from North Africa would leave a distinctive impact on Spain, particularly in the south.[28]

The Moorish invasion comprised of Muslim Arabs and Berbers was no brief event. In 711 the Moors entered, drove any resisting Christian Visigoths into the mountains of the distant north, and occupied virtually the entire peninsula. Despite introducing a radically different culture, including a new religion, language, customs, and architecture, the Muslims' long-term impact would diminish due to the Christian resurgence. From their mountain refuge near the Bay of Biscay, the Christians began the reconquest of their homeland, a series of wars against the Moors that would take well over seven hundred years and ultimately lead to the modern Spanish state. In this process, the Christians created many small kingdoms, including Portugal, often competing against each other as much as against the Muslims. Asturias, Leon, Navarre, Catalonia, Aragon, and Castile were the major evolving kingdoms that gradually merged to defeat the Moors, who, though at first united, also fragmented into smaller states often competing against each other as well. The fall of Granada, the last Moorish kingdom, completed the

---

[28] Roger Collins, *The Arab Conquest of Spain, 710–796*, A History of Spain (Cambridge, Mass.: Basil Blackwell, 1989), 10.

reconquest in 1492, but it did not eliminate the ethnic or regional variety of Spain, in spite of the oppressive measures taken by the monarchy to secure national unity.[29]

THE PROVINCE OF GRANADA

The marriage of Ferdinand of Aragon and Isabella of Castile ultimately joined their crowns in the Kingdom of Spain and turned that country from a Mediterranean to an Atlantic power. The mission of the Catholic Kings (their papal title) became the conquest of Granada, the climax of which Christopher Columbus witnessed: "I saw your Highnesses' banners victoriously raised on the towers of the Alhambra." But the unification of Spain as a Christian state continued after 1492. Incorporating Granada, a thoroughly Muslim land, into fanatically Christian Spain would not be easy, and despite previous repeated experience with benign incorporations, the case of Granada would be most intolerant. While Spain included many different regions and ethnic groups – indeed Castile and Aragon remained separate kingdoms in governance and language even after the death of the Catholic Kings – Ferdinand and Isabella sought religious conformity above cultural or national conformity. As a result, ethnic regions with distinct languages, such as the Basque Country and Catalonia, retained their cultures and even political autonomy for hundreds of years after 1492. Indeed, for centuries Spain would structurally remain a confederacy of autonomous ethnic regions. Granada, on the other hand, had the experience of a conquered province in a developing transatlantic empire.[30]

Boabdil, the Muslim king of Granada, had fought a long war with the Christians, but finding his nation besieged and his own situation precarious, he signed the Capitulations of 1491. According to an Arabic account, "Many people alleged that the emir of Granada and his ministers and military chiefs had already made an agreement [in secret] to hand over the city to the Christian king . . . but they feared the common people." The Capitulations offered the city a good deal of autonomy in order to encourage the resistant masses to lay down their arms, but the pact would finally remain effective only so long as Boabdil stayed on the

[29] Ibid., 230; and J. N. Hillgarth, *The Spanish Kingdoms, 1250–1560*, vol. 1, *1250–1410, Precarious Balance* (Oxford: Clarendon Press, 1976), vii–viii.

[30] Quoted in L[eonard] P[atrick] Harvey, *Islamic Spain: 1250–1500* (Chicago: Univ. of Chicago Press, 1990), 324–5.

peninsula. Initially, most local Moorish leaders remained in place, including the aristocratic ruling council. Property was respected for both
those choosing to stay in Spain and those wishing to depart. Even the
practice of Islam was tolerated, though not Judaism: "The Jews native to
Granada . . . and all other places contained in these Capitulations, will
benefit from them, on condition that those who do not become Christians cross to North Africa within three years." However, after Boabdil's
departure for Africa, Archbishop Francisco Jiménez de Cisneros began
to repress Muslim religious practices, which led to rebellion, an event
that rationalized the complete discarding of the Capitulations. This left
Granada a completely subordinate region, and the Moors, a conquered
people.[31]

Ironically, Granada came into being as a result of the earlier Moorish
conquest of the Iberian Peninsula; over the subsequent centuries the
Moors had made it a homeland. Interestingly, the Berbers and Arabs
who had crossed over from Africa never formed more than a small per-
centage of the peninsula's total population. As the conquering elite, they
naturally imposed their rule on the Hispanic natives, though that rule
was relatively tolerant. For example, the practice of Christianity and
Judaism were both permitted, though conversion to Islam was encouraged and accepted by many. The Moors intermixed ethnically and physically with the new converts in particular and in doing so also made
themselves natives of Iberia, or Al-Andaluz, as they termed it. Regardless
of this, the Hispanic Christians considered the Moors foreigners. Given
the religious fervor and developing nationalism of the Catholic Kings and
their followers, the autonomy promised in the Capitulations could not
last long. As a Muslim enclave, Granada clearly formed part of an ethnic
region in newly confederated Spain. In this it was not alone since other
Moorish areas – in Andalusia and Valencia, for example – had previously
been incorporated and remained in the developing national community
of Spain.[32]

In this process the Spanish monarchy embarked on a policy of
religious intolerance that finally led to an attempted ethnic and racial
purging of the nation. In 1492 Jews refusing to convert to Christianity
were expelled from Spain. A similar, but more gradual policy was aimed
at the Muslims, ending with their complete removal by the early

[31] *Nubdhat al-'aṣr* and Capitulations quoted in ibid., 311, 321, 326–31.
[32] Ibid; 6–9, and Nicholas Wade, "Gene Test Shows Spain's Jewish and Muslim
Mix," *New York Times*, 5 December 2008.

seventeenth century. Since many forced converts continued to practice their religion in secret, the Spanish Inquisition constantly investigated such people; even generations after the conversions occurred, descendants of former Muslims and Jews faced suspicion. Old Christians consequently began claiming "purity of blood" to deny any Jewish or Moorish ancestry, a concept that transformed religious background into racial difference. Ironically, most Moorish converts were descended from Visigothic Christians who had become Muslims during the earlier invasions from Africa. In Granada the remaining Moors would largely assimilate into Christian Spanish society. Arabic, Berber, and many other aspects of their culture were so suppressed they would not survive, even as other ethnically distinct, but Christian, regions did. The degree of suppression carried out by a state in its development virtually eradicated a nationality that inhabited the entire country. Despite this, the Moorish cultural influence remained strong in southern Spain, in the region of Andalusia, particularly in the province of Granada, where it marked the landscape indelibly with distinctive architecture and place names.[33]

The history of Spanish national development clearly demonstrates the role of imperialism in nation building. In seizing an ethnically distinct, if physically contiguous region, the Catholic monarchs sought to unify their state. They used religion and a historic geographical claim to justify the conquest. Continuation of the Capitulations would have ameliorated the conquest, and Granada might eventually have evolved into a perpetually autonomous region in a confederated state, but this was not to be. The new Spanish state could not tolerate such a degree of ethnic and especially religious difference: "These Moors are all very quiet," reported one official to the Catholic Kings. "However, I would rather there were not so many of them, not because I have any grounds for suspicion, thank God, but with an extra turn of the screw . . . your kingdoms might expel them." The region's proximity to Africa would forever have kept Granada a suspect province, so it was integrated and assimilated into Spain by unrelenting force.[34]

---

[33] Martha Menchaca, *Recovering History, Constructing Race: The Indian, Black, and White Roots of Mexican Americans*, Joe R. and Teresa Lozano Long Series in Latin American and Latino Art and Culture (Austin: Univ. of Texas Press, 2001), 40–1.

[34] Fernando de Zafra quoted in Harvey, 328; see also Leopoldo de Eguílaz Yanguas, *Reseña histórica de la conquista del Reino de Granada por los Reyes Católicos, según los cronistas árabes*, facsimile ed. (1894; reprint, Granada, Spain: Ediciones Albaida, 1986), 70–3.

KINGDOMS AND EMPIRES OF THE MAGHRIB

In the fifteenth century Castile, Aragon, and Portugal were only three of many kingdoms on the eastern side of the Atlantic. To the south of Granada extended a variety of African states governed by Muslim rulers, whose coastal towns and cities the Portuguese and other Christians had been raiding at least since the fourteenth century. By the late fifteenth century the Maghrib (Morocco and northwestern Africa) had fragmented into many states, changing hands and boundaries among competing factions. In Morocco the kingdoms of Fez and Marrakesh, struggling to hold together against internal usurpers, independent mountain groups, and dissident religious leaders, could not concern themselves with events in distant Iberia. Indeed, this fragmentation permitted the Christian reconquest of Granada, with little interference from the Muslim kingdoms in North Africa.[35]

This temporary situation had not always existed in the Maghrib, which had as long and complex a history as any other land on the shores of the Atlantic. Archeology suggests that recurrent waves of migrants occupied Northwest Africa over a million years ago. Some migrations came from Asia by way of the northern Mediterranean, others by way of East Africa along the southern Mediterranean. By 3000 B.C. peoples of mixed white and black ancestry formed the Berbers, the earliest recognizable ethnic group in this broad country. Though there exists no pre-Islamic folklore regarding Berber origins, such legends entered the literature of elite Berbers in the Middle Ages by way of Greek, Roman, and Arab influence.[36]

[35] Charles-André Julien, *History of North Africa: Tunisia, Algeria, Morocco from the Arab Conquest to 1830*, trans. John Petrie, ed. C. C. Stewart (New York: Praeger Publishers, 1970), 212–13; for a lucid treatment of historiographical issues in the general field, see John Parker and Richard Rathbone, *African History: A Very Short Introduction* (Oxford: Oxford Univ. Press, 2007).

[36] Abdallah Laroui, *The History of the Maghrib: An Interpretive Essay*, trans. Ralph Manheim, Princeton Studies on the Near East (Princeton, N.J.: Princeton Univ. Press, 1977), 17; Ernest Gellner, "Introduction," in *Arabs and Berbers: From Tribe to Nation in North Africa*, ed. Gellner and Charles Micaud, Race and Nations (Lexington, Mass.: D. C. Heath and Co., Lexington Books, 1972), 12; and Maya Shatzmiller, *The Berbers and the Islamic State: The Marinid Experience in Pre-Protectorate Morocco* (Princeton, N.J.: Markus Wiener Publishers, 2000), 18; see also BBC News, "Spain Dig Yields Ancient European," available from news.bbc.co.uk/1/hi/sci/tech/7313005.stm, accessed 21 December 2008.

As early as 150 B.C., Greeks and Hellenized Jews associated the Berbers with the Phoenicians, Philistines, or Canaanites as the people of Palestine were variously known; in the sixth century A.D. a Byzantine historian repeated this association, but added a connection to the Arabs. Middle Eastern scholars in the ninth and tenth centuries elaborated on this information by linking the Berbers to Arabs through Goliath, regarded as a member of an Arab tribe in Palestine, through an Arabic-speaking Noah, or through the Himyari of South Yemen, considered an original Arab tribe. In the eleventh century the account of Arab origin entered Berber consciousness by way of Andalusia, specifically the Berber court of Granada. An Arab Andalusian of the period commented on how a Granadan king thus "gave himself the aura of a literary man and tried to hide his pure Berber ancestry by claiming an Himyari origin" in order not to seem "less civilized than the Arab and hispanized [sic] kings of the Peninsula." In Andalusia where Berbers did not predominate culturally, this ethnic psychology allowed the Arab origin story to gain acceptance. In the Maghrib it did not because the Berber population predominated in the region and thus retained its ethnic self-esteem. There it was "said that God created our father Adam and our mother Eve from the earth from the Doukkala (the region between Mazagan and Marrakech)." Like Native Americans, the Berbers had resided in their homeland long enough to imagine themselves springing from their native soil.[37]

Indeed, despite the prestige of Arab culture, the Berbers had been critical to the expansion of Islamic civilization in northwestern Africa and Spain. After surviving and incorporating elements from invading Phoenicians, Greeks, Jews, Carthaginians, Romans, and Vandals, the Berbers also acculturated to Arabs and Islam but did not disappear as a distinct people with a distinct language. The Arabs arrived in Morocco in 682 A.D. and within thirty years had won over the Berbers for the assault on Spain. It was Tariq, a Berber under orders of an Arab governor, who in 711 crossed the strait bearing his name. His army included only four hundred Arabs, but seven thousand Berbers, who commenced the conquest of Spain, thus

[37] Elisa Chimenti, *Tales and Legends of Morocco*, trans. Arnon Benamy (New York: Ivan Obolensky, Astor Book, 1965), 12; Ibn Hayyān quoted in Shatzmiller, 20–5; and François Legey, *The Folklore of Morocco*, trans. Lucy Hotz (London: George Allen & Unwin, 1935), 102.

extending the empire of the caliph of Damascus, a city thousands of miles to the east.[38]

Submission to the caliphate did not last long. In 739 the Berbers of the Maghrib and Spain rebelled, largely retaining their independence until the eleventh century. At that point the Berbers launched the Moorish Empire from Granada, reaching peaks under the Almoravid (1053–1147) and Almohad (1147–1269) dynasties. Under the former the empire included southern Spain, Morocco, northern Algeria, and the western Sahara almost as far south as Cape Verde, with trade routes extending deep into the continent as well as across the Mediterranean. Under the latter dynasty the empire stretched close to Egypt. Though not as successful in territorial reach as the earlier dynasties, the Marinids (1269–1465) served Morocco and the Berbers well in other ways.[39]

By the time the Marinids came to power in Morocco, all that remained of Muslim Spain was the Kingdom of Granada. The emigration of Spanish Moors from Andalusia, however, benefited Morocco immensely because these refugees brought skills, training, and wealth to a dynasty springing from a relatively uncultivated tribe. (Indeed, even after the Marinids, Boabdil, "king that was of Granada . . . passed across to Barbary and resided with the King of Fez.") Particularly in Fez and the rest of northern Morocco, urban life improved with new elaborate buildings, better schools, more refined religious practice, and a flowering of literature. While much of the Andalusian influence tended to undermine Berber culture, the population benefited from the management of the state according to an Arabic and Islamic legal framework.[40]

As in most pre-industrial societies, the economic power of the Marinid kingdom rested on land and resources. Though Bedouins only recognized the communal lands where they camped or cultivated without measured boundaries, settled groups recognized both private and state property. Under the Marinids small landholders increased, due to ineffective state control of rural public lands, which paradoxically allowed for stability in the countryside. The Marinids were fortunate to have access to gold through trade across the Sahara, gold that allowed them to pay expenses without granting land to large landowners or

[38] Collins, *Arab Conquest*, 28–9.
[39] Julien, 78, 95, 212.
[40] Luis del Marmol Carvajal quoted in Harvey, 327; Julien, 204–5; and Shatzmiller, 132.

soldiers. To pay its military and other expenses, the state also effectively collected taxes in urban areas through orderly registration of taxable people, resources, and products. The solid organization of the kingdom naturally helped encourage commerce, both domestic and foreign. It should be no surprise that during this dynasty, chroniclers hailed their people and homeland, the Berbers and the Maghrib.[41]

THE JOLOF EMPIRE OF SENEGAMBIA

South of the Maghrib at the extreme western end of Africa, Cape Verde marks another homeland along the Atlantic. The coastal area surrounding the cape, between the Senegal and Gambia rivers, is often labeled Senegambia, "an enchanted corner [of which] . . . the inhabitants call the little paradise," suggesting an appreciative image of their homeland as a whole. The black Toucouleur, who occupied the Senegal Valley "since the beginning of the world" or at least since 3000 B.C., had regular interaction with the Berbers of the Sahara. Indeed, linguists disagree on whether "Senegal" derives from Senegana, the Toucouleur name for a local town, or from Zenaga, the name of a nearby Berber tribe. In the eleventh century A.D. migrating Berbers established a monastery at the Senegal River and converted the native Toucouleur to Islam, as the Almoravide dynasty extended its empire. After this empire fragmented in the thirteenth century, southern animistic tribes invaded the interior of the country. Muslim Arab tribes also infiltrated and by the 1400s had gained enough power to challenge the local Berbers. These migrations resulted in much political disunity among the communities of Senegambia.[42]

However, by the fifteenth century, the Wolof people, formerly subject to the Toucouleur, extended their empire throughout Senegambia. The Jolof Empire incorporated and drew tribute from a number of kingdoms beyond its core. From the Senegal River in the north, the Waalo, Kajoor, and Bawol realms extended south along the coast and were ruled by Wolof aristocracies. Siin and Saluum lying toward the Gambia were based on a different ethnic group,

---

[41] Ibid., 31, 125–7.
[42] André Terrisse, *Contes et légendes du Sénégal*, Collection des contes et legends de tous les pays (Paris: Fernand Nathan, Editeur, 1963), 218–19, my translation; and Lucie Gallistel Colvin, *Historical Dictionary of Senegal*, African Historical Dictionaries, no. 23 (Metuchen, N.J.: Scarecrow Press, 1981), 18.

the Sereer; these kingdoms nevertheless paid tribute to the Jolof Empire. Direct control of territory on the part of the emperor was unnecessary since land was plentiful. Instead, the ruler preferred to exact tribute from various social groups that enjoyed considerable autonomy as long as they paid the taxes, provided men for public works and the military, and recognized the officials of the ruling lineage whenever they appeared.[43]

Society tended to be highly stratified and based on lineage; free persons, servile artisans, and slaves comprised the three major social orders. Free persons, of both noble and common birth, were strongly attached to the land and thus primarily farmers; they were known as lamans, "masters of the land." Commoners were peasants without royal ancestry; the nobility ranked according to its descent from royalty traced through matrilineal lines. At the local level, Wolof elders who owned land as descendents of village founders formed a lesser nobility that nevertheless had a voice in the selection of any new king. While the aristocracy was stratified by descent, artisans were stratified by occupation. Jewelers had the highest status, then blacksmiths, weavers, leatherworkers, and singers in that order; women often worked at these same occupations and consequently enjoyed similar status. Individuals inherited their occupations and only rarely married outside their caste. Artisans made up only 10 percent of the population while slaves made up 50 to 65 percent. Though slaves had less social prestige as a group, they varied tremendously in terms of freedom. Born domestic slaves could not be sold, usually had land, and raised their own families. Slaves belonging to the crown might serve in the army, in the household, or in grueling tasks, such as fieldwork. Slaves who performed honorable service as warriors might merge into the aristocracy, but those captured in war were usually sold quickly, eventually in the transoceanic slave trade.[44]

---

[43] James F. Searing, *West African Slavery and Atlantic Commerce: The Senegal River Valley, 1700–1860*, African Studies Series, 77 (New York: Cambridge Univ. Press, 1993), 10–12.

[44] Ibid.; Boubacar Barry, "The Subordination of Power and the Mercantile Economy: The Kingdom of Waalo, 1600–1831," in *The Political Economy of Underdevelopment: Dependence in Senegal*, ed. Rita Cruise O'Brien, Sage Series on African Modernization and Development, vol. 3 (Beverly Hills, Calif.: Sage Publications, 1979), 43–4; and Sheldon Gellar, *Senegal: An African Nation Between Islam and the West*, Profiles, Nations of Contemporary Africa (Boulder, Colo.: Westview Press, 1982), 2, 4–5.

The economy of Senegambia varied by subregion, relying on agriculture, but also involving commerce. Free peasants basically farmed for subsistence and to pay taxes. Along the Senegal River, early communal farms produced crops to be exchanged for cattle and other livestock, particularly horses from the Berber nomads of the Sahara. Salt and salt fish were exchanged for millet up and down the river. Prior to direct contact with Europeans, slaves were sent across the Sahara, for horses and manufactured goods. In 1444 Portuguese voyagers arrived in the Cape Verde area where they set up posts to Christianize the locals, but more importantly to trade goods, including slaves. However, the Portuguese centered their commercial activities offshore on the Cape Verde Islands, directly west in the Atlantic.[45]

At the beginning of the sixteenth century the Jolof Empire began to break up into its formerly constituent kingdoms with Kajoor and Bawol first to gain their independence. The causes for the rebellion included resentment over the payment of tribute to Jolof and humiliations experienced by the local aristocracy. However, access to Portuguese trade along the coast allowed the coastal kingdoms to strengthen their positions relative to the Jolof in the interior and ultimately succeed in their rebellion. Subsequently, Senegambia would be divided among various independent kingdoms, despite the increasing presence of Muslims in the interior and Christians along the coast.[46]

THE TEMNE KINGDOMS OF SIERRA LEONE

The history of what would come to be known as Sierra Leone repeats the patterns of migration seen in other countries around the Atlantic. Located to the southeast of Senegambia, Romarong, the mountain as the inhabitants called it, was home to many peoples of whom the Temne gained in importance after their arrival. Apparently, the Temne migrated into Sierra Leone from neighboring Guinea in the early fifteenth century. According to Alhaji Kali Kamara, an elder of the Maforki chiefdom around Port Loko, "Our own great grandfather, this country was not his home. He came here for war, and after he had won

---

[45] Barry, 43–4; Gellar, 6; and Colvin, 19.
[46] Searing, 12–14; see also George E Brooks, *Eurafricans in Western Africa: Commerce, Social Status, Gender, and Religious Observance from the Sixteenth to the Eighteenth Century*, Western African Studies (Athens: Ohio Univ. Press, 2003), 82–3.

the war, he was crowned as king." After subjugating an area, by and large, the Temne farmed self-sufficiently, growing rice, as well as keeping goats, sheep, and cattle; however, they did establish themselves at important river mouths and at fords to engage in trade. Eventually, the Temne became the dominant group in the country, exercising power over cohesive territorial units through chiefs whom European visitors regarded as kings: "Then our people started chieftaincy, they got power from here up to Limba country, at that time one could walk from here to that country within the area of Temne power." They maintained their power by forming temporary confederacies for warfare.[47]

Europeans entered Sierra Leone repeatedly, but never entirely dislodged the Temne. In 1446 a Portuguese expedition sighted the shore, but not until 1462 did Pedro da Sintra map the coastline and name it, "Sierra Leona," the mountains of the lion. Da Sintra's expedition resulted from the well-known efforts of Portugal's Henry the Navigator, to explore the African coast. The Portuguese continued to visit the country, which they claimed the local people also called Pymto after a village in the mountains; by the early 1500s merchants had established trading posts along the coast. Initially, the Portuguese exchanged swords, household utensils, and clothing for ornaments made from ivory or imported gold, beeswax, and mats. The slave trade, though not as important here as elsewhere, would develop fully only after American plantations demanded the labor that imperial transoceanic commerce could supply.[48]

IMAGES OF COMMUNITY AND HOMELAND

As in America and Europe, complex processes in Africa affected the connection between peoples and the places they viewed as their homelands. Prior to the fifteenth-century transatlantic encounter, migrating peoples occupied lands that they would come to see as home. They would establish their cultures and governments in complex states often

---

[47] Joe A. D. Alie, *A New History of Sierra Leone* (New York: St. Martin's Press, 1990), 6–7, 38; Kenneth C. Wylie, *The Political Kingdoms of the Temne: Temne Government in Sierra Leone, 1825–1910* (New York: Africana Publishing Co., 1977), 3–5, 57; and "Selections from the Testimony of Alhaji Kali Kamara, an Elder of Maforki Chiefdom (Recorded at Port Loko, 21–22 September 1965)," in Wylie, 220.

[48] A. P. Kup, *A History of Sierra Leone, 1400–1787* (London: Cambridge Univ. Press, 1961), 1–2, 4, 7, 13; and Alie, 33.

through conquest, only to see themselves conquered by another wave of invaders. People beyond the village or tribe tended to unify through the force of a chief, a king, an emperor, or a dynasty. Of course, adherence to common religious institutions, such as secret societies among the Temne and neighboring groups, could also unify a population. Voluntary associations of tribes or states were rare, but did exist, as we have seen in various early alliances and confederations on both sides of the Atlantic. Still imperialism prevailed and indeed would reach global proportions with the expansion of Europe. The image of community, in the sense of a natural or voluntary association of individuals would remain a highly localized phenomenon for centuries. Yet on all these continents broader examples of federated community existed from earliest times, like a shadowy, unfocused background.[49]

---

[49] Diamond, 289–91; for a brief comment and sources on medieval and early modern European federalism, see Jan Erk, *Explaining Federalism: State, Society, and Congruence in Austria, Belgium, Canada, Germany, and Switzerland*, Routledge Series in Federal Studies (New York: Routledge, Taylor & Francis Group, 2008), 2–3.

CHAPTER THREE

DESIGNS FOR TRANSATLANTIC EMPIRE

THE COLONIAL ERA, 1400–1700

For millennia the Atlantic Ocean had set natural limits on human migrations across its waters. Notwithstanding the Viking colonies in Iceland, Greenland, and Newfoundland, most peoples imagined lands across the ocean, but lacked the means to seek them and to establish communities or homelands there. Naturally, the ocean had limited the imperial designs of many nations, including the Moors, English, Wolof, and Aztecs. However, by the fifteenth century improvements in seafaring encouraged Europeans to develop their images of lands across the ocean. Ultimately, navigational improvements, many borrowed from Asia, stimulated Europeans to act on their visions.[1]

Just as the English, French, and Spanish were uniting kingdoms under powerful monarchs, through conquest and confederation, a whole new world opened for their exploration, trade, and settlement. Vast collections of varied peoples and lands would come under the control of these nations, for their benefit, especially that of their elites. Colonialism, in the sense of settlement, would only be one form of this new overseas empire. More broadly, colonialism and imperialism were the same process, one that had already built states on both sides of the Atlantic. The process was one of conquest of foreign land and people,

---

[1] D[onald] W[illiam] Meinig, *The Shaping of America: A Geographical Perspective on 500 Years of History*, vol. 1, *Atlantic America, 1492–1800* (New Haven, Conn.: Yale Univ. Press, 1986), 6; and David Armitage, *The Ideological Origins of the British Empire*, Ideas in Context 59 (Cambridge: Cambridge Univ. Press, 2000), 41–2, 100–1.

resulting in a society where one nation dominated another – the subordinate group recognizable by its ethnicity or race. Colonialism was formal when a powerful state rationalized the process by claiming rights to another land, supporting a "just war" of conquest, and setting up a permanent government over the conquered. Native reactions, especially violent resistance, further fueled empire, a dynamo of evolving community.[2]

The imperial process had clearly developed early in the Mediterranean world, with the Roman Empire serving as the model for Europe, followed by the Franks and others. But the fifteenth century saw imperialism extend into the Atlantic, as the newly unified states of Western Europe developed new methods of navigation together with the desire to discover new commercial routes to the Far East. Needless to say, empire building had long been a process in the Americas, and African states had undertaken such political expansion as well. Nevertheless, it was European imperialism that would span the Atlantic and ultimately the globe over the next five to six hundred years. In that violent process, new settlements, new ethnic regions, and new states would form atop the homelands of native peoples, forming new nations but few federations.[3]

Colonies Along the African Coast

As we have seen, northwest Africans had experienced the rise and fall of many an empire over recorded history. In the fifteenth century they faced the Portuguese, a maritime empire with trading posts on the Atlantic coast. Initially, Prince Henry the Navigator (1394–1460) launched expeditions to explore the coast, hoping to find a route to the Indies. While that would be a prolonged search, the commercial possibilities immediately presented themselves as various coastal peoples showed an interest in trade. As the Portuguese advanced, they found penetration of the interior inadvisable because of the presence of various strong African nations and European

---

[2] Pablo González-Casanova, "Sociedad Plural, Colonialismo Interno y Desarrollo." *America Latina*, 6 (no. 3, 1963): 16, 18; for somewhat different definitions of colonialism and imperialism, see Armitage, 1, and Jurgen Osterhammel, *Colonialism: A Theoretical Overview*, trans. Shelley L. Frisch (1995; Princeton, N.J.: Markus Weiner Publishers, 1997), 16–17, 21.

[3] Armitage, 29–31; and Meinig, vol. 1, 7.

susceptibility to tropical diseases. Unsurprisingly, slavery became a major business of this maritime empire, as the first West African slaves reportedly arrived in Lisbon in 1441. The Portuguese reached and occupied the Madeira and Cape Verde Islands to the southwest and by 1462 had advanced to Romarong, modern-day Sierra Leone, at the big bend of the African coastline. Competing with the Portuguese, the French and the Spanish invaded the Canary Islands, as European imperialism spread down the west coast of Africa and out into the Atlantic.[4]

The people of Gomera, one of the chain of seven major Canary Islands, recounted "that a great prince, for no fault of theirs, caused them to be banished, and had their tongues cut out." This inauspicious view of their origins suggests Canarians saw their ancestors, if not themselves, as exiled, victimized, and isolated in what perforce became their homeland. Though told to French invaders between 1402 and 1405, this story apparently referred to a Roman banishment and torture of Berber rebels from Northwest Africa in the second century A.D. Since the islanders even centuries later had limited navigational skills and a distinctive whistling speech, the story somewhat supports the theory that the islands' settlement began as a penal colony of Europe's most legendary empire. Because communication between the islands remained intermittent for hundreds of years, their inhabitants developed relatively distinct insular societies. Indeed, some scholars have posited that there existed no single group of original Canarians – that they arrived in separate movements, during such migrations as resulted from the seventh-century Muslim conquests and the eleventh-century Almoravid Empire. (See Map 3.1.) Be that as it may, the Canarians did not adopt Islam and apparently spoke a common language in various dialects related to Berber, indicating the major group of arrivals was the Berber of Roman accounts, especially since those accounts described the islands as previously uninhabited. Though close together, the islands never developed a common native government; in fact, rarely did a single island have its own united government. The heritage of Roman colonialism had seemingly survived in the islands' isolation from one another. In the

---

[4]   Robert W. July, *A History of the African People* (New York: Charles Scribner's Sons, 1970), 150–1; and Basil Davidson, *Africa in History: Themes and Outlines*, rev. ed. (New York: Macmillan Co., Collier Books, 1991), 201–3.

fifteenth century that isolation was shattered by new waves of European imperialism.[5]

The persistent political fragmentation did not prevent the native Guanches from attempting unification of at least a single island through their own semiimperial process. Before the French invasion of Gran Canaria, Antidamana, a powerful mediator among the island's many ethnically similar tribes, married a nobleman named Gumidafe; together, through diplomacy and conquest, they united the largest of the Canaries and left it to their son, Artemis, who was king on the arrival of the French. Though matrilineal inheritance was commonly practiced on the Canaries, in this case power passed through the male line. As we have seen elsewhere, conquest tended to be the major, if not sole, way of unifying a homeland and expanding the state; moreover, imperialism usually concentrated strength in a monarchy that attempted to pass power to its heirs.[6]

Extending this incipient imperial state and dynasty proved difficult. After King Artemis's death at the hands of the French intruders in 1403, his sons split the kingdom in two, "but effective rule was still in the hands of the council of 190–200 nobles." As on the European continent, the nobility in this hierarchical society retained considerable power, to a degree representing the people of Gran Canaria, though through consanguinity, rather than democracy. Apparently, an elite "joint council" of a dozen nobles, half from the provinces, served based on the character of the individual, but this situation did not last. Joint administration of the kingdom failed as the brothers divided the state between them with the acquiescence of the nobility. As on the continent, dynastic struggles led to political divisions that undermined the ethnic unity of the community, even in the face of external threats.[7]

Relying on their sacred mountains, stone-built towns, neolithic weapons, and light clothing, the animistic and pastoral Canary

---

[5]   Pierre Bontier and Jean Le Verrier, *The Canarian, or Book of the Conquest and Conversion of the Canarians in the Year 1402, by Messire Jean de Bethencourt, Kt.*, trans. and ed. with notes and an introduction by Richard Henry Major, Works Issued by the Hakluyt Society, no. 46 (London: Hakluyt Society, 1872), 127–8; John Mercer, *The Canary Islanders: Their Prehistory and Survival* (London: Rex Collings, 1980), 22–3, 65–6; and Felipe Fernández-Armesto, *The Canary Islands after the Conquest: The Making of a Colonial Society in the Early Sixteenth Century* (Oxford: Clarendon Press, 1982), 6–9.

[6]   Mercer, 125, 184–5.

[7]   Ibid., 80, 184–5; cf. Fernández-Armesto, 8–9.

Map 3.1. The Almoravid Empire, c. 1100, with the Canary Islands and Senegambia. Adapted from Julien, *History of North Africa*. Cartography by Cassingham and Foxworth, courtesy of the Edwin J. Foscue Map Library, SMU.

Islanders would resist conquest successfully for some eighty years. Attempts by the French in 1403 and the Portuguese in 1443 failed to leave a lasting impression on the archipelago. In 1478 the Catholic Kings, Ferdinand and Isabella, took the conquest under their supervision. A series of would-be conquistadores appeared on the island, but ultimately Pedro de Vera completed the task. His success partially resulted from his co-opting of native factions, particularly those who had become Christians, and including one Fernando Guanarteme of the native royal family. In spite of valiant resistance, including the suicidal leaps of prominent men and women from their sacred peaks, the Spanish completed the conquest of Gran Canaria in 1483. Ferdinand and

Isabella had forged another piece of empire into a gradually unifying Spain.[8]

The seizure and division of native lands among the Spaniards followed the conquest of the Canaries, a standard imperial policy. Prior to the European invasions, the native Berber economy rested on sheep herding, but the Spanish plan for the islands involved first grain, then sugar production. A lucrative crop, sugar would provide the wealth that made the islands attractive. Of course, real estate took on higher value in an agricultural economy, particularly one based on a cash crop for export. In dividing the conquered lands, the Catholic Kings followed practices established in the long reconquest of the Iberian Peninsula from the Moors, practices that would continue on these island stepping-stones to America. The conquering officers and their soldiers expected rewards, and native supporters needed protection. Additional groups of value to the crown required accommodation. Portuguese settlers and Italian merchants had supported Spain and consequently stood to gain land. Not particularly large, the islands' arable land did best when irrigated, making access to water decisive in raising the value of any particular plot. As might be expected, wealthy European newcomers received the best irrigable lands since these could be developed most profitably; the natives got the least. The immigrant Portuguese and Italians, because of their capital, actually gained a more favorable position even than the Castilians. While some Guanches were permitted to keep land, they apparently could not engage in sugar production as could the immigrants, marking the natives as a colonized group and consequently a pool of subordinate labor.[9]

Naturally, labor was necessary to till the soil, but slavery became less institutionalized in the Canaries than elsewhere. For the diverse population that came to the islands, sharecropping, especially among the Portuguese, provided the most important labor. Needless to say, slavery played a role though not on the scale of large plantations. The native Guanches served often as household slaves in the cities, as did Africans, but they more often worked in the sugar mills. In the rural areas, natives experienced enslavement, deportation, and disease, consequently declining in numbers. Colonial attitudes towards the natives were captured in *Los Guanches de Tenerife* by Lope de Vega, "The land is beautiful and could/Have more bounty/Than produced by the

---

[8]   Mercer, 188–93.
[9]   Fernández-Armesto, 56, 60–1, 68, 202.

barbarians." Before the full opening of the Americas, the Canaries drew a settler population that tended to replace or assimilate native laborers, and natives in general.[10]

By the 1520s settlement of the Canaries dropped as New Spain became a magnet for Spanish immigrants. Moreover, the old independence in government and property enjoyed by the conquering generation disappeared as the crown united the islands under an *audiencia* directly under royal jurisdiction. As a frontline colony in Spain's battles with other powers, the Canaries identified more closely with Iberia than America. In 1586, for example, Francis Drake disembarked with three thousand men at La Palma Island, but noting the difficulty of the terrain, "he was forced to board again without doing any harm, . . . he had designs on the Indies, and his defeat [here] put him on the road to them." Relieved to have avoided violence, the lieutenant governor seemed content to see the enemy off and away from his islands and the peninsula. Geographical proximity would ultimately lead to the incorporation of the Canaries into Spain, rather than their separation with the end of the empire. Consequently, the effects of colonialism would vary from those in the New World, particularly in the identity of the people.[11]

By the 1520s the Guanches, outnumbered by the settlers, had acculturated and were rapidly assimilating into the dominant society. Elements of their culture survived in the diet, folklore, dances, and other attributes of island life, but peninsular and other European customs prevailed. By the end of the sixteenth century, the various European and native peoples had intermixed and little distinguished them any longer; in 1599 a public scribe referred to them proudly as "the locals of the Island of Gomera." As a result, the islanders would continue to identify as Spaniards when the New World's peoples rejected that nationality in the nineteenth century. The Canarians and their islands instead would evolve into an ethnic region within the developing nation of Spain. As residents of a territory beyond the Iberian Peninsula, their acceptability to other Spaniards nevertheless remained in doubt. Rather than an

[10] Quoted in ibid., 69, my translation.
[11] Ibid., 200–1; and "El licenciado Jerónimo de Salazar, . . . comunica a Felipe II el ataque de Francis Drake (8 de abril de 1585)," in Antonio Rumeu de Armas, *Piraterías y ataques navales contra las Islas Canarias*, vol. 3, pt. 2 (Madrid: Consejo Superior de Investgaciones Científicas, Instituto Jerónimo Zurita, [1950]), 950, my translation.

integral part of the evolving Spanish community, the Canaries would long seem the first and last colony of a vast overseas empire.[12]

The Indies or Homelands of the Arawaks

"They all go naked as their mothers bore them," wrote Christopher Columbus of the Arawaks, "they are the colour of the people of the Canaries, neither black nor white." After stopping at the Canary Islands, Columbus had launched into the unknown sea on his way to what he envisioned to be the Indies. Instead of the Spice Islands, today known as the East Indies off Southeast Asia, he encountered the homelands of the Arawaks, or the West Indies. After the ancient migrations of their varied ancestors from North, to Central and South America, specifically Ecuador and Colombia, the Arawaks had moved to the Caribbean islands through the Orinoco region of Venezuela, leaving the delta of that river before 900 B.C. and occupying the entire Lesser Antilles by A.D. 100–300. From there they eventually inhabited the Greater Antilles, occupying Puerto Rico, Hispaniola, Cuba, and Jamaica by A.D. 1000. Along the way, the Arawaks possibly conquered, displaced, and assimilated much of an earlier ethnic group, the Ciboney, an Arawakan word for "cave people." Skilled at fishing, foraging, and working stone, some Ciboney nevertheless continued to coexist alongside the Arawaks by the arrival of Columbus. More certain is that by A.D. 1000, the Caribs, also from Venezuela, had driven the Arawaks out of the Lesser Antilles and were attempting the conquest of Puerto Rico by 1492.[13]

The Arawaks identified closely with their early homelands, features of which they indelibly inscribed on religious figurines found by archeologists on many of the Caribbean islands. During their occupation of Guadeloupe and the other Lesser Antilles, the Arawaks developed

[12] Fernández-Armesto, 200–1; and "La segunda relación de lo que se prometió en lo de Canaria. Del hecho que hizieron [sic] los naturales de la Isla de la Gomera ... ," in Rumeu de Armas, 1102, my translation; for a description of the twentieth-century ethnic nationalist movement in the Canaries, see Mercer, 259–69.

[13] "Columbus on the Indians' 'Discovery' of the Spanish, 1492," in *Major Problems in American Indian History: Documents and Essays*, ed. Albert L. Hurtado and Peter Iverson. Major Problems in American History Series, 2nd ed. (Boston: Houghton Mifflin Co., 2001), 57; and Fred Olsen, *On the Trail of the Arawaks*, with a foreword by George Kubler and an introduction by Irving Rouse, Civilization of the American Indian (Norman: Univ. of Oklahoma Press, 1974), 180–1, 119, 233, 277.

a religion whose primary deity was Yocahú, the giver of manioc, their principle crop carried with them from South America; however, the islands' high, active, and imposing volcanoes personified him in conical stones and other images apparently used in religious observance. In addition, according to anthropolgist Fred Olsen, this people had "a female deity referred to as Atabeyra. Actually this goddess had several Arawakan names describing her functions: mother of moving waters – the sea, the tides, and the springs – the goddess of the moon, and the fertility goddess of childbirth." The temporal cycles of the moon, the tides, and menstruation all involved the flow of waters necessary for life. Surrounded by the immensity of the ocean, it should be no surprise that such a deity should inspire belief in an island people.[14]

Puerto Rico, Hispaniola, Cuba, Jamaica, and the Bahamas were the homelands of the Arawaks at Columbus's arrival. Having a common culture and language, these people traveled and traded between the islands, but structured their societies on a more local basis, best illustrated by Hispaniola. Its inhabitants apparently imagined it a paradise called, "Quisqeya," meaning "nothing greater" (seemingly, the Spanish thought otherwise, renaming it for their own motherland). The residents divided Quisqueya into five physical provinces with rough boundaries: Caizcimu, Huhabo, Cayabo, Bainoa, and Guacayarima. (See Map 3.2.) The name of the first province, in the east, meant the front of the island; the last province, in the west, meant the island's behind. Like the Micmacs, the island's Arawaks saw their homeland as a reflection of the human body. Caizimu, Cayabo, and Bainoa formed independent but allied kingdoms, with the latter having the most prestige; Huhabo and Guacayarima remained decentralized provinces likely occupied by free, aboriginal Ciboney. Internally, the kings – a queen, at one point, in the case of Caizcimu – ruled territorial subdivisions under lesser caciques or lords, forming hierarchical states based on matrilineal descent. According to geographer Carl Ortwin Sauer, all the islands of the Arawaks were similarly organized.[15]

Arawak villages could be large enough to have a temple and a ball court arranged loosely around an open space; some towns had more than one court. Usually rectangular, the public space served the

---

[14] Ibid., 92–3, 96–7, 102–3.
[15] Carl Ortwin Sauer, *The Early Spanish Main*, with a new foreword by Anthony Pagden, Centennial Book (1966; reprint, Berkeley and Los Angeles: Univ. of California Press, 1992), 37, 45–8, 50–1.

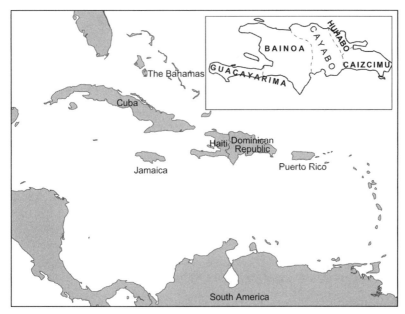

Map 3.2. The Present Caribbean with Inset of Provinces of Quisqueya. Inset adapted from Sauer, *The Early Spanish Main*, 46. Cartography by Cassingham and Foxworth, courtesy of the Edwin J. Foscue Map Library, SMU.

community for assemblies and festivities. The hereditary caciques and their nobility enjoyed the socioeconomic privileges of their rank, having relatively large houses fronting on the grassy public area. Unlike the smaller structures of commoners, the caciques' buildings served ceremonial purposes and were decorated with multicolored art. Steep, bell-shaped, thatched roofed houses, built of palm trunks and wooden siding, could also provide shelter for more than ten related nuclear families. The Arawaks thus lived settled lives in permanent locations.[16]

   To sustain their villages, the Arawaks practiced subsistence agriculture, based on slash-and-burn methods with ash as fertilizer, though on Hispaniola they also utilized some irrigation techniques. Slash-and-burn methods were used to clear fresh farmland, but soil was then piled up to form mounds that could be reused with fertilization. With the advantages of tropical fecundity, many crops resulted from this basic agriculture: maize, cassava, sweet potato, cotton, and tobacco, to name

[16] Ibid., 45, 63–4; cf. J[acques] N[icholas] Léger, *Haïti: Son histoire et ses détracteurs* (New York: Neale Publishing Co., 1907), 17–19.

the basics. Hunting, gathering, and fishing augmented the supply of food and other raw materials, such as bone and hides. Providing even more variety, the Arawaks participated in a network, including their Carib enemies, trading salted fish, vegetable products, captured game, and even manufactured goods, such as shell ornaments, wooden furniture, stone tools, and other "luxuries." Commerce sustained the cultural ties among the many Arawak homelands.[17]

On his first voyage to the Western Hemisphere, Columbus landed in the Bahamas; then under the guidance of "Indian" seamen proceeded to Cuba and then to Hispaniola, as he renamed it: "Its mountains and plains, and meadows, and fields, are so beautiful and rich for planting and sowing, and rearing cattle of all kinds, and for building towns and villages." After an unsuccessful search for rich cities in the Indies, Columbus had to abandon the *Santa Maria* that had run aground on the north side of the island. About forty men established the first Spanish settlement in the "New World," Puerto Navidad, when they built a fort to shelter them since the two remaining vessels could not carry all of Columbus's men home. Unfortunately for these first colonists, all died in hostilities with the Arawaks, as Columbus discovered on his second voyage to the Indies. The pattern of conflict at the core of colonialism had begun.[18]

After establishing a new settlement, named Isabella, Columbus proceeded to explore Jamaica and Cuba, but in his absence a full-fledged war broke out between the colonists and Hispaniola's natives. Since the settlers' efforts at farming had failed, they made incessant demands on the Arawaks' food supplies and abused them in other ways, which led to armed resistance. On his return Columbus launched a military campaign against the Indians, who quickly succumbed to superior arms. The Spanish conquest led to the demise of Hispaniola's Arawaks; by 1508 only sixty thousand of the original population of one million remained. Required to pay a tax in gold and cotton or provide free labor, the Indians faced their first imperial government. Such harsh treatment, further violence, and new diseases resulted from the conquest. The

---

[17] Bonham C. Richardson, *The Caribbean in the Wider World, 1492–1992: A Regional Geography*, Geography of the World Economy (New York: Cambridge Univ. Press, 1992), 22–3; and Sauer, 52, 54–8, 60, 64.

[18] "First Voyage of Columbus," in *Select Letters of Christopher Columbus, with Other Original Documents Relating to His Four Voyages to the New World*, trans. and ed. R[ichard] H[enry] Major, Works Issued by the Hakluyt Society, [no. 43], 2nd ed. (London: Hakluyt Society, 1870), 5; and Sauer, 20–1, 33, 72.

Spaniards came to completely dominate Hispaniola, but as only twenty-five hundred natives survived by 1519, the Europeans had to bring in African slaves to maintain their enterprises.[19]

Hispaniola became the base for further Spanish conquests in the homelands of the Arawaks. In 1509 Puerto Rico and Jamaica fell to the conquistadores; while they found some gold on Boriquén, the former island, they found none on the latter. Juan d'Esquivel led the conquest of Jamaica's Arawaks, parceling out the labors and lands to the few planters who bothered to stay with him there. Ponce de León, conquerer of Puerto Rico, sailed from that island and reconnoitered the southern tip of Florida in 1513. There he encountered the Calusa who had developed a powerful kingdom based on seafood and naturally growing plants; this resilient people successfully resisted Spanish encroachment for generations. Diego Velásquez's conquest of Cuba proved much more rapid and lucrative. There was actually some gold and much more land since this was the largest island in the Caribbean. However, Mexico began to draw settlers away from the Arawak homelands, especially the smaller islands.[20]

The Conquest of Mexico

It took the Spaniards some thirty years to reconnoiter the Caribbean and the Gulf of Mexico before coming upon the Aztec Empire. Hernando Cortés's epic conquest of the Aztec Empire is one of the most dramatic stories in history and central to the formation of the Atlantic World. Prior to contact with Mesoamerica, the Spanish had encountered peoples they regarded as primitive, but the civilizations of the Mayas and Aztecs exposed them to cultures competitive with their own. Indeed, cataclysmic warfare ultimately broke out between the Spanish and the Aztecs. Spanish victory over this society provided immense wealth that assured the dominance that transformed the peoples and places of the first transatlantic empire.[21]

[19] Ibid., 74, 62, 81, 83–4, 86, 295; and Richardson, 24.
[20] Sauer, 40, 178, 180, 182, 186, 190; and Randolph Widmer, *The Evolution of the Calusa: A Nonagricultural Chiefdom on the Southwest Florida Coast* (Tuscaloosa: Univ. of Alabama Press, 1988), 1, 3–8.
[21] Miguel León-Portilla, ed., *The Broken Spears: The Aztec Account of the Conquest of Mexico*, trans. Angel María Garibay K. and Lysander Kemp, with a foreword by J. Jorge Klor de Alva, rev. ed. (Mexico City: Univ. Nacional Autónoma de México, 1959; Boston: Beacon Press, 1992), xxv.

In 1519 an Aztec commoner from the imperial province of Cuet-laxtlan in the larger Totonac region of Cuextlan arrived at Moctezuma's court in Tenochtitlan to report a mysterious occurrence: "Our lord and king. . . . When I went to the shores of the great sea, there was a moun-tain range or small mountain floating in the midst of the water, and moving here and there without touching the shore. My lord, we have never seen the like of this, although we guard the coast and are always on watch." Apparently watching out for enemy rafts or canoes, the sentinel sought, by projecting the heights of interior Mexico onto the gulf, to have the emperor imagine a sight never before seen. Subsequent investigation by representatives of the emperor confirmed "that strange people" had "come to the shores of the great sea" in "great towers." These officials thus projected the high structures of their fortresses, temples, and cities onto the water to make the unknown recognizable. Through this process the foreign Spanish ships ironically reflected na-tive landmarks emblematic of homelands from the Gulf to the Valley of Mexico.[22]

Indeed, despite the wide extent of the Aztec Empire, Mesoamerica comprised many homelands and peoples whose divisions the Spaniards effectively manipulated. Central to this operation was Malintzin, the woman who interpreted and consequently provided the critical diplo-matic connection between Aztecs and the Spaniards. Born into a noble family along the Gulf on the southeastern frontier of the Aztec Empire, she was sold into slavery when her mother remarried. Malintzin found herself traded from one group to another along the coast until passed into the hands of Hernando Cortés. Speaking both Nahuatl and Mayan, acquired from living along the frontier between the empire and Yucatan, she linked with a Mayan-speaking Spaniard in a chain of communication between the Aztecs and Spanish.[23]

Thereafter as the native peoples faced the intrusive foreigners, they had to talk first with Malintzin, for as Moctezuma's officials informed him, "The strangers are accompanied by a woman from this land, who speaks our Nahuatl tongue. She is called La Malinche." Indeed, her

[22] Pedro Carrasco, *The Tenochca Empire of Ancient Mexico: The Triple Alliance of Tenochtilan, Tetzcoco, and Tlacopan*, Civilization of the American Indian Series, vol. 234 (Norman: Univ. of Oklahoma Press, 1999), 356; and León-Portilla, 16–17.

[23] Bernal Díaz del Castillo, *Historia verdadera de la conquista de la Nueva España*, with an introduction and notes by Joaquín Ramírez Cabañas, 2nd ed. (Mexico City: Editorial Porrua, Sepan Cuantos, 1962), 56–7.

image overlapped with that of Cortés so that the Indians came to call him Captain Malinche. The first official representatives of Moctezuma to Cortés, reaching his ship by canoe, included Pinotl, the Aztec governor of conquered Cuetlaxtlan. After exchanging salutations and gifts with Cortés at this and later meetings, Moctezuma's messengers witnessed the threatening power of Spanish horsemanship and firearms, which they eventually reported to their emperor. Both the governor and emperor would find the conquered Totonacs restive when presented with such alternatives to Aztec rule by the manipulative Spaniards.[24]

Faced with Cortés's request to meet Moctezuma, the Aztecs stalled, having heard of earlier Spanish victories against resistant Indians farther south on the Gulf Coast. Severing diplomatic contact, the Aztecs cut off supplies to the Spanish and abandoned surrounding towns when the latter sent men foraging for provisions. Meanwhile, learning of this diplomatic breach, nearby Totonac leaders sought an alliance with the Spanish against the Aztecs, using their own Nahuatl interpreters to join in the chain of communication through Malintzin to Cortés. Cortés then moved up the coast a bit to the semi-autonomous province of Cempoala from which the Totonac leaders had visited. There the Totonacs informed him of their distaste for Aztec rule and were convinced to resist imperial officials who sought to keep Cempoala, Cuetlaxtlan, and all of Cuextlan in submission. Thus was the first alliance formed in the rebellion against the Aztec Empire.[25]

"A man from Cempoala, who was known as Tlacochcalatl . . . . showed them [the Spaniards] the best routes" to Tenochtitlan, arguing that those lay through the independent country of Tlaxcala which they could enlist as a major ally against Moctezuma. However, the Tlaxcalans and their subordinate Otomi allies resisted Spanish encroachment into their territory. After several major battles that resulted in the burning of many towns and the deaths of many Tlaxcalans, they sued for peace with the invaders, deciding that the Spanish might indeed serve as formidable allies against the traditional Aztec enemy. Meeting with Captain Malinche, Tlaxcalan officials sent by Maxixcatzin, their ruler, identified themselves and their homeland. "You have entered our land. We are from Tlaxcala; our city is the City of the Eagle." This

---

[24] León-Portilla, 22–25, 35; Hernando Cortés, *Hernando Cortés: Five Letters, 1519–1526*, trans. J. Bayard Morris (New York: W. W. Norton & Co., 1969), 382 n.11; and Díaz del Castillo, 58–9.

[25] Ibid., 61–5, 69–70, 72–5.

reference to a noble bird, together with the etymology of the name – the place of maize tortillas – revealed the pride they felt in their fertile country. The officials invited the Malinche to their city which Cortés on his arrival described as "great and marvelous . . . . much larger than Granada." In the city Maxixcatzin decided to join the Spanish in their advance against Tenochtitlan, the capital city and traditional enemy of Tlaxcala. Opportunistically, the Aztecs' adversaries sought to use the foreigners' power against the empire.[26]

On the other hand, Moctezuma sought to halt the Spanish march with a combination of diplomacy, intrigue, and force. His messengers to Cortés suggested that he follow a route through the city of Cholula, where however the Tlaxcalans warned imperial troops lay in wait. Entering Cholula, just the same, Cortés ordered a preemptive attack, surprising and slaughtering three thousand lightly armed Cholulans. According to Aztec accounts, "When the massacre at Cholula was complete, the strangers set out again toward the City of Mexico . . . . as conquerors . . . glistening iron from head to foot; they terrified every-one who saw them." While some including Moctezuma himself were cowed, others stood willing to defend the empire; indeed, Cuitlahuac, the emperor's brother warned him not to "let the strangers into your house. They will cast you out of it and overthrow your rule."[27]

Meanwhile, other native towns welcomed the westward moving Spaniards and their increasing allies. Offering them provisions, warning them of the dangers, and suggesting ways of approaching Tenochtitlan, Huexotzinco, an independent state and ally of Tlaxcala, saw the advan-tages of siding with the seemingly fearless strangers. In that country Moctezuma's messengers diplomatically attempted to dissuade the Spanish from entering their city, but to no avail. The Spaniards, now with Huexotzincans at their side, descended the mountains into the Valley of Mexico and the core of the Aztec Empire. Successively, such Aztec towns as Amecameca, Cuitlahuac, Mixquic, and Ixtapalapan, under orders from Moctezuma, extended hospitality to the visitors though engaging in nighttime skirmishes among scouting parties along the shores of Lake Chalco.[28]

[26] León-Portilla, 38–40; Cortés, 48, 50–1, 55; and Díaz del Castillo, 125, 28.
[27] Cortés, 54, 57; and León-Portilla, 41, 54–5, 61.
[28] Richard F. Townsend, *The Aztecs*, Ancient Peoples and Places, rev. ed. (London: Thames & Hudson, 2000), 27; Cortés, 67; and Díaz del Castillo, 144.

Fatalistically, convinced that the Spanish were ancestral demi-gods returned to retake their kingdom, Moctezuma welcomed them at the entrance to Tenochtitlan: "You have come down from the sky. . . . Welcome to your land, my lords!" Moctezuma envisioned his land, his people, and empire as destined for rule by others – hardly an attitude of self-determination. Unsurprisingly, Cortés manipulated the emperor and soon had him captive in his own capital. While Cortés was able to rule through Moctezuma for a time, resistance quickly developed and exploded into violent rebellion among those Aztecs with a more re-alistic perception of the threat to their nation. According to Cortés, Moctezuma attempted to pacify the rebels but was stoned by his own people and died shortly thereafter.[29]

Encircled in the center of the Tenochtitlan, Cortés attempted to reason with the Aztecs: "we were burning and destroying their city and would have to continue. . . . To which they replied that they plainly perceive this but were determined to die to a man, if need be, to finish us." Indeed, the Mexica, after failing to exterminate the Spaniards, chased them from the capital, forcing them to flee for safety in Tlaxcala. Having themselves suffered two thousand casualties at the hands of the Aztecs, Maxixcatzin and the other Tlaxcalan leaders took in the Span-iards, seeing their alliance as firmer than ever, for "many women . . . of our towns will weep over the deaths of their sons, and husbands, and brothers, and relatives." Feelings were not unanimous, however, as at least one noble, Xicotencatl the younger, argued for union with the Aztecs, but was rebuked by his elders pointing out that Tlaxcala had regained prosperity after the Spaniards had eliminated Aztec trade barriers. Traditional international hatreds trumped the possibilities of a Nahua confederation against the foreign invaders, playing into the Spanish strategy of divide and conquer.[30]

While the Spanish recuperated in Tlaxcala, the Aztecs found it difficult to do the same as previously unknown small pox plagued Tenochtitlan. Though regaining the loyalties of the imperial core, the Aztecs in a debilitated state faced the reinforced Spanish in the final battle for their nation. Launching brigantines with cannon into the lakes surrounding the city, the Spanish and the Tlaxcalans besieged it, as their ground troops filled in the causeways to cross by land. According to the native chroniclers, "Nothing can compare with the

[29] León-Portilla, 35, 64, 76–7; and Cortés, 71, 74, 76–7, 80, 111–12.
[30] Ibid., 53, 115, 121; and Díaz del Castillo, 242, my translation, 244.

horrors of that siege and the agonies of the starving. . . . Little by little
they forced us to the wall." After house-to-house combat lasting days,
Cuauhtemoc, the young successor to Moctezuma, surrendered the city
to Cortés. An elegy written immediately after the conquest in 1523
captured the pathos of losing one's homeland and one's national identity: "How can we save our homes, my people?/The Aztecs are deserting
the city:/the city is in flames, and all/is darkness and destruction/ . . . /
know that with these disasters/we have lost the Mexican nation." All
this seemingly fulfilled the prophecies of a weeping woman said to have
wandered that streets of the city before the Spanish arrival: "'My children, we must flee far away from this city!' . . . 'My children, where shall
I take you?'" Indeed, the Aztecs would now be in search of a new place
and a new identity.[31]

Semiautonomous Tlaxcala

While the conquest of the Aztecs assured the subordination of that
group, the position of Tlaxcalans in the new Spanish imperial system
was anomalous for at least a century after the establishment of New
Spain. With the victory of that alliance, the Tlaxcalans, Spain's major
allies, experienced a peculiar relationship within the new empire.
Though the Tlaxcalans had been conquered by the Spanish, they had
also contributed to the conquest of the Aztecs. As a result of this and
their own incessant patriotism, Tlaxcala would early enjoy a measure of
autonomy unknown to other peoples in New Spain. Initially, the Spanish ruled through the Tlaxcalan leadership in a stratified system based
on that existing prior to their arrival. From 1521 to 1531, royal government was minimal. Tlaxcalan lands were protected as no grants were
made to Spaniards or others in the province. However, the encomienda
system of labor was implemented in practice, as Tlaxcalans had to provide workers to surrounding Spanish ranches and to government proj-
ects. During this ten-year period, there was some political instability in
the province as local government went through a transition to Spanish
administrative practices.[32]

---

[31] León-Portilla, 6, 92–3, 97–8, 109, 116–17, 146.
[32] Charles Gibson, *Tlaxcala in the Sixteenth Century*, Yale Historical Publications,
      miscellany 56 (New Haven, Conn.: Yale Univ. Press, 1952), 26, 62–5; the
      Viceroyalty of New Spain can be seen as an imperial colony or one kingdom
      federated with the multiple Hapsburg monarchy – see Armitage, 22–3.

Between 1531 and 1600 governance in the province stabilized as the system evolved. Tlaxcalans retained some political influence as an Indian *cabildo*, or council, advised the *corregidor*, or governor, appointed by the viceroy in Mexico City. After 1533, the *alguacil*, or mayor, was Indian. The *escribanos públicos*, or record keepers, often exploited the illiterate populace with regard to deeds, wills, and other legal documents. The government necessarily operated bilingually, as Spanish and Nahuatl shared the stage as public languages. Thus, government reflected a certain amount of autonomy gained as a result of Tlaxcala's persistent patriotism, as well as its support of the Spanish during the conquest of the Aztecs and in subsequent campaigns against other native peoples as far north as New Mexico.[33]

In spite of this ethnic regional autonomy, economic pressure on Tlaxcala escalated throughout the sixteenth century. Spanish and mestizo civilians gradually intruded on the lands of the province. A sign that the Tlaxcalans' favorable positon would erode was the first royal land grant made in the province to cattle raisers. Well before the era of fenced ranches, this grant led to the ruination of surrounding Indian crops. Following the cattlemen came non-Indian farmers, traders, and manufacturers. As early as 1550, the cabildo concurred that "this is the city of us Tlaxcalans only, and the Spaniards establish their cities in Mexico City, Puebla, and other places. Therefore . . . we should propose to the viceroy that he grant us the favor that no Spaniard be among us and they leave entirely." An Indian delegation did appeal directly to the viceroy with some success, but in the long run the intruders had far more influence in the centers of power than the Tlaxcalans. Tlaxcalan regional influence ultimately failed even to preserve Indian autonomy. By 1600 the province had been overrun by outsiders; it nevertheless retained its character as a distinct ethnic region and would survive as a separate state in the later Mexican republic.[34]

Significantly, Tlaxcalans and other Indians became agents of colonialism as the Spanish recruited them for further exploration, conquest, and settlement in the northern borderlands of Spain's growing

---

[33] Gibson, 65–72, 187–9; see also James Lockhart, *Nahuas and Spaniards: Postconquest Central Mexican History and Philology*, Nahuatl Studies, no. 3 (Stanford, Calif.: Stanford Univ. Press, UCLA Latin American Center, 1991), 23–38.

[34] Ibid., 83, 193; "Do Not Divulge Cabildo Business! August 8, 1550," in James Lockhart, Frances Berdan, and Arthur J. O. Anderson, *The Tlaxcalan Actas: A Compendium of the Records of the Cabildo of Tlaxcala (1545–1627)* (Salt Lake City: Univ. of Utah Press, 1986), 76, 30.

American empire. Loss of land and economic stresses at home caused emigration, sometimes to nearby cities such as Puebla, sometimes much farther away. In 1573 a group of men and women migrated north where they settled in six different areas including one called San Esteban de Nueva Tlaxcala near Saltillo. From this seminal group in later years and generations, Tlaxcalans would help settle New Mexico and Texas, including the cities of Santa Fe and San Antonio. As colonists, they naturally battled with Indians indigenous to the locales occupied, but political and social strife with Spaniards persisted in the north as well. The troubles of the old homeland persisted in the new ethnic communities on the frontiers, as older layers of dominance and subordination piled on new subjects, such as the Pueblos and Coahuiltecans.[35]

EXPANDING EMPIRES

Interestingly, in 1559 Tlaxcalans and other Indian allies of the Spanish participated in the early exploration of Florida. With the assistance of some veterans of the notorious Hernando de Soto expedition that explored much of the present southeastern United States (1539–43), Tristan de Luna y Arellano attempted a settlement at Pensacola Bay and reconnoitered much of Alabama, reaching into the Coosa or Cherokee country. Among his Indian assistants was a woman, taken from her homeland by the earlier De Soto expedition; like la Malinche, she served as the critically necessary interpreter. Although no permanent colony resulted from the Luna expedition, the Spaniards would found St. Augustine, with settlers directly from Spain a few years later in 1565.[36]

It was possible for an expedition from Spain to include Indians since some occasionally found themselves there, usually involuntarily. In

---

[35] Gibson, 185, 187–9; Amy Meschke, "Women's Lives through Women's Wills in the Spanish and Mexican Borderlands, 1750–1846" (Ph.D. diss., Southern Methodist Univ., 2004), 25–26; and Thomas D. Hall, *Social Change in the Southwest*, Studies in Historical Social Change (Lawrence: Univ. Press of Kansas, 1989), 4–5. Though New Mexico lay deep in the interior of North America, it became part of the Atlantic World by virtue of its trade connections through central Mexico to Vera Cruz and Spain; though New Mexico was the most important colony in the northern Spanish borderlands, Texas receives fuller attention in this work in keeping with the goal of highlighting the more marginal homelands nearer the Atlantic shores.

[36] Gibson, 159; David J. Weber, *The Spanish Frontier in North America*, Yale Western Americana (New Haven, Conn.: Yale Univ. Press, 1992), 67, 69.

1524 a Portuguese in Spain's service, Estevâo Gomes, officially explored
the North American coast between Cape Breton, in the land of the
Micmacs, and Buzzard's or Naragansett Bays. Failing to find the Northwest Passage that he sought, he enslaved some local Indians, probably
Algonkian speakers, and took them back to Spain doubtless to help
defray his costs. Indeed, native contacts with Europeans along the
Atlantic coast from Florida to Maine since about 1514 had consisted
almost exclusively of conflict with illegal Spanish slave hunters. In areas
farther north, on the other hand, including the Micmac country, contact seems to have been more benign.[37]

An early Micmac story "records the dream of a young girl in which
she saw an island of trees come floating to shore. Climbing among the
branches of the trees were animals that she thought were bears. When
the Micmac in her dream tried to shoot their weapons at the floating
island and the bears on it, the bears turned into men who paddled
ashore in a strange-looking canoe." Fanciful or not, the story suggests
the ways some Micmacs perceived the first European arrivals – as dan-
gerous beasts from foreign territory, invading the homeland. Regardless,
apparently some of the earliest contacts along the coasts of Labrador,
Newfoundland, and Nova Scotia were peaceful; fishermen from Ireland,
Brittany, and the Basque Country, possibly before 1492, stopped to
gather wood and water, dry the catch, and trade with the natives. Such
unofficial representatives of ethnic regions in Western Europe could be
more effective in intercultural relations than such official explorers as
John Cabot (1497) sailing for England, Giovanni da Verrazzano (1524)
for France, and Jacques Cartier (1534) also for France. The Micmacs
not only welcomed Cartier, himself from Brittany, but also sought to
monopolize trade with the French by squeezing out the Laurentian
Iroquois, their commercial rivals. Indeed, competition between these
two native nations led to a war in which the Micmacs drove the Iroquois into the interior where they prevented the French, then perceived
as Algonkian allies, from establishing settlements along the St. Lawrence for another seventy years.[38]

---

[37] Ibid., 35, 37; Meinig, vol. 1, 24–5; for the early impact of Spanish exploration on
      Indians, see Shirley A. Hollis, "Crafting Europe's 'Clean Slate' Advantage:
      World-System Expansion and the Indigenous Mississippians of North America,"
      American Indian Culture and Research Journal, 28(no. 3, 2004): 91–3.
[38] Meinig, vol. 1, 24–5; Weber, 38; and Kenneth R. Shepherd, "Micmac," in *Gale
      Encyclopedia of Native American Tribes*, ed. Sharon Malinowski et al., vol. 1,
      Northeast, Southeast, Caribbean (Detroit, Mich.: Gale Publishing, 1998), 135–6.

French Colonialism

Seeing the economic and military advantages of ties to the French, the Micmacs directly and indirectly assisted them in founding their first more or less permanent colonies at Port Royal on the Bay of Fundy in the Micmac country and at Quebec (1606–1608) on the St. Lawrence River in the interior. The French came to call their coastal colony "Acadia" from the Micmac word for place of abundance. "At Port Royal, the name of the Captain," according to a Frenchman, was "Membertou . . . [who ruled] not with so much authority as does our King over his subjects, but with sufficient power to . . . lead them to war." Chief and eventually Christian convert, Henri Membertou, aided the colonists in securing their settlements by using imported European weapons to repel the neighboring Abenaki. When the French under Samuel de Champlain moved inland from Acadia to found Quebec, they discovered the Iroquois of the St. Lawrence area had disappeared probably because of European diseases. Thus, the rich riverbanks of this former Indian homeland were open to become the core French-speaking region on the continent. The settlers, from northwestern France, set up independent long-lot farms extending from the riverfront to pasturage and woodland in the interior, leaving most farmers with access to the water and transportation provided by the river. Geography and the small population, rather than policy, dictated this pattern. The French government and its chartered Company of New France would have preferred a more feudal seigniorial arrangement of large estates, manor houses, and peasants. Such a formal social structure could not develop where the small population had access to much land.[39]

Politically and religiously, formality prevailed at Quebec City, the capital. As the imperial administrative center, Quebec represented monarchical and Roman Catholic France; no democratically representative government existed there. But geography dictated a looser society, especially away from the capital. Eventually the center of a vast empire extending from Acadia to New Orleans, Quebec could

---

[39] Marc Lescarbot, "La conversion des savvages qui ont esté baptizés en la Novvelle France cette anne 1610, avec un bref recit du voyage du Sieur de Poutrincout," in *Jesuit Relations and Allied Documents: Travels and Explorations of the Jesuit Missionaries in New France, 1610–1791*, ed. Reuben Gold Thwaites, vol. 1, *Acadia: 1610–1613* (New York: Pageant Book Co., 1959), 74–5; and Meinig, vol. 1, 36–7, 110.

not control this territory in an authoritarian fashion. Indeed, the commercial capital was Montreal, upriver and the base of an enormous hinterland, stretching westward up the Ottawa River across Canada, and southward through Niagara and Detroit, through the Illinois country, down the Ohio and Mississippi rivers. Another commercial route served the Great Lakes through Michilimackinac. This vast frontier empire rested on the fur trade and a riverine transportation network. Of course, the French/Indian alliance made the empire possible. Varied Huron, Algonkian, and other peoples throughout this huge North American empire provided the labor, skills, products, and markets that made the empire profitable. This decentralized system of alliances made the empire less oppressive than most even when the French resorted to open conquest as they did with the Natchez in Mississippi. Ultimately, the system still primarily served the interests of the French elite in their global struggles with competing empires.[40]

In Acadia during the late sixteenth century, small pox, dysentery, and respiratory infections had ravaged the Micmacs, dropping their population from 4,500 to 3,000, but somehow falling short of extermination. This led many Micmacs to accept Catholicism in hopes of finding new spiritual allies against the unknown illnesses. In the initial French settlement at Port Royal, the object had been to trade with the Indians for furs, but the colonists, as one recalled, immediately farmed: "I took in digging and tilling my gardens, fencing them in against the gluttony of the swine, making terraces, preparing straight alleys, building storehouses, sowing wheat, rye, barley, oats, beans, peas, garden plants, and watering them." In the 1630s another company with colonists from western France settled in the Micmac country, which by then had much depopulated territory. As these colonists had previously farmed along France's shores, they reclaimed land from the sea, consequently competing minimally with the Micmacs whose homeland they entered to develop their own. Lack of competition for space and growing trade relations led to relatively amicable relations. This pattern reflected French colonialism even in areas where fur trapping played a less important role in the economy. Thus, the two nations remained allies, even if

[40] Ibid., 109–17; cf. Kenneth J. Banks, *Chasing Empire across the Sea: Communications and the State in the French Atlantic, 1713–1763* (Montreal: McGill – Queen's Univ. Press, 2002), 7, 39.

unequal, until 1763 and the end of the French Empire in North America.[41]

A New English Region in Powhatan's Country

While the Micmacs were assisting the French, the Algonkians at Chesapeake Bay under King Powhatan, decided to coexist with the "Tassantasses," or English, who had established a trading post called Jamestown in 1607. Having destroyed an earlier Spanish mission in their homeland, Powhatan's people were aware of the dangers as well as the advantages of dealing with Europeans. Indeed, an Algonkian priest predicted that such men would "come and take away their country." Expecting to find gold as had Cortés, the English colonists failed to provide for themselves and had to rely on supplies from the Powhatans. When that was not enough, Captain John Smith and the English seized stores of food, causing Powhatan to retaliate in what had always been an uneasy relationship. A war of attrition followed with the Virginia Company eventually sending out enough supplies and reinforcements from England to allow the colonists to gain ground, with the assistance of European diseases. By 1614 Powhatan resigned himself to another tentative peace after his daughter, Pocahontas, was kidnapped and married to an Englishman. In learning her husband's customs, having his mestizo child, and even journeying to England, she became one of the earliest to imagine, create, and experience community between homelands across the Atlantic World. Unfortunately, on her way home she died shortly thereafter, prefiguring the demise of her people who would lose their state by 1646 after more warfare. Thus did the kingdom of the Powhatans become an Anglo-American homeland.[42]

---

[41] Shepherd, 136–7; Marc Lescarbot quoted in Margaret R. Conrad and James K. Hiller, *Atlantic Canada: A Region in the Making*, The Illustrated History of Canada (Toronto: Oxford Univ. Press, 2001), 58; and Meinig, vol.1, 36–7, 89–90.

[42] Quoted in James Axtell, *Natives and Newcomers: The Cultural Origins of North America* (New York: Oxford Univ. Press, 2001), 258, 234–8, 240, 242, 245, 248–50; for further expansion of the new Anglo-American homeland and its articulation with the Cherokee and larger Atlantic economies, see Wilma A. Dunaway, *The First American Frontier: Transition to Capitalism in Southern Appalachia, 1700–1860*, Fred W. Morrison Series in Southern Studies (Chapel Hill: Univ. of North Carolina Press, 1996), 23–7, 32–4.

Transitory Dutch Homeland

During the same period the Iroquois Confederacy faced similar pressures from European intrusion. The successes of the Micmacs, other Algonkians, and the Hurons in establishing alliances with the French pushed the Iroquois into becoming allies of France's enemies. Conveniently, in 1614 the Dutch established a fur trading post named Fort Orange (later Albany) at the navigation head of the river named for Henry Hudson, the Englishman who claimed it for the Netherlands. Conquering their Mohican rivals in the area, as the Dutch pushed aside smaller Algonkian tribes farther south, the Iroquois and their new European allies sought to wrench control of the fur trade, extending beyond the Great Lakes to the west and south, from the French. Furs could then be funneled from Fort Orange downriver to New Amsterdam, founded on Manhattan Island in 1623, then on to Europe. Gradually, Iroquois women interbred with Dutch backwoodsmen producing mixed offspring, such as Canaqueese, a.k.a. Smits John, who served as an interpreter among various peoples. In 1654 he informed the French that the front door to the Longhouse of the Iroquois was by way of the Mohawks' land to the east, rather than that of the Onondagas' at the smoke hole. Like mestizos and metis elsewhere, Canaqueese imagined the homeland of his mother as her people did and could represent them to outsiders. By controlling the vast region of present New York State, the Iroquois Confederacy was in a powerful position, not only between the French and Dutch, but the English, who were settling Massachusetts at the same time. Meanwhile, the Dutch were establishing an ethnic region along the Hudson River by the name of New Netherland.[43]

Attempting to establish a colonial system similar to that of the French, the Dutch encountered some of the same difficulties – a huge land and few settlers. The harbor attracted some colonists because Manhattan, the surrounding islands and estuaries reminded them of their European homeland, but the trading-post quality of the settlement reflected the character of their overall empire, one similar to that of the Portuguese, but less centralized. Rather unexpectedly, being a loosely federated republic itself, the Netherlands in the early 1600s developed a full overseas empire. The Dutch established far-flung trading posts,

---

[43] Meinig, vol. 1, 41, 119–21; and Francis Jennings et al. *The History and Culture of Iroquois Diplomacy: An Interdisciplinary Guide to the Treaties of the Six Nations and Their League* (Syracuse, N.Y.: Syracuse Univ. Press, 1985), 25.

from Africa, to India, the East Indies, the West Indies, and South America, virtually always along the coastline, but these rarely led to deeply rooted homelands.[44]

Similar to the French, the government of the Netherlands chartered the Dutch West India Company to establish a feudal land tenure system, but to no avail. While a few estates under patroons were established along the Hudson, their manor houses were hardly sumptuous and their workers hardly peasants. A scarcity of capital and settlers meant that the elite had trouble controlling a population that had access to land and could remain relatively independent. The local Indians were poor candidates for peasantry, and the fur-trapping economy encouraged freedom among all ethnic groups. Although some farming eventually took hold along the river, agriculture was based on free holding.[45]

New Amsterdam under company control had a mixed experience. The governors could be rather autocratic as long as that did not undermine the profitability of the enterprise. While the Netherlands would have preferred a homogeneous Dutch population, the company took settlers of any nationality as it needed their labor and skills. When one governor sought to exclude Jews, the Netherlands overturned his decision because Jewish talents were more valuable than the colony's religious purity. Indeed, while the Dutch Reformed Church had official standing, other Christians were admitted as long as they paid taxes for support of the church. Thus, from its earliest years, New Amsterdam had a mixed population more interested in commerce than in political, religious, or cultural designs; as one Dutch Lutheran lamented: "the fact is, alas, that many of the congregation begin to stray like sheep." Indeed, New Netherland served the interests of the metropolis rather poorly, and its population had little loyalty to the mother country.[46]

When the English arrived in New Amsterdam in 1664, the settlers refused to defend the city. They recognized that resistance would be futile and their city, not to mention their lives, would be lost. The interests of the larger Dutch Empire apparently did not merit the sacrifice of life and property. In spite of this, Dutch ethnicity, if not loyalty,

---

[44] Meinig, vol. 1, 41, 119–21; and A. T. van Deursen, "The Dutch Republic, 1588–1780," in *History of the Low Countries*, ed. J.C.H. Blom and E. Lamberts, trans. James C. Kennedy (New York: Berghahn Books, 1999), 143, 148–9.

[45] Meinig, vol. 1, 119–21; and Banks, 4.

[46] Quoted in Joyce D. Goodfriend, *Before the Melting Pot: Society and Culture in Colonial New York City, 1664–1730* (Princeton, N.J.: Princeton Univ. Press, 1992), 11, 8–21.

persisted. Up to the establishment of New York, immigrants to the city had acculturated, if not assimilated to the Dutch, but with that culture no longer dominant, immigrants assimilated to the English. The city fast became British; indeed, within a few decades New York was at the core of British North America. The Dutch could still be found in enclaves around Albany and a few other spots, but they now formed an ethnic region. Separated from the dominant culture of the Netherlands, the enclave survived where it was relatively isolated but disappeared in cosmopolitan New York City. Without the support of the Dutch state and its empire, Dutch ethnicity struggled to survive. This of course would be a common phenomenon in other ethnic regions.[47]

Ironically, after 1664 the Dutch confronted some of the same problems Native Americans had faced in their encounters with Europeans. But while the Dutch faced cultural erosion and assimilation due to British imperialism, the Indians faced extinction due to European colonialism. Competition over the fur trade between the French, Dutch, and British empires led to warfare among the Hurons, Algonkians, and Iroquois. The latter formed a powerful sovereign confederacy during the colonial era. In fact the confederacy had its own imperial ambitions as it attacked the surrounding Indian nations; however, these attacks had also resulted from the Iroquois' need to replenish their own population undermined by European diseases. Captive women, children, and even whole bands were incorporated into the confederacy; as one Jesuit noted, the Iroquois sought "to take, if they can, all the Hurons; and, having put to death the most considerable ones and a good part of the others, to make of them both but one people and only one land." Thus, European colonialism threatened Indian demographic, as well as cultural, extinction but also stimulated native imperialism as a mode of survival.[48]

EVOLVING CARIBBEAN COMMUNITIES

As the first area to experience European colonialism, the Caribbean revealed many of the results on the three races meeting there. As we have seen, the Spanish initially established settlements on Hispaniola; they conquered and enslaved the Indians, putting the natives to work

[47] Ibid.; Meinig, vol. 1, 121–4; and Armitage, 122.
[48] Father Jogues quoted in Susan Johnston, "Epidemics: The Forgotten Factor in Seventeenth Century Native Warfare in the St. Lawrence Region," in *Native Peoples, Native Lands: Canadian Indians, Inuit, and Metis*, ed. Bruce Alden Cox (Ottawa: Carleton Univ. Press, 1988), 28, 14–15, 24.

mining for gold. Deplorable conditions and diseases eliminated much of the native population in the Caribbean, though racial intermixture preserved some Indian traits in the later Cuban, Dominican, and Puerto Rican peoples. Depopulation made it necessary for the Spanish to purchase black slaves from the Portuguese who acquired them at their African trading posts by prompting wars in the interior for that purpose. The impact of imperialism on Africans thus proved disastrous as well. Removed from their original homelands in the Old World, individuals were isolated from other members of their own cultures to prevent rebellious conspiracies. As a result, individuals could not pass on whole cultures, as these were community phenomena. Detribalized people could not pass on either regional or larger cultures as a whole, but they could pass on distinct elements that would contribute to the creation of new African-American regional and ultimately national cultures.[49]

While the Spanish had conquered Quisqueya, renaming it Hispaniola, in the 1490s, the colony had suffered from mainland competition beginning in the 1520s. With colonists preferring more lucrative areas, much of western Hispaniola remained vacant. By the 1650s French pirates had stepped through this opening, subsisting between raids on stray Spanish cattle: "the meat was laid to be dried upon a wooden grate or hurdle which Indians call *barbecu*, placed at a good distance over a slow fire. The meat when cooked was called *boucan*." The buccaneers could also sell such dried meat, and thus they became entrepreneurs in their own private colonies, where sugar plantations would flourish. Eventually, imported African slaves would provide the labor and most of the population, since the natives had long died away.[50]

In 1664 the French government decided to assert direct control over these virtually independent Caribbean outposts. France bought out the proprietors and increased supplies of slaves by building more trading posts at such places as West Africa. The French West India Company was organized to handle trade, collect customs, and replace the Dutch who had monopolized trade. When resistance to this centralization arose in St. Domingue, France sent a fleet to suppress its own colonists

[49] Weber, 31–4, 82–3.
[50] Père du Tertre quoted in Robert Debs Heinl, Jr. and Nancy Gordon Heinl, *Written in Blood: The Story of the Haitan People, 1492–1971* (Boston: Houghton Mifflin Co., 1978), 16; Richardson, 1, 31; and J. H. Parry, P. M. Sherlock, and A. P. Maingot, *A Short History of the West Indies*, Macmillan Caribbean, 4th ed. (London: Macmillan, 1987), 78.

and the Dutch merchants who had rebelled. To secure control, France in the 1680s formed an alliance with Caribbean pirates to force Spain to give up its claim to St. Domingue, as well as settle other differences. After defeating Spain, France encouraged the pirates to establish sugar mills, purchase more slaves, join the navy – in other words to become respectable and productive subjects. A visiting aristocrat observed that to encourage marriage the governor imported "prostitutes from the hospitals, abandoned wretches raked up from the mud of the capital," a colonial pattern repeated from Virginia to Sierra Leone. By 1697 further Spanish and English attempts to dislodge the French had failed, and St. Domingue became the most profitable colony producing sugar in the Caribbean. The modern black nation of Haiti would eventually spring from this colony.[51]

As we have seen, Spain had early lost its monopoly in the Caribbean basin. Overextended in the Americas, it could not hold onto all its claims and concentrated on the most valuable, particularly on the mainland. In the 1650s Spain lost one of its larger possessions, Jamaica, to the English. After a failed attack on Hispaniola in 1654, the English turned on the less populated Jamaica in an attempt to force the Spanish to recognize England's position in the region. The English took over Kingston Harbor without a shot, but faced a protracted struggle with slave bands freed by the Spanish and armed by them in guerrilla re-sistance. Despite reinforcements from Mexico, the Spanish were forced to abandon the island in the face of an increasing British population. But the English did not secure control until they had settled with Lubolo, the key Maroon leader allied with the Spanish. He was allowed to take his people to the cockpit country in western Jamaica. With this treaty the Spanish in 1660 gave up hope of holding the island without local black support or new hardworking settlers "like those of the Canaries." For the next thirty years, Jamaica would serve as a base for pirates to raid the Spanish with on-and-off British support.[52]

Imperialism in the Caribbean did not become lucrative until the European powers cultivated sugar on a massive scale. Though the

[51] Richardson, 51, 78–9; Parry, Sherlock, and Maingot, 79–81, 89; and Baron de Wimpffen quoted in Thomas O. Ott, *The Haitian Revolution, 1789–1801* (Knoxville: Univ. of Tennessee Press, 1973), 5.

[52] Francisco de Leiva Isasi quoted in Francisco Morales Padrón, *Jamaica española* (Seville: Escuela de Estudios Hispano-Americanos de Sevilla, 1952), 373, 371–2, 374–5; and Parry, Sherlock, and Maingot, 58–9.

Spanish first introduced the industry, the Dutch, French, and English
gradually cut in on Spain's monopoly and improved on production
methods. Essentially, Caribbean islands were turned into agricultural
factories using black slave labor with a few white overseers in charge.
These overseers would do a tour of duty in what was perceived as a hot
uncomfortable environment. A minimum of "civilized" elements were
introduced into the environment as few Europeans settled on the islands. The result, however, was the creation of new African American
societies in new homelands. While European elements such as religion
and language persisted, these were permeated by aspects of many different African cultures. Thus, imperialism completely transformed the
relationship between ethnicity and homeland.[53]

SUPERIMPOSED HOMELANDS

From 1400 to 1700 native peoples and lands faced the spread of European imperialism along and then across the Atlantic. Conquered but
often resilient, Canarians, Arawaks, Totonacs, and Nahuas mixed with
Europeans and Africans, evolving into new peoples as the Spanish
Empire developed new colonies, new provinces, and new ethnic regions
in the occupied territories. Some ethnic regions seemingly disappeared –
Totonac Cuextlan obscured by Spanish-mestizo-mulatto Veracruz;
some reappeared in new form – Arawak Quisqueya replaced by Span-
ish-mestizo Hispaniola, then at least in part by French-African Haiti,
aboriginal traits persisting in the new communities. Through contact,
the Iroquois and Algonkians reconstructed identities in New Netherland and Acadia from contact with the Dutch and French empires.
Ironically, the French and Dutch found themselves and their New
World homelands displaced by the English – Acadia by Nova Scotia,
New Netherland by New York – as colonies built upon colonies. Unfortunately, these changes were usually forced, as images of confederation or federation found little place in the designs of transatlantic
empire.[54]

[53] Meinig, vol.1, 160–72; see also Banks, 218.
[54] For persistence of the Totonac in their homeland to the present, see Pablo
Valderrama Ruoy, "The Totonac," in *Native Peoples of the Gulf Coast of Mexico*,
Native Peoples of the Americas (Tucson: Univ. of Arizona Press, 2005), 188; cf.
Patrick J. Carroll, *Blacks in Colonial Veracruz: Race, Ethnicity, and Regional Development* (Austin: Univ. of Texas Press, 1991), 4–6, 108–9, 168; for one peri-
odization of modern colonialism, see Osterhammel, 27–38.

CHAPTER FOUR

ENVISIONING NATIONS

INCORPORATION OR INDEPENDENCE, 1700–1820

During the colonial era native peoples around the North Atlantic naturally saw and responded to the redesigning of their homelands by European empires. These responses varied from withdrawal and accommodation, to assimilation and resistance, all of which depended much on the opportunities afforded by the imperial powers themselves. Among the most important opportunities was the conflict among the European empires, a competition for dominance that often allowed native peoples to play one against another in defense of their homelands. In North America great wars and revolutions in the late eighteenth and early nineteenth centuries significantly altered the balance of power among the European empires and their colonies, permitting the formation of new independent states, but these were not controlled by indigenous peoples. Instead, Iroquoia, Quisqueya, Tlaxcala, and other native homelands were incorporated into new countries – the United States, Haiti, and Mexico, which envisioned themselves as new nations, but acted as old empires. In Europe the repercussions of imperial competition contributed to the transformation of confederated dynastic states into unitary national states based on the ethnic majorities, or nations, of the imperial cores. Replacing a monarchy with a republic did not automatically improve the lot of subordinate ethnic groups; indeed, this process would end the autonomy of the Bretons and the Basques in France. For a republic could be placed in the service of nation building, as ethnic majorities, "the people," asserted their sovereignty over "their land" in their own image, rather than in the king's. Nor did such changes end imperialism overseas, as colonialism

continued in Africa, illustrated by Sierra Leone. Despite this, the need
to join together disparate communities and regions eventually led new
states to consider the long-recognized geopolitical designs of confederation and federation.[1]

IROQUOIA, OTHER, AND NEWER HOMELANDS

Hostile toward the French since the early seventeenth century, the
Iroquois Confederacy – the Hodenosaunee, the People of the Longhouse – subsequently found it necessary to maintain their independence by maneuvering between the former and other European
powers. As we have seen, after the English dislodged the Dutch, the
Iroquois, given a fur trade geared to Albany and New York City,
naturally chose the English for business partners and military allies.
Repulsed by the French and their allies, the Iroquois signed a treaty of
neutrality with them in 1701. Their strength recovered by 1742, Canasatego, speaking for the confederacy, informed the British: "We assure you, the Governor of Canada pays our Nations great Court at this
Time ... he was uncovering the Hatchet, and sharpening it, and
hoped, if he should be obliged to lift it up against the English, our
Nations would remain neuter [sic], and assist neither Side. – But ... we
shall always be faithful and true to you our old and good Allies."
Hardly reciprocating in kind, the British claimed the lands of Iroquois
tributary tribes in the Ohio Valley to which Canasatego replied: "You
came out of the Ground in a Country that lies beyond the Seas, there
you must have a just Claim, but here ... the Lands ... belong to us."
Since the French effectively controlled the Ohio, he finally conceded
the territory to Britain. Thus, recurrent struggles between the European empires in the eighteenth century caught the Iroquois in the
middle, creating divisions among the nations of their confederacy
and its tributaries. The voluntary nature of the union gave it enough

---

[1] See Robert J. Rosenbaum, *Mexicano Resistance in the Southwest*, with a new
    foreword by John R. Chávez (Austin: Univ. of Texas Press, 1981; reprint,
    Dallas, Tex.: Southern Methodist Univ. Press, 1998), 14–15; Richard White,
    *The Middle Ground: Indians, Empires, and Republics in the Great Lakes Region,
    1650–1815*, Cambridge Studies in North American Indian History (New York:
    Cambridge Univ. Press, 1991), x; and Eugen Weber, *Peasants into Frenchmen:
    The Modernization of Rural France, 1870–1914* (Stanford, Calif.: Stanford Univ.
    Press, 1976), 72.

flexibility to remain independent, but not enough power to maintain an empire of its own for long.[2]

The Iroquois Confederacy nevertheless persisted throughout the colonial era and influenced the political vision of the British colonists. In 1744 at a meeting with officials from the disunited colonies, Canasatego argued that they should imitate his people's confederacy: "We heartily recommend Union and a good Agreement between you. ... Our wise Forefathers established Union and Amity between the Five Nations; this has given us great Weight and Authority with our neighbouring Nations." As idealized by Canasatego, the Iroquois Confederacy, in over a century of wars and plagues, had been strong when it maintained unity, adopted neighbors, and successfully resisted Europeans. However, the confederacy had been weak when acting as distinct nations, which its voluntary nature allowed. With another war threatening, a delegation of Iroquois met again with representatives of the British colonies at the Albany Conference of 1754 in an attempt to deal with issues of common concern. The Iroquois sought to resolve problems over white encroachment on Indian land, while the colonists sought military cooperation against the French. The Iroquois delegates, however, abandoned the meeting after land speculators in the background bribed minor Indian leaders to sign over vast tracks, which they had no authority to do. At this point the Iroquois refused to renew any military alliance with the British. Achieving unity within each racial group, let alone between them, appeared improbable.[3]

While the Iroquois had not succeeded in controlling their minor chiefs, the confederated nations had seemingly developed a common policy vis-à-vis the European powers for impending war. The British colonies, on the other hand, had neither controlled their land

---

[2] Francis Jennings et al., *The History and Culture of Iroquois Diplomacy: An Interdisciplinary Guide to the Treaties of the Six Nations and Their League* (Syracuse, N.Y.: Syracuse Univ. Press, 1985), 37, 39–41, 46–7; "The Treaty Held with the Indians of the Six Nations at Philadelphia in July, 1742," in Cadwallader Colden, *The History of the Five Indian Nations of Canada, Which Are Dependent on the Province of New York, and Are a Barrier between the English and the French in that Part of the World*, vol. 2, ed. Colden (New York: Allerton Book Co., 1922), 73; and "A Treaty Held at the Town of Lancaster, in Pennsylvania ... in June, 1744," in Colden, 138.

[3] Quoted in Samuel B. Payne, "The Iroquois League, the Articles of Confederation, and the Constitution," *William and Mary Quarterly*, 53(July 1996): 609; Jennings et al., *Iroquois Diplomacy*, 52.

speculators, nor established common policies with regard to Indian affairs, settlement, defense, or commerce. Indeed, in 1750 Pennsylvania's representative, Benjamin Franklin, had commented "It would be a very strange Thing, if six Nations of ignorant savages should be capable of forming a Scheme for such a Union ... and yet that a like Union should be impracticable for ten or a Dozen English Colonies." At Albany Franklin advanced a Plan of Union that was adopted by the conference, but subsequently vetoed by the colonial assemblies. While confederations, such as the United Provinces of the Netherlands, as well as the Swiss Confederacy, were geopolitical designs readily recognized by Anglo-Americans, independent development of a similar form among Native Americans inspired, if not shamed, the colonists into considering and ultimately implementing the design themselves.[4]

Paradoxically, for the first three years after the outbreak of the Great War for Empire, the Iroquois failed to maintain a unified policy, as some nations sided with the French and some remained neutral. Meanwhile the British colonists suffered repeated defeats at the hands of their enemies. Though experiencing setbacks along with their Micmac allies in Nova Scotia, the French and their other Indian allies successfully attacked the British in the Ohio Valley, deep into the coastal colonies, and significantly in New York around the Iroquois homeland. The disunity of the colonial militias made it difficult for the regular British army to counter the assaults, reflecting the political reality of colonial governance. Finally in 1759, fearing continued occupation by the French and their western Indian allies, the Iroquois turned against them when England offered to address complaints regarding land fraudulently acquired by colonists. The offer came as a result of a more centralized and aggressive war effort launched by the government in London.[5]

After British forces captured Louisburg in the Micmac homeland at the mouth of the St. Lawrence River, the Iroquois assisted in retaking New York. The French and their Algonkian allies then faced their enemies in the heart of Canada and New France. Pursuing a scorched earth campaign, the British destroyed the homes and farms of French

---

[4] Jennings et al., *Iroquois Diplomacy*, 50–2; Payne, 609, 612; see also Donald A. Grinde, Jr. and Bruce E. Lee, "Sauce for the Goose: Demand and Definitions for 'Proof' Regarding the Iroquois and Democracy," *William and Mary Quarterly*, 53(July 1996): 628.

[5] Francis Jennings, *Empire of Fortune: Crowns, Colonies, and Tribes in the Seven Years War in America* (New York: W. W. Norton & Co., 1988), 190–1, 406–7, 413–15.

colonists before besieging Quebec itself; one officer reported such action in a detached manner: "we marched fifty two Miles, and in that distance, burnt nine hundred and ninety eight good buildings ... and small craft, took fifteen prisoners (six of them women and five of them children), killed five of the enemy." In an epic battle the capital city fell in 1759 followed by Montreal in 1760, marking the end of the French Empire in North America. The Treaty of Paris in 1763 confirmed this event, leaving the Iroquois and surrounding Native Americans to face one European power where there had been two in competition.[6]

In 1758 the Iroquois had accepted the promises of royal officials of clear borders between the lands of the confederacy and the British settlements. (See Map 4.1.) A bit later the Micmacs had recognized "the jurisdiction and Dominion of His Majesty George the Second over the Territories of Nova Scotia or Acadia." In the Proclamation of 1763 the British attempted to extend these policies throughout their newly acquired western frontier in order to maintain peace with their other Indian allies and those who had supported the French. Essentially, the Indians received assurances that the colonists could not purchase land beyond the peaks of the Appalachians without specific permission of the crown. The need for such a policy had become evident, as a general rebellion, launched by Chief Pontiac of the Ottawa and other former French allies, had spread along the Ohio frontier. Except for the Seneca, the Iroquois, as major British supporters in the recent war, remained neutral, reflecting continuing divisions in the confederacy. Though the rebellion ended in a draw, it signaled to the Indians that their former policy of pitting Europeans against each other would be less effective in what England now claimed as British North America. While the Cherokee, Creeks, and Chickasaws in the southeast might still turn to Spain, the Iroquois and other northeastern Indians now had to accommodate a single European power in order to prevent their homelands from being overrun and preserve their independence.[7]

[6] Major George Scott quoted in John Dickinson and Brian Young, *A Short History of Quebec*, 3rd ed. (Montreal: McGill – Queen's Univ. Press, 2003), 47–8; Jennings, *Empire of Fortune*, 368, 419–25.

[7] Quoted in Margaret R. Conrad and James K. Hiller, *Atlantic Canada: A Region in the Making*, The Illustrated History of Canada (Toronto: Oxford Univ. Press, 2001), 88–9; and Jennings, *Empire of Fortune*, 461, 442–6, 451.

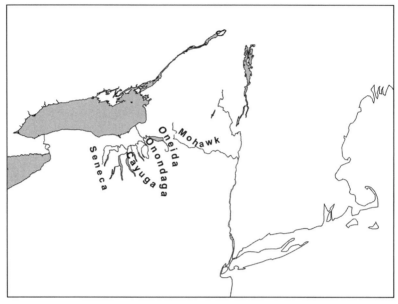

Map 4.1. The Longhouse of the Hodenosaunee, Seventeenth Century. Adapted from Jennings, et al., *The History and Culture of Iroquois Diplomacy*, 8. Cartography by Cassingham and Foxworth, courtesy of the Edwin J. Foscue Map Library, SMU.

OCCUPIED NEW FRANCE

Ironically, the French in North America to some degree now faced the same fate as that of their former Indian "allies" – that of a subject population. The vast colonies of Canada and Louisiana, which over some 150 years had at least in part transformed into the homelands of French Americans, had once again become the colonies of foreigners. This situation was not entirely new as France in 1713 had already ceded Acadia to England after an earlier war. Threatened with expulsion if they did not declare allegiance to their new overlords, the Acadians, and their weakened Micmac neighbors, largely withdrew from the newcomers in hopes of continuing their lives undisturbed. Renaming the region Nova Scotia, England had introduced new Protestant colonists of British, German, Swiss, and even French background, causing about a thousand Acadians to leave for nearby territory still in France's hands. Thus did imperialism lay homelands, one upon the other. Indeed, oppression made itself especially evident during the Great War for Empire when Britain, insisting on oaths of allegiance, ended in expelling about ten thousand peaceful Acadians. Forced to sell their homes and farms, they left for England,

France, the Caribbean, and most interestingly for Louisiana where they established a new "Cajun" ethnic enclave in an already French-speaking region. Unfortunately for these Acadians, Louisiana too experienced a change in imperial master, as France transferred in 1763 its huge territorial claim between the Rocky Mountains and the Mississippi River to Spain, its ally against England. French Louisiana thus became an ethnic region within the Spanish Empire. Such precedents did not bode well for the French of Quebec and the rest of Canada.[8]

Despite being the most populous part of the former French Empire in North America, Canada contained only seventy thousand widely dispersed colonists in 1760, compared with 1.6 million in England's coastal colonies, and was relatively underdeveloped in socioeconomic terms. The economy was based on the fur trade and subsistence farming with very few merchants, entrepreneurs, professionals, or even craftsmen. The departure of most of these with France's military and government officials left Quebec and the rest of former New France with a tiny landed elite and an insignificant middle class. Now dominant, British newcomers contributed to the class and racial divisions of Canada. Daniel Claus, an Indian agent from London, learned about the divisions while investigating a Huron land title. When he sent "two chiefs, Limanet and Athanas, with their interpreter, a French métis" to Lieutenant Governor Hector-Theophilus Cramahé, "the governor tossed the interpreter out the door and then sent for me. He told me he could not stand these half breeds and never let them come among the Hurons." Cramahé, second to British Governor Guy Carleton, clearly had little empathy for lower class, often racially mixed Canadians, as he ranked them even beneath Indians. Such attitudes led to a decline in support for the basic schooling begun under France, and whatever humanistic education remained failed to prepare French Canadians to compete economically with the English, even in the fur trade. Such conditions caused the former to withdraw increasingly into agriculture, the least dynamic sector of their homeland's economy.[9]

[8] D[onald] W[illiam] Meinig, *The Shaping of America: A Geographical Perspective on 500 Years of History*, vol. 1, *Atlantic America, 1492–1800* (New Haven, Conn.: Yale Univ. Press, 1986), 97–8; and Jennings, *Empire of Fortune*, 179–86.

[9] "Excerpts from the Journal of Daniel Claus, from July 26, 1773, to August 10, 1779," in Denis Vaugeois, *The Last French and Indian War: An Inquiry into a Safe-Conduct Issued in 1760 that Acquired the Value of a Treaty in 1990*, trans. Käthe Roth (1995; Montreal: McGill – Queen's Univ. Press, Septentrion, 2002), 234, my translation of quotation; and Edward M. Corbett, *Quebec Confronts Canada* (Baltimore, Md.: Johns Hopkins Univ. Press, 1967), 14–16.

Though London had planned severe restrictions on its new subjects' religious and civil rights, the British ultimately thought it unwise
to incite feelings of resistance among French Canadians, as the coastal
colonies were increasingly expressing dissent against new imperial
policies. In 1774 Parliament passed the Quebec Act centralizing control over the province, including taxation, continuing French civil
law, recognizing the privileges of Catholicism, but providing no
assembly. While this hardly allowed for autonomy, the new regulations were in keeping with former French governance and consequently acceptable to Canadians. Moreover, the borders of Quebec
were recognized as extending to the Ohio River, northwest of the
Indian country set aside in the Proclamation of 1763, consequently
embracing scattered French-speaking enclaves south of the Great
Lakes. Such early accommodation of the Quebecois helped guarantee
their long-term persistence as a distinct ethnic group that would one
day become a nation. Such would not be the case for the French in
the Ohio Valley, who would later assimilate with English-
speaking newcomers.[10]

INCORPORATION OF EUROPEAN HOMELANDS

While homelands and colonies changed imperial hands in North
America, in Western Europe dynastic states incorporated distinct
ethnic regions into larger territories dominated by ethnic majorities
increasingly claiming national preeminence. In 1707 previously under
the same royal house, Scotland "voluntarily" dissolved its parliament
and merged with England in the United Kingdom of Great Britain.
However, in the 1740s Charles Stuart's attempt to retake the British
crown led to the crushing of an insurrection in Scotland, effectively reducing that former Stuart kingdom into a conquered English
province. In 1769 Corsica lost its war for independence to France.
Transferred from Genoa, which Corsicans had resisted for decades,
a patriot asked: "how is it that the French ... would fall upon us to
annihilate a Nation"; Louis XV replied, "for the good of the people,"
without of course asking for their consent. While French and English
apologists deemed these benign, domestic actions, coercion if not
violence always remained an element in nation building. The wishes
of local communities or ethnic groups rarely mattered much as

[10] Ibid.; and Jennings, *Empire of Fortune*, 466–7.

dominant states at the national core made sweeping geopolitical changes.[11]

In the early eighteenth century, following the Bourbon ascendancy to the throne, Spain sought greater national unity. Guided by the ideas of French absolutism, in 1716 Philip V abolished the autonomy of Aragon and Catalonia, regions that had enjoyed their own systems of governance despite the unification of the Spanish monarchy in the fifteenth century. Spain, a declining power, feared further dismemberment as Britain in 1713 had seized Gibraltar on the Iberian Peninsula itself. Centralizing government and economic policy in Madrid, as France had sought in Paris, promised greater efficiency as well as unity. Spain, however, had always been a more diverse place than France or the British Isles and found union difficult to achieve.[12]

Despite increased Bourbon centralization, the Basque Country, on both sides of the Pyrenees, retained a great deal of independence until the late eighteenth century. Labourd, Basse Navarre, and Soule were *pays d'états* that continued local democracy despite the many attempts of the French monarchy to reconfigure them administratively. While the Bourbons had stripped the political rights of Spain's provinces elsewhere in 1706 and 1714, Basque support for the dynasty during the War of Spanish Succession had resulted in the region's continuing autonomy. As a people on the frontier between Spain and France, their loyalty had to be assured; consequently, Basques were required only to defend that frontier without the need to provide military service elsewhere. Madrid freed Vizcaya, Guipuzcoa, Alava, and Navarre from external taxation to stimulate the rapid growth of the region's population and economy. Politically, all four provinces had appointed governors, but the assemblies could legislate for their own region and even veto national laws. In general, Castile had taken over appointive

---

[11] Michael Hechter, *Internal Colonialism: The Celtic Fringe in British National Development, 1536–1966* (Berkeley and Los Angeles: Univ. of California Press, 1975), 71–2; Paoli and Louis XV quoted in Thadd E. Hall, *France and the Eighteenth-Century Corsican Question* (New York: New York Univ. Press, 1971), 189, 191; Benedict Anderson, *Imagined Communities: Reflections on the Origin and Spread of Nationalism*, rev. ed. (New York: Verso, 1991), 19–22.

[12] Ludger Mees, *Nationalism, Violence, and Democracy: The Basque Clash of Identities* (New York: Palgrave Macmillan, 2003), 6; and Peter Sahlins, *Boundaries: The Making of France and Spain in the Pyrenees* (Berkeley and Los Angeles: Univ. of California Press, 1989), 279–80.

military and judicial functions, but lawmaking and political institutions remained autonomous.[13]

This autonomy developed an ethnic region that did not follow the model of subordination so applicable elsewhere. Indeed, the Basque economy would evolve into one of the most prosperous in Spain, at times and in many ways more prosperous than the Madrid area itself. Freedom from outside taxation and Spanish customs duties allowed for the distinct development of the Basque commercial classes. Vizcaya, Guipuzcoa, and Alava until the nineteenth century remained a duty-free zone, importing food and merchandise without taxation. Only when goods moved on to Navarre or Castile were tariffs charged. Coupled with these early tax advantages were valuable natural resources. A position at the crossroads to areas east, west, and south, with natural harbors linked to vital sea lanes to northern Europe, favored trade through the Basque Country. Timber and later iron favored development of domestic manufacturing. Economically, this area did not fit the description of a subordinate region peripheral to a central state. By 1766 an enlightened sense of nationhood and unity began to arise from the prosperity, as illustrated by the founding of the Basque Society of Friends of the Country. Affiliated with other royal economic societies, this group of intellectuals sought to promote "the taste of the Basque nation for the sciences, letters, and arts . . . and to strengthen the union of the three Basque provinces of Alava, Guipuzcoa, and Vizcaya." On the other hand, this limited nationalism made little headway, despite provincial political and economic autonomy, as the Castilian language remained dominant in government.[14]

While Western European states formed more centralized unions in the eighteenth century, older confederated designs persisted not only in the Basque Country, but in Brittany as well. (See Map 4.2.) Despite Bourbon centralization, through most of the century, Brittany retained the autonomous provincial administration allowed since merger of the ducal and royal crowns. Among other rights, no Breton could be forced to serve in

---

[13] Alan Forrest, *The Revolution in Provincial France: Aquitaine, 1789–1799* (Oxford: Clarendon Press, 1996), 9; and Marianne Heiberg, *The Making of the Basque Nation*, Cambridge Studies in Social Anthroplogy, 66 (New York: Cambridge Univ. Press, 1989), 20–3.

[14] Ibid., 29, 24, 35–6, 38–9; "Los Estatutos de la Sociedad de Amigos del País" quoted in Maximiano García Venero, *Historia del nacionalismo vasco*, 3rd ed. (Madrid: Editora Nacional, 1969), 97, my translation; and Stanley G. Payne, *Basque Nationalism*, The Basque Series (Reno: Univ. of Nevada Press, 1975), 22.

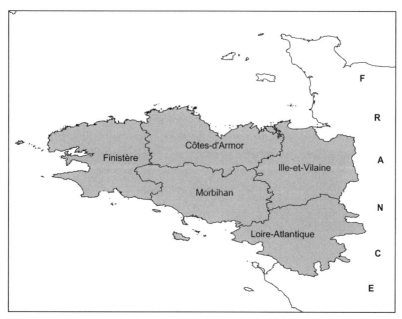

Map 4.2. The Present Departments of Brittany. Adapted from Reece, *The Bretons against France*, xxiv. Cartography by Cassingham and Foxworth, courtesy of the Edwin J. Foscue Map Library, SMU.

the military outside the province, and Paris could impose no changes in the institutions, laws, or significantly the customs of Brittany without approval of its aristocratic parliamentary bodies. Though the province was a dynastic holding, such guarantees helped preserve the region's ethnic autonomy. Nonetheless, such geopolitical designs did not yet reflect ethnic nationalism or centralized nations for that matter.[15]

Steps toward consolidation of dynastic territories did not eliminate ethnic differences. Regions, ethnically distinct from the dynastic or national core, persisted usually subordinate in status, as was the case of Ireland. The Reformation had dramatically intensified the ethnic distinctiveness and rebelliousness of the Irish as the Tudors began a policy of undermining Catholicism, including the planting of English

[15] Jack E. Reece, *The Bretons against France: Ethnic Minority Nationalism in Twentieth-Century Brittany* (Chapel Hill: Univ. of North Carolina Press, 1977), 17; for more on regionalism and Bourbon centralization, see Michel Vovell, *La chute de la monarchie, 1787–1792*, vol. 1 of *Nouvelle histoire de la France contemporaine*, ed. Michel Winock, Collection points, Série histoire (Paris: Editions du Seuil, 1972), 18–19, 38–9.

Protestant colonies in Ireland. Though the later Stuarts modified this trend, Oliver Cromwell, and then William and Mary pushed ahead more aggressively. In the eighteenth century this kingdom qua colony remained under the English crown governed by Anglo-Irish, upper-class Protestants. In 1731 aristocratic Mary Delaney described a state ball she attended in Dublin Castle, the seat of the viceroy's government: "I never saw more company in one place: abundance of finery, and indeed many very pretty women. . . . Vast profusion of meat and drink, which you may be sure has *gained the hearts* of all guzzlers!" Members of the subordinate Catholic majority, at 75 percent, were hardly welcome at such affairs since they could not vote, hold office, purchase land, marry Protestants, or participate in much of the rest of public life. There were, nevertheless, exceptions to these oppressive measures, as the continued existence of a small Gaelic gentry and Catholic seminaries attested. Despite their dominance, the Anglo-Irish complained of the island's poverty and their parliament's subordination to that of England. While monarchies had drawn varied regions and peoples together, the domi-nant nation as a state of mind shared by individuals with a common heritage only gradually gained importance.[16]

The development of European national states was often threatening for marginal ethnic homelands, such as Ireland. As the nationalism of a dominant people, such as the English, evolved, it usually became imperialism. The sense of confidence in a common French heritage, for example, engendered ethnocentric notions that served to the det-riment of weaker neighbors. In the face of the resulting expansion, outlying regions and peoples could react with ethnic solidarity or even full-blown nationalism, as in the Corsican case. On the other hand, the Basque Country through most of the eighteenth century illustrated that the legitimacy of the core state could be sustained by allowing regional autonomy in a confederated geopolitical structure. Overseas Great Britain would face the ultimate challenge to its imperial structure.[17]

---

[16] Nicholas Canny, "Early Modern Ireland, c. 1500–1700," in *The Oxford Illus-trated History of Ireland*, ed. R[obert] F[itzroy] Foster (New York: Oxford Univ. Press, 1989), 114–15, see also chronology on 358–62; quotation in Foster, "As-cendancy and Union," in Foster, 176 (caption to following fourth color plate), 163–7; and Meinig, vol. 1, 375–7.

[17] Ibid., 374; Hechter, 65, 73, 60; for an insightful discussion of the role of con-federation in the expansion and retention of empire, see David Armitage, *The Ideological Origins of the British Empire*, Ideas in Context (Cambridge: Cambridge Univ. Press, 2000), 129, 137–8, 156.

HOMELANDS AND ANGLO COLONIALISM

The American War for Independence was not an ethnic rebellion against an imperial power. Already independent, the Iroquois and Cherokees did not revolt against the British Empire, instead, most Indians allied themselves with it. The rebels were Anglo-Americans. While it could be argued that the colonists were developing a distinct culture, they were basically English; indeed they initially demanded their rights as Englishmen. According to geographer D. W. Meinig, Anglos occupied a domain, a territorial variant, rather than an ethnically peripheral region of the English cultural core. For this reason the American Revolution was a civil war between people generally more akin to each other, than even the Welsh and English. The attempts of the "thirteen" colonies to add the Caribbean colonies, Nova Scotia, Quebec, or even Ireland to their number against England, failed, not simply because of physical, but because of social geography. The large black majorities in the Caribbean left English colonists there fearful of losing their dominant positions. The Quebecois and Acadians of Canada saw little advantage to an alliance with their former enemies and continuing cultural adversaries, who were moreover too ethnically Anglo for the Irish. Indeed, the rebellion against England became a civil war of Anglo-American rebels against loyalists within the colonies themselves. Significantly, after the war thousands of the latter fled the new states to become English Canadians, a new ethnic group and ultimately a different nation. The rebellion then was not essentially of Cherokees or other Native Americans, indigenous by right of first arrival or precedence. In fact, the majority of the rebels were descendants of settlers, agents of colonialism, now claiming native status, through the process of migration, home-building, and naturalization we have seen over the millennia in the North Atlantic World.[18]

Among the Cherokees, the Anglo-American rebellion against the Empire meant a major assault on their homeland. In 1775, challenging London's right to negotiate treaties, the colonial Transylvania Company purchased much of present Kentucky and middle Tennessee from

[18] Meinig, vol.1, 378–9, 321, 399, 332; Edward Countryman, *The American Revolution*, rev. ed. (New York: Hill and Wang, 2003), 141–6, 154–5, 173; despite their internal cultural similarities, Anglo-Americans also had their own regional cleavages resulting from those in Britain; see for example David Hackett Fischer, *America, a Cultural History*, vol. 1, *Albion's Seed: Four British Folkways in America* (New York: Oxford Univ. Press, 1989), 605–8.

a faction of Cherokees. Outraged, Dragging Canoe, a rising leader, warned, "You have bought a fair land, but you will find its settlement dark and bloody." Once the colonies had moved to open rebellion, he allied himself with the Shawnees, other northern tribes, and the British to recover the lands lost. However, his actions did not win the support of Nancy Ward, the Beloved Woman, who feared the impending violence. Defeated in his initial attack, he moved north while the Peace Party conceded more land in a treaty with Virginia, Georgia, and South Carolina. Dragging Canoe fought with the British until they surrendered in 1781 and then sought a broad Indian confederation to continue resistance. Ward understandably persisted, "We are your mothers. You are our sons. Our cry is all for peace."[19]

In 1783 the Cherokees and other Native Americans faced thirteen loosely united but aggressive states along the Atlantic Coast. Though the United States was not officially founded on a specific ethnic heritage, in practice Anglo-American culture predominated, a culture first established and developed in the regions of Virginia and New England. While white settlers of other ethnicities resided throughout the new union – the Dutch in New York, the Scotch-Irish in the backcountry, Scots Highlanders in the Carolinas, Swiss and Germans in Pennsylvania – nowhere did these groups form a state based on that ethnicity, though they comprised significant founding groups in particular regions and urban enclaves. Beyond the Appalachians, English was a little-known language among the French, metis, Spanish, and mestizo remnants of earlier colonies claimed by the states. African American regions and enclaves existed throughout the confederation as well, but especially in the Carolinas where, besides English, blacks spoke Gullah and Creole French. The English, by virtue of being the largest ethnic group and having had the imperial support of their homeland, established their institutions, language, and general way of life as the norm in the original thirteen states. From its inception the Anglo-American union envisaged eliminating, removing, or assimilating competing communities in the process of its national development. Needless to say, Native American homelands, from the Shawnees' north of the Ohio River to the Cherokees' south of it, stood in the way of expanding Anglo regions that had already eroded Iroquoia and

[19] Quoted in Robert J. Conley, *The Cherokee Nation: A History* (Albuquerque: Univ. of New Mexico Press, 2005), 58–9, 65, 68–9.

its confederacy – broken, immersed, and pushed aside by the American Revolution.[20]

During the revolution, the states had formed their own confederacy under the Articles of Confederation. Following the old suggestions of Benjamin Franklin, and thus the designs of the Iroquois, the newly sovereign states had formed a loose union to prosecute the war against England and its attempts to centralize the empire. The Articles allowed the independence of each state, politically and economically, a situation that worked well enough while confronting a common enemy, but made collective action difficult after the war. Such decentralization allowed a white opportunist John Sevier to set up a "state," ironically named Franklin, on Cherokee land within boundaries claimed by the United States and North Carolina, without the authorization of their governments. In 1785 the Hopewell Treaty, the first between the United States and the Cherokees, permitted them to dislodge such intruders, but when they attempted that, the Franklinites resisted successfully. North Carolina ultimately suppressed Franklin, but the United States intervened only to the extent of keeping the land the bogus state had claimed. Despite its general weakness, the confederation could thus be effective in colonizing Indian homelands between the Appalachians and the Mississippi.[21]

Indeed, the most important acts passed by Congress under the Articles were the Land Ordinance of 1785 and the Northwest Ordinance of 1787, essentially blueprints for imperial expansion qua nation building. These acts were designs for the colonization of Indian lands, and their ultimate incorporation into the confederation. Though attempting to avoid the image of empire, the plans furthered imperialism as they legalized the extinguishing of Indian claims. Providing for the surveying of western lands into townships and sections, the Land Ordinance ultimately subdivided the landscape into squares for sale as a commodity to land companies, speculators, and then colonists. The Northwest Ordinance allowed for a territory of sufficient white population to form a government for ultimate admission into the confederacy and representation in Congress. The idea was to avoid restive colonies, similar to the original thirteen unrepresented in Parliament

---

[20] Meinig, vol. 1, 402, 160, 180, 426, 189, 209, 350.
[21] Bruce E. Johanson, "Native American Societies and the Evolution of Democracy in America, 1600–1800," *Ethnohistory*, 37(Summer 1990): 284–5; and Conley, 74–5.

and thus unequal members of the British Empire. Nonetheless, following the imperial model, this system rested on the colonization of Indian
territories and the formation of new states by the dominant, Anglo-
American population.[22]

Under the Constitution of 1787, Congress extended the territorial
ordinances passed under the Articles to western Cherokee lands. In
1790 Congress set up the Southwest Territory for later subdivision into
what are now Tennessee, Alabama, and Mississippi. With a powerful
executive, the central government had moved beyond a weak confederacy to a stronger federation, better capable of dealing with foreign and
Indian affairs. Empowered to raise sufficient revenues to support a military, the central government could now extend its law to all regions of
the country. While the states retained much of their autonomy within
their boundaries, the federal government expected to exercise more
effective control in the frontier territories. Under the new constitution
Secretary of War Henry Knox felt strong enough to condemn the violations of the Hopewell Treaty with the Cherokees: "If so direct and
manifest contempt of the authority of the United States be suffered with
impunity, it will be in vain to attempt to extend the arm of government
to the frontiers." With guarantees from this more powerful government,
in 1791 the Cherokees, including Dragging Canoe, agreed to the Treaty
of Holston, which nevertheless involved more land cessions.[23]

Thus, admission of Tennessee, Alabama, and Mississippi to the
Union followed the old confederation's territorial ordinances, peacefully or otherwise. The trans-Appalachian regions were settled through
the extinguishing of Indian possession, usually through coercion or
open warfare. Still concerned for the legitimacy of federal law, Henry
Knox in 1793 noted, "Captain John Beard, who had been called into
service by Governor Blount [of the Southwest Territory] with a view of
protecting the settlers, did ... in defiance of ... orders ... kill a number
of our best friends among the Indians." Reacting to this attack on his
home, Hanging Maw, the new Cherokee leader, wrote to President
George Washington: "We thought very well of your talk of restoring
peace, and our land being made safe to us; but the white people have
spoiled the talk at best." Through such intimidation from local residents

[22] Meinig, vol. 1, 342, 409.
[23] Ibid., 343–4; Knox quoted in Conley, 75–6; and Vicki Rozema, *Cherokee Voices:
      Early Accounts of Cherokee Life in the East* (Winston-Salem, N.C.: John F. Blair,
      2002), 86.

and authorities, the ordinance's requirement to extinguish land claims was carried out. In 1796 Tennessee became a state with Franklinite John Sevier as governor. With such foes coming to power, the remnants of the Cherokee homeland seemed likely to disappear before the expanding white states.[24]

To preserve their homeland, over the next three decades the Cherokees transformed their traditional state into a more centralized government, as had the United States. Acculturated merchants and planters pushed for more centralization, but the clan system, including its female leadership, provided the cohesion to bring the nation together in this endeavor. For example, in 1800 the clans, recognizing that local conflicts with whites led to land losses, transferred law enforcement to the National Council, comprised of village chiefs. Pressed to surrender the homeland entirely and remove to the West, the council in 1809 established the standing National Committee to handle relations with whites more effectively; still, the council remained close to the people: "The chiefs never conclude any very important business before they find the popular sentiments of their people." Despite the changes and their support for the United States in the War of 1812, the Cherokees lost more land due to pressures on a few local chiefs. Subsequently, the women's council, elected by the clans and holding the right to address the National Council on matters of war and peace, surrendered that right in a move to create a government recognizable to whites. More changes followed, such as switching the basis for National Council representation from the village to the district. This process culminated in 1827 with a formal constitution comparable to those of the surrounding Anglo-American states. However, the Cherokees were not only asserting state, but national, sovereignty.[25]

Native American peoples had often been treated as sovereign nations during the colonial era, but the United States strove to deny that status, attempting to reduce them to protectorates, as it had the Cherokees with the Treaty of Hopewell. Although some discussion of admitting American Indian states had occurred under the Articles of

---

[24] Knox quoted in Rozema, 87; "Letter from Hanging Maw to President George Washington, 15 June 1793," in Rozema, 94; and Conley, 83.

[25] Return Jonathan Meigs, U.S. Indian agent, quoted in Duane Champaign, *Social Order and Political Change: Constitutional Governments among the Cherokee, the Choctaw, the Chickasaw, and the Creek* (Stanford, Calif.: Stanford Univ. Press, 1992), 106, 93, 96, 100, 130–1, 135–8.

Confederation, the Constitution of 1787 never sanctioned ethnic states in the Union. Instead, a system of subordinate reservations would gradually develop, as the federal government exiled eastern tribes across the Mississippi in Indian Territory, far from their homelands. A reservation had the advantage of being temporary refuge from white intrusion, but it would never be a self-governing equal of the regular states. To gain that status would require an altering of the constitutional provision that made a citizen of one state a citizen of all, allowing for free movement and equal property rights in all states. Since this provision would have placed an Indian state at the mercy of white intruders, Native Americans did not seek statehood. Thus, the United States federal system privileged Anglo-American culture, supporting its expansion westward along a broad front, from the first regions colonized along the Atlantic.[26]

As we have noted, however, culture had earlier spread northward, when English loyalists moved into what is now Canada. In 1783 alone thirty-two thousand moved into Nova Scotia, followed by many more, including four thousand freed anglicized blacks, who expanded the earlier British settlements and established new ones – to the further disadvantage of the remaining Acadians and Micmacs. Most importantly, in the upper St. Lawrence, the loyalists founded a new ethnic region, eventually to become the core of English Canada, now known as Ontario. Curiously, this region would surround the Grand River Iroquois Reserve, established for loyalist remnants of the once great confederacy. North of Lakes Erie and Ontario and south of the Ottawa River, new towns formed, including present Toronto, which ultimately separated the region culturally from Lower Canada or Quebec. The Constitutional Act of 1791 made this cultural division political as London responded positively to loyalists' demands for their own separate colony. Thus, the political influence of the French-speaking was confined to a smaller part of North America. Moreover, in the new legislative and executive councils of Lower Canada, the French were kept a minority relative to elite English appointees, although the former controlled the less powerful assembly. Indeed, the loyalists secured Canada for themselves and the British Empire, by further

---

[26] Any thought of an African American state received little attention since that group was not simply subordinate, but enslaved, specifically in those regions where blacks had sufficient numbers to form states; Meinig, vol. 1, 358, 369–70; U.S. Constitution, art. 4, sec. 2.1, and art. 1, sec. 3.

subordinating the French and Indian communities in a new geopolitical arrangement.[27]

FREE HAITI IMAGINED

Revolutionary forces were rearranging the geopolitical landscape throughout the Atlantic World in the late eighteenth century: "At that time, men's hopes turned to France, whose first steps toward her regeneration promised them a happier future." In the French colony of St. Domingue, white planters in 1787 gained assemblies with an advisory role to the royal officials sent out from Paris, but this little satisfied the former. In a colony seriously divided by class and race, France controlled the islanders by manipulating their divisions. Occasionally supporting the royal officials were middle-class whites – shopkeepers and craftsmen – who clashed with the wealthy planters. The "free people of colour," who in some cases had become wealthy themselves, resented whites in general because social equality, even in such matters as dress and public celebrations, was denied. At the bottom of society, the black slaves naturally sought freedom and had rebelled repeatedly. Sharing many French cultural traits, the people of this compact colony also shared the class divisions of the metropolis, a situation that would bring both communities to revolution.[28]

When the Estates General met in Paris in 1789, the planters of St. Domingue sent representatives, against the orders of the royal governor, to demand the right to make their own laws. Denied this request, the representatives joined in undermining the French royal government through establishment of the new National Assembly. This active participation effectively meant that the Haitian and French Revolutions began simultaneously, as in 1790 the National Assembly granted autonomy to France's West Indian colonies, including St. Domingue. Limiting representation to white planters, however, the new French government could not initially bring itself to overthrow the racial order in the colonies, despite petitions to do so. Supported by abolitionists in

---

[27] Meinig, vol. 1, 325–6, 331–2; and Corbett, 16.

[28] "Letter to the Minister of Marine, 13 April 1799," in *Toussaint L'Ouverture, Great Lives Observed*, ed. George F. Tyson (Englewood Cliffs, N.J.: Prentice Hall, 1973), 30; J. H. Parry, P. M. Sherlock, and A. P. Maingot, *A Short History of the West Indies*, Macmillan Caribbean, 4th ed. (London: Macmillan, 1987), 138, 134–5.

France and England, and gun suppliers in the United States, coloreds in St. Domingue rebelled, leading to the arming of the slaves of both whites and coloreds, a situation clearly advantageous for the slaves. In 1791 a slave rebellion ensued that the white and colored planters were too disunited to suppress. Calling on France to crush the slave rebellion, the planters failed to cooperate with the French Army on its arrival; consequently, its commander, who actually embraced the rev-olutionary ideal of equality, emancipated the slaves and gained their support. In Paris the French Republic then declared, "negro slavery in all the colonies is abolished; in consequence, it decrees that all men, without distinction of color, who are domiciled in the colonies are French citizens and shall enjoy all the rights guaranteed by the constitution."[29]

Alarmed by the revolutionary challenges to monarchy and empire in both France and St. Domingue, Great Britain in 1794 invaded the French West Indies, to the delight of white planters who had lost their slaves. Coloreds, however, feared British discrimination against them and unexpectedly joined the ex-slaves and the French army. Despite initial British victories, a Maroon revolt in Jamaica limited their forces in St. Domingue. Meanwhile, François Dominique Toussaint L'Ouver-ture, a former slave of many talents, rose through the ranks and gained command of the French and black armies. Suspecting that French support was waning, he ordered their forces off the island, proceeded to expel the British by 1798, and conquered Spanish Santo Domingo in 1801: "seeking the means to throw off the shameful yoke of slavery that debased us. Did there not also want the addition to this glory, seeing the former Spanish part reunited to the French part ... ? This reunion has taken place. The island of St. Domingo is therefore under the same Government, it is entirely subject to the laws of the French Republic." At that point "St. Domingo" (Hispaniola) was effectively independent and united, though Toussaint kept it a nominal dominion of France because he respected that nation's revolutionary principles, but also feared further invasion. He nonetheless envisioned a state where the former slaves would determine their own fate: "What remains to be

[29] Ibid., 138, 140–1; Lester D. Langley, *The Americas in the Age of Revolution, 1750–1850* (New Haven, Conn.: Yale Univ. Press, 1996), 108–10; and "Decree upon Slavery," in *The Constitutions and Other Select Documents Illustrative of the History of France, 1789–1907*, ed. Frank Maloy Anderson, 2nd rev. ed. (Minneapolis, Minn.: H. W. Wilson Co, 1908), 204.

effected by you? The consolidation of liberty and the maintenance of order ... abundance and prosperity." While many if not most of the ex-slaves were actually natives of Africa, they within a very short time realized that their freedom depended on control of the place they were making a homeland.[30]

REGIONAL IDENTITY AND THE FRENCH REVOLUTION

Curiously, in 1789–1790 while St. Domingue gained autonomy from the new revolutionary government in Paris, Brittany and the Basque Country lost theirs. The new regime reorganized the regional political divisions of France: "the provinces which have had up to the present a common administration ... are divided among several departments." Thus, the National Assembly replaced the traditional domains of various noble houses, with geographical units more accountable to the people and the central government. As the revolution broadened French nationalism, the National Assembly sought to break down trade barriers, and equalize laws, taxes, and military service across class and regional lines within France. Brittany's delegation in Paris supported the move because the middle-class representatives sought to undermine the nobility that had controlled the Breton provincial government for centuries. The delegates clearly placed class and national interests against their ethnic regional interests, as the formerly unified province split into five departments. In the Basque Country, by contrast, the Garat brothers, to no avail, spoke against merging their areas with an adjacent French region, "They will end up splitting apart like the Tower of Babel." Divided between France and Spain already, Labourd, Soule, and Basse Navarre, under various names, continued to evolve separately in the new geopolitical arrangement without the local freedom each had enjoyed from Paris.[31]

With the French Revolution the sovereignty of the people over the monarchy gained currency. The king, who once personified the state, and the aristocracy lost position to the dominant ethnic community of

---

[30]   Parry, Sherlock, and Maingot, 142–3; Paul Fregosi, *Dreams of Empire: Napoleon and the First World War, 1792–1815* (London: Hutchinson, 1989), 86–9, 104–5; and "Address to the Military, 1801," in Tyson, 57.

[31]   "Decrees for Reorganizing the Local Government System," in Anderson, *Constitutions*, 33; Reece, 16–19; Philippe Veyrin, *Les Basques de Labourd, de Soule et de Basse Navarre: Leur histoire et leurs traditions*, new ed. (n.p.: Arthaud, 1955), 180; quoted in Forrest, 81.

France, the nation as exemplified at its core in Paris. Abolishing the nobility and its regional bases, the revolutionaries hoped to form one people, united under egalitarian principles, as well as a common culture. The culmination of this process was the beheading of the king and the establishment of a republic in 1793. Needless to say, local communities and ethnic regions lost ground in this process. As the nation-state became more centralized, opposition was demonized: "Federalism and superstition speak Breton; emigration and the hatred of the Republic speak German; counter-revolution speaks Italian; and fanaticism speaks Basque." As early as 1790 counterrevolutionaries had resisted the central government in Brittany and other provinces, but their goal was primarily to reestablish aristocratic privilege, rather than ethnic or regional autonomy. The loyalties of Breton individuals and other provincials seemed increasingly tied to class, or France as a whole, rather than to region.[32]

Significantly, as French nationalism consolidated, it acquired an imperial dimension. Threatened by monarchical neighbors, France had declared war on them in 1792 with a newly acquired sense of mission. The war went badly at first as Austria and Prussia invaded France; however, imbued with a deepened patriotism, everyday citizens formed volunteer armies that resisted the invaders. This popular resistance strengthened the advocates of the common people who established the republic, as well as those who undermined its idealism. During the radicals' infamous Reign of Terror, they imprisoned and executed thousands on mere suspicion of counterrevolutionary activity. Suspected of collaboration with émigrés in Spain, some Basque villages were destroyed and their inhabitants forcibly removed from the frontier to the interior. After the radicals were overthrown for their excesses in 1794, five years of reaction and instability prepared the way, first for dictatorship. Then monarchy returned, supposedly by the will of the people, rather than by divine right; the Constitution of the Year XII declared, "The government of the French Republic is entrusted to an emperor, who takes the title EMPEROR OF THE FRENCH."[33]

[32] François Furet, *The French Revolution, 1770–1814*, trans. Antonia Nevill, History of France (Malden, Mass.: Blackwell Publishers, 1996), 3–4, 7, 9, 121–2; Bertrand Barère quoted in Forrest, 234; and Reece, 18–20.

[33] Furet, 102–3, 107–9, 111, 135, 150–1; Forrest, 234–5; "Constitution of the Year XII" in Anderson, *Constitutions*, 342; *for more on perceptions of linguistic disunity, see Graham Robb, The Discovery of France: A Historical Geography from the Revolution to the First World War* (New York: W. W. Norton, 2007), 50–5.

The French masses accepted the rule of Napoleon Bonaparte because as a commoner he had been one of them and earned his position through his successful defense of the republic. Though a Corsican by birth, he had transcended his homeland and become the embodiment of French nationalism. He first seized power, naming himself First Consul in 1799, then declared himself emperor in 1804. This curious sequence of events illustrated the link between nationalism and imperialism. For example, during his dictatorship, further modifications in geopolitical administration of France occurred, most important of which was the assigning of a prefect, representing the First Consul, to each department, a change that cemented his rule in the former provinces. This resulted in a far more unitary state. A nation with a recently established representative form of government thus evolved into an empire, intent on spreading its ideals throughout Europe. Ironically, Napoleon and the French imagined they could unify the continent – under the progressive principles of liberty, fraternity, and equality – through imperialism, that is to say, conquest of other homelands.[34]

TRANSATLANTIC DESIGNS

Napoleon did not limit his imperial designs to Europe. Indeed, before he even claimed the throne, he sought to restore the French Empire in America. In 1800 he coerced Spain into returning Louisiana to France, and prepared to reassert French authority in St. Domingue, where Toussaint had established de facto independence, a constitution, and unfortunately his own dictatorship. When Napoleon's troops met effective resistance and bogged down in St. Domingue, he decided to cut back on his grandiose scheme, selling Louisiana to the United States since he could not defend the vast territory from the threatening British. Though the French succeeded in capturing Toussaint through trickery, the ex-slaves and coloreds continued resistance when they learned of a new Napoleonic act: "In the colonies restored to France ... slavery shall be maintained in conformity with the laws and regulations in force prior to 1789." Napoleon's plan to restore slavery, to make the colonial plantations once again lucrative, demonstrated the reactionary turn that the erstwhile republic had taken. Subsequently, the French lost the island to the insurgents, and St. Domingue declared itself

---

[34] Furet, 217, 251–2; and Joseph Barthélemy, *The Government of France*, trans. J. Bayard Morris (New York: Brentano's Publishers, [1924]), 132–3.

independent in 1804, imitating and perhaps mocking Napoleon by crowning its own Emperor Jean-Jacques I (Dessalines). Interestingly, recalling the native people's reverence for the landscape, the new nation-state was renamed "Haiti," Arawakan for a highland area of Hispaniola. As in the case of the United States, however, the second independent state in the Americas was not a creation of Quisqueya's native people. Haiti's population was overwhelmingly of African descent, but these people had secured a homeland in the place where they had been brought as slaves. A Franco-African ethnic region in the Americas had become a nation.[35]

While Napoleon's transatlantic scheme would fail, his empire building had wide ramifications. In 1801 Great Britain, hoping to avoid revolutionary upheavals in the British Isles, suppressed the Irish parliament, moved its members to Westminster, and formed the United Kingdom of Great Britain and Ireland. This centralization reflected trends on the continent, where Napoleon was rearranging the political geography. In 1808 the Emperor proclaimed his "well-beloved brother Joseph Napoleon, at present King of Naples and Sicily . . . King of Spain and the Indies." This act led to the Spanish War of Independence, which Basques interpreted as a defense of their regional rights under the lawful king, despite French attempts to co-opt them with a local constitution. On the other hand, other Spaniards ironically imbued with the French ideals of popular sovereignty and nationalism, formed a democratic parliament, the Cortes, to resist Napoleon and govern Spain and the colonies as a transatlantic federation. Temporarily at least, many Spaniards looked beyond region and recognized a larger nation. Curiously, the trend toward unity in Spain had the opposite effect in the Indies, its imperial possessions across the Atlantic.[36]

---

[35] Fregosi, 218, 203, 222, 213, 238; "Law for Re-establishing Slavery in the French Colonies," in Anderson, *Constitutions*, 339; Patrick Bellegarde-Smith, *Haiti: The Breached Citadel*, Westview Profiles: Nations of Contemporary Latin America (Boulder, Colo.: Westview Press, 1990), 44; and Carl Ortwin Sauer, *The Early Spanish Main*, with a new foreword by Anthony Pagden, Centennial Book (1966; reprint ed., Berkeley and Los Angeles: Univ. of California Press, 1992), 45.

[36] Hechter, 72–3; Furet, 237; "Documents upon the Overthrow of the Spanish Monarchy," in Anderson, *Constitutions*, 421; Mark Kurlansky, *The Basque History of the World* (New York: Walker & Co., 1999), 141–3; Payne, 36–7; and Peggy K. Liss, *Atlantic Empires: The Network of Trade and Revolution, 1713–1826*, Johns Hopkins Studies in Atlantic History and Culture (Baltimore, Md.: Johns Hopkins Univ. Press, 1983), 193.

With a usurper on the throne of Spain and French armies in its cities, its colonies naturally questioned their loyalties. Though the peninsulares and criollos of New Spain, especially Mexico City, hesitated to disobey Madrid, criollos, mestizos, and Indians in the provinces, from Tlaxcala to Texas and elsewhere, turned to their local cabildos, or town councils, to manage their affairs autonomously during the crisis. In 1808 the municipal council of Tlaxcala protested Napoleon's invasion of Spain and the following year elected a delegate to the Cortes. More radically, in 1810 west of Mexico City, Miguel Hidalgo y Costilla called together his Indian and mestizo parishioners and issued a call for independence, the *Grito de Dolores*: "Will you free yourselves? Will you recover the lands stolen three hundred years ago from your forefathers by the hated Spaniards? ... Long live Our Lady of Guadalupe!" The rhetorical appeal was clearly to the native heritage of the mixed Mexican people. Though led by a descendent of the Spanish, Mexico's War for Independence began as an indigenous uprising against the colonizing power, unlike the rebellions that led to the creation of the United States and Haiti. However, finding independence too radical, Tlaxcala's municipal council denounced the rebels.[37]

Failing to take Mexico City at an opportune moment, Hidalgo lost the support of his army, which gradually dissipated. Hoping to revive the movement in the north, he was instead captured by the Texas governor in Coahuila, sent to Chihuahua, and executed. In 1813 a follower of Hidalgo, José Bernardo Gutiérrez de Lara, nonetheless succeeded in reviving the movement with Anglo-American support, marched southwest from Louisiana, captured San Antonio, and issued his own declaration of independence: "We the people of the Province of Texas ... seize the moment which now offers itself, of shaking off the yoke of European domination, and of laboring in the cause of Mexican independence." Despite such efforts, independence did not come about until a change of government in Spain threatened conservatives in Mexico. When Spanish patriots forced King Ferdinand, restored after the defeat of Napoleon, to accept a liberal constitution based on the sovereignty of the people, conservative criollos decided they could better protect their class and racial privileges in an independent

---

[37] Ibid., 195–6; Ricardo Rendón Garcini, *Breve historia de Tlaxcala*, Serie breves historias de los estados de la república mexicana (Mexico City: Fondo de Cultura Económica, 1996), 165; and Michael C. Meyer and William L. Sherman, *The Course of Mexican History*, 5th ed. (New York: Oxford Univ. Press, 1995), 278–88.

Mexico. Though originally envisioned as an indigenous nation, the new state was in fact much more narrowly defined, as control rested on the white elite, native to the country, but with colonial attitudes. Indeed, the first head of state, Agustín de Iturbide, declared himself emperor. Though a constitutional monarch, he clearly had Napoleon and imperialism as his models for building a new nation, as did Haiti.[38]

IMPERIALISM RENEWED IN COLONIAL SIERRA LEONE

While colonialism was receding in the Americas, it renewed itself in Africa. As we have seen, the Temne people had had contact with Europeans since the arrival of the Portuguese in the fifteenth century. According to the elder Alhaji Kali Kamara, "The white men came here . . . . They found hunters here . . . and were welcomed by them." Nevertheless, full colonization of Sierra Leone did not commence until the late eighteenth century. Ironically, this colonial project resulted from the American War for Independence, an anticolonial process. Another ironic aspect of Sierra Leone's colonization was that it proceeded from the antislavery movement in Britain. In 1786 after the war, abolitionists in England founded the Society for Effecting the Abolition of the Slave Trade and a Committee for the Relief of the Black Poor, both of which became involved in the colonizing of Sierra Leone. Though abolitionism was profoundly anticolonial in its attack on the fundamental institution of the colonial labor system, the movement fostered further expropriation of the land and freedom of West African peoples.[39]

The white American colonists stimulated abolitionism because they demanded liberty for themselves, even as they continued the institution of slavery for blacks. Aware of this contradiction, the British military offered blacks their freedom if they enlisted in the loyalist cause. Though some American rebels made the same offer, particularly in

---

[38] Ibid., 294–7; and "The Declaration of Independence, April 6, 1813," in *Documents of Texas History*, eds. Ernest Wallace, David M. Vigness, and George B. Ward, Fred H. and Ella Mae Moore Texas History Reprint Series (1963; reprint, Austin: Texas State Historical Association, 2002), 39–40.

[39] "Selections from the Testimony of Alhaji Kali Kamara, an Elder of Maforki Chiefdom (Recorded at Port Loko, 21–22 September 1965)," in Kenneth C. Wylie, *The Political Kingdoms of the Temne: Temne Government in Sierra Leone, 1825–1910* (New York: Africana Publishing Co., 1977), 220; Parry, Sherlock, and Maingot, 153; and Joe A. D. Alie, *A New History of Sierra Leone* (New York: St. Martin's Press, 1990), 49.

the northern colonies, many blacks understandably joined the British side. With the final American victory in 1783, many freed blacks left for Nova Scotia and England itself. In England particularly, blacks found themselves unemployed and ineligible for poor relief, and consequently led miserable lives. Their visibility in the very streets of London encouraged English abolitionism, but also the desire to find some place other than Britain for these unfortunates to live.[40]

The Committee for the Relief of the Black Poor, which provided direct assistance to the freed slaves, took up a plan to colonize them in Sierra Leone. The idea for an agricultural settlement, including whites, appealed to many blacks, and they volunteered for the project. Called the "Province of Freedom," the colony would serve not only to settle the former slaves, but also to spread Christianity and European civilization to native Africans, the standard colonial mission. The colony's constitution was based on English law and traditions. The settlers would elect their own governor and the governing council that would make laws. Among the provisions for the judiciary was that juries would comprise at least half the members of the same ethnicity as the accused. The British government, happy to rid itself of impoverished blacks, agreed to fund the new settlement.[41]

In 1787 an expedition of four hundred blacks of both sexes and sixty mostly "abandoned" white women arrived in Sierra Leone; these "Original Settlers" disembarked on May 15. In exchange for rum, beads, tobacco, and iron bars, British naval officers eventually "cajoled" King Nembana of the Temne to forfeit a coastal section about ten miles long and twenty miles deep. As in the case of early Virginia and other colonies, the settlers suffered from ill health and death as they attempted to put up buildings and plant crops. As starvation loomed, the colonists had to negotiate with the native Temne for food. The elected government naturally had great difficulty dealing with these problems. The arrival of new settlers temporarily saved the colony, but in 1790 the Temne burned it to the ground in retaliation for a similar act on the part of a nearby European sea captain.[42]

---

[40] Ibid., 48–9; and Meinig, vol. 1, 331.

[41] Alie, 50–1; see also Leo Spitzer, *The Creoles of Sierra Leone: Responses to Colonialism, 1870–1945* (Madison: Univ. of Wisconsin Press, 1974), 9–10.

[42] Alie, 51–4; Robert W. July, *A History of the African People* (New York: Charles Scribner's Sons, 1970), 270; and Kevin Shillington, *History of Africa*, rev. 2nd ed. (New York: Palgrave Macmillan, 2005), 237–8.

Undaunted, the British abolitionists organized the Sierra Leone Company to reestablish the colony. Failing to gain further appropriations from the British government, they called on investors who would be interested in the commercial as well as the moral potential of the settlement. As a joint-stock company, the directors appointed a governor and seven councilmen to manage the colony, thereby denying the self-government initially established. Although only about fifty of the initial settlers joined the revived colony, they would eventually react negatively to the new nonrepresentative government. Clearly, the economic core of colonialism made itself evident in the top-down corporate structure of this enterprise, a structure commonly used in the founding of British colonies in North America.[43]

Just the same, since slavery was illegal in Sierra Leone, freed blacks continued to seek their fortunes in the colony. As we have seen, many black loyalists had also moved to Nova Scotia, where the British had promised land. Most, however, had not received it and continued to work for whites. Consequently, the British government encouraged the Sierra Leone Company to "repatriate" these blacks to Africa. Among the Nova Scotians deciding to emigrate, however, were over a hundred who already owned land, indicating that a desire for greater independence also motivated these people to go to Africa. Unfortunately, the Nova Scotians assumed they would govern themselves as had been the case under the original Sierra Leone constitution. In 1792 about 1200 black loyalists from Nova Scotia arrived in Sierra Leone, where they founded Freetown, eventually the capital of the colony. Ironically, blacks who had fought against American independence came to find freedom in Africa.[44]

Because of the diverse elements in the colony, a certain amount of social conflict inevitably developed. Thomas Peters, leader of the black Nova Scotians, derived his power from the religious congregations through which his people derived their community life. He came into conflict with Governor John Clarkson, who headed the white officials representing the company. Clarkson had promised, though not completely delivered, twenty acres for each man, ten for his spouse, and five for any child. He also organized the settlers into tithings and hundreds, which provided local democracy despite the company's attempts to retain

[43] The Massachusetts Bay Company was an important exception to top-down governance because its entire operations were moved to the colony and evolved into a broadly representative government; July, 270.

[44] Ibid., 270–1; and Alie, 54–7.

all control. The Nova Scotians nevertheless preferred that one of their own run the colony, since they were the majority. Clarkson successfully retained his position despite the opposition, only to be removed by the company for giving away land, free of charge, to the colonists.[45]

The land issue would haunt the colonists and officials for years to come. In 1796 Governor Zachary Macaulay received authority to impose quit-rents to rebuild Freetown after the French had bombarded it. Arguing that they had been promised their land free of charge, the Nova Scotians in particular resisted, despite being offered the full amount of land originally promised though with quit-rents attached. Rather than accept the company's authority, many Nova Scotians abandoned farming altogether. Moreover, the local governments, comprised of tithingmen and hundredors, were deprived of their powers under a new charter in 1799 that centralized authority in the company. This act caused the Nova Scotians to rebel, a rebellion suppressed only with the arrival of the Royal African Corps and new settlers, Maroons from Jamaica. This was another irony in the history of Sierra Leone – the use of these escaped slaves to quash a rebellion.[46]

Despite the internal turmoil of the colony, its fundamentally imperialist purpose revealed itself in its relations with the native Temne. The Temne had originally conceived of their land cession to the colony as a lease not a sale. When they refused to give up their claim forever, hostilities broke out in 1801. Despite assistance from a Nova Scotian leader, the Temne eventually lost the war and signed a forced peace treaty in 1807, in which they conceded the sale of the land claimed by the colony after the destruction of many of their villages. Despite this defeat, the Temne continued to occupy the rest of their chiefdoms throughout the colonial period, though not without further violence, as one of their histories lamented: "the Masimerah country has been a scene of bloodshed ever since this settlement was colonized in 1787."[47]

Curiously, the British abolished the slave trade throughout the empire in 1807, but ended any hope of self-government for mostly black Sierra Leone the next year. The company's continued financial problems and Britain's need for another naval base converted the territory

[45] Ibid., 57–8; and Spitzer, 10.
[46] Alie, 60–1; July, 271; for a full discussion of subsequent interactions between these varied colonizing groups, see Spitzer.
[47] Alie, 61–2; Wylie, 7; and abstract from "History of Masimerah Country," comp. W.T.G. Lawson (Freetown, 1878), in Wylie, 233.

into a Crown Colony ruled directly from London. When the British
Navy captured slave ships, the released prisoners, called Recaptives or
Liberated Africans, were often brought to Freetown, which consequently grew from two thousand to forty thousand in about two decades.
The colonial government sent Recaptives to found villages on the outer
edges of the colony, while unattached children became apprentices and
servants to earlier residents. Though stigmatized as savages on their
arrival, the Recaptives received land, schools, and churches from the
government who perceived them as a counter weight to the rebellious
early settlers and interior natives. Once again, Sierra Leone provided
ironies on ironies, as freed captives were used to suppress earlier rebels
and free natives in the interior. Though all were black, the colonial
relationship of dominance and subordination continued to operate
along ethnic if not racial lines.[48]

LIMITED VISIONS

The appearance of many new states in North America and Europe between 1776 and 1821 fulfilled the dreams of many patriots, but the new
nations did not end imperialism on either side of the Atlantic. The
French Republic evolved into Napoleon's empire, independent Temne-
land became the colony of Sierra Leone, and the new multiethnic states
of North America imitated their former masters in a process of nation
building quite similar to colonialism. During this period many men and
women moved from the status of slaves and subjects, to free persons and
citizens, as their homelands moved from colonies to independent
nations. But for others the process of subordination began or continued,
as their ethnic regions disappeared in the designs of stronger neighbors or
completely foreign powers. Despite this, peoples, such as the Iroquois and
Anglo-Americans, continued to imagine and experiment with confederations and federations that joined communities and allegiances harmo-
niously. The success of such experiments was limited, given more popular
visions of empire.[49]

[48] Alie, 65–8; and Philip D. Curtin, *The Atlantic Slave Trade: A Census* (Madison:
Univ. of Wisconsin Press, 1969), 231, 245, 249–50, 253.
[49] Langley, 285–7; after independence national development proceeded with the
continued subordination of peoples, such as the Mayas in peripheral regions of
Mexico and Guatemala – Rodolfo Stavenhagen, "Classes, Colonialism, and
Acculturation," *Studies in Comparative International Development*, 1 (no. 6,
1965): 71–2, 74–6.

CHAPTER FIVE

CONCEIVING FEDERATIONS

NATIONAL DEVELOPMENT, 1820–1880

The foundation of so many new states in the Atlantic World involved continual experimentation with various geopolitical forms throughout the nineteenth century. The early revolutions that rearranged that entire global region stimulated searches for alternatives to empire, but usually only altered its form rather than its substance. As we have seen, revolutions in Haiti, France, and Mexico shook up or broke away from imperial cores only to produce emperors in imitation of the monarchs they had initially challenged. Though the emperors did not last long, the imperial process persisted even where republicanism and federalism seemed clearly to triumph. As we have also seen, in the United States a federal system was implemented to avoid the problems of both imperialism and regionalism. The new system had nevertheless continued colonial patterns of migration into Indian homelands in the trans-Appalachian West. Moreover, in Canada and Sierra Leone, the British Empire renewed its expansion, albeit under more representative and abolitionist principles. Despite the persistence of imperial patterns, centrifugal forces over the century continued to challenge core states. Peoples of marginal ethnic regions increasingly insisted on the recognition of the geopolitical rights of their homelands. Both old and new states sought to deal with these restive sections of their national or imperial territories. The results were a series of struggles between centralists and federalists, unionists and confederates, not to mention the continuing tensions between colonizers and colonized.

Unfortunately, even dreams of federation took forms that led to violent realities.[1]

LIBERIA: AN AMERICAN AFRICAN STATE

The independence of the United States marked a gradual, but significant change in the imperial process, from formal to informal colonialism. Ostensibly, founded on anticolonial principles, the United States nevertheless had expansionist plans from its inception. To the satisfaction of whites, the Northwest and Land ordinances that removed native Indians also excluded blacks from new states entering the Union from the region of the Great Lakes. Though the legislation did not permit slavery in the new states, neither did it permit the immigration of free blacks. Indeed, where to put free blacks in the new Anglo-American nation was a concern, especially for abolitionists. In the late eighteenth century they decided to solve the "problem" by removing blacks from America entirely, by "returning" them to Africa. Thus was Liberia first imagined, as a state for free blacks on the Atlantic Coast of that continent.[2]

Although dreams of "repatriating" blacks became popular after U.S. independence, not until 1816 did a practical organization for that purpose appear – the American Colonization Society. The name had historical significance since the basic plan involved settling freed American blacks on African soil, following the patterns set by white colonists when they settled in America. Another similarity unfortunately would be the settlement of these American colonists on lands that belonged to the black individuals and peoples indigenous to that specific stretch of African coast. Historically, according to Stephen Hlophe, "shifting centres of power resulted in the political and economic ascendancy of different groups; beginning with the coastal De and Vai in the fifteenth and sixteenth centuries, the Temne and the Mande in the seventeenth century, the Mandingo Confederacy of

---

[1]   D[onald] W[illiam] Meinig, *The Shaping of America: A Geographical Perspective on 500 Years of History*, vol. 2, *Continental America, 1800–1867* (New Haven, Conn.: Yale Univ. Press, 1993), 489–90; and Andrés Reséndez, *Changing National Identities at the Frontier: Texas and New Mexico, 1800–1850* (Cambridge: Cambridge Univ. Press, 2005), 2–3, 264.

[2]   Library of Congress, *The Federalist Papers*, no. 14, available from Thomas.loc. gov/home/histdox/fed_14.html, accessed 1 July 2008; and Kevin Shillington, *History of Africa*, rev. 2nd ed. (New York: Palgrave Macmillan, 2005), 238–9.

Condo at Bopolu in the nineteenth century." Speaking many languages, these ethnic groups had formed many political structures from towns, to kingdoms, and federations interspersed among each other as they migrated and vied for control of trade and homelands. Into this complex of ethnic enclaves, the Colonization Society would introduce African American settlers with imperial ambitions. The success of the British colony of freed blacks in Sierra Leone (1786–1794) offered an example that one Dr. William Thornton had suggested to James Madison as early as 1788. In 1811 a black American merchant, Paul Cuffe, apparently transported some fellow freedmen to Sierra Leone. But not until after the War of 1812 did the American Society for the Colonizing of Free People of Color (its official name) appear.[3]

The list of founders of the American Colonization Society included such prominent names as Henry Clay, Daniel Webster, John Randolph, and Richard and Henry Lee. The society argued freed blacks had to be removed because they threatened white racial purity, caused social turmoil, competed with white labor, and increased to unacceptable numbers; overseas they might Christianize Africans and better their own lives. Although established as a private effort, U.S. President James Monroe provided the Society with $100,000 in federal funds under the Anti-Slave Trade Act of 1807 since illegally trafficked slaves could be freed and settled in the proposed colony. Although the founders were all white, some black churches initially joined the cause, though others felt it was simply a plot to rid the United States of blacks, a view even reflected by the society's first president, Bushrod Washington.[4]

In 1821 the Society sent agents to Africa to negotiate with the natives for the purchase of land for a colony, a process clearly analogous to the attempts to acquire Indian lands in North America. The agents, Ephraim Bacon and Joseph R. Andros, attempted to purchase land from King Jack Ben of the Bassa people, as well as other leaders along the Pepper Coast (later Liberia), but without success. Given the slave trade,

[3]   Stephen Hlophe, "The Significance of Barth and Geertz' Model of Ethnicity in the Analysis of Nationalism in Liberia," *La Revue canadienne des Études africaines/Canadian Journal of African Studies*, 7 (no. 2, 1973): 247; and G[eorge] E[utychianus] Saigbe Boley, *Liberia: The Rise and Fall of the First Republic* (New York: St. Martin's Press, 1983), 10–11, 13.

[4]   Ibid., 6–7, 12–13; and Tom W. Shick, *Behold the Promised Land: A History of Afro-American Settler Society in Nineteenth-Century Liberia*, Johns Hopkins Studies in Atlantic History and Culture (Baltimore, Md.: Johns Hopkins Univ. Press, 1980), 6.

West Africans, by this time, had learned to distrust white negotiators; moreover, the sale of tribal land for the settlement of outsiders threatened the very existence of the indigenous people. After this failure, the U.S. government instructed its navy to negotiate for the society, apparently at gunpoint. Again, despite the fact the settlers would be black, colonialism would advance through force, in the age-old imperial pattern.[5]

Captain Robert F. Stockton and Eli Ayers, a surgeon in the navy, arrived at Cape Mesurado (later Monrovia) and attempted to buy a stretch of land 130 miles long and 40 deep. Although the accounts of what happened vary, including the name of the native chief and the amount of land, apparently the negotiations went poorly as the naval officers failed to convince the locals that the colonists would be benefactors, rather than enemies. Supposedly, the Americans then threatened to shoot Zolu Duma (King Peter to the colonists), because of his confederacy's resistance. In any case, the local people apparently agreed to the sale under duress since they later attempted to get out of the deal with colonists already in transit at Sierra Leone. The exact amount of land and the sales price were never clear even to the first director, Jehudi J. Ashmun, of the new colony called Liberia in 1824.[6]

The first settlement at Cape Mesurado eventually developed into Monrovia, Liberia's capital city named after U.S. President James Monroe. Several other groups joined the American Colonization Society in establishing "plantations," agricultural settlements in Liberia. Interestingly, many of these organizations, including the first, originated in Southern states because in those areas there existed the greatest fear that freed blacks would encourage slaves to rebel. Despite this, the political rhetoric of the U.S. South appeared in the documents of these organizations. For example, the Colonization Society of the State of Virginia, with state funds, sought to establish a New Virginia in Africa: "'a free, sovereign and independent state' . . . but bearing such relation to Liberia . . . as our State does to the United

---

[5] Santosh C. Saha, *Culture in Liberia: An Afrocentric View of the Cultural Interaction between the Indigenous Liberians and the Americo-Liberians*, African Studies, vol. 46 (Lewiston, N.Y.: Edwin Mellen Press, 1998), vi–vii; and Boley, 13–14.

[6] Ibid., 13–17; for descriptions of the "confederacies" of Zolu Duma and Sao Boso (Condo), apparently developed through imperial conquest, see Amos Sawyer, *The Emergence of Autocracy in Liberia: Tragedy and Challenge*, Publication of the Center for Self – Governance (San Francisco: CS Press, Institute for Contemporary Studies, 1992), 66–7, 77–9.

States." Apparently, this society believed free blacks could function autonomously within a confederation under the Southern principles of states' rights.[7]

As other societies, from states such as Maryland and Mississippi, established plantations, they impinged on native peoples and lands. By 1827 somewhat fewer than twenty thousand blacks from America settled in Liberia, a tiny figure compared with the millions remaining in the United States, but they were enough to significantly impact the surrounding peoples. About 30 percent of the settlers, however, were Africans, taken by the U.S. Navy from slavers illegally operating in U.S. waters. These "recaptured" slaves had never acculturated to Anglo-American society and were consequently regarded as inferior by the freed black American settlers. These recaptured Africans, on the other hand, mingled well with the native population, often intermarrying with the locals. However, a class system developed from inception, with the Americanized at the top, the recaptured Africans in between, and the natives at the bottom.[8]

Land was acquired from the indigenous people, through negotiation or warfare as was the case in America. The land thus acquired, the societies apportioned it among the settlers as had the joint stock companies in the colonial era of the United States. A colonist settling in Monrovia, for example, received a lot for a townhouse and five acres outside for farming. As settlers moved out of Monrovia, they received fifty acres under the condition that they build a house and farm two acres within a set period. Recaptured Africans, on the other hand, received no such benefits. They lived in segregated, closely supervised quarters, where they were Christianized and made to work in the fields as indentured servants. In 1826 and 1837, respectively, New Georgia and Marshall were established as exclusive settlements for the recaptured slaves who had completed their terms of service.[9]

---

[7] Boley, 17–18; for the demographic impact of colonization, see Antonio McDaniel, *Swing Low, Sweet Chariot: The Mortality Cost of Colonizing Liberia in the Nineteenth Century*, Population and Development (Chicago: Univ. of Chicago Press, 1995), 74, 136–8.

[8] Boley, 22–3; and Philip D. Curtin, *The Atlantic Slave Trade: A Census* (Madison: Univ. of Wisconsin Press, 1969), 249–50.

[9] Boley, 23–4; though the indigenous peoples did not hold private property, and they often shifted location, "Land was the bond linking the ancestors with the present and future"; the founding ancestors were called "the masters of the land," thus defining the people and legitimizing their leaders – Sawyer, 55–6.

Clearly, the black American settlers had learned the principles of imperialism from the colonization societies. One disapproving missionary noted that these settlers had come to behave toward Africans as whites did toward blacks in the United States: "A colonist of any dye (and many there are of darker hue than the Vey, or Dey, or Kree, or Basso), would if at all respectable, think himself degraded by marrying a native. The natives are in fact menials, (I mean those in town)." In the case of Liberia, the line between the colonizer and the colonized was ethnic rather than racial, but it nevertheless established a relationship of dominance and subordination. The role of gender in this relationship echoed in the words of a Gola chief from Liberia's interior: "the Americans have bad men as constables; they come out here, take our women, sleep with them . . . and when we attempt to put a stop to it, then they go . . . trying to set up war." The Americo-Liberians benefited from this relationship, but so did the larger colonizing society of the United States. As the metropolis, the United States, specifically its white elite, gained by ridding itself of an undesirable population, as Britain had sent her convicts to early Virginia. One difference was that the colonization societies regarded themselves as philanthropic organizations, rather than as for-profit joint stock companies. Moreover, the U.S. government never took political possession of Liberia, though the latter remained a protectorate of the former in dealings with other powers. Liberia thus remained an informal or neo-colony of the United States.[10]

In 1837 various settlements established by the colonization societies formally united into the Commonwealth of Liberia with a federal constitution modeled on that of the United States. A few years later the American Colonization Society relinquished its remaining authority over the Commonwealth, and in 1847, Liberia became the first independent black republic in Africa. Though recognized by Britain in 1848, other countries only gradually acknowledged Liberia's sovereignty. Indeed, the United States waited until 1862 after the South had seceded from the Union. Unfortunately, for Liberia, 95 percent of the population remained colonized natives subject to constant Americo-Liberian attacks on their lands and lives. The colonies first established on the coastal lands of the Vai, Dei, Bassa, Kru, and Grebo were organized as Americo-Liberian counties with the hinterland remaining in native hands. After numerous wars of conquest, the

[10] Boley, 25–6; "Dwallah Zeppie to President Hilary Richard Wright Johnson, August 1, 1887," in Shick, 91.

Liberian government would in the twentieth century organize a central-ized "chieftancy" in the interior, followed by provinces for later admis-sion into the federation as counties. This was a territorial system analogous to those of the United States and Canada as they expanded into their frontiers. Internal colonialism persisted in independent Liberia, but unlike the Indians of North America, the natives were too numerous to exclude from control of the entire federation forever.[11]

JAMAICA: FROM AUTONOMOUS TO CROWN COLONY

When Britain's North American colonies rebelled and secured their independence, its Caribbean outposts stayed loyal, a phenomenon hav-ing much to do with their racial composition. While British colonies such as Jamaica had autonomy similar to that of their North American neighbors, the ratio of the white to black population differed dramat-ically. In Jamaica fewer than 10 percent in 1775 were white. When the North Americans broke into open rebellion, the Jamaican assembly, which had supported the northern colonies earlier, recanted. With such a small white population, the planters could not hope to prevent slave uprisings without the British military. While the principle of represen-tative government was established in Jamaica, only the wealthy, land-holding, white elite could vote or hold seats in the assembly. Edward Long, a contemporary historian defending the rights of the Jamaican slaveholders against the Crown, nevertheless justified government as "an association of the opulent and the good for better preserving their acquisitions against the poor and the wicked." As London left local affairs to the assembly, and as the assembly would not tax the elite for the general public good, the colony remained undeveloped in terms of schools, roads, hospitals, and other public works. The riches of sugar remained in the hands of the planters, a situation that autonomy perpetuated.[12]

However, white hegemony in Jamaica was far from complete. As we have seen, from the departure of the Spanish, Maroons had run their

[11] Boley, 27–9; see D. Elwood Dunn and Svend E. Holsoe, *Historical Dictionary of Liberia*, African Historical Dictionaries, no. 38 (Metuchen, N.J.: Scarcrow Press, 1985), xiv–xv, xxii–xxiii, 50, 90.

[12] J. H. Parry, P. M. Sherlock, and A. P. Maingot, *A Short History of the West Indies*, Macmillan Caribbean, 4th ed. (London: Macmillan, 1987), 115–16; Curtin, 159–60; and Edward Long quoted in Denis M. Benn, *The Caribbean: An In-tellectual History, 1774–2003* (Kingston, Jam.: Ian Randle Publishers, 2004), 18.

own "illegal," independent communities on the island, augmented by constantly escaping slaves and periodic slave rebellions. Repeated conflict forced the English to formalize an autonomous preserve where the Maroons might officially make their own laws and elect their own leaders. In return the Maroons agreed to stop accepting more runaways, stop raiding plantations, and help put down slave rebellions. In 1795 war broke out again when the British governor feared a relatively minor disagreement would lead to another sovereign state like Haiti, a revolution another contemporary described as "written in colours too lasting to be obliterated." Although the British won some victories, shipping about five hundred surrendered Maroons first to Nova Scotia, then Sierra Leone, autonomous communities of free blacks continued to exist well after the end of slavery. Indeed, as late as 1831, after abolition of the slave trade, one unsuccessful slave rebellion sought to establish an independent, black state in Jamaica, once again asserting the right to a sovereign ethnic homeland.[13]

While the nineteenth century saw major independence movements sweep Latin America, the Caribbean in some ways experienced a loss of autonomy, which ironically had the result of promoting equality. In 1833 Britain officially ended slavery in the empire, though a period of apprenticeship (six to eight years) was required before full freedom would be allowed. The end of slavery would be the beginning of individual liberty for blacks, though their ability to function as sovereign groups had already been established by the Maroons in Jamaica. With the end of slavery, the plantation system and sugar production fell off, causing many whites to emigrate. Despite emancipation, the Colonial Office did not believe blacks could "have political power, or communicate it through any exercise of the right of a constituency." Since race, property, and social class dictated the size of the electorate, as well as the right to serve in the assembly, in 1864, only 1,457 voters chose an assembly governing 450,000 citizens. Because the white population had dropped precipitously, coloreds came to form two-thirds of the legislature by the 1860s. Naturally, whites objected to this, and unfortunately the majority of blacks benefited little since coloreds did not identify with

[13] Bonham C. Richardson, *The Caribbean in the Wider World, 1492–1992: A Regional Geography*, Geography of the World Economy (New York: Cambridge Univ. Press, 1992), 164–5; Bryan Edwards quoted in Benn, 21; and Parry, Sherlock, and Maingot, 70, 129.

them. Since the assembly represented the rich, Jamaica lacked public services, a decent transportation network, and education. Thus, Jamaica's geopolitical autonomy was undemocratic, promoting inequality, and economic underdevelopment.[14]

Recognizing these problems, London sought to turn Jamaica and its other Caribbean possessions into Crown colonies, essentially ruled by an appointed governor with an advisory council. Curiously, this outcome resulted from black militancy, rather than the simple wishes of Britain. Blacks constantly complained that the local administrators denied them the opportunity to own land, leading to what the Colonial Office described as "barbarous squatting in wild situations." Although much abandoned plantation land lay vacant, the planter government had refused to open it to black, small farmers. Even when blacks purchased land outright, local officials delayed the transfers of title. Baptist missionaries complained to London about such conditions, which deteriorated further with the rise in food prices caused by the U.S. Civil War.[15]

Instead of acting to ameliorate the situation, London relied on Jamaica's current governor, who was in league with the elite, to carry out an even more oppressive policy. Droughts and wage cuts for farm labor caused small landholders to occupy land illegally, which led to arrests for trespassing and theft. In 1865 this situation caused spontaneous rioting, which Governor John Eyre used as an excuse for violent suppression, including the execution of six hundred people. Threatening further resistance, one anonymous group bitterly complained, "the governor sent to shot every man and woman, old and young, and to burn down every house. . . without law, not to seek for the rebels alone and the rioters." Fearing further black outbreaks, the Jamaican assembly voted to disband, replacing itself with a council of twelve elected and twelve appointed members. Needless to say, coloreds were excluded, shifting power completely back into the hands of the wealthy white elite. An added benefit was transfer of Jamaica's debt to Britain. In 1866 Britain eliminated elections and elected councilmen altogether, converting Jamaica into a Crown colony. According to historian, Denis M. Benn, "Crown Colony government made no pretence of being democratic. On the contrary, the doctrine of imperial trusteeship positively affirmed the need for a benevolent autocracy." Jamaica had completely

---

[14] Ibid., 161, 186–9; Henry Taylor quoted in Benn, 34; and Richardson, 164.
[15] Carnarvon quoted in Benn, 40; and Parry, Sherlock, and Maingot, 189–90.

lost its autonomy, after independence had advanced elsewhere in the
Americas.[16]

Though centralized and undemocratic, between 1866 and 1874 the
new government did more for Jamaica and its people than the earlier
assembly had. (This situation was somewhat analogous to the Reconstruction governments imposed on the U.S. South, though a Crown
colony was not at all representative.) Removing the previous governor
for his mismanagement, Britain appointed Sir John Peter Grant. He
removed many of the local officials who had abused blacks, by restruc-
turing local government. He replaced abusive local militias with a new,
fairer police force. He improved the infrastructure both in rural and
urban areas. Moreover, he increased spending on public health and
provided the poor with jobs on many new public works. Thus, the
population of Jamaica, a predominantly black homeland within the
British Empire, received better treatment from the Crown than from
the previously autonomous local government.[17]

SOVEREIGN SOUTHERN STATES

Autonomy also had a negative impact on the minority black population
of the vast and growing southern section of the United States. Though
not a single ethnic region, the section's plantation economy gave its
many and increasing states much in common vis-à-vis the North; indeed, a territorial variant of Anglo-American culture, founded on the
values of the white landed elite, had evolved, a variant based on the
subordination of blacks. While the northern states had abolished slavery following the American Revolution, Delaware, Maryland, Virginia,
the Carolinas, and Georgia had retained the institution and would
spread it westward, eventually as far as Texas. To preserve slavery in
the face of northern criticism, Southerners increasingly interpreted the
Constitution of 1787 in terms of confederation, rather than federation.
Advancing the doctrine of states' rights, the South argued that each
of its states was sovereign, rather than simply autonomous. They
denied the supremacy of the national government, threatening in
effect to return the country to the Articles of Confederation. By the

[16] Ibid.; group quoted in Mimi Sheller, *Democracy after Slavery: Black Politics and Peasant Radicalism in Haiti and Jamaica*, Warwick Univ. Caribbean Studies (London: Macmillan Education, 2000), 223; and Benn, 44.
[17] Ibid., 45; and Parry, Sherlock, and Maingot, 189–90.

mid-nineteenth century, the Southern states used the autonomy they enjoyed to threaten independence for the preservation of a way of life based on domestic colonialism. Though Africans as a people were no more indigenous to the South than to the Caribbean Islands, they had made the section a collection of homelands, just as whites had. In the colonial process, however, whites had forced blacks to migrate with them and colonize new homelands together. Ultimately, from Virginia to Texas, whites would argue Africans "were rightfully held and regarded as an inferior and dependent race, and in that condition only could their existence in this country be rendered beneficial and tolerable." As in Jamaica, geopolitical autonomy licensed the white elite to maintain its dominance, though in a process of Southern internal colonialism.[18]

CHEROKEE HOMELAND LOST

Another form of internal colonialism in the South was the removal of the section's native peoples, with the acquiescence of the federal government, specifically the presidency. By 1819 the vast Cherokee homeland had been reduced to a reservation overlapping edges of Georgia, North Carolina, Alabama, and Tennessee. (See Map 5.1.) There, hoping to avoid further losses, the Cherokees consciously adopted many white customs, including Christianity, Anglo-American dress, English, and ironically black slavery. Traditionally an agricultural people, they focused more than ever on farming, further accommodating white notions of civilization. Consequently, Elias Boudinot, a Cherokee newspaper editor, mocked the hypocrisy of removal proponents who, denying this acculturation, argued: "it is impossible to enlighten the Indians, surrounded as they are by the white population, and that they assuredly will become extinct, unless they are removed." Refuting such arguments, the Cherokees, as we have seen, established a government with a constitution modeled on that of the United States. However, such an ethnic state asserting sovereignty threatened the surrounding white governments. When

[18] Meinig, vol. 2, 475–6; and "A Declaration of the Causes which Impel the State of Texas to Secede from the Federal Union," in *Documents of Texas History*, ed. Ernest Wallace, David M. Vigness, and George B. Ward, Fred H. and Ella Mae Moore Texas History Reprint Series (1963; reprint, Austin: Texas State Historical Association, 2002), 196.

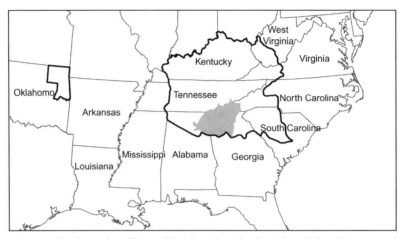

Map 5.1. Traditional and Later Cherokee Homelands. Adapted from Duncan and Riggs, *Cherokee Heritage Trails Guidebook*, 14–15. Cartography by Cassingham and Foxworth, Courtesy of the Edwin J. Foscue Map Library, SMU.

white miners encroached on the reservation with the discovery of gold, President Andrew Jackson supported Georgia's claim to sovereignty over the Cherokee homeland.[19]

Reflecting their own cultural sophistication, as well as their accommodation to white ways, the Cherokees took the matter to court in the 1830s. In two cases, Worchester vs. Georgia and the Cherokee Nation vs. Georgia, they argued that, as a sovereign nation, they were not subject to the laws of either the national or state governments. They asserted not merely autonomy within, but independence from, the United States; they asserted that relations between the nations rested on negotiated treaties. The Supreme Court denied Cherokee independence, but recognized that a special relationship existed between Indian peoples and the federal government. Indeed, in the decision in the first case, Chief Justice John Marshall labeled the Cherokees, a "domestic dependent nation," in other words, an autonomous ethnic people and region, an "internal colony." Despite the loss of their full claim to sovereignty, the Cherokees

[19] Duane H. King, "The Origin of the Eastern Cherokee as a Social and Political Entity," in *The Cherokee Indian Nation: A Troubled History*, ed. King (Knoxville: Univ. of Tennessee Press, 1979), 164; and "Cherokee Editor Elias Boudinot Opposes Removal, 1828," in *Major Problems in American Indian History: Documents and Essays*, ed. Albert L. Hurtado and Peter Iverson, Major Problems in American History Series, 2nd ed. (Boston: Hougton Mifflin Co., 2001), 204.

used the court's definition to win the second case, arguing for United States rather than Georgian jurisdiction over the reservation.[20]

In spite of the legal victory, President Jackson's refusal to enforce the decision meant that the Cherokees had to emigrate to Indian Territory west of the Mississippi River. Since the presidency of Thomas Jefferson, national Indian policy had followed the British colonial model of establishing a western reserve for Indians, beyond the frontier of white settlement, along the lines of the Proclamation of 1763. Jackson's innovation was to permit the states, especially in the South, to instigate removal even from reservations supposedly secured through federal treaties. Cherokee observer, Speckled Snake, reacted bitterly to the President's removal policy, "'go beyond the Oconee . . . ; there is a pleasant country.' He also said, 'It shall be yours forever.' Now he says, 'The land you live on is not yours; go beyond the Mississippi; there is game; there you may remain.'" Of the Great Southern Tribes the Chickasaws, Choctaws, and Creeks moved from their homelands peacefully on the whole; the Cherokees suffered illness and death during the infamous Trail of Tears; the Seminoles resisted violently and to some extent successfully in Florida. Centuries had tied the Great Southern Tribes to their homelands near the Atlantic; then they were uprooted and transplanted in the Great Plains, in the lands of nomadic cultures, such as the Arapaho. Indeed, white society required the Cherokees to colonize these "foreign" lands and make them their own. Despite differences with local Indians and similarities with other tribes removed to Indian Territory, the Cherokees would make Oklahoma a homeland, established through forced resettlement, rather than conquest, a situation analogous to that of blacks, rather than whites, in many new homelands about the Atlantic.[21]

In forcibly creating new homelands for the Great Southern Tribes, the United States nevertheless failed to eradicate the old ethnic regions entirely. Deep in the Florida Everglades, a branch of the Seminoles (a mixed people of much African descent) succeeded in maintaining itself in the face of one of the costliest U.S. military campaigns, resisting the government for over a hundred years before securing the right to stay in

---

[20] Angie Debo, A *History of the Indians of the United States*, Civilization of the American Indians Series (Norman: Univ. of Oklahoma Press, 1970), 121; and Hurtado and Iverson, 199.

[21] Debo, 120–5; and "Speckled Snake's (Cherokee) Reply to President Jackson, 1830," in Hurtado and Iverson, 204.

place. Furthermore, in the mountains of North Carolina, a band later known as the Eastern Cherokees escaped removal because they occupied some of the least desirable land in the area. These two marginal groups would cling to their homelands, resisting pressures to acculturate to the Anglo-American nation-state. Though these tribes would eventually gain federal recognition, their homelands would remain places dependent on the United States, rather than autonomous regions federated with the states.[22]

TEXAS BETWEEN FEDERATIONS

Hoping to avoid Anglo-American imperialism entirely, another band of Cherokees migrated west of the Mississippi, but instead of Oklahoma, they entered Texas. In that northeastern borderland of Mexico, they settled among the nomadic Wichitas, south of the Red River, rather than among the Spanish-speaking, mestizo population concentrated in Nacogdoches, Goliad, and San Antonio. (See Map 5.2.) Despite earlier attempts at settlement, the Spanish-speaking population, including Tlaxcalans and Canary Islanders, had settled San Antonio in the first half of the eighteenth century. A hundred years of residence had furthered the mestizaje, begun in central Mexico, by mixing in the local Coahuiltecan Indians, among the many other native peoples Spain sought to incorporate or displace. This distinctive aspect of Spanish colonialism created a population that was curiously both immigrant and indigenous to its evolving homeland. Though never densely settled, Texas lost population during Mexico's War for Independence (1810–21) as a result of several expeditions organized by Mexican rebels and Anglo-American adventurers to drive the royalists from New Spain – or possibly separate the province, if the larger objective could not be achieved. Subsequently, the government in Mexico City, as well as Tejanos themselves, hoped to repopulate the province, by making grants of land to settlers, including possibly the Cherokees.[23]

[22] King, 165.
[23] Debo, 129–30; and Ana Carolina Castillo Crimm, *De León: A Tejano Family History* (Austin: Univ. of Texas Press, 2003), 24, 57–60, 71–3; and Gilberto M. Hinojosa and Anne A. Fox, "Indians and their Culture in San Fernando de Bexar," in *Tejano Origins in Eighteenth-Century San Antonio*, ed. Gerald E. Poyo and Gilberto M. Hinojosa (Austin: Univ. of Texas Press for the Institute of Texan Cultures, 1991), 107–10.

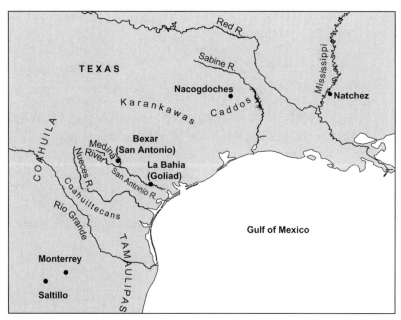

Map 5.2. Northeastern Mexico, c. 1830. Adapted from Poyo and Hinojosa, *Tejano Origins in Eighteenth-Century San Antonio*, viii. Cartography by Cassingham and Foxworth, Courtesy of the Edwin J. Foscue Map Library, SMU.

Between 1810 and 1836 Texas's fate was tied to the geopolitical development of Mexico. That development arose from patterns that had been established by Spain, the former "mother country," but also from the federal model presented by the United States. Unlike the thirteen colonies that became the United States, the Viceroyalty of New Spain, extending across much of North America from Panama to California and Texas, was centralized. Despite this, the huge land mass governed from Mexico City, had administrative subdivisions, reflected in the subsequent national state. For example, the distant northern borderlands, including Texas, had been administered for defensive purposes within a viceregal subdivision, called the *Provincias Internas*. After Mexican independence, most of the internal provinces retained their colonial frontier character, and thus became territories patterned on those of the Anglo-American frontier; that is territories preparing for admission as autonomous states within the new federal republic. Following the U.S. model regarding population size, Texas was denied separate statehood, but rather than territorial status, the province was merged with Coahuila in a single state in 1824. The national government made these decisions in Mexico City, following the centralized patterns of the Spanish era.[24]

Indeed, after independence Mexico, like the United States, resorted to time-honored imperial policies to solve its immense problems of national development. Mexico planned to subdue Indians and settle its vast borderlands, including Texas, following the methods of Spanish colonialism. While missions and presidios were no longer favored, towns and especially ranches were the institutions that would hopefully populate the distant north with "civilized," that is hispanicized citizens. Land grants became the single most important tool in Mexican plans for colonization. Hoping to lure citizens and foreigners with free land, the government made grants to individuals and communities on condition that the grantees make the land productive. Local Indians could receive grants to their own lands, if they settled down to agriculture, christianized, and accepted Mexican authority. Cherokees and other "immigrant" Indians from the United States qualified for grants in Texas, as well as Anglos.[25]

In its plan for national development, the new Mexican republic envisioned a federalism based on the individual citizen; accordingly, the constitution of Coahuila y Texas stipulated that "Every man who inhabits the territory of the State, although he may be but a traveler, enjoys the imprescriptible rights of *Liberty, Security, Property* and *Equality*." In practice, Mexico City sought to transform individual Indians, mestizos, and immigrant Anglos into loyal Mexican citizens, imagined

---

[24] Central America enjoyed relative autonomy under the colonial Audiencia of Guatemala; consequently, shortly after independence from Spain, that large region seceded from Mexico; Michael C. Meyer and William L. Sherman, *The Course of Mexican History* (New York: Oxford Univ. Press, 1979), 314–15; see also Pedro Pérez Herrero, "Regional Conformation in Mexico, 1700–1850: Models and Hypotheses," trans. Jane Walter, in *Mexico's Regions: Comparative History and Development*, ed. Eric Van Young, U.S – Mexico Contemporary Perspectives Series, 4 (San Diego: Center for U.S – Mexican Studies, Univ. of California, 1992), 128–31.

[25] Pablo González-Casanova, "Internal Colonialism and National Development," *Studies in Comparative International Development*, 1 (no. 4, 1965): 33; David J. Weber, *The Mexican Frontier, 1821–1846: The American Southwest under Mexico*, Histories of the American Frontier (Albuquerque: Univ. of New Mexico Press, 1982), 162–3, 102; needless to say, violence against Indians persisted – see Kelly F. Himmel, *The Conquest of the Karankawas and the Tonkawas, 1821–1859*, Elma Dill Russell Spencer Series in the West and Southwest, no. 20 (College Station: Texas A&M Univ. Press, 1999), 60–1.

as hispanicized males. Consequently, in 1824 the states generally formed around concentrations of individuals, historic population centers, rather than around ethnic groups, and Texas was no exception. Indeed, the national government kept Texas tied to populous Coahuila because it wished to prevent the increasing Anglo-Texans from developing their ethnicity into a nationality competitive with the Mexican image. While Texas's traditional population included nomadic tribes, such as the Comanches and Apaches; mission Indians, such as the Coahuiltecans; and mestizo Tejanos with family ties to the native Indians and the criollo elite, the national government feared Anglo-Texans would dominate a separate state through sheer numbers of immigrants. Moreover, an autonomous ethnically Anglo Texas challenged the Mexican federal ideal because the immigrants threatened to shift their allegiance to the United States.[26]

The flaws of Mexico's vision of national development showed by 1830 as Anglos outnumbered ethnic Mexicans in Texas, five to one. Indeed, the colonization plan created an Anglo homeland in Mexico almost overnight, as Stephen F. Austin noted, "The whole of this country, with exception of the small towns of Bexar and Goliad, has been settled and redeemed from the wilderness within a few years by the enterprise of immigrants." Joined with much more populous Coahuila, he and other Anglos felt underrepresented and thus requested Texas "be organised as a separate State of the Mexican confederation." Among the many reasons advanced for the separation was significantly the "dissimilarity of habits occupation and language," suggesting the desire to establish an autonomous ethnic homeland. Furthermore, use of the term "confederation" reflected a view of Mexico as a loose set of sovereign states, following the states-rights ideology of the U.S. South.[27]

The Texans' movement for separate statehood became moot when Mexico's federalist constitution was overthrown in favor of a centralized

[26] Some traditional indigenous regions, such as Tlaxcala, eventually became states – Ricardo Rendón Garcini, *Breve historia de Tlaxcala,* Serie breves historias de los estados de la república mexicana (Mexico City: Fondo de Cultura Económica, 1996), 72; "Constitution of Coahuila and Texas, March 11, 1827," in Wallace, Vigness, and Ward, 61; and Claudio Lomnitz-Adler, "Concepts for the Study of Regional Culture," in *Mexico's Regions,* ed. Van Young, 64–5.
[27] "Austin's Address Explaining Why the Convention Was Called, April 1, 1833," in Wallace, Vigness, and Ward, 74–6; for a nuanced description of the competing ethnic, racial, and national loyalties in Texas, see Reséndez, 146–70.

structure. In 1834 centralists established a system modeled on the
French Republic, which replaced federated states with departments
administered from the capital. Geographically distant and ethnically
distinct, Anglo-Texans rejected that structure, joining with other federalists to restore the constitution of 1824. Some Tejano supporters,
especially among the wealthy, believed "the ideas of government held
by North Americans are in general better adapted to those of the
Mexicans than are the ideas of European immigrants." These joined
Anglos in their cause, but other Mexicans suspected the national loyalties of the latter all along. Mexico's Secretary of War José María
Tornel y Mendívil believed, "At the time when Stephen Austin was
promoting and encouraging the independence of Texas, the Mexican
republic was under a federal government." He argued that the movement for a separate state was simply a justification for independence.
Given Anglos' states-rights beliefs and their subsequent acts, his view
had merit.[28]

In fact, Anglo federalists ultimately became secessionists and declared Texas independent, successfully severing the region from Mexico
in 1836. Imbued with a radical belief in regional sovereignty, rather
than simply autonomy, vis-à-vis a central government, the Texans
nevertheless designed a unitary constitution for their new republic,
despite its huge size, probably because they expected annexation to
the United States as a unitary state. No autonomy was envisioned for
the former department of Bexar where Tejanos predominated, or for
Spanish-speaking pockets, such as Nacogdoches, let alone the Indian
homelands in West and North Texas. While members of the elite, like
Francisco Ruiz of San Antonio, signed the new constitution, other
Tejanos, like Vicente Córdova, feeling desperate isolation, issued their
own proclamation. Denied their civil and property rights, "The citizens
of Nacogdoches . . . having gathered together with their weapons in
hand . . . are determined to shed their last drop of blood in order to
protect their individual rights and those of the Nation to which they
belong. . . they have no knowledge of the current laws by which

[28] Weber, *Mexican Frontier*, 243–5, 255; Ayuntamiento of San Antonio, "Indus-
trious, Honest, North American Settlers," in *Foreigners in Their Native Land:
Historical Roots of the Mexican Americans*, ed. David J. Weber, with a foreword by
Ramón Eduardo Ruiz (Albuquerque: Univ. of New Mexico Press, 1973), 84; and
José María Tornel y Mendívil, "Relations between Texas, the United States of
America, and Mexico," in *The Mexican Side of the Texan Revolution*, trans. with
notes by Carlos E. Castañeda (Dallas, Tex.: P. L. Turner Co., 1928), 334.

guarantees of their lives and property are offered." Reduced to an ethnic minority in Texas, Tejanos under Córdova rebelled against the new republic in 1838. In the process, they formed alliances with some Cherokees and other Indians and sought to reconnect with the Mexican nation to the south. Though their effort ultimately failed, it reflected their resistance to disinheritance, as one Tejana reminded her descendants, "Always remember these words: Texas is ours. Texas is our home."[29]

Having requested annexation to the United States as early as 1836, Texas clearly preferred admission to an Anglo-American union. There Anglo Texas would be no ethnic region; it would be a territorial variant of the dominant nation. On the other hand, Tejano South Texas severed from Mexico would remain an ethnic region without autonomy, for the United States was not a federation that granted statehood to the homelands of ethnic minorities. Federation, as in Mexico, meant a union of regions controlled by citizens of the nation's dominant culture. While denying citizenship to "Indians not taxed, Africans and descendants," the new state constitution made no direct mention of its now Mexican American citizens. Sustaining their ethnic rights as a regional group within the U.S. federal system would be a daunting task.[30]

Before annexation to the United States, the Texas Republic had dreamed of its own empire, claiming the entire length of the Rio Grande as its boundary, in the process claiming half of the neighboring provinces of New Mexico and Tamaulipas, including their Mexican populations. After annexation, Texas convinced the United States to press that claim, merging the imperial visions of these Anglo-American states. The U.S./Mexican War, a clash between imagined North American empires, realized the visions of Anglo-Americans, rather than Mexicans. Both peoples had sought to expand into the vast reaches of the continent, following the imperial patterns of Britain and Spain;

[29] "The Constitution of the Republic of Texas, March 17, 1836," in Wallace, Vigness, and Ward, 100, 103, 106; proclamation quoted in Paul Lack, "The Córdova Revolt," in *Tejano Journey, 1770–1850*, ed. Gerald E. Poyo (Austin: Univ. of Texas Press, 1996), 97; and Ramoncita, great-grandmother of Jovita González de Mireles, quoted in Teresa Palomo Acosta and Ruthe Winegarten, *Las Tejanas: 300 Years of History*, Jack and Doris Smothers Series in Texas History, Life, and Culture, no. 10 (Austin: Univ. of Texas Press, 2003), 46.

[30] "The Texas State Constitution of 1845, August 28, 1845," in Wallace, Vigness, and Ward, 150.

as a result, competition between these peoples in the borderlands, especially Texas, finally led to war. Though about ready to accept the loss of Texas, Mexico opted to defend itself when it could not continence further territorial losses, especially when the United States sought to acquire California and New Mexico in addition to the disputed Rio Grande areas. Successfully invading Mexico, the United States realized its imagined empire in 1848 under the Treaty of Guadalupe Hidalgo; in this process the victor acquired a vast region comprised of many American Indian homelands and Mexican subregions. These would remain restive through much of the nineteenth century, with the violent resistance of Navajos, Comanches, Apaches, and other Indian tribes; and into the twentieth, in the case of ethnic Mexicans, with uprisings of Californios, Nuevomexicanos, and especially Tejanos.[31]

The loss of Texas and its other far northern borderlands assured that Mexico's national development would continue in a smaller geographical space. Contraction, rather than expansion, had followed independence from Spain. Despite this, Mexico still had much territory to colonize, and the nation pushed to further hispanicize its diverse Indian populations, from Yaquis in the north to Mayas in the south. In its first constitution Mexico had made Tlaxcala a territory, refusing to grant the autonomy of statehood to an indigenous homeland. With a governor appointed by Mexico City, native Tlaxcalans nevertheless retained municipal self-government in the federalist system, avoided absorption by neighboring states, and maintained the region's ancient geographical integrity. But the region's status would alternate – between territory, department, and state – over the next fifty years in the struggles between federalists and centralists. Fearing fragmentation, further loss of territory, or even complete loss of sovereignty, Mexico struggled to maintain its own integrity. In 1854 the nation lost more land to the United States, through the Gadsden Purchase, and in 1862 faced total conquest again in the face of a French invasion. In tandem with these external threats, divisions between federalists and centralists returned to earlier

---

[31] Mario Barrera, *Race and Class in the Southwest: A Theory of Racial Inequality* (Notre Dame Ind.: Univ. of Notre Dame Press, 1979), 11, 13–14; David Montejano, *Anglos and Mexicans in the Making of Texas, 1836–1986* (Austin: Univ. of Texas Press, 1987), 15–19; and Thomas D. Hall, *Social Change in the Southwest,* Studies in Historical Social Change (Lawrence: Univ. Press of Kansas, 1989), 175. Anglo-American desire for California ports for trade with Asia also contributed to the U.S./Mexican War and illustrate that these economic interests transcended the Atlantic World.

divisions between republicans and monarchists as the latter attempted to strengthen the center through the crowning of Maximilian as emperor of Mexico, backed by French bayonets. Similarly, Texas and the United States would face further challenges to their national unity.[32]

The imperialism that included the occupation of Texas exacerbated the regional problems of the United States. The admission of Texas together with Maine was in keeping with the compromises between free and slave states that kept the sectional balance of power; however, the admission of California as a free state in 1850 upset the balance by restricting the spread of slavery into the West. Further containment caused Texas and ten other Southern states to secede from the Union and form the Confederate States of America in 1861. That the fundamental cause of discord was the colonial system of slavery was evident from Texas's own justification for secession: "the Federal Government . . . has so administered the same as to exclude the citizens of the Southern States . . . from all the immense territory . . . on the Pacific Ocean . . . as a means of destroying the institutions of Texas and her sister slave-holding States."[33]

In the Confederate States true sovereignty returned to Texas from the central government, and the loyalties of individuals lay in their specific states. As we have seen with Texas, the Southern states were Anglo-American regional variants of the United States, but even as they also shared elements of a general Southern regional heritage, these were not enough to effect sovereignty. While ethnic subregions existed throughout the Confederacy, such as the black Gullah area of the Carolinas and the Cajun area of Louisiana, nowhere did such a distinct culture play a significant role in secession from the Union. On the other hand, race certainly did, as in every Confederate state the desire to maintain white supremacy and black slavery underlay the demand for states' rights – that is the insistence that sovereignty resided in the white population of a specific state and secondarily in the nation-state as a whole: "We hold as undeniable truths that the governments of the various states, and of the confederacy itself, were established exclusively

---

[32] Rendón Garcini, 68–72, 77, 80; Meyer and Sherman, 352–3; and Edward H. Spicer, *Cycles of Conquest: The Impact of Spain, Mexico, and the United States on the Indians of the Southwest, 1533–1960* (Tucson: Univ. of Arizona Press, 1962), 83–5.

[33] Meinig, vol. 2, 456–7; and "A Declaration of the Causes," in Wallace, Vigness, and Ward, 195.

by the white race, for themselves." The Confederates imagined a voluntary alliance of white states resting on a "dependent race," rather
than the indivisible white Union of free labor imagined by the Federals,
a difference leading to the War Between the States.[34]

In the Civil War, Texas Mexicans did not see the conflict as directly
related to the autonomy of their ethnic group since Anglos dominated
both Federal and Confederate causes. Concentrated in their South
Texas homeland, where slaveholding was minimal, Tejanos had traditionally given support to runaway slaves on their way to Mexico. They
were, however, recruited to fight by both sides using financial inducements to sign up poor vaqueros and small farmers. On the other hand,
their political loyalties were doubtless influenced by local Tejano
patrones, like Colonel Santos Benavides of Laredo who fought with
the Anglo Confederates. Some support for secession was evident in
December 1860 when a gathering, including Tejano officeholders, in
Carrizo near Laredo issued a denunciation of the "felonious aggression
of the Abolitionists of the north upon southern institutions." Less than
four months later, however, forty Tejanos entered the town, unsuccessfully attempting to kill Pedro Díaz, the Confederate sheriff, and drive
his Anglo supporters out of the county. The divisions immediately
across the border in Mexico between monarchists and republicans,
Confederate and Federal sympathizers respectively, no doubt led some
Tejanos to volunteer for one or the other army in Texas. Their allegiance, as was the case for many Anglos, was often less based on ethnicity or federalism, than on a calculation of the individual benefits of
signing up for a particular side.[35]

Ultimately, resorting to the methods of imperialism, the Union
conquered the South, imposing Reconstruction governments hardly
reflective of the will of the section's white majority. Texas, for example, had to admit to "the heresies of nullification and secession" in its
Constitution of 1869. In the final analysis, the Union could justify
limiting the sovereignty of the Southern states through its liberation
of enslaved blacks. Through its victory, the North established the

[34] Ibid.; and Meinig, vol. 2, 476–8.
[35] Daniel D. Arreola, *Tejano South Texas: A Mexican American Cultural Province*,
Jack and Doris Smothers Series in Texas History, Life, and Culture, no. 5
(Austin: Univ. of Texas Press, 2002), 34, 38, 44; and *Ranchero* (Corpus Christi),
12 January 1861, quoted in Jerry D. Thompson, *Mexican Texans in the Union
Army*, Southwestern Studies, no. 78 (El Paso: Texas Western Press, 1986), 2–3,
see also vii–viii.

principle that the sovereignty of a state, its freedom to control its destiny, could not be used to deny freedom to minority communities within its borders. Ideally, federation allowed for the greatest freedom of individuals and their concentric communities and should thus be voluntary, but in practice coercion and even force played a role in settling intractable issues, especially those threatening the federation itself. The re-subordination of African Americans after the withdrawal from the South of Union troops by 1877 underscored the need for enforcement of human rights in the face of oppressive regionalism.[36]

FRENCH CANADA AND FEDERATION

Questions of union also played a major role in the nineteenth-century history of Canada, with ethnicity and region as major considerations. A French Canadian ethnicity, focused on customs, had predominated between 1759 and 1800 with little nationalism reactive to the British occupation. As English settlers dominated government and the economy, French Canadians tended to withdraw into rural communities. With the Catholic Church reflecting their ethnicity, the French held to very conservative traditions. Under church influence, the French romanticized an inefficient agricultural life. The church controlled education, causing the population's better-educated people to focus on the humanities and such careers as barrister and priest, rather than merchant. The training of barristers, however, created an increasingly active political elite though open conflict with the English in Upper Canada (Ontario) and in the urban areas of Lower Canada (Quebec) developed slowly.[37]

In the early nineteenth century, French animosity in the face of increasing English dominance gradually developed, though the War

---

[36] Eric Foner, *Reconstruction: America's Unfinished Revolution, 1863–1877*, New American Nation (New York: Harper & Row, 1988), xxvi, 602–3; "The Constitution of 1869, February 8, 1869," in Wallace, Vigness, and Ward, 213; and D[onald] W[illiam] Meinig, *The Shaping of America: A Geographical Perspective on 500 Years of History*, vol. 3, *Trancontinental America 1850–1915* (New Haven, Conn.: Yale Univ. Press, 1998), 188–9, 209.

[37] Edward M. Corbett, *Quebec Confronts Canada* (Baltimore, Md.: Johns Hopkins Univ. Press, 1967), 16; see also Susan Mann [Trofimenkoff], *The Dream of Nation: A Social and Intellectual History of Quebec*, Carleton Library Series, 1982, 2nd ed. (Montreal: McGill – Queen's Univ. Press, 2002), 33–47.

of 1812 temporarily unified Canadians. Angered at British seizure of its shipping during the Napoleonic Wars, the United States invaded Canada, in hopes of conquering Britain's remaining North American colonies, but failed in this imperialistic adventure. Other ramifications of the French Revolution affected Canada in 1837, when a small group of rebels took up arms, seeking to establish a French republic on the St. Lawrence. Stating that "one nation should never govern another," Louis Joseph Papineau led the unsuccessful struggle to gain sovereignty for Lower Canada. To squelch further French resistance, the British Parliament merged Upper (West) and Lower (East) Canada in the Act of Union of 1840, dividing the new single legislature evenly between the two peoples, but establishing English as the official language. Before long the English-speaking legislators demanded the majority in the assembly because their numbers had increased, but the French naturally feared any political rearrangement that would worsen their status as a subordinate minority in Canada. Although Canada secured increased self-government from Britain in 1849, the biethnic union worked poorly.[38]

In 1867 London passed the British North America Act designed to alleviate the French problem by creating a larger federation with an even larger English-speaking majority. New Brunswick and Nova Scotia, with their Acadian and Micmac minorities, joined Upper Canada, now Ontario, and Lower Canada, now Quebec, as provinces in the new union. Moreover, as the Dominion of Canada, the new state still recognized the sovereignty of Britain's Queen Victoria. Despite losing power in the overall federation, the French regained their legislature in Quebec, albeit with a strong English presence. Acadians, on the other hand, bitterly resented Ottawa's tacit support of nonsectarian common schools, judged an affront to Catholicism, a controversy that stimulated ethnic nationalism. Longfellow's *Evangeline,* recalling the eighteenth-century Acadian dispersal, became the collective myth of this regional identity:

> Still stands the forest primeval; but under the shade of its branches
> Dwells another race, with other customs and language,
> Only along the shore of the mournful and misty Atlantic
> Linger a few Acadian peasants, whose fathers from exile
> Wandered back to their native land to die in its bosom.

[38] Corbett, 17; and Ramsay Cook et al., *Histoire générale du Canada,* Boréal compact, 18, trans. from English to French, Michel Buttiens et al. ([Montreal]: Éditions du Boréal, 1990), 251–2.

The Micmacs also regained a bit of their old homeland, a reserve acquired through private efforts in 1870, continuing the long process of recovery for a First Nation. Thus, the still rigid federation became the geopolitical framework of a Canada constantly challenged by ethnic regionalism.[39]

The federation added new provinces over time, a process that recreated the ethnic problem since the new members usually sought English as the official language. In 1869 on the distant, western Red River, Louis Riel led the *métis*, the mixed French/Indian majority of the region, in a rebellion to secure their language, religious, and property rights. Anticipating the establishment of a pro-English province, he operated a provisional government until driven from the country by Canadian troops. In 1870 the Manitoba Act assured French-language rights and Catholic schools, but strife continued when English settlers challenged these provisions. In 1885 the *métis* recalled Riel from exile to lead another rebellious provisional government in Saskatchewan, where he called on the Blackfeet and Cree Indians to join him in preserving the land and buffalo from encroachment by the railroad. His defeat and execution convinced the French that the national government in Ottawa was pro-English and would confine their culture to the eastern part Canada, Quebec in particular. Despite these fears, the next fifty years saw the stabilization of their culture within the federation as the French survived what had seemed inevitable assimilation by a dynamically growing English Canada.[40]

THE BASQUE PROVINCES

In the nineteenth century the Basque Country faced the same issues of sovereignty, autonomy, regionalism, centralization, and federation confronting Quebec and so many other parts of the Atlantic World. Yet among these many lands, the Basque Country of Spain, if not France, was unique in its relationship to the political center, in this case,

[39] Corbett, 19; Margaret R. Conrad and James K. Hiller, *Atlantic Canada: A Region in the Making*, The Illustrated History of Canada (Toronto: Oxford Univ. Press, 2001), 131–2, 148–50, 112; and Henry Wadsworth Longfellow, *Evangeline* (Indianapolis, Ind.: Bobbs–Merrill Co., 1905), 132.

[40] Corbett, 19; and John Dickinson and Brian Young, *A Short History of Quebec*, 3rd ed. (Montreal: McGill – Queen's Univ. Press, 2003), 154, 249–51.

Madrid. As we have seen, the traditional autonomy enjoyed by this ethnic region had given it significant commercial, if not cultural advantages. These advantages, however, varied by hispanization, class, urbanization, and religious position. Significant alterations in the relationship between the region and the central state began to occur after 1795 when Napoleon and the wars for independence virtually dismantled the Spanish Empire.[41]

Long reliant on commerce with Spain's formal colonies, Basque merchants found that trade had disappeared with the independence of the Latin American nations in the 1820s. The free trade with the colonies and northern Europe that the region had enjoyed through its politically autonomous status now seemed slowly but increasingly disadvantageous. Merchants who moved their investments into manufacturing found potential markets restricted by trade barriers between their region and the rest of Spain. Domestic industry based on mining was improving but also faced stiff foreign competition due to the region's position outside the protective tariff walls of the nation-state. Consequently, incipient manufacturers sought fuller integration into Spain as a whole.[42]

In this effort, however, the merchants faced powerful resistance from traditional sectors of Basque society based in rural areas. Rural landowners and peasants feared agricultural competition from the rest of Spain and feared loss of communal lands. Neither did they wish to pay taxes imposed by the central government. Especially onerous for the budding manufacturers was municipal control of lumber and iron ore, which in some locales, both rural and urban, were not exportable. Manufacturers faced a confusing array of local regulations when trying to gain access to these critical natural resources. The local clergy sided with the rural interests, among whom it exercised power and influence, rather than with the new, rising class of hispanicized industrialists.[43]

These socioeconomic divisions split the Basque Country as all of Spain broke out in the Carlist civil wars (1833–9, 1872–6), dynastic

[41] Marianne Heiberg, *The Making of the Basque Nation*, Cambridge Studies in Social Anthroplogy, 66 (New York: Cambridge Univ. Press, 1989), 35.

[42] Ibid., 35–6; cf. Juan Díez Medrano, *Divided Nations: Class, Politics, and Nationalism in the Basque Country and Catalonia*, Wilder House Series in Politics, History, and Culture (Ithaca, N.Y.: Cornell Univ. Press, 1995), 70–1.

[43] Ibid.; cf. Maximiano García Venero, *Historia del nacionalismo vasco*, 3rd ed. (Madrid: Editora Nacional, 1969), 155–7.

struggles that involved many issues, especially regional autonomy. The supporters of Don Carlos Borbón for the throne fought for a traditional society against the liberal government in Madrid, supporting Isabella II. Backing a decentralized monarchy, the Carlists defended the ancient autonomy of Spain's ethnic regions when Madrid subdivided them into uniform provinces, akin to French departments, limited in legislative and executive power. As he fought for the pretender, General José Antonio Muñagorri reminded Basques that "Our first objective is the total restoration of the Fueros [regional rights]." The pro-Catholic, rural interests lost the first war to the central government and the urban liberals who favored the manufacturing sector. Consequently, Madrid moved the tariff wall to the coast, commercially enclosing the region with the rest of Spain. The Basque Country's autonomy thus eroded, though it remained on paper.[44]

Curiously, the Second Carlist War broke out when the Basque Country insisted on the semblance of its traditional autonomy when Madrid offered a measure of real self-governance under a new federal Spanish constitution. With the Carlists' second defeat even the formal autonomy of Vizcaya, Guipúzcoa, and Alava came to an end; only Navarre, ironically less ethnically Basque, managed to keep this geopolitical status. Because of the urban elite's support of centralization, Madrid did allow the Basques to negotiate taxes lower than those applied to other regions. This, together with greater protective trade barriers against foreign competition, allowed industry to boom. Moreover, municipalities lost control over iron ore, allowing private companies to extract and export it to the UK in exchange for investment from that country. In some ways, the Basque Country thus seemed more an economic colony of Britain than of Spain.[45]

The export of raw materials, however, did not lead to dependency on Britain because enough capital accumulated, particularly in Bilbao, to make Basque capitalists independent and the most powerful in Spain. The end of the nineteenth century saw the depletion of iron ore, but by then these capitalists had made metallurgical improvements,

---

[44] Heiberg, 36–8; Muñagorri quoted in Mark Kurlansky, *The Basque History of the World* (New York: Walker & Co., 1999), 151.

[45] Heiberg, 36–8; Stanley G. Payne, *Basque Nationalism*, The Basque Series (Reno: Univ. of Nevada Press, 1975), 53–5; and Díez Medrano, 71.

constructed new ports, established shipbuilding, and opened banks, so that the economy had moved beyond the early extractive stage. Significantly, this development occurred after the end of autonomous rule and suggests that the region benefited more from closer integration with the Spanish state, but the hispanicized urban elite derived the major benefits from this arrangement. For the new urban industrial economy rested on the migration of cheap labor, especially from impoverished rural areas of Castile.[46]

Thus, through Spanish centralization a new complex class and ethnic structure arose in the Basque Country, one riddled with social problems. The new industrial Basque elite descended from a few, old, commercial and landed families; it controlled wealth through monopolies, rather than the competitive market; the hispanicized elite also controlled politics through a boss system that favored the appointment of incoming Spaniards to administrative posts. Smaller Basque family businesses tended to hire working-class Basques, who remained impoverished because these enterprises had difficulty competing in the monopolized economy. With little social mobility an autonomous class culture among Basque shopkeepers and artisans did not develop, as education remained minimal and regional culture proletarian. Within the Basque and migrant Spanish proletariat, living and working conditions worsened as this class increased, affecting the quality of life for the entire region. "The factory worker is a virtual slave," wrote not some Marxist, but Carlist journalist V. Manterola, "good only to produce, but without regard for his morale." Labor unrest followed among the Spanish newcomers against the regional elite, while the Basque lower classes remained unorganized in smaller companies. Curiously, this made Basques as a whole appear as the oppressive nationality, hardly the situation of a theoretical internal colony.[47]

In actuality the majority of Basques existed as a subordinate, regional, ethnic group because their own elite aligned its interests with the larger Spanish capitalist class. The end of autonomy had not benefited the group as a whole. As we have seen, migration had eroded its political power, as newcomers held most of the government positions. Demographically Castilians and other Spaniards increased relative to the locals, undermining the latter's political power. Economically, Basques found themselves in peripheral industries, which also excluded

[46] Heiberg, 39–40.
[47] Ibid., 41–4; and Manterola quoted in Kurlansky, 157.

them from participation in union organizing. Ethnically, the dominant language began to eclipse the regional tongue as it and other elements of the local culture lost prestige. In Castilian the great Spanish writer Miguel de Unamuno described Basque nationalism as "exclusivist regionalism, blind to all broader visions," a nationalism he had shared in his youth. The immense power of the Basque elite did little to maintain the region as distinct, allowing later Basque nationalists to define it as an internal colony.[48]

Dreams of Sovereignty

The evolution of colonized communities in the nineteenth century followed different trajectories as contradictory forms of political development filled the imaginations of various nationalities. In West Africa native peoples, such as the Basso, resisted free black colonists using imperial methods to build the federated nation envisioned as Liberia. Likewise, white and colored Jamaicans in the Caribbean and rural Basques in Western Europe unsuccessfully resisted the encroachment of British imperial and Spanish national centralization with mixed ethical purposes and results. In North America where large multiethnic states developed, Mexico, Canada, and the United States used traditional colonial methods in their attempts to control Anglo-Texans, Manitoban *métis*, and Cherokees, respectively. Nor were these large states averse to the use of such methods against regional variants of the dominant nationality if they threatened the center, as in the case of the Confederate States. Despite the prevalence of imperialism, different nations and nationalities imagined and experimented with various unions, from loose confederate to tight federal forms. The latter achieved the most success in unifying states under dominant nations, such as the Castilians in Spain, but not in allowing for ethnic autonomy. If many peoples dreamed of self-determination for their homelands within a multiethnic state, sovereignty could not remain exclusively in the hands of one nationality. Around the North Atlantic, full recognition of ethnic autonomy within federalism remained somewhat imaginary.[49]

[48] Heiberg, 44; cf. Payne, 61–2; Unamuno quoted in Kurlansky, 164.
[49] Meinig, vol. 2, 516; for institutional changes that decentralize power in a unitary state, see Amos Sawyer, *Beyond Plunder: Toward Democratic Governance in Liberia* (Boulder, Colo.: L. Rienner, 2005), 88–9.

CHAPTER SIX

Imperial Designs Revived

The Second Colonial Era, 1880–1945

Colonialism, both formal and informal, resurged in the late nineteenth century as new technology, including steamboats, railroads, telegraphs, machine guns, and improved drugs, permitted the great powers to penetrate heretofore inaccessible regions in the Sahara, the Caribbean, and the rest of the world. This competition for new territory led to catastrophic world wars and clashes of empire in the first half of the twentieth century. After World War I, consequently, Cameroun and other German colonies, nominal mandates of the League of Nations, went to the British and French Empires. In counterpoint, advocacy of world federation and national self-determination prepared the way for the collapse of formal imperialism. For example, after the Great War sections of Prussia returned to a reconstituted Poland, while Austria, Hungary, and other nations emerged from the former Hapsburg realm. Meanwhile, a multitude of Atlantic peoples and lands, "domestic" and "foreign," remained subject to France, Britain, the United States, and other empires.[1]

West Africa from Sovereign States to Colonies

As we have seen, native peoples in West Africa had had contact with European empires at least since the fifteenth century, but conquest

---

[1] E[ric] J. Hobsbawm, *Nations and Nationalism since 1780: Programme, Myth, Reality*, 2nd ed. (Cambridge: Cambridge Univ. Press, 1992), 164–5; David Armitage, *The Declaration of Independence: A Global History* (Cambridge, Mass.: Harvard Univ. Press, 2007), 132; and Albert Memmi, *Portrait du colonisé précédé du portrait du colonisateur* (Paris: Buchet/Chastel, Correa, 1957), 114, 190–2.

would not proceed, as it had in the Americas, until the nineteenth because of the strength of native states, not to mention the inaccessibility of the physical environment to whites. In 1872 in Sierra Leone, for example, in response to French expansion in Guinea, the British pushed farther into the hinterland occupied by nearly twenty interspersed native peoples. From their Freetown enclave among the Temne, the British enlisted an anglicized black doctor, Edward W. Blyden, to visit the Yalunka-speaking Muslims of Falaba, thus marking the British colony's northeastern frontier with the French. (See Map 6.1.) Incorporating so many ethnic groups into a crown colony the size of Scotland necessitated another exercise in conquest. In the late 1890s the Temne unsuccessfully rebelled against a British "hut tax:" "It was decided that this should not be paid," according to subchief Pa Kapr Bundu, "for the simple reason that the houses on which the tax was based belonged to our people." A similar insurrection followed among the Mende, who, like the Temne, comprised about a third of Sierra Leone's population. However, astutely seeing resistance as futile, "The leading chief . . . Madam Yoko" secretly collaborated with the government, for which she "became chief not only of Moyamba, but of Banya and Mano." Thus did the British expand their empire.[2]

In Senegambia after the breakup of the Jolof Empire in the sixteenth century, the kingdoms of Kajoor, Bawol, and Jolof had nevertheless remained politically independent of Europe and engaged in that most imperial of ventures, the slave trade. (See Map 6.2.) The Portuguese and then the Dutch continued the trade along and across the Atlantic with the Senegambian kingdoms supplying large numbers of slaves until about 1600, when the Europeans found more lucrative areas farther south. Relations among these sovereign peoples were complex, not yet those of complete European domination. For instance, from the time of the Portuguese arrival, their resident traders, who could not own land, often relied on local women to provide invaluable services as interpreters, cultural brokers, and even business partners. These alliances produced Luso-African children who, often finding themselves unwanted by either of their parents' peoples further developed their mothers' roles as intermediaries. Thus, imperialism had its impact well before the actual

[2] "Testimony of Pa Kapr Bundu, a subchief at Rogbongba, in Yoni (Mamela) chiefdom (recorded at Rogbongba, 11 November 1970)," in Kenneth C. Wylie, *The Political Kingdoms of the Temne: Temne Government in Sierra Leone, 1825–1910* (New York: Africana Publishing Co., 1977), 230–1, 111–13, 153–4.

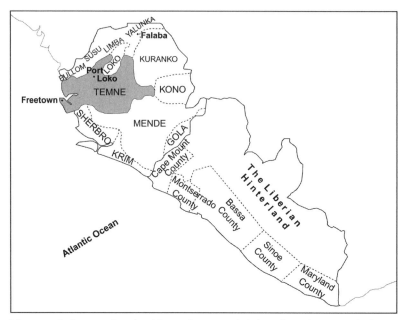

Map 6.1. Indigenous Lands of Sierra Leone and Colonial Settlements of Liberia, c. 1850. Adapted from Wylie, *The Political Kingdoms of the Temne*, xiv, and Saha, *Culture in Liberia*, vi. Cartography by Cassingham and Foxworth, courtesy of the Edwin J. Foscue Map Library, SMU.

European conquest of Africa. Indeed, the prevalence of slavery in traditional Senegambian societies had much to do with its transformation into a fully capitalist venture in the hands of the European empires.[3]

With slaves over half of the populations of Kajoor, Bawol, and Jolof, these people were more than a commodity in traditional Senegambia. Since individuals born into domestic slavery could not be sold, they were more similar to peons tied to their masters, rather than goods for the market. Since slaves could belong to the government, some served as soldiers and actually became a warrior class from which the

---

[3] Boubacar Barry, "The Subordination of Power and the Mercantile Economy: The Kingdom of Waalo, 1600–1831," in *The Political Economy of Underdevelopment: Dependence in Senegal*, ed. Rita Cruise O'Brien, Sage Series on African Modernization and Development, vol. 3 (Beverly Hills, Calif.: Sage Publications, 1979), 43–4; and George E. Brooks, *Eurafricans in Western Africa: Commerce, Social Status, Gender, and Religious Observance from the Sixteenth to the Eighteenth Century*, Western African Studies (Athens: Ohio Univ. Press, 2003), 50–2, 104.

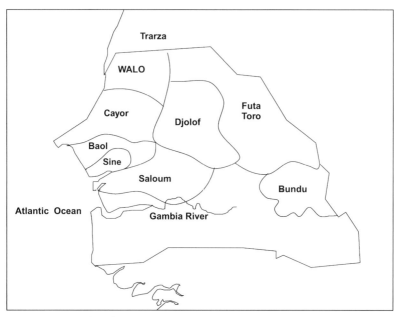

Map 6.2. Pre-Colonial States of Senegal, c. 1850. Adapted from Gellar, *Senegal*, 3. Cartography by Cassingham and Foxworth, courtesy of the Edwin J. Foscue Map Library, SMU.

aristocracy sometimes drew exceptional leaders. In this way nonchattel slaves provided both military and political power to the Senegambian kingdoms and their noble matrilineal families. Nevertheless, chattel slavery, which had always provided labor as well as profits at sale, became lucrative with expansion of the market across the Atlantic. Because the African kingdoms acquired chattel slaves as prisoners of war, conflict increased as it became highly profitable. Thus, chattel slavery produced great wealth for the elites of Senegambia and their imperial trading partners.[4]

Before European colonization, though men dominated the Jolof Empire and the succeeding kingdoms, women derived significant power through matrilineage. Apparently, the importance of matrilineal descent in the monarchies stemmed from polygamy. The offspring of different mothers in the same household competed with one another for power and naturally relied on maternal relatives for support.

[4]   Sheldon Gellar, *Senegal: An African Nation Between Islam and the West*, Profiles, Nations of Contemporary Africa (Boulder, Colo.: Westview Press, 1982), 3–6.

Maternal families owned property, especially cattle and slaves, which meant economic power rested in that line of descent. A king's mother, moreover, played an important political and financial role in the state, naturally more than his first wife did. An aunt or sister could also exercise the functions of the king's mother if she were absent. Such women received revenues allocated specifically to them from the provinces. In general aristocratic women administered the household, including both domestic and field slaves. Because property and titles passed on through their daughters, women could also exercise important power beyond their own lives. European colonialism would challenge such traditions.[5]

Though many of the Wolof people held to their traditional religion based on reverence for ancestors and nature spirits, Islam rather than Christianity increasingly influenced their beliefs. On the edge of the Sahara, Senegambia was recurrently affected by Muslim movements that acted as counterweights to the European presence on the Atlantic coast. For instance, from 1673 to 1677, Muslim leaders in Senegal led a grassroots rebellion against the aristocracies of Kajoor, Jolof, and Waalo, a rebellion partially incited by the participation of those kingdoms in the transatlantic slave trade. Needless to say, Europeans assisted the local elites by supplying firearms to crush the rebellion. Interestingly, these Maraboutic Wars had begun in Mauritania, in the Saharan interior, partially in reaction to the loss of trade to the Atlantic merchants, suggesting that the conflict had as much to do with commercial rivalry as religious antislavery sentiment. In any case, European religious influences faced strong competition in Senegambia.[6]

With the decline of Dutch power, other European states intervened in Senegambia, most notably France. In 1659 the French established St. Louis, a trading post and fort at the mouth of the Senegal River, thus gaining a colonial beachhead. Within twenty years they drove the competing Dutch from Cape Verde, but would continue to struggle for the Atlantic trade with the English. Though the French did not fully occupy Senegal for another two centuries, their influence along the coast had a powerful impact from their arrival. For example, in 1695 assisted by the wealth, weapons, and iron the French provided, King

[5]   Ibid., 4–5; and James F. Searing, *West African Slavery and Atlantic Commerce: The Senegal River Valley, 1700–1860*, African Studies Series, 77 (New York: Cambridge Univ. Press, 1993), 15–16.
[6]   Barry, 49–50, 55.

Latsukaabe of Bawol conquered the Sereer ethnic regions to the south, and united the monarchies of his state and Kajoor, an imperial union lasting nearly two hundred years.[7]

As with the Portuguese, French power was mediated by local people, particularly women called "signares." At the settlements of Gorée and St. Louis in the eighteenth century, free African and Eurafrican women with property often married officials of European companies for mutual economic advantage. One Frenchman observed that "the majority live in considerable affluence, and many African women own thirty to forty slaves which they hire to the Compagnie." Like their Luso-African predecessors, these women, often of French and English ancestry, served as interpreters and cultural brokers, but they had greater prestige and power in colonial society. Known for their beauty, they were more independent of their husbands and true entrepreneurs. Older, established signares often had large households of domestic slaves that effectively comprised major manufacturing compounds, including the workshops of carpenters, masons, tailors, weavers, and other skilled craftsmen. The products of these workshops entered the commercial networks through which these women traded for other goods and slaves (those integrated into the local community were not sold overseas). As a local elite, these women illustrated the complex hybrid hierarchies often established through colonialism.[8]

By the beginning of the nineteenth century, penetration of Senegal seemed necessary for the French to make their beach head profitable, as the transatlantic slave trade had begun to decline due to the successful Haitian independence movement. Given increasing British and even U.S. opposition to the trade, France looked to develop an agricultural colony in Senegal, specifically in Waalo, the kingdom closest to St. Louis. The French believed cotton, sugar, or tobacco plantations could thrive with local supplies of slaves. In 1819 Waalo granted land for that purpose and essentially became a protectorate of France; however, the enterprise failed when native landowners refused to cede their property, labor could not be got, and neighboring states objected to the European intrusion. Subsequently, the French launched a war of conquest in 1854, annexing all of Waalo the next year, but the war lasted until 1886 when the Wolof armies of all Senegal finally surrendered. The Serer ethnic regions kept some autonomy for a time, but were

---

[7] Gellar, 6; and Searing, 18–19.
[8] Antoine Edmé Pruneau de Pommegorge quoted in Brooks, 214, 206, 270–1.

eventually centralized into the French colonial system. Though formal colonialism had ended in most of the Americas in the early nineteenth century, it was reaching a peak in West Africa. Self-determination had disappeared in Senegal.[9]

This intensified colonialism resulted in the continued reproduction of a mixed population, including one Leopold Panet. A native of Senegal, the "orphan" was fortunate to receive an education, an experience that acculturated him thoroughly in the ways of the French and earned him a position in the colonial administration. In that capacity in 1850, he was assigned to explore the vast territory between his homeland and Algiers on the Mediterranean Coast. Apparently, his mixed appearance and knowledge of Arabic allowed him to pass as a Muslim Algerian, though not without incident, across borders and through regions hostile to Christian Europeans. Crossing Mauritania and the Western Sahara, he got as far as Mogador on the southwestern coast of Morocco, whence he shipped to France to present his report: "I have thrown a bit of light on more than 200 [myriametres] of a region entirely unexplored." Despite serving French imperialism, Panet's hybridity allowed him to open a road between the local and the global. Remote ethnic regions, such as the homeland of the Trarza Moors, north of Senegal, became possibilities for future federation.[10]

MAURITANIA, WESTERN SAHARA, MOROCCO – LATE COLONIES

Once the French had subdued Senegal, they sought control of virtually all West Africa, which meant penetration of the Sahara to the north of the Senegal River, the country now called Mauritania. Basically, "a vast plain strewn with rocks" and sand dunes, Mauritania had arable lands only at a few depressions and oases beyond the Senegal River Valley. The desert to the north and east, and a barren shore to the west meant that access to the country was easiest from the south, at least for the French. Long before their arrival, local Berber groups had traded, fought, and otherwise interacted with the blacks near the

---

[9] Barry, 56–8; Gellar, 6–8; and Searing, 18–19.
[10] Quoted in Robert Cornevin, *Littératures d'Afrique noire de langue française*, Littératures modernes 10 ([Paris]: Presses Universitaires de France, 1976), 111–12, my translation.

Senegal. By the fifteenth century the Ben Maql Arabs (hassane) had infiltrated the region and gained enough power to challenge the native Sanhadja Berbers. After two centuries of intermittent conflict, the Arabs decisively defeated the Berbers in 1674, after which the latter ethnic group became subordinate. No longer permitted to be warriors, the Berbers engaged in religious, scholarly, commercial, and livestock-raising occupations, paid tribute, and served the hassane. Despite the inequality between them, Arabs and Berbers formed a Caucasian caste, subdivided by clan, but distinct from the black slaves. The Arabs had the most political power and owned most of the cultivated land, as well as controlling fishing and water rights; as warriors, the Arabs also had access to booty in slaves and animals. Blacks concentrated along the Senegal River served as targets of raids from the north for hundreds of years. The fragmented nature of Mauritanian society at the end of the nineteenth century would leave it open to conquest by France, a conquest albeit not completed until the early twentieth century.[11]

Northwest of Mauritania and south of Morocco stretched an even more isolated and challenging territory known in the late twentieth century as Western Sahara. Though the Portuguese and Spanish had visited its barren coastline, near the Canary Islands, at least since the fifteenth century, the desolate landscape proved so forbidding that the major European powers bypassed the country in their global expansion. Though these states carried out periodic raids for slaves, and engaged in some trade, their meager attempts at permanent settlement failed. Not until the late nineteenth century did Spain finally establish a successful colony in order to forestall other European occupation of an African land so close to Spain itself.[12]

Meanwhile, French forces moved up from Senegal across Mauritania and into Morocco; they also moved west from Algeria and directly across the Mediterranean. In so doing they entered one of Africa's most colonized countries, one occupied by many empires, including the Roman. On the other hand, Morocco had also been the core of the Moorish Empire, which had included Spain. In the twentieth century the French coerced Morocco into becoming a protectorate in their empire,

[11] Virginia Thompson and Richard Adloff, *The Western Saharans: Background to Conflict* (Totowa, N.J.: Croom Helm, Barnes & Noble Books, 1980), 33–4, 41–4.
[12] Tony Hodges, *Western Sahara: The Roots of a Desert War* (Westport, Conn.: Lawrence Hill & Co., 1983), 17, 19–20, 22.

another forced collection of many distinct nations. Mohammed ben Abd el Krim el Khatabi, a leader of the resistance against France and Spain, called their division of Morocco "a preposterous act of totally unjustified and unjustifiable imperialism." While the French would later attempt a West African Federation of their colonies, such a geo-political model was doomed to failure, seen as a foreign imposition by the native peoples, rather than a voluntary union. To them the civiliz-ing mission of this second great era of European colonialism seemed nothing less than hypocrisy.[13]

Internal Colonialism in the American Southwest

As the French and other European empires renewed their colonial expansion overseas, Mexico and the United States had enough terri-tory within the continental span of their boundaries to occupy their imperial energies at least until the end of the nineteenth century. As we have seen, the empire claimed by Mexico, though still larger than most European countries, was much reduced, but that nation contin-ued to colonize its Indian territories. Though indigenous Tlaxcala achieved statehood permanently by late century, the civilizing mis-sion of President Porfirio Díaz made autonomy more difficult, but not impossible; his support of a native Tlaxcalan governor meant that Indians continued to control property, though the dictator's interfer-ence in their local governments would eventually contribute to rev-olution. Across the border, the United States developed its own internal empire including a vast southwestern region with a sparse and varied population of Indians, ethnic Mexicans, and Anglo-Amer-icans. A landmass larger than the countries of Western Europe com-bined, the Southwest naturally encompassed many subregions, including a multitude of Indian cultures, as well as Anglo and Mex-ican subcultures. The Pueblos of New Mexico had little in common with the Gabrielinos of California; the Mormons of Utah certainly differed from white, not to mention black Texans, in customs and beliefs; and Mexicans also varied between Californios and Tejanos. Nevertheless, of the three major groups, Mexicans had the most in

---

[13] Quoted in Eleanor Hoffmann, *Realm of the Evening Star: A History of Morocco and the Lands of the Moors* (Philadelphia: Chilton Books, 1965), 214–15, 198, 219; see also Henri Terrasse, *Histoire du Moroc des origines à l'établissement du Protectorat français*, vol. 2 (1950; reprint, New York: AMS Press, 1975), 399.

common among themselves. Consequently, it was their heritage that gave this macro-region, especially the borderlands, its most distinctive ethnic imprint. Defining the Southwest historically as all the land gained by the United States from Mexico, we recognize the role of imperialism in the region's creation.[14]

Of the various Mexican subcultures in the Southwest, Tejanos continued to evolve as a distinct community in the nineteenth century. Their homeland, compressed into South Texas, as the result of displacement and out-numbering by Anglo-Americans farther north, had all the markings of the larger internal colony, as well as an ethnic region. During the late 1800s, Tejanos experienced internal colonialism in many ways, including continued armed conflict along the border. As we have seen, the U.S. Army had crossed the Nueces River into northern Tamaulipas, successfully transferring the Texas Republic's territorial claim to the United States. But the conquest and occupation of the trans-Nueces area remained incomplete, as resistance and repression continued. In 1875, for example, a band of Mexicans had crossed the Rio Grande, ridden to Corpus Christi, killed ranchers, and stolen livestock. In response, according to a Texas Ranger, "Large parties of mounted and well-armed men, residents of Nueces County, were riding over the country, committing the most brutal outrages, murdering peaceable Mexican farmers and stockmen who had lived all their lives in Texas. These . . . vigilance committees . . . pretended that they were acting in the cause of law and order." The Mexican raiders obviously disregarded the "new" international boundary; even twenty-seven years after formal establishment of the border, the legitimacy of Anglo-American rule was still in dispute. On the other hand, the new Anglo residents clearly disregarded the new U.S. citizenship of the local "Tejanos," not to mention their historical roots in Tamaulipas. In Tejano eyes, even the Texas Rangers came to be seen as an oppressive state police force, as their methods too often echoed those of the vigilance committees. Displeased with the occupation, some local

---

[14] Ricardo Rendón Garcini, *Breve historia de Tlaxcala*, Serie breves historias de los estados de la república mexicana (Mexico City: Fondo de Cultura Económica, 1996), 83, 85; D[onald] W[illiam] Meinig, *Southwest: Three Peoples in Geographical Change, 1600–1970* (New York: Oxford Univ. Press, 1971), 3–6; and Mario Barrera, *Race and Class in the Southwest: A Theory of Racial Inequality* (Notre Dame, Ind.: Univ. of Notre Dame Press, 1979), 7–12.

Mexicans periodically rebelled, reflecting a South Texas not yet completely subdued by force of arms.[15]

With military and police control of the core of the state, Anglos sought to secure that control in South Texas, and to exert their dominance over civic institutions as well. In San Antonio that had occurred early as many Tejanos fled the city during the revolution and immigrants moved in from the United States and Europe, making the former a minority in their old capital city. Such demographic change shifted electoral power to Anglos there, but that change did not occur so readily across the Nueces. In Laredo, the major city on the border, civic positions remained in Mexican American hands, despite the attempts of newcomers to take control. In the mid-1870s, when a U.S. official pressured the Tejano mayor to appoint an Anglo chief of police, resistance developed. While attempting to arrest a drunk, Chief N. A. Jennings recalled, "two women ran up to me and threw their arms around my neck. . . . When I finally did get into their heads the fact that I was a police officer . . . he had disappeared." Jennings soon discovered capturing the man was a mistake, as he had apparently been protected by the women. A week later, the chief "was shot at five times," by "unknown assailants," whom he suspected were his own officers. Needless to say, Jennings resigned his position, realizing that the local community did not recognize his authority.[16]

Regardless of such difficulties, colonizing Texas was an attractive proposition; it had plenty of land, the basis for its traditional economy of cattle and sheep ranching. Shortly after the U.S. conquest, the state had sought to clarify titles to land for purposes of taxation and sale when its Bourland-Miller Commission had checked the validity of Spanish and Mexican land grants in South Texas. Requiring proof of ownership and clear boundaries, the commission nevertheless held to flexible

[15] N. A. Jennings, "A Set Policy of Terrorizing Mexicans," in *Foreigners in Their Native Land: Historical Roots of the Mexican Americans*, ed. David J. Weber, with a foreword by Ramón Eduardo Ruiz (Albuquerque: Univ. of New Mexico Press, 1973), 188; and Robert J. Rosenbaum, *Mexicano Resistance in the Southwest*, with a new foreword by John R. Chávez (1981; reprint, Dallas, Tex.: Southern Methodist Univ. Press, 1998), 37–9.

[16] Armando C. Alonzo, *Tejano Legacy: Rancheros and Settlers in South Texas, 1734–1900* (Albuquerque: Univ. of New Mexico Press, 1998), 10, 95–6, 280 (Alonzo opposes colonial theory); David Montejano, *Anglos and Mexicans in the Making of Texas, 1836–1986* (Austin: Univ. of Texas Press, 1987), 35, 38, 40–1; and Jennings, "In Sympathy," in Weber, 240.

standards that recognized the legally destabilizing effects of recent wars and approved most of the land grants. However, over time, land grants came to rest in the hands of Anglo-Americans because of their control of the market; their acquisitions increased with financial support from eastern and even European investors. The marriage of Anglo business-men and lawyers to wealthy Tejanas offered the latter expertise in the new regime in exchange for land; examples were the marriages of John Young, and after his death, of John McAllen to heiress Salomé Ballí of Rancho Santa Anita on the Gulf of Mexico. While fraudulent and even violent "land grabbing" also occurred, Anglos usually bought up prop-erties with purchasing power that cash- and credit-poor Mexicans lacked. Following the military and political occupation, economic co-lonialism thus advanced.[17]

As long as the cattle and sheep economy persisted, Anglo-Americans who moved into the subregion adjusted somewhat to Tejano life. By the turn of the century, however, commercial farming began to compete with stockraising in economic importance. Land speculators bought up ranches, subdivided them into farms for sale to Midwesterners to grow cotton and citrus fruit: "Tons of 'literature' were scattered through the agricultural states of the Mississippi Val-ley. Special rates were made for homeseekers' 'excursions.'" The inducements to colonize were fertile land at good prices and cheap labor, both from the local area and Mexico. With the building of railroads, U.S. labor contractors encouraged Mexican immigration, thus reinforcing the subregion's Tejano culture, even as Anglo-American farmers came to form a growing and powerful minority in South Texas.[18]

Commercial farming significantly worsened relations between Anglos and Tejanos as real estate developers designed a segregated society, lacking even the paternalistic aspects of the Anglo-dominated ranching society that had nevertheless remained culturally Hispanic. Brought in as farmworkers, Mexicans in agricultural counties lived in separate housing, attended separate schools, and were barred from

---

[17] Alonzo, 152–4, 222; Montejano, 38; for precedents of such intermarriage as related to land acquisition, see Andrés Reséndez, *Changing National Identities at the Frontier: Texas and New Mexico, 1800–1850* (Cambridge: Cambridge Univ. Press, 2005), 130–1.

[18] Charles Harger quoted in ibid., 106–10; and Daniel D. Arreola, *Tejano South Texas: A Mexican American Cultural Province*, Jack and Doris Smothers Series in Texas History, Life, and Culture, no. 5 (Austin: Univ. of Texas Press, 2002), 41.

public facilities, in the same fashion as blacks in the Deep South. According to historian David Montejano, "The first 'Mexican school' was established in Central Texas in 1902 (in Seguin) and the practice continued unabated until Mexican ward schools existed throughout the state. By 1930, 90 percent of South Texas schools were segregated." Resistance to this practice arose as early as 1911, when the Congreso Mexicanista, a statewide convention, declared, "It remains for us to say something of the exclusion of Mexican children from the Anglo-Saxon schools in the majority of the counties of the State of Texas." Such schools represented a deepening of the internal colony established in the previous century, a state into which later immigrants stepped.[19]

Open rebellion recurred along the border from 1915 to 1916 because Tejanos resented their eroding situation and were inspired by the Mexican Revolution of the same period. Problems over landownership, segregation, and general ill treatment led to the organization of a guerrilla group known as the *sediciosos*. The rebels proclaimed the Plan of San Diego, calling for "the independence and segregation of the States bordering upon the Mexican Nation, which are: TEXAS, NEW MEXICO, ARIZONA, COLORADO, AND UPPER CALIFORNIA, OF WHICH States the Republic of MEXICO was robbed in a most perfidious manner by North American imperialism." The sediciosos clearly recognized the Southwest as the conquered ethnic region, even as they confined their activities largely to their South Texas homeland. Their anarchist politics led them to challenge the modern nation-state, only thinking to annex their proposed republic to Mexico if such were later deemed appropriate. Comprised of Mexicans from both sides of the border, the sediciosos destroyed the property of both Anglos and Tejano ranchers who supported them. Vigilantes and the Rangers retaliated against Tejanos in general, with the U.S. Army attempting to secure the border. As World War I loomed in the background, the status of South Texas as an internal colony was rarely so evident.[20]

[19] Montejano, 160; and Rev. Pedro Grado, "Por la raza y para la raza," in Weber, 251.
[20] Quoted in John R. Chávez, *The Lost Land: The Chicano Image of the Southwest* (Albuquerque: Univ. of New Mexico Press, 1984), 79; Rosenbaum, 49–52; despite the ethnic conflict, many Mexican Americans served loyally in the U.S. armed forces – José A. Ramírez, "'To the Line of Fire, Mexican-Texans': The Tejano Community and World War I" (Ph.D. diss., Southern Methodist Univ., 2007), 226–31.

As in Quebec, Jamaica, or Ireland, the colonized population did not react to repression in the same way. While some Tejanos resisted violently, others withdrew to their small towns and ranches hoping to avoid confrontation. Some accommodated the authorities, assisting them enough to maintain peace, yet others sought assimilation into Anglo-American society. World War I provided many Tejanos an opportunity to show loyalty to the United States through military service, even as their relatives sometimes resisted the draft, as did many Quebecois and Irish. After the war, returning veterans and middle-class Tejanos made a concerted effort to organize groups dedicated to Americanization, merging several into the League of United Latin American Citizens (LULAC), at Corpus Christi in 1929. Indeed, LULAC's goal was "to develop within the members of our race the best, purest and most perfect type of a true and loyal citizen of the United States of America." LULAC stressed the learning of English and the acquiring of civic values for greater acceptance in the United States. To the extent that modernization and inclusion aimed at social equality, LULAC's goals helped the community. Women, for example, gradually gained fuller participation in the organization, as Alice Dickerson Montemayor argued, "If a woman is qualified to fill a general office and some of our membership draw the line on her just because of her sex, then they are not true Lulackers." On the other hand, traditionalists believed that LULAC's assimilationist outlook supported Anglo-American cultural hegemony, the final step in successful colonialism.[21]

Assimilation increased somewhat during the Great Depression when local, state, and national governments pressured Mexicans who had immigrated to the United States in the previous decades to depart. Known as repatriation, the policy was designed to rid the relief roles of Mexicans who had previously been recruited to work, especially in agriculture. Since jobs had disappeared, many Mexicans voluntarily left, some departed under threat of losing relief, others faced formal deportation. Most unfortunate was the "repatriation" of the Mexican American children of the immigrants. In 1931, when one Angeles Hernández de Sánchez, having lived in the United States for fourteen years, sought reentry into Texas after a visit to Mexico, a doctor falsely

---

[21] LULAC constitution quoted in Chávez, 113–16; and Montemayor quoted in Teresa Palomo Acosta and Ruthe Winegarten, *Las Tejanas: 300 Years of History,* Jack and Doris Smothers Series in Texas History, Life, and Culture, no. 10 (Austin: Univ. of Texas Press, 2003), 91.

reported that she had venereal disease. This led to her deportation with her two children, despite their being U.S.-born. With thousands of immigrants repatriated from their ethnically Mexican subregion, the remaining Tejanos tended to be more acculturated, though hardly assimilated into Anglo-American life.[22]

The intense patriotism of World War II furthered the acculturation of Mexican Americans as they served in the armed forces with distinction. The internal colony of South Texas showed signs of integration into the larger state and nation, as Tejanos increasingly sought assimilation, rather than the separation once desired by the sediciosos. Of a family in Texas before 1846, Private Armando Flores initially experienced inclusion in the United States in 1942, through military service: "That was the first time in my life that I had been called an American." Much larger than the World War I group before them, returning veterans joined LULAC and other acculturated organizations, such as the American GI Forum. The veterans and their allies at home struggled to overthrow school segregation and the other Jim Crow practices that subordinated Tejanos. Though they made important gains, complete success eluded them because of renewed recruitment of migrants from Mexico through the Bracero Program, designed to bring in temporary workers who usually became permanent.[23]

Tejanos could not completely assimilate, as had the Irish or Italians, because their homeland was attached to the country that continued to reinforce their Mexican culture through constant contact, especially immigration. This persistent ethnicity and Mexican precedence in Texas gave Tejanos a regional sense of identity not easily erased. Moreover, immigration of Mexicans into the Southwest as a whole constantly threatened to turn regional ethnicity into irredentism. Such a prospect, going against U.S. ideals of assimilation, frightened Anglo-Americans who worried their country would face the problems of nationality seen in Europe and elsewhere. Ironically, by continually recruiting Mexican labor, the United States kept South Texas an internal colony, and by repressing Tejano ethnicity, it fostered reactive solidarity among ethnic Mexicans. Domestically, then, the United

[22] Rodolfo Acuña, *Occupied America: A History of Chicanos*, 5th ed. (New York: Pearson/Longman, 2004), 211.
[23] Quoted in Maggie Rivas-Rodríguez, ed., *Mexican Americans and World War II* (Austin: Univ. of Texas Press, 2005), xvii.

States, like Mexico and Canada in the mid-twentieth century, contained ethnic regions that it had not satisfactorily incorporated despite a federal geopolitical framework.[24]

From Spanish to American Empire

Though still digesting internal colonies like South Texas, the United States entered another phase of imperialism, one more readily recognized as such because it reached overseas. Anglo-Americans had long considered expansion into the Caribbean; before the Civil War Southerners had particularly liked the idea of acquiring Cuba as a potential slave state. Although such interest receded after the war, by the 1890s as European powers rapidly picked up new colonies in Africa and Asia, their example influenced U.S. policy. Also, Spain's harsh treatment of Cuba repeatedly caused rebellion, which drew U.S. sympathy for a New World republican cause against an Old World monarchy. Finally, in 1898 the United States intervened on the side of the rebels, quickly dispatching the forces of declining Spain in the brief Spanish-American War. In the Caribbean the result was replacement of the aging Spanish Empire with a modern, more vigorous American Empire.[25]

In keeping with the stated purpose of its intervention, the United States granted Cuba formal independence after three years of occupation, but the relationship between the two states remained neocolonial. The new Cuban constitution included the Platt Amendment, a provision that relegated the island to the status of protectorate. Before U.S. forces departed, Cubans had to agree that its northern neighbor could return at will to preserve the new state's independence and constitutional provisions, especially the right to property (including U.S. investments). The Platt Amendment limited Cuba's freedom to conduct its own foreign and even domestic affairs. Indeed, the United States would intervene militarily in Cuba repeatedly until the 1930s when the Platt Amendment was repealed. Despite that, a neocolonial economic dependency continued until the 1950s.[26]

[24] D[onald] W[illiam] Meinig, *The Shaping of America: A Geographical Perspective on 500 Years of History*, vol. 3, *Transcontinental America, 1850–1915* (New Haven, Conn.: Yale Univ. Press, 1998), 352–3.

[25] Gordon K. Lewis, *Puerto Rico: Freedom and Power in the Caribbean*, with an introduction by Anthony Maingot, rev. ed. (Kingston, Jam.: Ian Randle Publishers, 2004), 73–4.

[26] Ibid., 78.

Though never as restive under Spain as Cubans, Puerto Ricans did repeatedly lobby for greater self-government within the empire until seized along with Cuba by the United States in 1898. Intense debate in Congress during and after the war focused around the future of the overseas colonies acquired from Spain. Were they to be prepared for statehood or independence? The debate centered on the race and ethnicity of the populations of Cuba and Puerto Rico, not to mention the Philippines and Guam. These populous lands had large cities and settled farms; removal, extermination, or assimilation, the policies applied to Indians seemed unworkable. Anglo-American pioneers could hardly overwhelm these places with sheer numbers as they had on the continent. Ultimately, Cuba (1901) and the Philippines (1946) gained independence, but Puerto Rico, as well as Guam, would remain colonies in all but name throughout the twentieth century.[27]

When U.S. forces landed in Puerto Rico in 1898, they received some local support from the populace that expected the same independence promised Cuba; however, the people would have to wait half a century before being allowed to vote on the issue. Over a two-year period, the U.S. military government immediately implemented some improvements. It built roads, distributed emergency food supplies, and fought small pox and yellow fever. Such concrete benefits, were unfortunately offset by regressive constitutional policies, including censorship of the press and elimination of Puerto Rico's Autonomous Charter, through which Spain had granted greater self-governance, albeit belatedly, to the island.[28]

In 1900 the U.S. Congress passed the Foraker Act providing for formal governance of the new U.S. possession. The Puerto Rican elite that had generally supported the U.S. invasion did not look favorably on the act because it was less democratic than the Autonomous Charter

[27] José Trías Monge, *Puerto Rico: The Trials of the Oldest Colony in the World* (New Haven, Conn.: Yale Univ. Press, 1997), 20; and Lewis, 80; interestingly, the debate delayed the admission of New Mexico to statehood, as that territory in light of the new colonies was also perceived as too hispanized – see John M. Nieto-Philips, *The Language of Blood: The Making of Spanish-American Identity in New Mexico, 1880s–1930s* (Albuquerque: Univ. of New Mexico Press, 2004), 83–5.

[28] Lewis, 88, 90, 69; and Diane Christopulos, "Puerto Rico in the Twentieth Century: A Historical Survey," in *Puerto Rico and Puerto Ricans: Studies in History and Society*, ed. Adalberto López and James Petras (New York: Schenkman Publishing Co., John Wiley & Sons, Halsted Press, 1974), 123.

of 1897. Though drawn up to preempt an independence movement on the island and scarcely implemented, the Spanish document set the standard for governance expected by the elite. The charter had provided for a stronger and more representative upper house than the Foraker Act did; moreover, Puerto Rico had possessed a vote in the Spanish parliament, but gained none in the U.S. Congress. Under the Foraker Act individual Puerto Ricans could vote for island, but not national, offices because the islanders lacked U.S. citizenship, considered an especially offensive situation since Congress could tax them. Under the act, Puerto Ricans also lacked trial by jury, another sign of their continuing status as a colonized people in a new empire.[29]

In 1917 the Jones Act improved the constitutional status of Puerto Rico relative to the United States, but not the colonial essence of the relationship. The upper house of the assembly became more representative, and significantly Puerto Ricans received U.S. citizenship. The latter reform permitted easier migration to the mainland and greater integration of individuals into U.S. society; the change also implied future statehood rather than independence for the island, which did not sit well with nationalists. To the chagrin of these and other Puerto Ricans, citizenship came together with the draft for World War I. Despite the reforms, power remained concentrated in the executive branch of government appointed by Washington, thus perpetuating the island's colonial status. From 1904 to 1924 the island's political parties divided over this constitutional issue. The Federalist/Unionist Party, which enjoyed a majority, favored independence or greater autonomy for Puerto Rico; on the other hand, the island's Republican Party, supported by planters and other business groups, favored statehood. At that time neither organization preferred the colonial status quo, politically or economically.[30]

Educationally, administration of the island by the United States led to some definite improvements, but also to some regressive conditions. By 1930 attendance at school jumped from 8 to 50 percent of youth, indicating progress. But since teachers and preachers from the mainland taught all classes in English, Puerto Ricans received little reinforcement of their culture. Moreover, the efficacy and utility of an English-only education in an overwhelmingly Spanish-speaking land was dubious. If

[29] Ibid., 124–6; see also Eugenio Fernández Méndez, *Historia cultural de Puerto Rico, 1493–1968* (San Juan, P.R.: Ediciones "El Cemí," 1970), 323–42.
[30] Christopulos, 129, 134.

one sought employment with the federal government, a U.S. corporation, or on the mainland, English might be necessary; otherwise an
individual communicated in Spanish in government, business, and society on the island. However, intellectuals feared that through such
education and economic development, Anglo-Americans would in
the long run impose the dominant culture of the United States on
Puerto Rico: "In the future there will be abundance, physical well-
being, a richness of fruits and metals; but there will be no country.
And if there is, it will belong to Americans and their sons and grandsons." Since the Puerto Rican wealthy and creole intellectuals were
overwhelmingly male, they imagined the island as feminine and, consequently, saw their impending dispossession as emasculation.[31]

Economically, the island became more subordinate to the powerful
U.S. economy than it had been to the Spanish. Mainland capitalists
purchased large amounts of land, putting even greater emphasis on
sugar than had Spain; about 44 percent of farmland came under cultivation of the crop. Subsidized by a tariff that squeezed out foreign
competitors, sugar became as lucrative for the United States as it had
been for the Caribbean's previous colonial rulers. Coffee and tobacco
were other cash crops that proved profitable for outside corporations.
Significantly, by 1930 subsistence crops dropped from 32 to 14 percent
of output as large planters bought out small farmers.[32]

Consequently, after the U.S. occupation of Puerto Rico, the land-
less and poverty-stricken population grew. Ironically, part of the problem resulted from the benefits of somewhat better health care provided
by the United States. Improved control of infectious diseases caused
a decline in the death rate (though less than in the rest of the hemisphere), which led to a larger population relative to the land base;
consequently, unemployment rose from 17 to 30 percent by 1930. In
addition, it took 104 days to buy food for a family, compared with the 70
days previously necessary. One major reason for the rise in the cost of
living was Puerto Rico's inclusion behind the U.S. tariff wall. With only
10 percent of the mainland's per capita income, Puerto Ricans had to
pay mainland prices since the tariff artificially increased the cost of
foreign products. Ironically, this harmed public health by denying the

[31] Luis Muñoz Rivera quoted in ibid., 133; and Magali Roy-Féquière, *Women,
Creole Identity, and Intellectual Life in Early Twentieth-Century Puerto Rico*. Puerto
Rican Studies (Philadelphia: Temple Univ. Press, 2004), 155–6.
[32] Christopulos, 129, 130–1.

population access to goods that could prevent certain diseases, such as hookworm. Due to the tariff, one quarter of the people could not afford shoes, a simple preventative for this foot disease. Thus, policies deemed good for the United States could prove injurious to an underrepresented colony. "One cannot observe Puerto Rican life close up without reaching the conclusion that every form of tutelage is morally degrading," remarked future Governor Luis Muñoz Marín, "This is the political illness of Puerto Rico and its only cure is a dose of unadulterated sovereignty."[33]

Significantly, the colonized status of Puerto Rico would ultimately lead to a colonized population of Puerto Ricans on the mainland. The socioeconomic changes fostered by the United States on the island stimulated immigration. By 1910 only 1500 islanders had left for the mainland, and even after the granting of citizenship, only 12,000 islanders departed by 1920. By 1930 50,000 left, and the pattern was set, as emigration boomed in the 1950s, ultimately creating a mainland Puerto Rican population as large as the island's. Though concentrated in the Northeast, Puerto Ricans did not form the same kind of ethnic region on the mainland as existed among ethnic Mexicans in the Southwest; their migratory settlement was more like that of African Americans who had previously moved to some of the same neighborhoods in the northeastern cities. As citizens, Puerto Ricans came and went from a homeland, in relative proximity to the Northeast, in ways that no "foreign" immigrant group could. Distinctly, the continued existence of Puerto Rico as a U.S. possession meant that all Puerto Ricans both on and off the island remained colonized.[34]

JAMAICA: FORMAL COLONIALISM

Although the American empire had replaced the Spanish in 1898, the British, who had started displacing Spain over two hundred years earlier, remained a colonial power in the West Indies into the twentieth century. While Great Britain expanded its empire in Africa and Asia in the nineteenth century, it continued to hold colonies from an earlier period of expansion in the Caribbean. In 1866 after Britain had

[33] Quoted in ibid., 138, 131–2.
[34] Ibid., 152; and Jorge Duany, *The Puerto Rican Nation on the Move: Identities on the Island and in the United States* (Chapel Hill: Univ. of North Carolina Press, 2002), 1–2.

declared Jamaica a Crown colony, a complete political dependency, all elected representation disappeared as the royal governor assumed full powers. London restored some self-government by 1884 when a legislative council, eventually with some elected members, began advising the governor and passing local laws. By 1900 a growing middle class, resulting from a more diverse economy and better education, began to lobby for a more representative government. Though this middle class was comprised of whites and coloreds, it saw its interests as counter to those of the small, controlling, white elite. In response, in 1921 the Wood Commission appointed by London recommended greater elective representation on the council, warning, nonetheless, "that the stability and progress of the West Indies are largely dependent upon the presence of the European element." The reform was implemented, but major changes did not occur until World War II.[35]

In 1944 the labor parties of Jamaica successfully pressured Britain into granting universal suffrage, demonstrating the increasing powers of working-class blacks. Having survived the worst of Nazi Germany's attacks, a weakened Britain nevertheless doubted its ability to hold together its empire. Despite this, only gradually did Jamaica win complete control over domestic affairs; the British only reluctantly relinquished executive powers because "Representative Government in the colonial empire was never intended to foreshadow any real transfer of power from the home government to some local authority." Although Britain eventually committed itself to granting independence to its colonies, the plans for this tended to be incremental and unfocused. For example, an experimental attempt at confederating Jamaica with the other British West Indian colonies would occur before full independence.[36]

QUEBEC: A PROVINCE IN FEDERATION AND EMPIRE

Even as the British expanded their empire worldwide in the nineteenth century, Canada, one of their earlier colonial acquisitions, served as an on-going geopolitical experiment in balancing global and regional

[35] Jean Grugel, *Politics and Development in the Caribbean Basin: Central America and the Caribbean in the New World Order* (Bloomington: Indiana Univ. Press, 1995), 58, 167; quoted in Denis M. Benn, *The Caribbean: An Intellectual History, 1774–2003* (Kingston, Jam.: Ian Randle Publishers, 2004), 52.

[36] Grugel, 117; and E. W. Evans quoted in Benn, 56–7.

visions. The province of Quebec, Canada's most salient ethnic region, had been the raison d'etre for federation. Ottawa attempted to incorporate the francophones by promoting the image of two founding nations in a transcontinental state, but the reality of multiple English provinces, an anglophone majority, and increasing power in the capital made that notion a myth. Though subordinate to the English, French culture in Canada continued to survive mainly because federation allowed French-speaking institutions, such as the school, farm, and the church to persist in Quebec. Generally residing in rural areas of both the region and the dominion, French Canadians continued to identify with an agricultural life, Roman Catholicism, and of course their language. Though farming declined as the century passed, the status of the French, especially in Quebec, remained distinct; the British did not assimilate them. In the 1880s one ethnic nationalist described the importance of the region thus: "the French race in America will never have any real influence for good unless it is solidly based in the province of Quebec, as in a fortress."[37]

Besides constant disputes with English Canadians over language, religion, and education, the French resented Canada's involvement in the British Empire, especially its military adventures. Representing the anglophone view in the 1890s, one politician gushed, "There is no doubt that we are in the age of empire. We will attend (in twenty-five years possibly) the birth of a sort of imperial assembly at Westminster. The grandest federation ever seen in the world." Recognizing their own historic victimization by the empire, French Canadians saw a larger British union making their voice even smaller than in their present federation. They especially opposed contributing to imperialism elsewhere, particularly if it threatened the conscription of their own youth. This was evident in the Boer War of 1899, when French Canadian opposition forced Britain to pay directly for any Canadian volunteers sent to South Africa. The grandson of the insurgent Papineau, Henri Bourassa, though a supporter of the federation under the crown, led the opposition on the Boer issue. Subsequently, he also resisted Canadian involvement in naval defense of the empire and denounced the draft during World War I. Beyond him, radicals in the provincial legislature

[37] Edward M. Corbett, *Quebec Confronts Canada* (Baltimore, Md.: Johns Hopkins Univ. Press, 1967), 20; and Jules-Paul Tardivel quoted in John Dickinson and Brian Young, *A Short History of Quebec*, 3rd ed. (Montreal: McGill – Queen's Univ. Press, 2003), 255, 250–3.

moved that Quebec accept breakup of the federation if the other provinces considered Quebec an obstacle to Canadian goals. Though federalism permitted much autonomy to Quebec, the province was tied to
the foreign policies of the British Empire. Despite this, the federation
survived as the twentieth century began.[38]

Throughout the nineteenth century, soil depletion and a shortage of
new farmland had caused many Quebecois to migrate to New England
or to Canada's cities, gradually loosening ties to both land and religion.
By 1919 the French-Canadian population reached a balance between
rural and urban areas, a phenomenon that required a rethinking of the
traditional rural strategy for survival. In the cities the French-speaking
basically provided unskilled labor for English manufacturing, slowly
making it obvious that the pastoral ideal was obsolete – workers needed
to improve their lives in the urban areas where they now lived. The
cultural bias against business as an English activity was gradually discarded as industrialization transformed Canada. Still, rather than large
private enterprises, cooperatives, especially credit unions, developed
successfully in Quebec; according to historian Susan Mann, "the family
served as a model, less in this instance for its hierarchical structure than
for its communitarian practice. The woman's devotion to the common
good taught children in particular the benefits of familial co-operation
and her contacts with other women in village and church organizations
formed the basic lines of social support." Under the continuing influence of the church, French ethnicity reflected a corporatist mentality
toward economics in the twenties and thirties. However, the provincial
economy changed dramatically when World War II created great demand in the United States for pulpwood, nonferrous metals, and hy-
droelectric power, all abundant in Quebec. Consequently, industry
boomed, the population urbanized further, and the ethnic region became increasingly prosperous, secular, and autonomous. This evolution
would lead the province of Quebec repeatedly to challenge its status in
the federation, just as Canada increasingly asserted its sovereignty vis-à-
vis the empire.[39]

---

[38] William Lyon Mackenzie King quoted in Ramsay Cook et al., *Histoire générale du
Canada*, Boréal compact, 18, trans. from English to French, Michel Buttiens
et al. ([Montreal]: Éditions du Boréal, 1990), 485, my translation of quotation;
Dickinson and Young, 250–3; and Corbett, 29–30.

[39] Ibid., 22–3; and Susan Mann [Trofimenkoff], *The Dream of Nation: A Social and
Intellectual History of Quebec*, Carleton Library Series, 1982, 2nd ed. (Montreal:
McGill – Queen's Univ. Press, 2002), 241–2.

THE IRISH FREE STATE

As Great Britain expanded globally in the nineteenth century, its oldest overseas colony remained Ireland, particularly Ulster, the "plantation" established by Protestant English and lowland Scots. Though the Irish, dominated by Anglo lords, had acknowledged the suzerainty of the English monarch, direct British control beyond Dublin and Ulster remained limited until 1801. Threatened by Irish Catholic unrest during the French Revolution, Britain imposed the Act of Union on Ireland, forcing the island into the United Kingdom, supposedly on an equal basis with England, Wales, and Scotland. This was, however, no federation since the union denied regional self-government; Britain dissolved the Irish parliament in Dublin, replacing it with parliamentary representation in London. Prime Minister William Pitt candidly expressed Britain's motives: "The Union is the only answer to preventing Ireland becoming too great and powerful." Although the Protestant Anglo-Irish had controlled the Dublin parliament, all semblance of Irish sovereignty disappeared with union.[40]

Unfortunately for the vast Irish Catholic majority, all political and economic power remained in the hands of Protestants under the new geopolitical arrangement, as well as the old. A whole series of restrictions depriving Catholics of their civil rights continued; for example, they were denied the vote, barred from parliament, excluded from the legal profession, prohibited firearms, and forbidden to keep public schools. Though Catholics were officially emancipated from many of these onerous civil restrictions in 1829, the economic oppression went on for decades. Protestants, who owned virtually all the land, would transfer it only to their own, keeping Catholics in their traditional roles as laborers or tenant farmers. Squeezed onto tiny farms that they could not improve, the poor became dependent on the potato for survival, a crop that failed in 1846-7. The result was the Great Famine that killed thousands, led to massive emigration to North America, as well as a failed rebellion in 1848. Despite reforms in the late nineteenth century, agitation for Irish home rule increased; indeed, the threat

[40] Quoted in Michael Hechter, *Internal Colonialism: The Celtic Fringe in British National Development, 1536–1966* (Berkeley and Los Angeles: Univ. of California Press, 1975), 72–3.

of violent resistance confronted the British Empire at its very doorstep.[41]

In the 1890s with the political push for home rule, Ireland experienced an ethnic resurgence in culture and economics, becoming a full-blown nationalist movement. Linguists revived the Gaelic tongue with greater consequent interest in Irish literature and history. In economics nationalists launched a cooperative movement in agriculture and developed specifically Irish industry. While pushing to develop the homeland internally, Irish nationalists, like French Canadians, made parallels between themselves and the Boers of South Africa, defending their transplanted Dutch homeland against British imperialism. All of this Protestants in the north perceived with alarm since their own positions would deteriorate and the Catholic majority would gain the upper hand in any new state governed from Dublin. By the eve of World War I when the British parliament seemed likely to pass home rule, Protestant military forces formed to prevent Ulster from leaving the United Kingdom with the rest of Ireland. In response Irish nationalists also organized themselves militarily for possible civil war.[42]

While thousands of Irishmen, both Protestant and Catholic, enlisted in the British army to fight the Germans, radical nationalists with Irish American support saw the opportunity of conflict overseas to overthrow British rule in Ireland. In the Easter Uprising of 1916, British forces, over the course of a week, succeeded in finally crushing an Irish rebellion that had received some German support. The subsequent execution and deportation of political dissidents led to greater popular support of the rebels than might otherwise have been the case. British application of the draft to Ireland in 1918 only exacerbated discontent. Significantly, Sinn Fein, the nationalist political party, demanded an independent republic based on the principle of self-determination advocated by U.S. President Woodrow Wilson. Irish guerillas soon engaged in wide-ranging attacks on British installations, attacks that naturally led to reprisals by the empire.[43]

---

[41] Ibid., 76; for a comparison between colonial rule in Ireland and India, see Barbara Bush, *Imperialism and Colonialism*, History: Concepts, Theory, and Practice (Harlow, UK: Pearson, Longman, 2006), 70–1.

[42] David Fitzpatrick, "Ireland since 1870," in *The Oxford Illustrated History of Ireland*, ed. R[obert] F[itzroy] Foster (New York: Oxford Univ. Press, 1989), 225–7.

[43] Ibid., 235, 237–9, 241; and Bush, 72–3.

With the end of World War I, increasing international negative publicity pressured Britain to settle the matter of Ireland's status. The United Kingdom offered to create the Irish Free State as a dominion under the Crown on a par with others, such as Canada. However, since Ulster would have separate statehood with its own parliament, nationalists found the dual statehood proposal unacceptable. Consequently, while Northern Ireland began operations as a dominion under the proposal in 1921, violence continued both in the south and north for several years. In 1922 a majority of Irish nationalists resigned themselves to the truncated Irish Free State, a dominion of the crown but only until 1949. Then the Republic of Ireland declared its complete independence, to which Britain ominously responded, "in no event will Northern Ireland or any part thereof cease to be part of His Majesty's dominions and of the United Kingdom without the consent of the parliament of Northern Ireland."[44]

Even as the British Empire achieved its greatest extent at the opening of the twentieth century, Ireland gained its independence after nearly eight hundred years of colonialism by its British neighbor. Exhibiting the extremely complex evolution of an ethnic regional community – a loose assortment of independent chiefdoms, a titular kingdom, a collection of autonomous earldoms, a semidependent realm of a foreign monarch, a colonial plantation, a fully dependent realm, an imperial dominion, an independent republic – Ireland illustrated the multiplicity of geopolitical patterns possible by the early twentieth century. Including Ulster, Ireland also reflected the complex allegiances of individuals to the entities they viewed as their homelands, nations, and states. The harmonious aligning of these loyalties proved nearly impossible because of the competing forces involved. Because of colonialism, in Ulster Protestants and Catholics claimed the same homeland, even as they gave their allegiance to separate sovereign states, the United Kingdom and the Republic, respectively. Even a federal solution to this conundrum escaped the imagination.[45]

BRITTANY: ETHNIC REGION

The development of nationalism in Brittany, an ethnic region within the boundaries of the French state, occurred amidst the rise of similar

[44] Ireland Act quoted in Foster, 267, 250–2.
[45] Ibid., 252; and Bush, 62.

anti-imperial movements in Ireland and other parts of Europe just before World War I. In the nineteenth century there had been Breton regionalists who had sought decentralization autonomy from Paris especially in cultural affairs. Regionalists reacted negatively to the colonial paternalism of Parisian educators touting their methods, "as applicable to little Flemings, little Basques, little Bretons, as to little Arabs and little Berbers." Between 1910 and 1914, however, the Parti Nacionaliste Breton appeared, a party that hoped to become a mass-based movement for independence. Though hoping to avoid fragmentation, the movement in its various guises would fail to achieve its aims, in the long run remaining a loose collection of small splinter groups. These nevertheless kept Bretons conscious of their distinct regional ethnicity at a time when empires straddled the globe.[46]

The earliest Breton nationalists exhibited some of the problems their movement would face throughout its twentieth-century history – an excess of idealism with little practical connection to the masses of Bretons whose primary identity remained French. In 1910 the ethnic issue arose rather innocuously over a statue depicting a Breton maid at the knees of a French maiden. In 1911 one Camille Le Mercier d'Erm, in an act of political theater designed to avenge this insult to Breton sovereignty, disrupted the unveiling ceremony for the statue. Though he went to jail, his act of civil disobedience failed to fire much interest among his compatriots. In his writing a few years later, he compared his homeland to Finland, Poland, Bohemia, and Ireland, all ethnic regions that would one day become independent states.[47]

Unfortunately for their movement, Breton nationalists could not form a coherent program to achieve their goals. Thinkers more than activists, these "leaders" did not know how to win followers and organize them. While all the patriots shared a love for Brittany, they divided their meager numbers over ideological issues. Some thought of themselves primarily as regionalists, desiring autonomy within France; others were fundamentally separatists. Bretonnants stressed the

---

[46] Quoted in Eugen Weber, *Peasants into Frenchmen: The Modernization of Rural France, 1870–1914* (Stanford, Calif.: Stanford Univ. Press, 1976), 489–90; Jack E. Reece, *The Bretons against France: Ethnic Minority Nationalism in Twentieth-Century Brittany* (Chapel Hill: Univ. of North Carolina Press, 1977), 80.

[47] Ibid., 81–82; Weber, 490; for further comment on national personification, see Jack Hayward, *Fragmented France: Two Centuries of Disputed Identity* (Oxford: Oxford Univ. Press, 2007), 55–6.

importance of learning the language as a sign of ethnic identity, while Gallos emphasized the greater significance of history, since they themselves often did not know the ancestral tongue: "it is thanks to Breton history that our language has survived." The groups also divided over the significance of customs, the church, and socialist ideals. Such factionalism reflected a collection of highly individualistic intellectuals and did not bode well for a cohesive mass movement. Consequently, before 1914 ethnic nationalism had a negligible impact in Brittany.[48]

The first Breton nationalist movement ended when World War I stimulated French patriotism against the invading Germans. However, the Allies' emphasis on self-determination for subject nationalities, not to mention the Irish example, encouraged a second Breton movement to get underway in 1918. Disproportionately high casualties among Bretons led ethnic nationalists to blame Paris, as well as the region's own elite for the poor educational and vocational skills that placed the region's soldiers on the front lines. As in Quebec and Ireland, activists resented the conscription used to fill the French army with Bretons. As middle-class intellectuals, they identified with the working class that filled the ranks, though they had few ties with common laborers. The role of class in ethnic regionalism was evident in the activists' charges that the Breton elite identified more with the French state than the region.[49]

Formed in 1918 the Group, Regionaliste Breton, influenced by the movement for the Irish Free State, admired German culture believed to be rooted in a common Celtic heritage with Brittany's. The group demanded Celtic history and language courses in the schools of the region, but split over other issues along ideological lines. The more radical elements called for independence from France, seeing Paris as a cultural, as well as administrative and political enemy; in 1919 one delegation went before Woodrow Wilson insisting on "the right of national self-determination." Interestingly, the radicals, known as the Gallos, had assimilated most to French culture. But this fact made them feel more subordinated and hostile because they had lost much of their

---

[48] Quoted in Reece, 83–4; see also Hayward, 64–5.
[49] Reece, 86–8; for more on the impact of growing national unity on the ethnic regions of France, see Graham Robb, *The Discovery of France: A Historical Geography from the Revolution to the First World War* (New York: W. W. Norton, 2007), 324–8.

Breton culture to the larger nation. Federalists, on the other hand, sought greater autonomy for their region and tended personally to re-tain more of their Breton heritage. Similar relationships of accultura-tion to ethnic political stance could be seen in other regions throughout the Atlantic World.[50]

In the interwar period the Breton nationalists survived and had some influence. Organized locally, their councils published small newspapers promoting their ideas. In their press the separatist Gallos especially criticized the Breton-speaking clergy for exercising their cultural advan-tages to promote conservative pro-French positions; regionalists came under attack for a romantic love of country that lacked a political agenda. Increasingly, the Breton nationalists became frustrated with their own middle class, "half French in blood values and conduct," for its lack of financial support. This naturally meant the councils remained too weak to seriously challenge the unitary state that remained at the core of the global French Empire.[51]

Despite their fascist inclinations, such as their belief in Germanic cultural superiority, the Breton nationalists advanced some ideas rele-vant to their peers elsewhere. Pacifists, they condemned the militarism of dominant nation-states that not only led to war, but to the imperial subordination of nationalities like their own. Significantly, reflecting the influence of anarchism, Breton nationalists called for a federation of European ethnic groups, rather than of the current multiethnic states ruled by dominant nations. As a result, these Breton activists supported the desire of Alsatians, reacquired from Germany after World War I, for autonomy within France. Pro-French Bretons in the National Assembly roundly condemned the ethnic nationalists for supporting Germanic customs in Alsace. Breton nationalists likely earned much animosity over this issue from the French, given that nation's continuing fear of Germany. In spite of their marginal position in French politics, these activists did successfully encourage Breton cultural revival within one of the world's most cohesive nation-states at a height in its imperial trajectory.[52]

---

[50] Quoted in Weber, 100; Reece, 89–91.
[51] Quoted in ibid., 96–7; cf. Hayward, 47.
[52] Reece, 98–100; for a comparison of the impact on regions of French and U.S. constitutions, see Louis Rougier, *La France à la recherche d'une constitution* (Paris: Recueil Sirey, 1952), 165.

Antiimperial Dreams

Roughly between 1880 and 1945, natives and homelands about the Atlantic – the Wolof of Senegal, the Tejanos of South Texas, the Bretons of Brittany – experienced the weight of empire increasing globally. Though formal colonialism as seen in Jamaica and Senegal spread more commonly beyond the North Atlantic World, where it had seen its heyday earlier, informal colonialism persisted in Cuba, Liberia, and Tlaxcala. There the processes of socioeconomic subordination based on race and ethnicity survived in neocolonial or internal colonial patterns despite official political independence or regional autonomy. These situations indicated that even after the peak of formal empire and colonialism, their underlying processes would continue. Yet anti-imperial trends appeared in these places as well as others – U.S. citizenship in Puerto Rico, home rule in Ireland, and national development in Quebec. Though self-determination and federalism were largely dreams before World War II, fuller implementation of these ideals would follow.[53]

[53] Frantz Fanon, *Les damnés de la terre* (Paris: François Maspero, 1961), 113–14; Amílcar A. Barreto, *Language, Elites, and the State: Nationalism in Puerto Rico and Quebec* (Westport, Conn.: Praeger, 1998), 7–8, 19–21; for a comparison of federalism in Germany before and after World War II, see David McKay, *Designing Europe: Comparative Lessons from the Federal Experience* (Oxford: Oxford Univ. Press, 2001), 87–90.

CHAPTER SEVEN

POSTCOLONIAL VISIONS

INTERNATIONALISM AND DECOLONIZATION, 1945–1975

In the 1930s formal imperialism reached its zenith with the rise of Fascist Italy, Nazi Germany, Imperial Japan, and Falangist Spain, the last a figment of its former – transatlantic expanse. Taking on the very symbols of imperial Rome, these countries, especially Germany, asserted a right of conquest based on scientific racism. Rather than simply rationalizing their aggression on the grounds of religion or civilization, as had most previous European powers, these states at least tacitly defended their actions based on the innate superiority of their dominant peoples. Predictably, in World War II they clashed with the traditional empires and their updated equivalents, the United States and the Soviet Union. The defeat of the Axis powers would have the effect not only of discrediting racist ideologies, but the very designs of empire itself, designs they had taken to the extreme. Among the imperial possessions taken from the Axis were Libya from Italy, Korea from Japan, and East Prussia from Germany. More surprising, seeking a new anti-imperialist order, the victorious Allies would liberate many of their own colonies and again envision global federation through the United Nations. Thus encouraged, colonized peoples and their homelands about the Atlantic and elsewhere would openly strive for self-determination and a place in the new world order.[1]

---

[1]   Edward W. Said, *Orientalism* (New York: Random House, Vintage Books, 1978–9), 36, 39, 55, 63; and Walter D. Mignolo, *Local Histories/Global Designs: Coloniality, Subaltern Knowledges, and Border Thinking*, Princeton Studies in Culture/Power/ History (Princeton, N.J.: Princeton Univ. Press, 2000), 280–1; for practical applications of postcolonial theory, see Amos Sawyer, *Beyond Plunder: Toward Democratic Governance in Liberia* (Boulder, Colo.: L. Rienner, 2005), 6, 59–60, 78.

The Protectorate of Morocco

Among the late acquisitions in the European Scramble for Africa, Morocco would lose, then regain self-determination from 1904 to 1956. Though the country had experienced European imperialism as early as the fifteenth century when the Portuguese and Spanish seized the ports of Ceuta and Melilla, respectively, Morocco's independence began seriously eroding in the nineteenth century. (See Map 7.1.) Most influential in the nation's affairs then were the British. The sultanate lost sovereign control of the realm to France and Spain after repeated interference in Moroccan affairs by those countries, as well as Britain and Germany. In 1904 France and Spain agreed to spheres of influence within Morocco, by 1908 the overthrow of the Sultan Abdel Aziz in a dynastic struggle permitted the complete invasion of the country by these European powers; and in 1912 they agreed to separate protectorates over Morocco, permitting complete military occupation of its territory.[2]

Under indigenous rule, the sultan had a functioning state that varied, depending on the period, in its control of a country comprised of Berbers who spoke their own language and those who spoke Arabic. The sultan appointed caids to lead nomadic tribes and small towns, with the consultation of elders, and pashas to administer large towns. The Berber-speakers, autonomous compared with the speakers of Arabic, relied more on elders in a more representative political administration. One late nineteenth-century Moroccan commented that the Middle Atlas region had a "habit of submitting when the Makhzan [central authority] was there and of revolting once its back was turned." By the early twentieth century, dynastic rivalries, partially instigated by European interventions, had weakened the sultanate further. For example, in the Rif, a mountainous area of northern Morocco, the sultan's troops had no control over a local pretender to the throne, though the Berbers there continued to pay tribute and taxes, as well as trade with the rest of the nation. The Moroccan state's inability to stop assaults on Europeans in its own territory or control tribal raids into Algeria provided Spain and France with pretexts for intervention.[3]

[2]   Sebastian Balfour, *Deadly Embrace: Morocco and the Road to the Spanish Civil War* (New York: Oxford Univ. Press, 2002), 6–7.
[3]   Quoted in C. R. Pennell, *Morocco: From Empire to Independence* (Oxford, U.K.: Oneworld Publications, 2003), 125–6, 131–2; and Balfour, 6, 13.

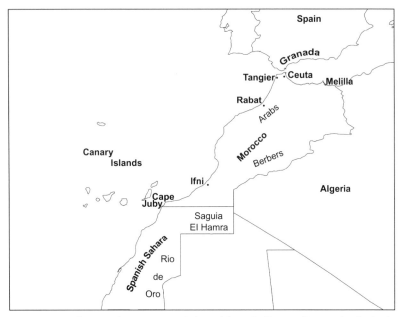

Map 7.1. Northwest Africa, c. 1900. Adapted from Gellner and Micaud, eds. *Arabs and Berbers*, 16–17. Cartography by Cassingham and Foxworth, Courtesy of the Edwin J. Foscue Map Library, SMU.

By 1912 the French, primarily from Algeria, occupied the vast majority of Morocco and instituted a thorough colonial administration, going well beyond the usual protectorate involving outside control of a nation's foreign affairs. The French resident general approved all appointments made by the sultan, who was reduced to a figurehead; French civil officials supervised all Moroccan leaders at all levels wherever possible; in the cities of Fez and Casablanca, Europeans controlled all aspects of governance though they did not form majorities in either place. In these and other cities colonists from France, as well as Italy, would settle in substantial numbers with several thousand more in the countryside as farmers. As early as 1919, these colonists received an elected assembly, that eventually expanded to include native members, but exercised little power. Nevertheless, the new socioeconomic order assured European dominance. Unsurprisingly, Moroccan military resistance continued in the interior until crushed by French forces in 1936.[4]

---

[4]   Pennell, 141, 148, 152–3.

Advancing from its historic enclaves at Ceuta and Melilla in 1908, Spain's occupation of northern Morocco resulted partially from the loss of the remnants of the Spanish Empire in America to the United States in 1898. Fearing further losses, Spain secured its late nineteenth-century African colonies in Guinea and Western Sahara (Rio de Oro) by convincing France to recognize these as Spanish possessions. Also, anticipating foreign encroachment on the metropolis itself, Spain persuaded France to agree to the partition of Morocco, allowing Spanish control of the African territory directly across the Strait of Gibraltar, as well as a southern stretch of territory connected to Rio de Oro. Moreover, after 1898 Spain, fearing for its own unity as Basque and Catalan regionalists increasingly called for autonomy, saw imperialism as a way to rebuild Spanish nationalism. Consequently, the desire to recover imperial prestige, not to mention economic advantage, played into the decision to embark on a new colonial venture.[5]

The Spanish military that had lost prestige and experienced the problems of readjustment to the metropolis after 1898 saw the venture in Morocco as redemptive, but imperialism was not entirely popular on the peninsula. By early 1909 the occupation required additional troops, so Madrid called up the reserves, but in so doing caused rioting against "conscription" in the Catalan regionalist stronghold of Barcelona. The central government reacted by declaring martial law throughout Spain, thus using the army as police against its own people. Within two years the army was drafting striking Spanish railway workers and securing the borders of the Moroccan colony (a protectorate in name only) in the face of French competition. Only a year into the colonial venture, imperialism was coming home to roost.[6]

SPANISH INTERNAL COLONIALISM

However, the conquest of northern Morocco would involve years of warfare. Though neutral during World War I, Spain still found itself fighting recalcitrant tribes that threatened mining operations in the colony. In 1921 resistance reached a peak when a Spanish force met crushing defeat at the battle of Anual. Blaming politicians for the disaster, Captain General Primo de Rivera subsequently rebelled against

[5] Balfour, 4, 8–9.
[6] Shlomo Ben-Ami, *The Origins of the Second Republic in Spain* (New York: Oxford Univ. Press, 1978), 2.

the parliamentary government, establishing a dictatorship in cooperation with King Alfonso XIII, to end corruption in the metropolis and
solve the problem of Morocco. Between 1924 and 1927, Primo de
Rivera, personally in command at the decisive battle in Alhucemas
Bay, succeeded in pacifying all of Spanish Morocco, thereby restoring
the army's prestige. Reflecting the army's renewed self-image as the
nation's unifying force, the dictator proceeded to abolish a measure of
Catalan autonomy instituted the previous decade. Thus did Spain's
colonial venture continue to impact domestic events.[7]

By 1930, however, Primo de Rivera went into exile because his regime had lost popularity due to his oppressive policies and the worldwide depression. A year later the king abdicated in the face of his
complicity with the dictator and the rise of republican and regionalist
sympathies. Though the desire for regional autonomy existed in Galicia
and Valencia, as well as the Basque Country, Catalonia proved to be the
most insistent in its demands during the 1930s. In that northeastern
region, insurgents immediately declared a "Catalan state" within what
they imagined as a "confederation with other Spanish Republics."
Though the new central government would not implement a confederation for all of Spain, Madrid did return autonomy to Catalonia, permitting it to pass regional legislation, to police itself, to establish its own
universities, and to make Catalan an official language with Castilian.
This devolution of power, or internal decolonization, satisfied the region to the point of making it the most stable in Spain from 1931 to
1936, the period of the Second Republic. Unfortunately, extremist
politics from communist to fascist, fragmented the country's republican
dream, leading to the Spanish Civil War of 1936–9, a conflict having
deep roots in the Moroccan colonial adventure.[8]

Domestic unrest fueled fascism, represented by the Falangist Party,
which demanded law and order in a unitary state stressing traditional
Spanish values and nationalism, to the point of imagining a Hispanic
race. Needless to say, army officers found this ideology appealing, and
a mutiny led by General Francisco Franco Bahamonde broke out in
Morocco. Though right-wing rebellions against the republic exploded
throughout Spain, with early successes in provinces of the north and

[7] Ibid., 3–4; and Balfour, 9.
[8] Quoted in Ben-Ami, 249–50; Stanley G. Payne, *Spain's First Democracy: The
     Second Republic, 1931–1936* (Madison: Univ. of Wisconsin Press, 1993), 22, 33,
     201–6.

west, the Army of Africa assumed leadership of the nationalist insurgents as it crossed the Straits of Gibraltar from Ceuta. Comprised of
officers and men who had "pacified" Morocco under Primo de Rivera,
an army that identified with empire returned to apply oppressive colonial tactics at home. Indeed, Franco himself would later characterize
himself in colonial terms: "My years in Africa live within me with
indescribable force."[9]

The geopolitical issues of empire involved in the civil war revealed
themselves in both external and domestic affairs. Internationally, the
conflict became a preview for the imperial clashes of World War II as
fascist Germany and Italy supported Franco while the Soviet Union,
Mexico, and leftist American, British, and other volunteers joined the
Second Republic. Internally, the nationalists' imperial vision of a unitary Spain and the republicans' regionalist vision reflected their geopolitical differences, but these issues intermixed with others to create
complex alignments. At the beginning of the Civil War, the republic
offered the Basque Provinces renewed autonomy, as an inducement to
keep them loyal; Vizcaya and Guipuzcoa accepted, but Alava and Navarre, valuing their traditional Carlist Catholicism more highly than
autonomy, joined the Falangists under Franco. In Vizcaya and Guipuzcoa where "Basque nationalists" found themselves caught between left-
wing labor unions and right-wing religious, landed, and business groups;
their party nevertheless supported the republic: "Given the struggle
between the citizens and fascism, between the Republic and monarchy,
the principles of the PNV [Partido Nacionalista Vasco] lead unavoid-
ably to the side of citizens." On the other hand, Basque identification
with monarchical Carlism and hierarchical clericalism turned Alava
and Navarre toward the Falange and its ideas of Spanish national consolidation built on imperialism. Across the international border, French
Basques sympathized with the plight of their relatives, but dared not
support any movement toward regional autonomy as the unitary French
state strongly opposed separatist politics. Wisely, aware of explosive
possibilities of such regional and international politics, France sought
to keep itself and other states neutral during the Spanish Civil War.[10]

[9] Quoted in Balfour, 202.
[10] Quoted in Marianne Heiberg, *The Making of the Basque Nation*, Cambridge
Studies in Social Anthroplogy, 66 (New York: Cambridge Univ. Press, 1989),
87, 85–6; and Philippe Veyrin, *Les Basques de Labourd, de Soule et de Basse
Navarre: Leur histoire et leurs traditions*, new ed. (n.p.: Arthaud, 1955), 192.

Basque refugees streamed across the Pyrenees, as Franco's forces
overcame the Basque republicans early. Isolated and divided, some of
these Basques sought to negotiate a settlement with Franco's Carlist
and Italian allies, but failed to get the guarantee of autonomy sought.
The major fighting centered on Bilbao where the attacking "nationalist" army included Basque brigades from Navarre, a division of
Italians, German air support, Spanish foreign legionnaires, and
Moroccan troops. Clearly, that army reflected the imperialism, rather
than the nationalism, of Franco's movement; indeed, the colonial
troops were known for their Moorish attire. During the battle, the
Germans carried out the infamous aerial bombardment of Guernica,
presaging World War II's new tactics of total warfare on civilian
populations. After the fall Bilbao, its new mayor gave the nationalists' victory its imperial significance: "This horrible, evil nightmare
called Euzkadi ... has been defeated forever . . . Vizcaya is again
a piece of Spain through pure and simple military conquest." The
dream of an autonomous Basque homeland would have no place in
Franco's unitary Spain.[11]

In 1939 Catalans fled into France as Barcelona fell to the nationalists
with Madrid following a few months later. Of course, Franco's victorious regime quashed all regional autonomy as it centralized power in the
national capital. Under his dictatorship Spanish nationalism was such
that languages and customs other than the Castilian were suppressed:
"It is the obligation of the public authorities to repress, to the extent
possible, these practices ... which help obscure the Spanish con-
science." Even Basque given names and Catalan greetings were forbidden in the new totalitarian society. Beyond regionalism, the public
practice of religions other than Catholicism was also prohibited, in
a policy reminiscent of the anti-Semitism of the Catholic Kings in
fifteenth-century Granada. To enforce social conformity and govern-
mental uniformity a vast administrative apparatus, akin to the colonial
bureaucracy of Morocco, reached deep into the local level. Despite the
regime's totalitarianism, the post-colonial dream of Basque, not to mention Catalan, self-determination, survived because the regime needed
the industrial and commercial strength of these regions too much to
destroy their economic underpinnings.[12]

---

[11] Quoted in Heiberg, 89, 88; and Balfour, 202.
[12] Quoted in Heiberg, 90–1; cf. Maximiano García Venero, *Historia del nacionalismo vasco*, 3rd ed. (Madrid: Editora Nacional, 1969), 622–5.

Since World War II broke out only months after the end of the Spanish Civil War, Franco declared neutrality knowing his country was weakened from its own struggle and exposed to British and French attack. His sympathies, however, clearly lay with the Axis powers. In late 1940, for example, he used the war as an opportunity to annex the international city of Tangier briefly to Spanish Morocco, and a year later he actually sent a division of volunteers to fight with Germany against the Soviets. The regime set up the Council of Hispanity attempting to recoup Spain's prestige among its former transatlantic colonies by appealing to their common racial heritage, but, except for Argentina, those nations reacted negatively and aligned themselves with the Allies. Germany's occupation of France stimulated further imperial fantasies within the Falangist imagination. In the event of victory by the Axis, Spain saw itself taking over French Morocco and even advancing into the rest of the French and British colonies of West Africa – "that daughter caressed by the sun" – thus reasserting sexist and racist medieval imperial ambitions that had been distracted by the lure of the Americas. Unfortunately for such imperialistic visionaries, in late 1942 the Allies landed in Morocco, meeting only token resistance from the forces of Vichy France. After 1945 the Falangist party and its symbols reflecting Roman imperialism, receded into the background.[13]

Occupied Brittany

The German invasion of France during World War II threatened that nation not merely with the loss of its empire in Morocco and West Africa, but with the loss of its own territorial integrity. With the German advance, militant Breton nationalists saw an opportunity to establish an autonomous or even an independent Brittany in the event of a Nazi victory. Seeing Paris rather than Berlin as the enemy, militant Bretons, by no means all regionalists, decided to collaborate with the Germans against France. Even before the invasion two Breton leaders, Olier Mordrel and Fanch Debauvais, went to Berlin hoping to secure provincial independence in case of a German victory; they even spread propaganda to French troops, arguing that "No true Breton has the right to die for France." Such activities naturally caused the French government to suppress other Breton activists at home. With the German advance, these collaborators received permission to recruit Breton

[13] Donoso Cortés quoted in Balfour, 317.

prisoners of war for a regional military force to assist in the occupation of the hopefully soon-to-be "autonomous" Brittany. Though fewer than 150 prisoners joined the force, they followed the German army into the province.[14]

Unfortunately for the militants, the fall of Paris and the establishment of the Vichy government occurred without the complete dismemberment of France. German armies, however, would occupy the north and west, including Brittany, allowing the militants some room to maneuver. They set up the Conseil National Breton to coordinate their activities. They imagined this organization as the nucleus of a future "authoritarian, hierarchical, corporative, and anti-Semitic state," obviously catering to the Nazi occupiers, as well as reflecting their own attitudes. Playing the Vichy government and the Breton militants against each other, the Nazis did not formally recognize the new organization, but funded some of its publishing activities. As Vichy officials gained the upper hand in this game, moderate Breton nationalists replaced the militants. As Marshal Pétain hinted at "administrative decentralization and reconstitution of France's historic provinces," Breton moderates saw an opportunity for autonomy under the Vichy government in contrast to the highly centralized French republics that had previously divided Brittany into five disconnected departments.[15]

Under the Vichy government Breton nationalism reached a climax as a modern political movement. By early 1942 under moderate leadership, calling for autonomy rather than independence, the Breton Nationalist Party had three thousand to four thousand members, many times the number before the war. The organization extended throughout Brittany; the group's publications and radio broadcasts gained wide audiences; voluntary contributions poured into the coffers; and the party actually staged a large rally of fifteen hundred in Paris. Furthermore, behind the moderates operated a disgruntled faction of militants who still desired independence and actually formed paramilitary units, modeled on the Irish Republican Army. The militants trained secretly in remote areas, but since their hopes necessarily lay with a final

---

[14] Quoted in Jack E. Reece, *The Bretons against France: Ethnic Minority Nationalism in Twentieth-Century Brittany* (Chapel Hill: Univ. of North Carolina Press, 1977), 151, 149–50, 152–3.

[15] Ibid., 156–8; for more context, see Roger Price, *A Concise History of France*, 2nd ed. Cambridge Concise Histories (Cambridge: Cambridge Univ. Press, 2005), 282–314.

German victory in the war, the occupation authorities did not overreact to reports of their activities.[16]

Indeed, the Vichy government began making concessions to the increasingly powerful Breton movement. The regime approved the teaching of the peninsula's history, as well as the use of the Breton language, in the schools; optional courses in the language and extra pay for instructors were also implemented. In addition, Vichy named an official sympathetic to Brittany as prefect of the whole region, implicitly recognizing the peninsula's historic integrity. Subsequently, the prefect established the Comité Consultatif de Bretagne to advise him on matters relating to Breton culture, again acknowledging a distinct ethnic region within France, a policy essentially taboo since the French Revolution. As a result, about a hundred folklore societies became active in the traditional province. To the new council, however, the prefect appointed no activists, militant or moderate, only regionalists interested in cultural preservation rather than political autonomy or independence.[17]

These regionalist successes proved short lived as German prospects of winning World War II dimmed by early 1943. Breton nationalists began to pull back from their open support for the occupation forces, as violence between the Nazis, their collaborators, and the French resistance intensified. Nationalist neutrality appeared feigned to all sides, consequently the Breton paramilitary units broke with the moderates and actually donned Nazi uniforms to help track down members of the resistance: "war is declared between ourselves and the enemies of Brittany wherever they may be found." The allied landings in Normandy, however, caused these units to disintegrate and their members to disperse internationally. While the top leadership escaped, their followers faced the violence of the resistance, as about thirty Breton nationalists were summarily executed in the summer of 1944; subsequently, about a thousand were placed in internment camps.[18]

The collaboration, especially of the paramilitary units, with the Nazis gave all Breton regionalists a bad name, despite Charles De

---

[16] Reece, 157–60; see David Fitzpatrick, "Ireland since 1870," in *The Oxford Illustrated History of Ireland*, ed. R[obert] F[itzroy] Foster (New York: Oxford Univ. Press, 1989), 251, 253–4.

[17] Reece, 159–62, 175; and Jack Hayward, *Fragmented France: Two Centuries of Disputed Identity* (Oxford: Oxford Univ. Press, 2007), 371–2.

[18] Célestin Laîné quoted in Reece, 165, 163–4, 166–8.

Gaulle's call for fairness: "if the Breton autonomists have committed treason, they will be punished for it; if they have only been autonomists without having betrayed France, that is another matter." The liberation authorities purged the nationalist movement, to the point of firing civic employees with such sympathies and even harassing children wearing Celtic clothing. The collapse of the Vichy regime naturally led to the abrogation of all concessions made by that government to Breton regionalism, regardless of their triviality. In 1945 it seemed that Breton nationalism was doomed, despite the popularity it had shown during the war. But, regardless of the setback, so many Bretons had supported France against Germany that their ethnic nationalism in the context of an overarching French nationalism would quickly regain legitimacy.[19]

INTERNATIONALISM

During the Spanish Civil War and World War II, ethnic regionalism in Western Europe manifested itself in a variety of forms in the face of the internal and external imperialism practiced by the dominant states of Spain, France, Britain, Italy, Germany, the United States, and the Soviet Union. As we have seen, substantial numbers of Catalans, Basques, and Bretons sought political alignments that would permit them to preserve their cultures and identities in the continuing confrontation with the larger more powerful ethnic groups, the "nations" that sought to impose their norms on all other nationalities within the territory claimed by the "nation-state." Many ethnic regionalists supported reactionary forces in hopes of freeing their homelands by siding with the enemies of the state they found immediately oppressive; for example, Basque Navarrans joined the Falangists and Breton militants the Nazis. Indeed, even the Irish Free State, though recently independent of Britain, refused to join it against Germany, despite offers of a post-war union with Northern Ireland. Many ethnic nationalists gambled, of course, that the reactionary imperialists would be more pliable than the liberal imperialist states that controlled the ethnic homeland. Caught between empires, the right-wing regionalists lost their gamble at the end of World War II, but the victory of the more progressive

[19] Quoted in ibid., 167, 165, 168, 176-7; see also Luc Capdevila, "Violence et société en Bretagne dans l'aprè-Libération (automne 1944–automne 1945)," Modern and Contemporary France 7 (no. 4, 1999): 454.

empires set the stage for decolonization, first beyond Europe, then in the metropolis as well.[20]

Colonizing many of the world's nationalities were the more modern empires – the British Commonwealth of Nations and the United States of America, progressive in terms of individual freedom, and the Union of Soviet Socialist Republics, in terms of collective ideals. The full names of these three empires indicated they shared certain geopolitical similarities; all three had experience governing vast lands and peoples of great diversity, practice they would call on to establish order after World War II. In 1942 calling their alliance the United Nations, these great powers led twenty-six nations against the re-actionary Axis. From this military alliance would grow the successor to the failed League of Nations, the confederation idealists had hoped would establish and enforce international law after World War I. Even before the entry of the United States into World War II, President Franklin Roosevelt and British Prime Minister Winston Churchill enunciated the UN's set of governing international principles in the Atlantic Charter on August 14, 1941. While affirming the rights of all peoples to determine their governments, with a voice in setting the boundaries of these states, the two leaders called for greater international economic cooperation and a better "system of general security." These statements, especially those regarding self-determination and boundaries, had important ramifications for the colonized homelands and peoples of the world, first for those occupied by Germany, Italy, and Japan, but later for those occupied by the Allies themselves, both externally and internally.[21]

During the war various visions regarding the geopolitical structure of the new world order appeared, with major differences arising among the United States, the Soviet Union, and Britain. These ideas involved not only the future of the defeated empires, their metropolises, and their colonies, but the global system of empires, nation-states, and international alliances. Roosevelt imagined three or four major powers disarming the rest of the world and policing it. Churchill envisioned a structure built on global regions – Europe, the Far East, and the Americas – with the major powers in each controlling councils of states

[20] Reece, 150; and Jonathan Tonge, *Northern Ireland: Conflict and Change*, 2nd ed. (London: Pearson Education, Longman, 2002), 34.
[21] Evan Luard, *A History of the United Nations*, vol. 1, *The Years of Western Domination, 1945–1955* (New York: St. Martin's Press, 1982), 17.

"for peoples who are without history" in a pattern resembling imperial spheres of influence. Interestingly, Josef Stalin of the Soviet Union objected to the lack of power and representation assigned less powerful states in such proposals. Realistically, he recognized that smaller nations, current colonies, and restive regions would not readily comply with such neocolonial forms.[22]

Ultimately, the great powers compromised their visions of the new world order by incorporating in the new United Nations many of the structures of the old League, though somewhat strengthened. A Security Council, comprised of the great powers, would make the major decisions, particularly with regard to policing the world. On the other hand, the General Assembly would give all member states a voice in the affairs of the world, a democratic principle curiously supported first by dictator Stalin. A Secretary-General would serve as the chief executive of the new organization. Significantly, while the UN established itself, other independent international organizations also arose, for example, the International Monetary Fund and the World Bank, dealing with financial matters. The great powers did not expect the UN to centralize all these activities in a huge bureaucracy. Nevertheless, while the UN's central mission remained preserving the peace, it would have certain tasks of a social and even a cultural nature, most of which would evolve over time. In 1944 the major erstwhile empires agreed to the main elements of the UN charter at the Dumbarton Oaks Conference in Washington, with ratification coming from the world at large in San Francisco the next year, followed by establishment of a permanent site in New York City, all cities within the United States.[23]

Clearly, the great powers – Britain, the USSR, and especially the United States – envisioned, designed, and implemented the plans for the United Nations; consequently, they controlled it, at least until they fell out among themselves and allowed the many members of the assembly, increasingly former colonies, a greater voice. The

---

[22] Ibid., 19–24; quoted in Neil Smith, *American Empire: Roosevelt's Geographer and the Prelude to Globalization*, California Studies in Critical Human Geography (Berkeley and Los Angeles: Univ. of California Press, 2003), 363, 349, 380, 382, 390–1.

[23] Luard, 30–1, 37–8, 44; cf. "Covenant of the League of Nations, January 10, 1920," with "Charter of the United Nations, June 26, 1945" in *Documents Relating to International Organization*, ed. Werner Levi, rev. ed. (Minneapolis, Minn.: Burgess Publishing Co., 1947), 1–32.

dominance of the great powers reflected the colonialism of the past, as each remained an imperial power under modern guise. The hopes for world community faltered in the late forties as the Cold War developed between the United States and the Soviet Union, the superpowers – erstwhile empires – that soon divided the world into two huge spheres of influence. At the same time, however, nationalism insidiously worked against this bipolar hegemony as newly independent states broke up the British, French, Spanish and other formal empires and played the superpowers off against each other. Despite the apprehensions of the western powers, in 1952 the General Assembly, driven by Afro-Asian countries, resolved that "the States Members of the United Nations shall recognize and promote the realization of the right of self-determination of the peoples of Non-Self-Governing and Trust Territories who are under their administration . . . through plebiscites." Though limited to formal colonies, such UN resolutions would also inspire ethnic regions in the metropolises to seek self-determination as well.[24]

Among the first issues facing the United Nations was the application of the reactionary Spanish state for admission to the organization. As the war had turned against Germany, Spain had retreated from nonbelligerent status with pro-Axis leanings to stricter neutrality, but the Allies, formally the United Nations, suspected Franco's sincerity. Consequently, at the Potsdam conference in 1945, the Allies branded his regime, fascist despite some superficial changes, as unfit for membership in the UN. The following year this opinion was confirmed by a vote of the General Assembly, demanding a return to government by the people in Spain and recommending the withdrawal of the ambassadors of member states from Madrid. Given that nearly a third of the members were former Spanish colonies, Spain found itself truly isolated in the early postwar era, though still holding onto its African possessions. However, rather than undermining the regime, the ostracism tended to increase support for it, leading the UN to rescind its ban on Spanish membership in 1950. By that time the post-war order in Europe had evolved through trying times.[25]

[24] Luard, 383; quoted in Yassin El-Ayouty, *The United Nations and Decolonization: The Role of Afro-Asia* (The Hague: Martinus Nijhoff, 1971), 59, 221–2.
[25] Stanley G. Payne, *The Franco Regime, 1936–1975* (Madison: Univ. of Wisconsin Press, 1987), 338–9, 358, 361, 383.

The European Common Market

Though part of the victorious United Nations at the end of World War II, Britain and France no longer had the military might to compete with the United States and the Soviet Union. The economy of Europe lay in shambles, with factories, utilities, stores, and infrastructure destroyed, allowing little support for military establishments. Labor markets were in disarray due to the casualties of war and the return of discharged, job-seeking veterans. Consequently, maintaining overseas empires and their commitments became increasingly burdensome. To make matters worse, Europe faced the possibility of renewed warfare as the two superpowers threatened to use the continent as the major battlefield between them. By 1947 the United States had taken over Britain's military commitments to Greece and Turkey to prevent these nations from becoming Soviet protectorates. Gradually, necessity bred further geopolitical adjustments that allowed Western European countries to benefit from the Cold War, rather than remaining neocolonies of the American empire. Contrary to imperialistic tradition, according to European visionary Jean Monnet, the United States "instead of basing its power on ruling by dividing . . . consistently and resolutely backed the creation of a large Community uniting peoples previously apart."[26]

Fearing Soviet expansion westward, either through military invasion or communist subversion, the United States implemented a foreign policy of containment that included military alliance and economic aid. The North Atlantic Treaty Organization allied the United States, Canada, and Western Europe to block Soviet imperialism. But more significant was the European Economic Recovery Program (the Marshall Plan) proposed in 1947 to prop up capitalist economies and make communism less attractive. Although the United States initially offered economic aid to Eastern Europe including the Soviets as well, Americans knew full well that these states would reject the offer. Recognizing that the aid would come only within a capitalist framework, the communist nations perceived the help as economic imperialism designed to undermine socialism, an undeniable charge. With the subsequent drawing of the Iron Curtain, the Marshall Plan

[26] Elizabeth Pond, *The Rebirth of Europe* (Washington, D.C.: Brookings Institution Press, 1999), 24–5, 29; quoted in Geir Lundestad, *"Empire" by Integration: The United States and European Integration, 1945–1997* (New York: Oxford Univ. Press, 1998), 3.

proceeded in Western Europe, excluding Spain of course. In 1948 the European Organization of Economic Cooperation was set up to coordinate efforts to restore Europe's economy under the Marshall Plan. Though a forum for the discussion of economic issues, the new organization also implemented practical measures. Initially, the members sought to allocate scarce resources among the depressed states. But more importantly, they succeeded in abolishing some trade restrictions, barriers that had historically led to severe competition between nation-states, contributing to hostilities that led to war. Between 1948 and 1951 the United States spent $12 billion under the European Recovery Program that would lead to major geopolitical as well as economic change on the continent.[27]

By 1952 the cooperative ideas engendered by the Marshall Plan led to creation of the European Coal and Steel Community, a rather mundane title for an institution that germinated visions of continental geopolitical confederation. France, Belgium, the Netherlands, Luxemburg, Italy, and West Germany sought to integrate their coal and steel industries in a common market with headquarters in Brussels. While the idea was to lower trade barriers, the exchange of technology and materials drew the industries into much closer relationships. Interestingly, this community included members that less than ten years earlier had been fatal enemies for centuries. Most significant was that the members envisaged the evolution of a "United States of Europe" to reduce the tensions that had led to World War II. Indeed, contrary to the imperialistic tradition of nation-building based on conquest, this new international confederation was based on voluntary economic cooperation.[28]

Within five years the same nations that established the coal and steel block founded the European Economic Community (the EEC, better known as the Common Market). In the Treaties of Rome, the member states essentially agreed to facilitate commerce; they sought to remove more trade barriers, both public and private. They sought to assure the mobility not only of capital and entrepreneurs, but also of labor. Policies

---

[27] Pond, 24–5; and Michael J. Hogan, *The Marshall Plan: America, Britain, and the Reconstruction of Western Europe, 1947–1952*, Studies in Economic History and Policy: The United States in the Twentieth Century (New York: Cambridge Univ. Press, 1987), 1, 29, 43–5, 127.

[28] Lundestad, 6–7; Hogan, 427; and Michael Burgess, *Federalism and European Union: The Building of Europe, 1950–2000* (New York: Taylor & Francis Group, Routledge, 2000), 64–5.

regarding transportation, agriculture, and other sectors of the economy would be coordinated internationally. Revealing strong unity among themselves, the members would establish unitary policies toward non-members. Parallel with but initially separate from the Common Market, the same European member states had established the Council of Ministers, Court of Justice, and Parliament. Such institutions, reflecting those of a sovereign state, went beyond management of a trading block; they were the seeds of an interstate political confederation, one that would perforate the boundaries of old nation-states and even their ethnic regions. In his Grand Design presented in Philadelphia in 1962, President John F. Kennedy welcomed "a concrete Atlantic partnership . . . between the new union now emerging in Europe and the old American Union founded here 175 years ago." The old federation, influenced by the Iroquois, had served as a model in the redesign of Europe.[29]

Decolonizing West Africa

As Western Europe turned inward to deal with the problems resulting from World War II and the Cold War, the colonial peripheries of the old colonial empires began to demand independence. The internal economic and military weaknesses of Britain, France, and Spain, not to mention Belgium and the Netherlands, made their continued overseas empires difficult to retain. Moreover, the rhetoric of self-determination, anti-imperialism, liberation, and antiracism used in defeating the Axis and in constructing the UN pressured the old mother countries to release their territorial possessions. The metropolises, however, with justifications as diverse as their individual colonies, often held onto them for unnecessarily long periods. As a result, indigenous movements to decolonize homelands lost patience and became violent.[30]

In the Atlantic World France and Spain faced similar problems in Morocco, Western Sahara, and the Maghreb in general. In late 1942 the brief conflict between Anglo-American armies and the Vichy French led the indigenous peoples of northwestern Africa to believe erroneously that the Allies would support their movements for

---

[29] Ibid., 76; Pond, 28; quoted in Lundestad, 64.
[30] Tony Hodges, *Western Sahara: The Roots of a Desert War* (Westport, Conn.: Lawrence Hill & Co., 1983), 68–9.

self-determination. Consequently, political parties for that purpose got underway; the next year Moroccan activists demanded complete independence with a constitutional monarchy, after a short transition under the French. Lack of a positive response caused rioting that, despite punitive suppression, led France to begin a series of reforms in the mid- to late 1940s that allowed the local people greater partic- ipation in government. Meanwhile the sultan steadfastly opposed Morocco's incorporation into the French republic, as had occurred with Algeria. Renewed violence against the protectorate impelled the French to move against nationalists in the government. When the sultan refused to cooperate, he was replaced and exiled in 1953, an event that would launch a guerrilla movement in both French and Spanish Morocco.[31]

Following the outbreak of the Algerian Civil War, in 1955 Moroccan partisans created the Army of Liberation in imitation of the Algerian National Liberation Front. Recruiting in the Middle Atlas and Rif mountains, partially in the Spanish protectorate, the Moroccan insurgents engaged in attacks that required an inordinate number of French forces to repel. Facing rebellion on two fronts, Paris chose to negotiate in Morocco, culminating in the return of the sul- tan. Rather than let up the pressure, the insurgents continued their offensive by attacking loyalists, capturing French troops, and even recruiting native auxiliaries by the thousands. On March 3, 1956 France recognized Morocco's independence as the rebels then occu- pied the Atlas and Rif mountain ranges and distant southern areas, overlapping Spanish territory.[32]

Perforce the following month Spain followed France's example, ac- knowledging that northern Morocco belonged to the newly indepen- dent nation, pledging to "respect the territorial unity of the empire," but resisting evacuation of all the land occupied by Franco's forces. On the Mediterranean Spain would not turn over its ancient outposts at Ceuta and Melilla, nor would Franco surrender Ifni, a port on the Atlantic coast, ceded "in perpetuity" by the sultan in 1860. Eventually, in 1958 Spain conceded a sliver of southern Morocco previously held as part of the protectorate. However, Franco refused to recognize Moroccan sovereignty over Western Sahara, the vast desert territory

[31] Ibid., 73.
[32] Ibid.; and Eleanor Hoffmann, *Realm of the Evening Star: A History of Morocco and the Lands of the Moors* (Philadelphia: Chilton Books, 1965), 253.

stretching south along the Atlantic coast toward Senegal. In that region
the Moroccan sultans had apparently never exercised suzerainty over
the nomadic Saharawis, whose territory the Spanish partly colonized
only in the twentieth century.[33]

While the Saharawis did not necessarily see themselves as Moroccans or their homeland as a Moroccan region, some had fought with
the Army of Liberation envisioning it as a pan-Arab movement for the
independence of the entire Maghreb. In 1957 units including Saharawis operated out of southern Morocco across Spanish Sahara, often
attacking French posts across the border in Algeria and even into
Mauritania. While the new Moroccan government disavowed the
activities of the guerrillas, Spanish authorities, fearing rebellion in
Western Sahara, began cooperating with the French. Their fears were
warranted as attacks commenced on Ifni and sites in Spanish Sahara
itself. Fortunately for the Spanish, dissension broke out in the Army of
Liberation, apparently between the Moroccan leadership and the
Saharawis troops. A Saharawi sheik, Khatri Ould Said Ould el-
Joumani, who had been imprisoned by the Moroccan command, escaped and sought help against the rebel army's attacks from the French
and Spanish counterinsurgency forces. He asked the colonial powers
for assistance in defending "our territory, which extends from the
Kharawi to the Atlantic Ocean, and from the coast to Adrar Soutouf,
and to the Kediat of Idjil, to Bir Moghrein, to Tindouf and to the Oued
Draa." Claiming to represent all the chiefs of the region's major tribe,
the Reguibat of Zemmour, the sheik included virtually all of Western
Sahara, southern Morocco, and slices of Mauritania within these landmarks. This region did not correspond precisely with Spanish, French,
or Moroccan claims, suggesting that the Saharawis, nomadic or not,
imagined their homeland in their own terms even if influenced by the
colonial powers.[34]

The divisions within the Army of Liberation between Moroccans
and Saharawis prevented their effective resistance to a counteroffen-
sive launched by Spanish and French forces in early 1958, a campaign
that ended any chance of Western Sahara becoming immediately

[33] Quoted in Hodges, 74, 26; Hoffmann, 259; for more on Spain's nineteenth-
century expansion in Morocco, see Henri Terrasse, *Histoire du Moroc des origines
à l'établissement du Protectorat français*, vol. 2 (1950; reprint, New York: AMS Press,
1975), 326–7.
[34] Quoted in Hodges, 79, 74–8.

independent or part of Morocco. Spanish troops moving out of the coastal positions recovered areas of the interior previously lost, while French forces from Algeria and Mauritania dispersed the guerrillas. Many rebels returned to their homes in Spanish Sahara, sought refuge in Morocco, or even Mauritania, where the French encouraged desertion. The dispersal of these activists would create conflicts in the post-colonial era as their specific places of residence affected their identities in the new states created with boundaries established under European direction. For example, Khatri Ould Said joined in a meeting of former guerrilla leader Mokhtar Ould Daddha, who declared: "You Reguibat ... are the people of this region of northern Mauritania, but you are members of Greater Mauritania because we want to create the Mauritanian nation, which implies that Mauritania will become a large tribe in which the present tribes are simply families." Khatri Ould Said had not previously declared his homeland as part of Mauritania, but now seemed interested in building a new nation-state separate from Spain, France, and Morrocco. Mauritanian independence shortly thereafter with Saharawi citizens would create disputes with Morocco over the future status of Spanish Sahara.[35]

The disunity of the Army of Liberation in terms of personnel and goals left Western Sahara in Spain's hands; indeed, Franco in 1958 declared the region and Ifni no longer colonies, but provinces of that unitary state, much as France had done unsuccessfully with Algeria. Given that he had had to re-deploy some 175,000 restive officers and troops from Morocco, to these territories and the Canary Islands, Franco had the forces necessary to control Spain's remaining colonies, whether defined as external or internal. Though Ifni had little economic value, Western Sahara had significant phosphate deposits and fisheries important to Canarians off the coast. Only gradually would Spain release its hold, ceding Ifni to Morocco in 1968 and abandoning Western Sahara in the mid-1970s after renewed insurrection there and instability on the Iberian Peninsula itself.[36]

---

[35] Quoted in ibid., 81, 79–80, 82; for dreams of a Greater Morocco, see Hoffman, 264–5.

[36] Hodges, 80, 74, 83; for the continuing postcolonial conflict involving Morocco, Algeria, and the local population, see U.S. Institute of Peace, "The United Nations and Western Sahara: A Never-Ending Affair," Special Report 166 (July 2006), pp. 18–20. Available from www.usip.org/pubs/specialreports/sr16.pdf, accessed 24 July 2008.

Compared with Spain, defeats in Morocco and Algeria, not to mention Vietnam, led France to relinquish "voluntarily" most of its overseas
empire in the late 1950s and regularly thereafter. Britain's problems
with India in the late forties led it also to pursue a policy of decolonization. In West Africa among the many newly independent states
France recognized were Mauritania and Senegal in 1959–60, while
Sierra Leone and Gambia were recognized by Britain in 1961 and
1965, respectively. With minimal success the metropolises encouraged
their former colonies to remain in their erstwhile empires – now voluntary international communities – the British Commonwealth of
Nations and the French Community of Nations. Initially, the British
had envisioned a confederation of dominions tied together by allegiance to the crown, with institutions, foreign policy, and markets
in common. After World War II, however, nationalism intensified to
the point where the Commonwealth and its French equivalent became
very loose organizations of countries with a common colonial heritage,
even less capable of unified action than the United Nations. After
a century of European imperial domination, global centrifugal forces
seemingly compelled nations and ethnic groups to seek their destinies
independently.[37]

Liberia faced some of the same centrifugal forces, at first limited,
since the country had gained independence in 1847. As we have seen,
its government and economy had remained in the hands of the colonizing Americo-Liberians and their descendents. Forcibly subordinating more than sixteen indigenous ethnic groups, including the Bassa,
Krahn, Gio, Mende, Gola, Vai, and Mandingo, the ruling minority had
established plantations with absentee landlords on the lands and with
the labor of the native peoples. During the long-term presidency of
William Tubman (1944–71), however, the restive native peoples
gained the vote, legislative representation, access to the civil service,
better education, and more respect for their cultures. As they gained
prestige, indigenous groups identified more with Liberia than their
homelands because the national state offered more advantages than
could regional governments. Moreover, only a few of the fifteen counties, such as Grand Bassa and Grand Kru, had formed out of the non-
contiguous, native enclaves, limiting calls for regional autonomy.

[37] John Darwin, *Britain and Decolonisation: The Retreat from Empire in the Post-War
World*, Making of the Twentieth Century (New York: St. Martin's Press, 1988),
251, 61, 146–8.

Rather than developing separatist sentiments then, individuals increasingly identified with the nation, for good or ill, as had Americo-Liberians. "In 1978 . . . I became a candidate for mayor of Monrovia," recalled scholar-activist Amos Sawyer of his optimistic youth, "one element of a broader movement for democratic reform." Unfortunately, though officially an English-speaking country like Sierra Leone, Liberia lacked a common religion, numerically predominant ethnicity, stable economy, or sufficiently flexible government to maintain unity toward the twenty-first century.[38]

FREE QUEBEC?

As the British Commonwealth lost hold on its members in Africa and elsewhere, some of these appeared to lose their cohesion as well. After World War II Canada, long divided between English and French nationalities, saw gradual erosion of Ottawa's power relative to Quebec. French Canadian sentiments against conscription to fight in a war on Britain's behalf had subsided with victory, and the post-war economy built the province's prosperity to the point where it had achieved modernity. However, French Canadians now recognized more than ever that their socioeconomic position continued to be inferior to that of the English. Through the early 1960s the Quebecois in particular called for a fair proportion of federal employment, preservation of their natural resources, public ownership of utilities, improved social welfare, equality of French with English, and "an autonomous 'Laurentian' state." While a few radicals tossed bombs in the cause of an independent Quebec, the seriousness of this "anticolonial" movement became evident in 1976 with the election of the separatist Parti québécois to govern the province with plans for a referendum on its status in Canada. "For many federalists . . . ," according to historian Susan Mann, "separatism was unthinkable precisely because, without quite realizing it, they compared Quebec to a woman. Neither she, nor, by analogy, *la belle province*, had the right to independence." The federation was a family, including French Canadian children outside the province that she must not abandon. (See Map 7.2.) The analogy revealed the inequality and

---

[38] Stephen Hlophe, "The Significance of Barth and Geertz' Model of Ethnicity in the Analysis of Nationalism in Liberia," *La Revue canadienne des Études africaines/Canadian Journal of African Studies* 7(no. 2, 1973): 251–4; and Sawyer, 13–17.

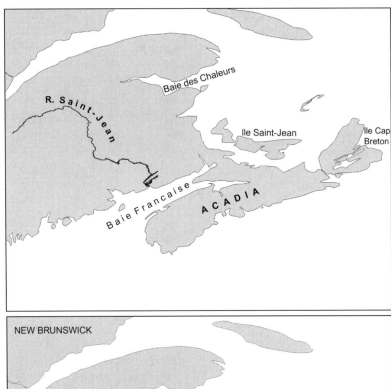

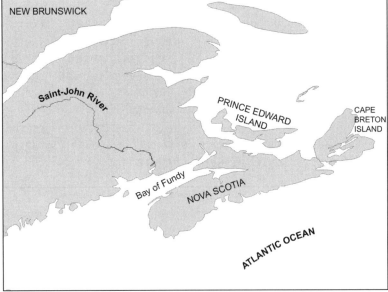

Map 7.2. Acadia, Nova Scotia by the Early Eighteenth Century. Adapted from Conrad and Hiller, *Atlantic Canada*, 54, 96. Cartography by Cassingham and Foxworth, Courtesy of the Edwin J. Foscue Map Library, SMU.

limited freedom of the union, as well as the wanderings of members from the "home," circumstances that forced Canadians to imagine federation as more than a geographical house with regional rooms.[39]

Decolonizing the Caribbean

Unlike Quebec, many American nations had achieved independence in the early nineteenth century, but not in the Caribbean; there various colonies renewed their dreams of self-determination in the receptive atmosphere after World War II. Among the most important was the old English colony of Jamaica. After many discussions regarding the size appropriate for new nations, Britain decided to experiment with a confederation of its Caribbean colonies. Located on the mainland, British Honduras in Central America and Guiana in South America refused to participate, citing their distinct geographical circumstances. In 1958, however, Jamaica joined Trinidad and Tobago, Barbados, and several smaller islands in the Federation of the British West Indies. Unfortunately for its visionaries, this confederation in practice was short lived because the central government lacked powers to tax, to engage in foreign affairs, or to control immigration. Trinidad sought a stronger central government with a national bank and customs union, but Jamaica ultimately seemed more concerned with its own self-interest, seeking a majority in the assembly to control the West Indian polity. Economically, Jamaica also sought to build an oil refinery that threatened to compete with similar facilities in Trinidad, competition that went against the plans the central government had for the whole confederacy's economy. The positions proved irreconcilable, and Jamaica withdrew from the union in 1961, reflecting the centrifugal tendencies of the period's nationalist movements.[40]

The failure of the Federation of the British West Indies showed the difficulty of such voluntary associations. Clearly, this geopolitical entity was more akin to a confederation, than a federal union. Despite having

---

[39] Edward M. Corbett, *Quebec Confronts Canada* (Baltimore, Md.: Johns Hopkins Univ. Press, 1967), 30; Susan Mann [Trofimenkoff], *The Dream of Nation: A Social and Intellectual History of Quebec*, Carlton Library Series 1982, 2nd ed. (Montreal: McGill – Queen's Univ. Press, 2002), 330, 312, 328–9; for further ethnic complexities involving Quebec, see Leslie Laczko, "Attitudes towards Aboriginal Issues in Canada: The Changing Role of the Language Cleavage," *Québec Studies* 23(Spring 1997): 4–5.

[40] Darwin, 219–20.

similar ethnic, racial, linguistic, geographic, and cultural backgrounds, economic competition between the territories sundered the combination. Such problems were similar to those faced by the United States under the Articles of Confederation, but rather than overcome these difficulties with a stronger federal union, the islands chose different paths. In 1962 Trinidad and Tobago formed one independent state while Jamaica went its own way in another, though both remained members of Britain's loose Commonwealth of Nations. Varied efforts at uniting the islands nevertheless continued, for as Jamaican statesman, Michael Manley, commented: "The choice, . . . in the long run of history lies between a low road of self-imposed, insular impotence and a high road of adventure into Caribbean regionalism leading on to the wider possibilities of third-world strength."[41]

The desire for self-determination in the Caribbean transcended the formal British, French, and Dutch colonies of the region, affecting the informal colonies of the United States as well, including Puerto Rico, a territory in name, and Cuba, an independent republic, neocolonial in status. The Philippines having gained its independence from the United States after their common effort against the Japanese invasion, Puerto Ricans also dreamed of nationhood. With the principle of self-determination highlighted at that time, the U.S. Congress in 1947 expanded self-governance on the island, permitting election of the governor by Puerto Ricans themselves, though keeping the offices of auditor and supreme court justices appointive. Puerto Rico's delegate to Congress remained a non-voting member of the House of Representatives. Puerto Rico thus became a U.S. "commonwealth," inferior in terms of autonomy to an American state or an independent nation-state.[42]

The first native elected governor, Luis Muñoz Marín launched Operation Bootstrap, an economic development program designed to pull Puerto Rico out of the depressed conditions that had continued even during and after World War II. While the island's economy had improved somewhat during the conflict due to defense spending on roads and airfields, the return of sixty thousand Puerto Rican veterans

---

[41] Ibid.; and Michael Manley, "Overcoming Insularity in Jamaica," in *The Birth of Caribbean Civilisation: A Century of Ideas about Culture and Identity, Nation and Society*, ed. O. Nigel Bolland (Kingston, Jam.: Ian Randle Publishers, 2004), 503.

[42] José Trías Monge, *Puerto Rico: The Trials of the Oldest Colony in the World* (New Haven, Conn.: Yale Univ. Press, 1997), 104–6.

had also caused the return of traditionally high unemployment. Taking advantage of the island's exemption from income and other federal taxes, Muñoz Marín invited mainland firms, particularly pharmaceutical companies, to move to the island. Though this improved employment somewhat in the 1950s, these corporations were not nearly as labor intensive as necessary to provide all the jobs needed. The governor consequently encouraged migration to the booming northeastern United States by encouraging low-cost airlines, put together with left-over military aircraft, to offer cheap flights to the mainland. Such policies, particularly free access to U.S. markets, eventually raised the island's economy above those of independent Latin American countries, but not quite to the level of the poorest state in the Union.[43]

But nationalist currents were not easily disbursed. In 1950 at the beginning of Muñoz Marín's administration, Puerto Rican nationalists unsuccessfully attempted to assassinate President Harry S. Truman, causing the death of one of their own and a secret service agent. One result of the assassination attempt was the first plebiscite on the political standing of the island, with choices for statehood, independence, or continuing commonwealth status. Significantly, among the political organizations on the island, there existed an Independence party, in addition to the Statehood Republican, and Popular Democratic parties. As the island's economy – with labor and goods dependent on access to the mainland – was improving by then, Puerto Ricans voted for the status quo, with independence receiving the lowest number of votes. Apparently limited autonomy, even if it implied continuing colonialism, was preferable to statehood that threatened elimination of tax exemptions and cultural assimilation or independence that endangered political and economic stability.[44]

---

[43] Morris Morley, "Dependence and Development in Puerto Rico," in *Puerto Rico and Puerto Ricans: Studies in History and Society*, ed. Adalberto López and James Petras (New York: Schenkman Publishing Co., John Wiley & Sons, Halsted Press, 1974), 222–4, 234.

[44] Diane Christopulos, "Puerto Rico in the Twentieth Century: A Historical Survey," in López and Petras, 154, 151, 153; in joining a "symmetrical" federation that allows little differentiation between states, Puerto Rico might transform the United States into a more multinational, "asymmetrical" union, like that of Canada or Spain – see Alfred Stepan, "Federalism and Democracy: Beyond the US Model," in *Federalism and Territorial Cleavages*, ed. Ugo M. Amoretti and Nancy Bermeo (Baltimore, Md.: Johns Hopkins Univ. Press, 2004), 452.

Of course, Puerto Ricans were aware that independence within the
U.S. sphere of influence in the Caribbean could be meaningless. Ever
since the Spanish-American War and the construction of the Panama
Canal at the turn of the twentieth century, Cuba, Haiti, the Dominican
Republic, not to mention the mainland republics bordering the
Caribbean basin, had effectively been neocolonies of the United States.
The dollar and gunboat diplomacy of the early century had involved
repeated U.S. military intervention in and occupation of those countries. While the Good Neighbor Policy from 1933 to 1954 had re-
strained this imperialism, the Cold War caused its resurgence when
the Central Intelligence Agency helped overthrow a democratically
elected leftist government in Guatemala out of fear that it would give
the Soviets a communist beachhead within the U.S. sphere of
influence.[45]

In 1958 this fear crystallized when Fidel Castro's Marxist revolution
exploded in Cuba. However, as had been the case in Algeria and Vietnam, the revolution's driving motivation was nationalist, rather than
communist, though the latter provided a small nation with a block of
allies previously unavailable. (His Marxist ideology provided a thorough
critique of the forces behind U.S., if not Soviet, imperialism.) Though
Castro aligned himself with the Soviets in order to prevent a full-scale
U.S. invasion, he saw Cuba as an anti-imperial model for other Latin
American, and later African, nations. He offered his homeland as an
example of successful military and political resistance to neocolonialism
and later as an example of a self-sufficient economy and society. Despite
its dictatorial nature, Castro's Cuba had a powerful influence on the
nationalist imagination everywhere, including the United States
itself.[46]

FRAGMENTS OF EMPIRE

During the 1960s the nationalist revolutions of Algeria, Cuba, and Vietnam had a tremendous impact on the movements for civil rights of
minorities in North America. Indeed, those nationalist models sometimes transformed domestic movements from integrationist to separatist

---

[45] Gordon K. Lewis, *Puerto Rico: Freedom and Power in the Caribbean*, with an introduction by Anthony Maingot, rev. ed. (Kingston, Jam.: Ian Randle Publishers,
2004), 72.

[46] Ibid., 531–7.

struggles. Black Muslims, for example, argued for an autonomous black nation within the confines of the United States; though not territorially specific, they sometimes thought of such a homeland somewhere in the Deep South where blacks had formed a core population. Chicano activists in the Southwest, including Texas, reminded Mexican Americans that they were not simply migrants in the region but a native people entitled to self-determination in the land that had once been far northern Mexico. Acadians and Micmacs established new organizations to reassert their rights to their ancient overlapping homelands in the Maritime Provinces. Other Indians, from the Iroquois of Ontario to the Cherokees of North Carolina reminded their fellow citizens that they were the First Nations or Native Americans, colonized for centuries. In Mexico Tlaxcalans once again spoke of themselves as an autonomous indigenous nation. Thus, while decolonization proceeded between core and periphery in overseas empires, internal colonies, or conquered ethnic regions, within ostensibly unified nation states became restive as well.[47]

While the global resurgence of nationalism spread, the multiethnic states that had fought World War II and continued with the Cold War faced similar anticolonial movements within their own boundaries. France, the United Kingdom, the United States, and Canada, some of the world's most developed states could not take their unity for granted. Nor could Spain and Mexico. The old imperialism across the Atlantic that had built these states revealed itself in the continuing existence of ethnically distinct regional populations, increasingly influenced by twentieth-century anticolonialism. Northern Ireland and Quebec were some of the regions that had long gained publicity for their nationalist causes, but more surprising to outsiders were the ethnic movements that gained ground in places such as Brittany and Texas. Such movements with their calls for independence or autonomy forced the multiethnic state to reconsider the bonds that held it together.

---

[47] Melani McAlister, "'One Black Allah': The Middle East in the Cultural Politics of African American Liberation, 1955–1970," in *Bodies in Contact: Rethinking Colonial Encounters in World History*, ed. Tony Ballantyne and Antoinette Burton (Durham, N.C.: Duke Univ. Press, 2005), 383, 386; Margaret R. Conrad and James K. Hiller, *Atlantic Canada: A Region in the Making*, The Illustrated History of Canada (Toronto: Oxford Univ. Press, 2001), 201–5; Stephen Cornell, *The Return of the Native: American Indian Political Resurgence* (New York: Oxford Univ. Press, 1988), 215–17; and Ricardo Rendón Garcini, *Breve historia de Tlaxcala*, Serie breves historias de los estados de la república mexicana (Mexico City: Fondo de Cultura Económica, 1996), 141–2.

Indeed, decolonization involved fragmentation of the world order. Once comprised of a limited number of empires holding colonies in involuntary subordination, the international order after World War II shattered. While this allowed for greater self-determination on the surface, it also created unnecessary competition, barriers among states and citizens, and military realignment. Any vision of global federation faced powerful centrifugal forces, as the confederated UN could attest.[48]

[48] Darwin, 334; Sawyer, 96; and Edward Murguía, *Assimilation, Colonialism, and the Mexican American People*, Mexican American Monograph Series, no. 1 (Austin: Center for Mexican American Studies, Univ. of Texas, 1975), 4, 106–12; see also Leela Gandhi, *Postcolonial Theory: A Critical Introduction* (New York: Columbia Univ. Press, 1998), 4.

CHAPTER EIGHT

SUPRANATIONAL CONCEPTIONS

CONTINENTAL CONFEDERATIONS, 1975–2000

As we have seen, recognition of the independence of many former colonies around the Atlantic and elsewhere after World War II created unrest within the boundaries of even the most powerful, well-established states. By the 1970s ethnic unrest among Chicanos and Indians in the United States had definite territorial components, and resistance to internal colonialism was by no means confined to that country. Mexico, a state older than Germany or Italy, faced similar problems in Tlaxcala and Chiapas – ranging from organized cultural nationalism in the first case, to guerrilla warfare in the last – though the issues revolved strongly around class, historic regional grievances also played a part. In Canada the traditional divide between French and English Canadians not only intensified but became more complicated as the First Nations, including not just the Micmacs and Iroquois but also the Inuits, advanced their arguments for self-determination. In Western Europe, Northern Ireland, and the Basque Country, ethnic nationalism became violent, but it remained mild in Brittany. Unfortunately, on the West African coast, Sierra Leone and Liberia experienced violent ethnic conflict.[1]

Despite these centrifugal forces, new counter tendencies intensified in the late twentieth century. These centripetal forces pulled toward the economic magnets of France, Germany, and the United States. As

---

[1] Walker Connor, *Ethnonationalism: The Quest for Understanding* (Princeton , N.J.: Princeton Univ. Press, 1994), 214, 220; for a sophisticated treatment of federal ideas as "polycentric governance," see Amos Sawyer, *Beyond Plunder: Toward Democratic Governance in Liberia* (Boulder, Colo.: L. Rienner, 2005), 6, 124, 128, 159–60.

well-established states with powerful economies, these nations became the centers of vast new trading blocks that increasingly took on the structures of supranational states or continental confederations. The European Common Market evolved into the much more cohesive European Union, while the North American Free Trade Agreement established a similar model on the western side of the Atlantic. Hoping to imitate their more powerful neighbors, the Economic Community of West African States also appeared. Significantly, these vast collections of varied lands and peoples envisioned voluntary union for the benefit of all, rather than for a single dominant nation, as in empire. Based on economic rather than military force, these new continental trading blocks, evolving into political confederations, offered renewed possibilities for international community. These confederations suggested fruitful ways of merging the interests and loyalties of nations, homelands, and individuals, while minimizing conflict.[2]

THE EUROPEAN COMMUNITY

Between 1958 and 1968 the commercial advantages of the European Economic Community (the Common Market) became evident as trade quadrupled among the members – France, Italy, Belgium, Luxemburg, and the Netherlands – through the elimination of all tariffs. Hoping to build on this economic foundation, the members decided to move beyond a simple trading block and construct a political edifice. In 1967 they merged several major continental institutions, including the Commission of the European Coal and Steel Community, the Council of Ministers, the Court of Justice, and the Parliament into a new entity calling itself the European Communities. By incorporating judicial and legislative functions into their organization, the members began transforming their common market into a continental confederation; the stage was then set for expansion beyond the original members. In 1973 Britain, Denmark, and Ireland joined, followed in 1981 by Greece and in 1986 by Spain and Portugal. In the 1980s the European "Communities" became the European "Community," the singular form of the noun denoting the increased unity of this supranational state.[3]

---

[2] For the Caribbean Community and Common Market (CARICOM), see Michael Manley, "Overcoming Insularity in Jamaica," in *The Birth of Caribbean Civilisation: A Century of Ideas about Culture and Identity, Nation and Society*, ed. O. Nigel Bolland (Kingston, Jam.: Ian Randle Publishers, 2004), 503 n.2.

[3] Geir Lundestad, *"Empire" by Integration: The United States and European Integration, 1945–1997* (New York: Oxford Univ. Press, 1998), 9, 104, 110.

THE SIX COUNTIES OF ULSTER

While these trends toward continental unity progressed, old, seemingly irreconcilable ethnic and regional differences resurfaced in Europe. The establishment of the Republic of Ireland and its separation from the British Commonwealth of Nations after World War II had not completely settled the issue of Irish nationalism. The six northern counties, as Irish Catholics called them – Ulster or Northern Ireland, as Irish Protestants preferred – remained a self-governing dominion under the British Crown. Neither the republic nor Catholics in the north accepted this state of affairs, even during the relatively calm decades from the early 1920s through the 1950s. The Irish Republican Army continued its activities just the same, undertaking a "Border Campaign" between 1956 and 1962 to undermine the northern regime, but gaining little support from Catholics north of the line.[4]

However, socioeconomic conditions in Northern Ireland provided fuel that would reignite Irish nationalism in the region. Although the division within the region's population was usually framed in religious or sectarian terms, the differences could be interpreted from an ethnic perspective as well. As we have seen, English and lowland Scots had colonized Ulster bringing the Anglican and Presbyterian denominations with them. The colonists intermarried with the native Irish to some extent; nevertheless, separate communities that assimilated individuals to both sides developed, thus evolving separate customs and histories beyond religion. More seriously, Irish Catholics comprised the majority of the working class, with only a tiny middle class; as such Catholics experienced discrimination in employment, housing, education, and political representation. Despite few if any differences in race or language, the population divided along classic colonial lines, a relationship of dominance and subordination based on an ethnic difference focused on religion.[5]

---

[4] Jonathan Tonge, *Northern Ireland: Conflict and Change*, 2nd ed. (London: Pearson Education, Longman, 2002), 36.

[5] Ibid., 36; and Michael Hechter, "Introduction to the Transaction Edition," *Internal Colonialism: The Celtic Fringe in British National Development, 1536–1966* (Berkeley and Los Angeles: Univ. of California Press, 1975; reprint, New Brunswick, N.J.: Transaction Publishers, 1999), xiv–xviii; Hechter's view of Ireland as an internal colony of the United Kingdom has resurged, see for example Barbara Bush, *Imperialism and Colonialism*, History: Concepts, Theory, and Practice (Harlow, UK: Pearson, Longman, 2006), 74–6.

The examples of decolonization in the British Empire and the civil rights movement in the United States stimulated similar activism in Northern Ireland during the 1960s. The election of Catholic, Irish American President John F. Kennedy raised the confidence of Irish everywhere, but his support for the black civil rights movement encouraged Irish Catholics to see their own situation in Ulster in a similar light. As in America, the movement began with requests for moderate reform; the Campaign for Social Justice in 1964 began lobbying members of Parliament in London for betterment of the lives of northern Irish Catholics, without reference to their region's separation from the republic to the south. Civil disobedience became a tactic by 1967 with the founding of the Northern Ireland Civil Rights Association, still a reformist group acknowledging the state of Ulster in its very name. Staging a protest march the following year, this organization encountered physical force from the police; by 1969 a more radical group was attacked by Protestants, apparently with the assistance of undercover police. Subsequently, wholesale violence broke out over historic Loyalist parades, and Catholics seized a section of the city of Derry and held it against the security forces. A full-scale colonial rebellion seemed underway, and the British Army entered the fray.[6]

Because Irish Catholics completely distrusted the Ulster police, initially activists welcomed the British troops, suggesting that the broader issue of the partition of Ireland had not yet come to the foreground. This situation changed especially after a Conservative government took control in London, a government more supportive of the Unionists in Ulster. Not trained as peacekeepers, soldiers soon made enemies of the Catholic working class through forceful tactics in the search for arms, detention of suspects, and imposition of curfews. Finally, in 1972 after the army shot to death thirteen unarmed marchers in Ulster, Irish in Dublin burned down the British embassy, effectively signaling conversion of the northern conflict into a continuation of the colonial struggle for independence. The movement for civil rights within Northern

[6] Tonge, 37–9; distrustful of "anachronistic myths such as that of 'Ireland's 800-year struggle'" against colonialism is Michael Keating, "The United Kingdom: Political Institutions and Territorial Cleavages," in *Federalism and Territorial Cleavages*, ed. Ugo M. Amoretti and Nancy Bermeo (Baltimore, Md.: Johns Hopkins Univ. Press, 2004), 157.

Ireland had reverted to the historic struggle of all Ireland against English imperial subjugation.[7]

By 1972 Catholics and Protestants had become polarized as radical and reactionary forces picked up arms in the escalating violence. The Protestant Unionist Party and Loyalist paramilitary groups, such as the Ulster Protestant Volunteers and the Ulster Defence Association, formed to defend the province from incorporation into the republic. In their view, "the Roman Catholic population do not regard themselves as part of Ulster. They regard themselves as part of the Republic of Ireland. They are on the side of murder, terrorism, intimidation, and the total destruction of loyalists"; regardless of this statement, both sides engaged in violence. The previously quiescent Irish Republican Army (IRA) took up arms in the six counties, though it fragmented. The Provisional IRA, with its Sinn Fein political wing, broke away from the official IRA because the latter had abandoned the organization's traditional agenda. Catholic, vaguely socialist, nationalist, and militant, the Provisionals objected to the atheist, Marxist, interethnic, and electoral approach of the official IRA. Despite these political differences, both factions engaged in bombings and killings. When the tougher security measures of the Unionist government in Belfast failed to end the violence, London decided to rule Northern Ireland directly. The Irish nationalists thus succeeded in undermining local Protestant political control, and in making London the colonial oppressor once more.[8]

For the next thirty years the troubles would continue in Northern Ireland, the violence rising and falling according to circumstances. Segregation intensified behind high fences, called "peace lines" that supposedly marked safe zones, but sometimes made neighborhoods targets. One young woman recalled, "I got a petrol bomb put through my window. . . our house was on fire. . . we live at the back of a 'peace line'. . . now we have guards up on the windows." Despite living in the same region, the residents of Belfast and other cities and towns were locally divided, not only along religious, but ethnic, lines between Irish and British transnational identities that overlapped geographically. Such a situation called for a federalism of the mind beyond mere

[7] Tonge, 39–40; though my work has followed the colonial paradigm, I recognize that there are valid alternatives – see Hugh F. Kearney, *Ireland: Contested Ideas of Nationalism and History* (New York: New York Univ. Press, 2007), 287–9.
[8] Quoted in Tonge, 46, 40–3, 48–9.

geography. Having resided in Ulster for hundreds of years, the Protestant population continued to claim the rights of indigenous status despite its intense loyalty to London. As a dominant minority during the colonial period, Protestants had controlled the entire island, but as a minority in a unified Republic of Ireland, their political power would virtually disappear. They thus avidly defended the enclave remaining to them in Ulster where they were the majority and where the Catholic minority remained subordinate by every socioeconomic index. Unfortunately for Ulster's Protestants, the Catholics continued to grow in population, thus constituting an internal threat to Loyalist hegemony. The presence of supporters in the nearby southern republic, not to mention the United States, meant that resistance among Catholics in Northern Ireland could continue indefinitely. By 2000 Britain and Ireland, having joined the European Communities in 1973, agreed to set up a new government in Belfast under their joint supervision. All paramilitary groups were required to surrender their arms and engage one another through the new parliament, but such surrender was slow in coming. Protestants realized that demographics would assure that a democratic Ulster would eventually join a republican Ireland; militant Catholics resisted giving up any advantage. Significantly, in the late nineties, in what amounted to a preemptive strike, the United Kingdom reestablished legislative bodies in Scotland and Wales, acknowledging their autonomy before any serious nationalist movements commenced there. Northern Ireland had taught the English a lesson – power centralized in London could be counterproductive.[9]

BRETON AND BASQUE HOMELANDS

While Irish nationalists were achieving real sovereignty in a modern nation-state, their Celtic cousins in Brittany remained frustrated in the unitary French state. Despite the collaborationist debacle of World War II, Breton nationalism survived because many of its proponents had served France loyally. In the 1960s, influenced by anticolonial and civil rights movements in places such as Algeria, Ireland, Vietnam, and the

---

[9] Quoted in Mike Morrissey and Marie Smyth, *Northern Ireland after the Good Friday Agreement: Victims, Grievance, and Blame* (London: Pluto Press, 2002), 148; Tonge, 182, 213–14; Hechter, xviii; and Jonathan Hearn, *Claiming Scotland: National Identity and Liberal Culture* (Edinburgh, U.K.: Polygon at Edinburgh, 2000), 70–1.

United States, Breton patriots, more leftist than before, pushed harder for regional autonomy. Better communication and wider exposure to revolutionary rhetoric contributed to the renewed nationalism. As in earlier years, intellectuals, especially linguists and historians, studied and placed greater value on Brittany's culture. However, claiming cultural oppression was not as effective as arguing that the larger state oppressed Brittany economically and politically. On the other hand, demands for independence could sound ridiculous in highly patriotic France, though calls for autonomy might catch the ears of a few. In general, gaining mass support for Breton nationalism continued to be a frustrating endeavor for those who favored it. Into the twenty-first century, French nationalism retained an uncommon hold on the individual Breton, and the new allegiance to Europe as a whole gained headway as well.[10]

The situation in the Basque Country of France after World War II had similarities to that of Brittany, but the proximity of Spain's Basque provinces created a more peculiar situation as always. Although the autonomous Basque government of the Spanish republic escaped to Bayonne in 1937, the exiles apparently roused little nationalistic sentiment among the locals against France, given that the latter provided refuge to the republicans. The nearly forty-year Franco dictatorship in Spain made that regime almost the exclusive target of Basque nationalist animosity. Despite their political and cultural subordination under Franco, the Basques nevertheless thrived economically because they had successfully defended their industrial infrastructure during the civil war. Spain's isolation after World War II encouraged protectionism and self-sufficiency, which made Madrid especially anxious to further develop Basque manufacturing. Although obsolete methods and poor goods resulted from the lack of competition during the 1950s, reforms in the next decade improved the situation again so that by 1975 Spain, propelled by the Basque region, had developed among the world's ten most industrialized economies. In a peculiarly Basque historical tradition, this culturally peripheral homeland continued to be at the core of

---

[10] Jack E. Reece, *The Bretons against France: Ethnic Minority Nationalism in Twentieth-Century Brittany* (Chapel Hill: Univ. of North Carolina Press, 1977), 177; in the late twentieth-century economic development, cooperation with central authorities in Paris and the EU improved the lot of Brittany – Marc Smyrl, "France: Challenging the Unitary State," in *Federalism and Territorial Cleavages*, 210, 215–16.

Spanish economic development, despite the complaints of oppression by nationalists.[11]

However, industrial development led to major demographic changes that gave credence to nationalist complaints of cultural subordination by the Franco regime. Migration of labor from other parts of Spain, to the point where nearly half of the region's residents were non-Basques, threatened to undermine the ethnic identity of the region. Accustomed to earlier migrations, Basques by the 1960s had become alarmed by the sheer numbers of the latest wave, lamenting that "Our house is no longer our own!" Basques feared economic competition, though the migrants generally filled plentiful jobs for low-skilled labor, and the political support supposedly given by the migrants to the regime. On the other hand, migrants lacked upward mobility since Basques controlled the upper rungs of the class ladder. Indeed, the former thought it necessary to adopt or at least acquiesce to Basque customs in order to improve their lot in life. Curiously, adopting Basque nationalism was an acceptable way of doing that because the regional identity was somewhat fluid, even though some placed great emphasis on genealogy. For example, rural Basques who often spoke Euskera seemed ashamed of their rustic customs on arrival in the city and sought to shed them; however, urban Basques who had often lost the language sought to recover their culture. In this context, other Spaniards could adopt the regional identity and be accepted, especially if they learned Euskera and supported the political aspirations of nationalists. Under Franco the great fear was that official opposition to use of the language in the schools and the media, together with migration, was destroying Euskera.[12]

After Franco's death and restoration of the monarchy, King Juan Carlos helped institute constitutional reforms that brought democracy back to Spain in 1977. As part of an overall plan for modernization, Spain then joined the European Community and the North Atlantic Treaty Organization. Thus, this previously centralized fascist state gave up a level of national sovereignty to international economic and military alliances. More surprising was the new democracy's willingness to

---

[11] Philippe Veyrin, *Les Basques de Labourd, de Soule et de Basse Navarre: Leur histoire et leurs traditions*, new ed. (n.p.: Arthaud, 1955), 194; and Marianne Heiberg, *The Making of the Basque Nation*, Cambridge Studies in Social Anthropology, 66 (New York: Cambridge Univ. Press, 1989), 92–4.

[12] Quoted in ibid., 96, 95, 97, 99, 101, 100.

devolve power to Spain's ethnic regions. Catalonia and the Basque Country recovered regional autonomy in a geopolitical rearrangement that granted the same status to all of Spain's traditional regions. However, much of this resulted from a violent, ongoing Basque movement for independence, a movement not satisfied with mere autonomy.[13]

Despite this dissatisfaction, the Basque Country under the new constitution received about as much autonomy as a region could have without outright independence. The province controlled its own police and its own schools, and even levied its own taxes, a power no other region possessed. Moreover, nationalists had been elected to all political offices in the region. They even monopolized businesses, unions, social organizations, and the government bureaucracy, something that had never occurred under previous autonomous governments. But as with the earlier regimes, autonomy did not solve all the region's social problems.[14]

The early promise of autonomy seemed unfulfilled by 1988 as economic and social decline set into the Basque Country. The formerly powerful manufacturing economy had turned into an industrial wasteland because of obsolescence and foreign competition, a transformation that some attributed to the undermining of protectionism with entry into the European Community. Naturally, unemployment and urban crime rose, phenomena that the authoritarian state had previously controlled. The very social fabric of the Basque Country seemed rent as drugs penetrated the region as never before. In response to these problems, the governing Basque nationalists seemed unable to develop sound economic and social policy.[15]

This debilitating situation contributed to the Basque independence movement led by the ETA. Despite its violent tactics, the ETA drew support from rural areas where the desire to preserve traditions persevered and from the urban poor regardless of ethnicity because of the group's radical socialist stance. A major reason that simple autonomy within Spain had not satisfied the ETA was the continued division of the region with France. Any resolution to the conflict thus required the

---

[13] Jonathan Story, "Spain's External Relations Redefined," in *Democratic Spain: Reshaping External Relations in a Changing World*, European Public Policy Series, ed. Richard Gillespie, Fernando Rodrigo, and Jonathan Story (New York: Routledge, 1995), 32–3.

[14] Heiberg, 125, 129.

[15] Ibid., 227–30.

cooperation of a second nation-state, fortunately an economic and military ally of Spain. One lesson drawn from this ethnic region seemed to be that autonomy could not solve all of a region's problems because many of these remained international rather than national in character.[16]

On the other hand, an independent Basque nation spanning the Pyrenees, but remaining within the European Union might be more viable, similar to Slovenia, formerly of Yugoslavia. Whether Spanish or French nationalism would tolerate such dismemberment, given that other regions might follow, was a serious question. Perhaps a European federation based on ethnic regions, such as Castile, Corsica, and Scotland, rather than nation-states, would resolve many ancient inter-ethnic animosities. Unfortunately for ethnic nationalists, the existence of many interspersed groups, such as Castilians in Basque cities, made clear homelands with neat boundaries difficult to divide. The concept of even loosely segregated regions also made the free movement of labor much more difficult. In any case, the socioeconomic situation of the Basque Country by the twenty-first century improved as all of Spain went through a period of sustained growth; this together with the new threat of Islamic fundamentalist terrorism finally led extreme Basque nationalists to renounce violent tactics in 2006.[17]

THE EUROPEAN UNION

In fact, by the 1990s Basques, Catalans, and other Spaniards were forced to consider allegiance to a larger political entity – the European Union. Momentum toward a truly continental federation accelerated with the collapse of the Soviet Union. When formerly communist East Germany merged with its western counterpart, the European Community formally transcended the old Iron Curtain. Envisioning a new post–Cold War order, in 1991 the members signed the Maastricht Treaty formally committing themselves to further political as well as economic integration. Signifying this new commitment was the change in name from "community" to "union" and especially the evolution of continental

[16] Ibid., 228, 230; and Philip W. Silver, "¡Malditos pueblos!: Apuntes sobre los vascos al final del siglo XX," in *Disremembering the Dictatorship: The Politics of Memory in the Spanish Transition to Democracy*, Portada Hispánica 8, ed. Joan Ramon Resina (Atlanta, Ga.: Rodopi, 2000), 56.

[17] Connor, 213.

institutions. Real power remained in the Council of Ministers including one representative from each nation-state, a body complemented by the European Council made up of the national heads of state. More important, however, was the democratic institution transcending the nation-states – the popularly elected European Parliament, which made all citizens of the member states citizens of Europe.[18]

Significantly, Europe was successfully moving toward unity through economics, rather than militarism. Voluntary incentives, rather than conquest, had drawn these nation-states together in a trading block, as opposed to an empire. Furthermore, the original economic alliance had become a political confederation that increasingly was developing into a supranational federation. By the turn of the millennium, the EU was implementing a central bank and a common currency, monetary instruments previously utilized only by nation-states. Acting more and more like a unified sovereign state, the EU was also attempting to implement common foreign and security policies. These federal efforts were on a geographical scale that made Europe competitive with the largest of traditional nation-states, Russia, China, and the United States. Powerful forces were drawing Europe together, even as its people seemed increasingly to value their particular ethnic regions.[19]

The North American Free Trade Agreement

The success of the European Union led to imitation across the Atlantic, where Canada, the United States, and Mexico would implement the North American Free Trade Agreement (NAFTA) in the 1990s. In the early twentieth century, nation building had reached stability with these core states achieving control over the many Native American and other ethnic homelands within their geographical limits, though migration was a continuing concern. While some French Canadians crossed the northeastern boundary of the United States, forming small enclaves in Maine and other areas once part of New France, such small-scale migration and settlement did not become a major problem between the two predominantly English-speaking nation-states. However, during the century the single most important issue in U.S.-Mexico

[18] Lundestad, 116.
[19] Ibid.,117; for a discussion of confederation and federation in the complexity of EU governance, see David M. Wood and Birol A. Yeşilada, *The Emerging European Union*, 4th ed. (New York: Pearson Longman, 2007), 2–3.

relations was migration from the latter to the former. The importance of immigration and the borderlands to international politics increased in the late 1970s when businessmen and liberal activists first publicly discussed the idea of a common market between the United States and Mexico. They imagined resolving problems of oil shortages and illegal immigration by opening the border for the greater exchange of both goods and labor, thus stimulating business. This vision was clearly modeled on the European Community that had dealt with both factors. Although protectionists in the United States undermined implementation of the idea during the administration of President Jimmy Carter, the plan would reappear in the 1980s, but then with little consideration of immigration, let alone ethnic regions.[20]

What developed into the North American Free Trade Agreement began in 1988 between the United States and Canada, rather than Mexico. The agreement had to do strictly with trade and nothing to do with labor, or ethnic issues, such as Quebec nationalism. In this sense the treaty was most similar to the earliest forerunner of the European Union – the European Organization of Economic Cooperation. In 1992 Canadian Prime Minister Brian Mulroney, U.S. President George H. W. Bush, and Mexican President Carlos Salinas de Gortarí negotiated and signed NAFTA. Ratified in 1993, the treaty called for a gradual reduction in tariffs, customs duties, and other trade barriers, some immediately, others over fifteen years. Clearly, the treaty was made in the interests of business, as labor issues received no consideration. Indeed, labor leaders in the United States opposed the treaty for fear of losing jobs to Mexico where unemployment had been high for decades. Canadians did not relish the treaty either since their heretofore exclusive relationship with the United States had broadened. In Mexico, however, opposition arose most dramatically in the southern state of Chiapas where guerrilla warfare broke out on the first day of NAFTA's implementation in 1994. Clearly, one ethnic region perceived this grand trading block as a threat.[21]

[20] John R. Chávez, *The Lost Land: The Chicano Image of the Southwest* (Albuquerque: Univ. of New Mexico Press, 1984), 155; and Carey McWilliams, "A Way Out of the Energy Squeeze?" *Los Angeles Times*, 8 April 1979.

[21] Maxwell A. Cameron and Brian W. Tomlin, *The Making of NAFTA: How the Deal Was Done* (Ithaca, N.Y.: Cornell Univ. Press, 2000), xiii–xv; and James W. Russell, *After the Fifth Sun: Class and Race in North America* (Englewood Cliffs, N.J.: Prentice Hall, 1994), 199–205.

Chiapas and nafta

Bordering on Guatemala, Chiapas remained one of the most indigenous of Mexico's states. Though Mexicans are largely of Indian ancestry, most are mestizos who identify with the national culture. Those Mexicans who continue to speak native languages, practice native customs, and identify with their ancient peoples are considered indigenous. A populous and urbanized area, Chiapas retained its Mayan character after the conquest of the 1500s because of its isolation from the Spanish settlements even after the demographic decline of the colonial era. Needless to say, the descendents of the conquistadors took over the land and labor of the region and continued to dominate after Mexico's independence even after the Revolution of 1910. The land reform promised by the revolution failed to take place, and petitioners for land redistribution were sent into the forest to carve out new farms. The mestizo bosses and native caciques controlled the peasants with paramilitary forces.[22]

This situation persisted into the 1970s when the immediate conditions leading to the 1994 uprising developed. With the elite continuing to control large estates, the problem of land distribution became acute as the population increased. Somewhat better health care and food had caused the population to grow, exacerbating the land problem and raising unemployment. In addition to overuse of the land, the increasing use of chemicals by farmers also caused ecological problems. To make matters worse, by 1980 Guatemalan refugees from civil war in their country began to move into Chiapas causing greater competition for work.[23]

These material factors gave the message of new activists in the region a larger audience. The theology of liberation, a philosophy that merged Christian principles with socialist, even Marxist–Leninist ideals, caught hold. Grassroots organizing followed in the villages of the region, with teachers' unions influencing the *campesinos*. Educated people, the teachers, often from other parts of Mexico, had direct contact with the peasants and could transmit the philosophy and techniques of unionized labor. In addition to the unions, churches, and other nongovernmental agencies offered support both material and social.

---

[22] Thomas Benjamin, *Chiapas: Tierra rica, pueblo pobre – Historia política y social* (Mexico City: Grijalbo, 1995), 164–5, 249.
[23] Ibid., 276–81.

Some government agencies, such as the Instituto Nacional Indigenista, also assisted the native peoples, but Chiapa's own state agencies would not.[24]

Chiapas's state agencies remained under the control of the landholding elite that opposed any reforms to benefit the poor. When the national government under President Carlos Salinas de Gortarí attempted to redistribute land, the state government blocked such measures in addition to other federal funds allocated for Indians and other peasants. The elite not only controlled most of the land, but also expelled small landholders by accusing them of having invaded the larger estates. These events suggest one of the problems with regional political autonomy; it can be used by local elites to suppress certain sectors of their own population, even in the face of national opposition. Mexico's federal system permitted Chiapas's elite to oppress Indians, much as the states of the U.S. South had used the principle of states' rights to deny the civil rights of blacks. Nation-states had traditionally expanded through imperialism; however, by the late twentieth century national governments had begun to pay closer attention to the interests of colonized peoples.[25]

By 1990 conditions in Chiapas had deteriorated from their historically woeful levels. The prices of the region's major products – timber, coffee, cattle, and corn – dropped under the free market policies of the Salinas administration. In this case the national policies hurt the poor of Chiapas, as well as the whole country. Indeed, opposition to both national and state policies developed among the newly organized Indians and peasants. These groups particularly feared the coming of NAFTA, which would open the local economy to foreign products, causing further price erosion accompanied by more unemployment and lower wages. At the bottom of the social scale, the indigenous peoples felt oppressed by all policies of government – state, national, and international. Indeed, this intensified a desire for local autonomy along village lines.[26]

Significantly, organizations mobilized under "a utopic desire of recovering a lost Indian nation." The Indians could understand an

[24] For this section I owe much to Luis Hernández Navarro, "The Chiapas Uprising," trans. William Rhett Mariscal in *Rebellion in Chiapas*, ed. Neil Harvey, Transformation of Rural Mexico Series, no. 5 (San Diego: Ejido Reform Research Project, Center for U.S.–Mexican Studies, University of California, 1994), 53.

[25] Benjamin, 276–7.

[26] Hernández Navarro, 57–8,

interpretation of their present conditions based on the Spanish conquest. On Columbus Day 1992, dissidents toppled a statue of a local Spanish conquistador, a symbolic act stressing the colonial interpretation. While many local organizations worked for peaceful resolution to the historic problems of the region, frustrations rose to a point where armed struggle seemed the answer. Old problems regarding land, resources, poverty, and violent discrimination had previously led to revolts, and in 1994 these factors did again. The Zapatista rebellion, named for the agrarian hero Emiliano Zapata of the 1910 revolution, exploded in opposition to the conditions imposed by the original conquest, but also against the threats posed by the new capitalist world order represented by NAFTA. For good reason, the Zapatistas saw no more advantages accruing to indigenous peoples from this international trading block than they had seen from the nation-state or the regional state. Clearly, a vast federation, global in scale, could not succeed if it did not integrate local ethnic communities on a voluntary basis in ways that benefited them at the grassroots.[27]

According to Luis Hernández Navarro, the solutions to the region's problems depended on the involvement of all key sectors of the society. Campesino organizations, nongovernmental groups, churches, teachers' unions, political parties, human rights activists, governments, and finally the oligarchy, had a role to play. Of course, the latter would find itself in opposition to reform and most of the other groups because the colonial system benefited the elite. Ironically, NAFTA would seem a critical factor in bringing the oligarchy to change, for foreign competition could also hurt its interests, though clearly it had more resources to adapt than did the peasants. Balancing the interests of all the groups seemed necessary for the success of NAFTA, as well as the region.[28]

According to Hernández Navarro, even moderate reform required many changes. Fundamentally, land redistribution seemed necessary to give the peasants a greater stake in society, but national and even international policies favored the larger more productive farms of agribusiness. Comprehensive regional development taking into consideration cultural as well as economic attitudes was needed. Thus, peasants needed to be incorporated into any redevelopment planning

---

[27] Ibid., 58, 51–2.
[28] Ibid., 60; see also Guillermo Trejo, "Mexico: The Indigenous Foundations of Indigenous Mobilization and Ethnoterritorial Conflict (1975–2000)," in *Federalism and Territorial Cleavages*, 379–84.

and execution. Of course, any reform of this nature required competent officials, a fair police force, and a just judiciary. Such changes on the local level were only likely to occur with a more democratic system, at all levels, one respecting native forms as well as internationally recognized patterns. Thus, Chiapas illustrated that self-determination rested on the local community, then the region. To the degree federalism balanced those local interests with national and international interests, the more likely confederacies, such as NAFTA would succeed.[29]

TEJANOS IN CONCENTRIC AND INTERSECTING COMMUNITIES

Across Mexico's northern border, NAFTA and the United States faced other ethnic challenges. As we have seen, South Texas clearly formed the homeland of a people sometimes called Tejanos. As a subculture of the much larger group called Mexican Americans, Tejanos also lived within a greater ethnic borderland stretching from the Gulf of Mexico to the Pacific; they were moreover part of a Hispanic/Latino population dispersed across the United States by the late twentieth century. The heterogeneous Latino population had concentrations in many subregions of the country, but it was a minority in large regions, as was the case with Mexican Americans even in the Southwest. With a population constantly augmented by immigration from Mexico, Mexican Americans were less likely than French Canadians to have their historic ties to region acknowledged. While insiders might view Tejanos as pioneer settlers, outsiders would not see them as native because of Tejanos' family ties to Mexico. Like other ethnic Mexicans, Tejanos were usually seen as immigrants. But Mexican Americans repeatedly and sometimes aggressively challenged that image, as in "El plan espiritual de Aztlán": "Conscious . . . of the brutal 'Gringo' invasion of our territories, we, the Chicano inhabitants and civilizers of the northern land of Aztlán, from whence came our forefathers, reclaiming the land of their birth. . . . We [who] do not recognize capricious frontiers on the bronze continent . . . we declare the independence of our mestizo nation."[30]

---

[29] Hernández Navarro, 62–3.

[30] Daniel D. Arreola, *Tejano South Texas: A Mexican American Cultural Province*, Jack and Doris Smothers Series in Texas History, Life, and Culture, no. 5 (Austin: Univ. of Texas Press, 2002), 44; quoted in Chávez, *Lost Land*, 143.

By the mid-1960s in Texas and elsewhere, children of the Mexican American generation we have studied rejected their parents' acceptance of acculturation, as well as their subordinate place in U.S. society. Chicanos, as these activists called themselves, asserted their status as natives of the Southwest, based on Mexico's prior ownership of the region. Moreover, the activists based their assertion on their Indian, rather than Spanish ancestors, referring to the Southwest as Aztlán, the mythical homeland from which the Aztecs had migrated to Mexico City. In this they differed from the Mexican American generation, and earlier regional elites such as those of Laredo or San Antonio, that rested their claims simply on U.S. citizenship or Spanish settlement. Activists refused to identify with Spanish colonists who had conquered the native peoples and lands of Mexico and the Southwest. While Chicanos recognized their Spanish language and cultural traits, they identified primarily with the colonized Indians because it was their traits that distinguished Mexicans ethnically from others, including other Latins. Furthermore, identification with their Indian ancestors gave Chicanos a more legitimate claim to the Southwest, including Texas, one not based on the imperialism of Spain. Clearly, by the 1960s Mexican Americans had been influenced by colonial theories then gaining popularity in Africa, Latin America, and among other American minorities.[31]

José Angel Gutiérrez and La Raza Unida Party chose Crystal City, a small town in South Texas "to begin Aztlán!" – to show that ethnic Mexicans could regain control of their homelands north of the U.S.–Mexico border. In the early 1970s he led an electoral revolt that gained control of the local school board, the city council, and county government for the majority Tejano community. La Raza Unida established a micro society based on communitarian principles that served as a model for what might be established on a regional level; indeed, the party ran candidates statewide and in other parts of the Southwest. This activism reflected the desire for autonomy among Tejanos and other Mexican Americans; self-determination required a land base, and there was no more solid place for such a claim than South Texas. However, the U.S. government and society in general would not readily tolerate autonomy for an ethnic group regarded as immigrant, or even pioneer,

---

[31] Ibid., 30; see also Neil Foley and John R. Chávez, *Teaching Mexican American History*, Teaching Diversity: People of Color (Washington, D.C.: American Historical Association, 2002), 39–43.

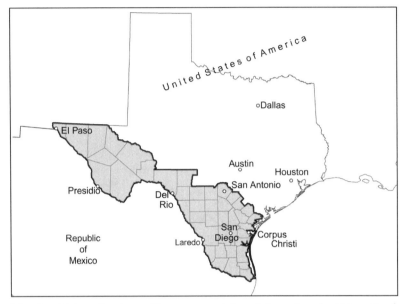

Map 8.1. Tejano Southwest Texas, 2000. Adapted from Arreola, *Tejano South Texas*, 60–1. Cartography by Cassingham and Foxworth, Courtesy of the Edwin J. Foscue Map Library, SMU.

in the Southwest. The authorities eventually undermined the Chicano movement, as did its internal disagreements. The young activists none-theless went into mainstream politics giving Mexican Americans an increasing presence at all levels of government, with growing demo-graphic clout that promised wider movements in the future.[32]

In the late twentieth century the status of ethnic Mexicans was constantly in contention in Texas and elsewhere as they increasingly migrated beyond the Southwest to other parts of the United States. Bilingual education, affirmative action, political redistricting, and other successful outcomes of the Chicano movement seemed threatening to Anglo-American regional and national hegemony and created a con-tinuing conservative reaction. Even feminism seemed ethnically men-acing; as early as 1971, Francisca Flores stated, "The issue of equality, freedom and self-determination of the Chicana – like the right of self-determination, equality, and liberation of the Mexican community – is not negotiable." Although such issues reverberated in Texas, immigra-tion repeatedly rang out nationally. The dramatic increase in the

---

[32] Quoted in Chávez, *Lost Land*, 145.

Mexican population in the Southwest, especially through illegal immigration, made Aztlán as threatening to Anglo-Americans as Quebec
was to English Canadians. Though openly separatist arguments had
flourished during the Chicano movement, they lay dormant during
the rest of the century despite increasing concentrations of ethnic
Mexicans in states such as Texas. Since so many had moved beyond
the region, the "Mexican problem" became national in scope.[33]

But what would autonomy mean for ethnic Mexicans, especially
with the increasing international integration caused by NAFTA? A
separate nation-state of Aztlán comprising the Southwest, such as that
proposed for Quebec, was impossible because the Mexican origin population was too disbursed among other groups, including other Latinos,
to form a cohesive geographical whole. Reactionary fears that such
a state would revert to Mexico seemed absurd given that so many of
that country's people had sought escape from its problems. However,
political control of entire states, such as California, New Mexico, and
Texas was distinctly possible as demographers estimated that ethnic
Mexicans would form majorities in those subregions early rather than
late in the twenty-first century. (See Map 8.1.) Though U.S. federalism,
as we have seen, had not allowed the admission of ethnic minority
states, it might not prevent their evolution. At a minimum, greater
control of local governments, schools, and businesses offered to help
Mexican Americans sustain their culture in the face of Anglo hegemony. By 2000 they had significantly acculturated to U.S. society, but
assimilation threatened their distinctiveness. On the other hand,
NAFTA positioned them well between two nations, economically
and politically. It offered them business opportunities and political
advantages that Mexico recognized first. That nation offered ethnic
Mexicans in the United States dual nationality, as a way of keeping
their economic as well as national loyalties. Significantly, in 2006 as
hundreds of thousands of undocumented workers demonstrated for
legalization of their status in the United States, Mexico lobbied to open
the border more widely for labor as well as goods, in imitation of EU
policies. Such a step would more rapidly gain Mexican Americans
political autonomy in subregions like Texas, without the creation of
an independent Aztlán. Increasing prosperity also promised them

[33] Quoted in Teresa Palomo Acosta and Ruthe Winegarten, *Las Tejanas: 300 Years
of History*, Jack and Doris Smothers Series in Texas History, Life, and Culture,
no. 10 (Austin: Univ. of Texas Press, 2003), 234; and Chávez, *Lost Land*, 154–5.

a more powerful role in the economic revitalization of Mexico through supranational NAFTA.[34]

MULTIETHNIC QUEBEC

The continuing saga of nationalism in Quebec illustrated the need for a more flexible federalism within multiethnic and supranational states. Throughout the 1980s Ottawa and the province negotiated a series of accords attempting to recognize the distinct status that Quebec sought within the Canadian federation, but all floundered in the face of opposition from the other provinces. In 1990 and again in 1995 referenda on independence for Quebec failed, the second essentially because of the opposing votes of non-French immigrant communities in Montreal. Despite this, Quebec had gained informal recognition as a nation, based on its language and territory. Over two centuries the ethnic struggle of the French-speaking in North America had become focused on the St. Lawrence because there, as nowhere else, they had the population to control the state; thus, they succeeded in preserving their language and culture through control of the schools and other government bodies. This permitted the Quebecois to acculturate the children of immigrants to French, even as the state respected the latter's diverse backgrounds. This civic nationalism permitted the growth of a Quebecois society beyond the specific ethnic group. Whether the newly acculturated population would support the aspirations of the natives for independence remained to be seen. Moreover, it seemed an independent Quebec would escape the Canadian federation only to find itself still a weak member of the larger confederation gradually coalescing under NAFTA.[35]

[34] Daniel D. Arreola, ed., *Hispanic Spaces, Latino Places: Community and Cultural Diversity in Contemporary America* (Austin: Univ. of Texas Press, 2004), 33–5; for a more critical view of these developments, see Gilbert G. González and Raul A. Fernández, *A Century of Chicano History: Empire, Nations, and Migration* (New York: Routledge, 2003), 186.

[35] Susan Mann [Trofimenkoff], *The Dream of Nation: A Social and Intellectual History of Quebec*, Carleton Library Series, 1982, 2nd ed. (Montreal: McGill – Queen's Univ. Press, 2002), xi; and Robert A. Young, *The Secession of Quebec and the Future of Canada* (Montreal & Kingston: McGill – Queen's Univ. Press with the Institute of Intergovernmental Relations, 1995), 294–5.

Map 8.2. Nunavut, Nunavik, and Quebec, 2000. Adapted from www.theodora. com/maps/new/nunavut16.gif, accessed 29 June 2005, and en.wikipedia.org/wiki/ Nunavik, accessed 21 September 2006. Cartography by Cassingham and Foxworth, Courtesy of the Edwin J. Foscue Map Library, SMU.

INUIT NATIONALISM

In the late twentieth century the role of indigenous peoples and their homelands had not fully matured in the multiethnic state, let alone the supranational state into which NAFTA might evolve. Neither Canada, Mexico, nor the United States had evolved just and efficient means of incorporating these ethnic regions into the larger societies. The reservation systems of these countries have helped preserve the cultures of these peoples, even when the reservations were designed to assimilate the people. But true autonomy has come slowly since these entities had usually been administrative units of the national governments, rather than self-governing regions. Canada, however, took major steps to allow self-determination for its native peoples. Partly because of its problems with Quebec, the central government felt impelled to recognize the rights of native peoples to autonomy. (See Map 8.2.) The Inuits, formerly known as the Eskimos, were a case in point.[36]

Before 1945 the Inuits, natives of the Arctic Circle, had limited contact with outsiders, mostly French and British trappers, and government agents. During that period, all aspects of their culture were nevertheless affected by European culture, though language seemed the least touched. This contact followed the French colonial pattern in North America, based on the fur trade. Open conflict was limited, but the Inuits were drawn into the market economy to the degree that when the fur industry collapsed, they experienced famine and other health problems. In response the Canadian government intervened with time-honored imperial policies that saved many Inuits from starvation, but more fully exposed their culture to the outside world. Ottawa decided to relocate the native peoples to government settlements, where the population did increase with improved health care. But the government also promoted assimilation with schools taught in English to the exclusion of the native language. For a generation this approach continued until the general upheavals of the 1960s caused reconsideration, but only then in Quebec. Given the desire of the Quebequois to defend their own language, they recognized that the Inuits deserved a right to their language as well. That province, followed by other provinces in the 1970s, first used Inuktitut in the schools and the media.[37]

Sociologist Marybelle Mitchell argues that nationalism among the Inuit ironically resulted partially from the initiation in 1959 of cooperatives by the Canadian state: "The official policy was that the Eskimo people should, with all deliberate haste, have control over these organizations in all of their aspects, and should regain their self-sufficiency." In response to the dire circumstances of the native people, the George

---

[36] Jean-Philippe Chartrand, "Survival and Adaptation of the Inuit Ethnic Identity: The Importance of Inuktitut," in *Native People, Native Lands: Canadian Indians, Inuit, and Meti*, ed. Bruce Alden Cox (Ottawa: Carleton Univ. Press, 1988), 241–2.

[37] Ibid.; and Leslie S. Laczko, *Pluralism and Inequality in Quebec* (Toronto: Univ. of Toronto Press, 1995), 202–3.

River Cooperative, established in northeastern Canada, built on the fishing and logging resources of the area with investment directly from Ottawa. This began a rather rapid movement that reached virtually all the Inuits. The federal government implemented cooperatives directly, rather than allowing them to be creations of the people themselves, as is the ideal of proponents of the institutions. The ideals of cooperatives in Canada included open membership; election and democratic control of officers; shares with limited interest; surpluses for development, common benefits or dividends; collective education; and the federation of cooperatives locally, nationally, and internationally. The government implemented these institutions with the notion that they would function in line with the perceived communal traditions of the aboriginal people. Mitchell, however, points out that the traditional culture had both individualistic as well as communal components; moreover, the cooperative structure was completely alien to the Inuit who had very little experience with formal business. The cooperative, nevertheless, had the advantage of being a hybrid form, fusing capitalist practices with collectivist goals. This would permit fuller integration of the Inuit into the larger society.[38]

Despite the principles of Canadian cooperatives in general, the reality differed in the north. While members elected officers, the latter and their agents often had to be outsiders with technical knowledge. About 1970, Pitseolak, an Inuit artist, described how she produced and marketed her work: "The Co-op sends the carvings and prints to the south, and it is owned by Eskimos. I don't know exactly how it works but there is a board of directors who are Eskimos. Terry [a white agent] gives out the pens and the papers for drawing, and later when we bring him our work, he pays." Shares rarely produced much interest or dividends, given the low profit margins of the enterprises established. Despite this, Pitseolak commented, "Terry at the Co-op . . . gives me money . . . with which I can buy clothes and tea and food for the family. . . . I am happy to have the money and I am glad we have a Co-op." Gradually, members did gain more knowledge of business practices, but this tended to create a small savvy elite and a large low-skilled work force. Moreover, the national federations tended to have excessive power in the

---

[38] For this section, I am heavily indebted to Marybelle Mitchell, *From Talking Chiefs to a Native Corporate Elite: The Birth of Class and Nationalism among Canadian Inuit*, McGill – Queen's Native and Northern Series (Montreal: McGill – Queen's Univ. Press, 1996), 164, 167, 155, 154.

operations of local cooperatives, in terms of product development and marketing.[39]

Regardless of these problems, the cooperatives did bring a measure of economic improvement to the northern communities and promoted a larger sense of ethnic, though not Canadian, identity. Traditional Inuit culture had stressed immediate family and extended kinship ties, in nomadic bands. Despite a common way of life and a diverse though common language, the Inuit had not developed a sense of ethnic identity stretching across northern Quebec, let alone northern Canada. Drawn into settled communities by the Canadian government and introduced to cooperatives, the Inuit had greater contact with groups beyond their kin. Indeed, relations of authority were transformed as social contacts expanded, forming an elite that had self-interest in and could see the benefits of a broader ethnic identity. But this identity took a truncated form because provincial governments and co-op federations failed to encourage Canadian national unity. While the government sought self-sufficiency of the native peoples partly to free itself of welfare costs, it feared separatism would arise, especially given the situation of the Quebecois. The federal government also sought to assert its sovereignty over the entire national domain, particularly as the Cold War made the north contested territory with the Soviet Union across the Arctic and North Atlantic.[40]

In 1973 after some agitation particularly on the part of Canada's Indians, the federal government sought to settle the various land claims of its indigenous peoples. Even though the land conflict had a long history with Indians, it had never been a major issue with the Inuits because settlers had not populated the distant north in great numbers given its challenging nature. The situation changed as multinational corporations became interested in the nonrenewable resources of the northern lands, especially oil and gas. The first government settlement with the Inuit – a treaty, in other words – was the James Bay and Northern Quebec Agreement, signed in 1975. This modern treaty involved rights to game animals, sacred grounds, settlement, marketable

[39] Ibid.; and Pitseolak [Ashoona], *Pitseolak: Pictures out of my Life*, with Dorothy Harley Eber, 2nd ed. (Montreal: McGill – Queen's Univ. Press, 2003), 74, ix, 121.

[40] Mitchell, 448; for similar internal problems in an ethnic community development corporation in a different country and region, cf. John R. Chávez, *Eastside Landmark: A History of the East Los Angeles Community Union* (Stanford, Calif.: Stanford Univ. Press, 1998), 257–9.

products, resource revenue, and property. Services of various sorts, such as welfare, education, language, and security, entered the agreements as well. Critical to the evolution of ethnic nationalism was the requirement that beneficiaries of the treaties prove their Inuit heritage, to the point of receiving identity cards. Clearly, such a requirement would engender a sense of ethnic identity as nothing else had.[41]

The state recognized undefined Inuit title to the lands under the national government's sovereignty, but sought to define title clearly so that the land might be developed according to capitalist methods. In practice this meant convincing the natives to transfer their rights for concrete benefits from the state. In exchange for vast stretches of territory and the "potential for generating internal capital," the Inuits generally received financial compensation ($90 million at James Bay, about $1,500 per person), use of land, self-government, educational control, social services, and economic development. To handle the compensation funds, the government instituted development corporations that included all present and future Inuits as shareholders. While the policies and revenues of the corporations remained primarily in the hands of government officials, these institutions again supplied a collective identity to the Inuits. Ethnic nationalism thus evolved within and because of cooperatives and development corporations, ostensibly economic, but clearly political entities as well.[42]

This nationalism, of course, meant self-determination for the Inuit homeland. In 1992 an accord between the national government and the Inuits of the Eastern Arctic divided the Northwest Territory and created Nunavut, an Inuit-dominated territory. As might be expected, this occurred as part of a broad treaty in which the local Inuits gave up title to land elsewhere. The Inuits of northern Quebec had earlier sought a similar agreement with the provincial government, but met with greater resistance, given the desire of the French-speaking for the territorial integrity of a province many hoped to separate from Canada. In 1983, however, the provincial government had offered greater autonomy to its Inuit population in a homeland called Nunavik. Among the

---

[41] Mitchell, 342; and Claude Meillassoux, "Comment se sont perpétués les Inuit?" in *Population, reproduction, sociétés: Perspectives et enjeux de démographie sociale – Mélanges en l'honneur de Joel W. Gregory*, ed. Dennis D. Cordell, Danielle Gauvreau, Raymond R. Gervais, and Céline Le Bourdais (Montreal: Les Presses de l'Université de Montréal, 1993), 19–23.

[42] Mitchell, 364, 352.

organizations involved in the negotiations for self-government was the Makivik Development Corporation, demonstrating the role of economic institutions in the ethnic nationalist movement for self-determination.[43]

Significantly, cooperatives and development corporations also played a role in the formation of a pan-Eskimo movement. Indeed, just after the founding of the first cooperatives, Inuits from throughout Canada met in 1963 at Frobisher Bay to discuss issues regarding cooperatives, the first such meeting in Inuit history. About this time the co-op movement in Quebec had assumed the role of underground Inuit governance; ethnic nationalism thus developed at various geographical levels. By 1977 the pan-Eskimo movement had become transnational. The first Inuit Circumpolar Conference (ICC) met at Barrow, Alaska, including delegates from Greenland, as well as the United States and Canada. Eventually, Inuit from Siberia would also meet in such conferences.[44]

In their relatively short history of intensive contact with the dominant society, Inuits had moved from a starving disorganized collection of colonized people, totally dependent on the national government, to an assertive ethnic group showing all the signs of becoming a nation. Their ethnic nationalism, nevertheless, showed signs of transcendence through the pan-Eskimo movement. Numbering fewer than two hundred thousand throughout the Arctic, Inuits could not continue to think only in terms of local homelands, regardless of their vast geographical extent. Self-government in Nunavut and Nunavik rested on Inuit majorities that might quickly erode with the next gold rush into the Arctic. The survival of ethnic groups culturally and otherwise depended on events beyond local regions and even national states. With multinational corporations seeking to develop the Arctic's resources, Inuits and other ethnic groups needed to cooperate transcontinentally. United Nations' acceptance of the ICC as a nongovernmental organization exemplified steps possible for federation at the global level.[45]

[43] Ibid., 358, 368; cf. Chávez, *Eastside Landmark*, 259–62.
[44] Mitchell, 322–3, 429–30; the importance of indigenous community-based organizations, including those run by women, in Liberia is evident in Sawyer, 68–70, 72.
[45] Mitchell, 429–30; cf. Chávez, *Eastside Landmark*, 263–4; and Sandra Faiman-Silva, *Choctaws at the Crossroads: The Political Economy of Class and Culture in the Oklahoma Timber Region* (Lincoln: Univ. of Nebraska Press, 1997), 214–18.

The Economic Community of West African States

The need for a confederation along the lines of the European Community, at least for economic development, was recognized in Africa even before North America. In the 1970s the Economic Community of West African States (ECOWAS) had formed combining various former colonies, sixteen by 1990. Various Francophone states, including Senegal and Mali to the north, had joined Anglophone countries to the south and east, such as Sierra Leone, Liberia, and Nigeria hoping to break down trade barriers, establish a monetary union, and undertake other such policies modeled on Western Europe. However, border disputes, interethnic rivalry, dictatorship, general poverty, uneven socioeconomic development, and fear of domination by powerful Nigeria made effective confederation difficult.[46]

The importance of international and interethnic community to the internal stability of independent states was nevertheless undeniable. Senegal, for example, evolved from independence in 1960 into a successful, democratic, multiethnic state through such cooperation. Its long history, as the Jolof Empire and a major French colony, had given it some geopolitical coherence. Though representing Toucouleur, Serer, Mandingo, and other groups, the state coalesced around an urban Wolof plurality, a Francophone elite, and a common Muslim religion. The unitary state allowed regional assemblies under appointed governors, but this administration reflected ethnic regions less than commercial centers and their hinterlands. With this regional system, Senegal succeeded as a multiethnic state because its varied groups felt sufficiently represented through local departments and rural councils. In this small country, ethnic groups, even the Wolof, formed interspersed enclaves, rather than fully contiguous homelands, which made ethnic separatism less likely, despite a brief rebellion of that sort along the Casamance River. Loyalty to one's ethnic group did not preclude loyalty to Senegal, with an official language that connected it to the rest of Francophone Africa and the outer world. Since Dakar had been the capital of the French West African Federation, Senegal was very willing to experiment with federalism, twice merging with neighboring states,

---

[46] Adekeye Adebajo, *Liberia's Civil War: Nigeria, ECOMAG, and Regional Security in West Africa* (Boulder, Colo.: L. Rienner, 2002), 60; and Department of Foreign Affairs, "Economic Community of West African States," available from www.dfa.za/for-relations/ multilateral/ecowas.htm, accessed 31 December 2003.

Mali in 1960 and Gambia in 1982, but finding common interests insufficient to maintain the unions.[47]

Though cross-border refugees from authoritarian Mauritania added to the interethnic complexity, Senegal's political harmony was more threatened by its own extremes of class. With over half of the population impoverished, a tiny elite controlled the economy and its links to the outer world. Largely rural with few natural resources, Senegal depended on foreign assistance for about a third of government spending in 2000, monies coming from France, the United States, the World Bank, and the International Monetary Fund. Benefiting from such aid in 2003, Senegal electrified some rural areas, thus allowing micro businesses to operate. Then able to plug in a refrigerator, villager Astou Diagne could sell plastic bags of ice to her neighbors: "For someone who was making zero money, it makes a big difference," she remarked. This woman's situation illustrated the socioeconomic foundations necessary to build stable geopolitical structures, from the individual to the regional, national, and global. Given foreign aid, Senegal participated actively in international organizations, such as ECOWAS, including sending troops on peacekeeping missions to Liberia and Sierra Leone. Having dealt successfully with domestic ethnic diversity, Senegal became an active proponent of confederation at the international level.[48]

Liberia and Sierra Leone were far less stable than Senegal. By the late twentieth century the Americo-Liberians could no longer enforce the unity we saw established in the nineteenth. As indigenous groups became increasingly aware of their disadvantages, slow change built further animosity against the still oppressive system. President William R. Tolbert continued reforms started by his predecessor, but a deteriorating economy undermined the Americo-Liberian regime's ability to meet increasing ethnic and other demands. When iron ore and rubber

---

[47] Sheldon Gellar, *Senegal: An African Nation Between Islam and the West*, Profiles, Nations of Contemporary Africa (Boulder, Colo.: Westview Press, 1982), 8–10; U.S. Department of State, Bureau of African Affairs, "Background Note: Senegal," available from www.state.gov/r/pa/ei/bgn/2862.htm, accessed 21 December 2003; and République du Sénégal, Site officiel du Gouvernement, available from www.gouv.sn/integration/index.html, accessed 27 June 2005.

[48] Ibid.; quoted in Nafi Diouf, "Debt Relief Means Electricity for Senegal," *Seattle Post-Intelligencer*, 15 June 2005; for more on the role of women, see Frederick Cooper, *Africa Since 1940: The Past of the Future*, New Approaches to African History (New York: Cambridge Univ. Press, 2002), 125–7.

export prices dropped, Tolbert could not afford to import the rice needed to feed the population, causing unrest. In 1980 a coup, led by native junior army officers, finally ended Americo-Liberian political, if not economic, dominance. Ethnic leaders and groups thus competed for power over the central government, rather than to gain regional autonomy.[49]

Unfortunately for Liberia, indigenous rule proved no more just than the previous regime. Initially "stressing class over ethnicity," Samuel Kanyon Doe, the coup leader, nevertheless filled strategic posts in the army and government with Krahns (his own ethnic group) and his allies, including some Mandingos and Americo-Liberians. Instead of serving the nation as a whole, Doe's supporters proceeded illegally to obtain land, natural resource concessions, and even U.S. food assistance, using the state to enrich themselves and deepening the economic crisis. This naturally angered Doe's rivals, ethnic, and otherwise. Violations of civil and human rights increased, as Doe murdered and imprisoned his opponents. In 1985 an attempted coup led to violence between Gios and Manos on the rebel side, and Krahns and Mandingos on Doe's, culminating in the government's killing of three thousand. Such chaos illustrated the limits of the sovereign state and the need for federated international institutions to control the anarchy.[50]

In 1990 Charles Taylor, Americo-Liberian and Gola in ancestry, led Doe's rivals in overthrowing the government, again demonstrating the need for legitimate intervention. Eventually, ECOWAS stepped in because the violence threatened neighboring states, such as Sierra Leone. With minor support from the United Nations, European Union, United States, and nongovernmental organizations, ECOWAS was able to stabilize the situation in the nineties with an interim government and an election in 1997, which put Taylor officially in office. Unfortunately, no more a statesman than Doe, Taylor claimed, "Once you are in, because of the chaos created from outside, you become undemocratic in the preservation of power." His support for Sierra Leonean rebels caused civil war to spread to that country, plagued by similar divisions. Finally, Taylor was forced into exile in 2003 under

---

[49] Central Intelligence Agency, "World Factbook – Liberia," available from www.cia.gov/cia/publications/factbook/geos/li.html, accessed 28 June 2005; and Adebajo, 21–5.

[50] Ibid., 25–8, 36; see also Sawyer, 17–20.

pressure from the international community after violence erupted again
in Liberia. Though ECOWAS proved too weak to control the situation
alone, this confederation's West African membership had given the
international community the legitimacy to act where even UN intervention might have seemed imperialistic. In 2006 Taylor was put on
trial by Sierra Leone and the UN; and Liberia had elected Ellen John-
son-Sirleaf president to reconstruct the country after years of rule by
"strongmen."[51]

Small countries in West Africa, Senegal, Sierra Leone, and Liberia
were each a composite of many homelands forced together by imperialism, rather than voluntary union. As we have seen, native states, such
as the Jolof Empire and the Temne Kingdoms, had held these lands
and peoples together over centuries only to have them fragment. In
the modern era the French, British, and Americans had imposed their
own imperial systems, arbitrarily joining native homelands for external reasons. For instance, in the twentieth century the British com-
bined the multi-ethnic "chiefdoms" of Sierra Leone, granted some
representation in the legislative council, and allowed some self-government, though under white district commissioners. After ten years
of seeming preparation, in 1961 Sierra Leone gained independence,
divided into the Freetown area and three nonethnic provinces, but
with ethnic representation in parliament, along the colonial model.
Despite a common creole English and wealth in diamonds, the country
fell into dictatorship and disorder, as strongmen sought control of the
central government, using gendered, ethnic, class, and other rivalries
to advance personal fortunes – a situation culminating in the 1990s
with civil war similar to Liberia's. On departure, the colonial powers
had left disparate communities and lands grouped into so-called nation-states with little ethnic or other unity. Even where democracy
and federalism had seemingly been implemented as in Sierra Leone,
dire poverty and masculine ambitions could waylay the country. In the
resulting rape, mutilation, and general internecine violence, one ex-
soldier said there was "no sense of belonging." Sierra Leone and
Liberia, despite the latter's long history as an independent state, lost

---

[51] Quoted in Adebajo, 236, 62, 217, 248–9; BBC News, "Timeline, Sierra Leone:
     A Chronology of Key Events," available from news.bbc.co.uk/1/hi/world/Africa/
     country_ profiles/1065898.stm, accessed 30 June 2005; and "Liberia: President
     Orders Ministers to Oust Corrupt Staff," available from allafrica.com/stories/
     200604280505.html, accessed 1 May 2006.

"national" unity, illustrating the need for legitimate intervention by the international institutions with which these countries were federated.[52]

The Economic Community of West African States was an indigenous African attempt at international confederation to encourage more local unity. Though far from the supranational state evolving in Europe, ECOWAS had shown the ability to intervene and bring peace to states destabilized by interethnic and other conflict. Though struggling as an economic union, ECOWAS had of necessity become an international military alliance playing a role curiously more like that of the North Atlantic Treaty Organization. Being African meant ECOWAS had relatively more legitimacy in any intervention within its own continental area, even though particular nation-states and ethnic groups disputed that. In theory the balance between the local, the national, and international was better served by ECOWAS than through intervention by the United States or European Union. Given the weak economies of ECOWAS's members, however, material support for peacekeeping had to come from outside powers. In addition, international nongovernmental organizations – Catholic Relief Services, Action Contre la Faim, International Rescue Committee, Médecins du Monde – remained essential for humanitarian assistance. Finally, the weak financial and military resources of the West African states led the UN, the ultimate global confederation, to take over peacekeeping in 2003. Unfortunately, at the local level, external influences could be seen as renewed imperialism even when carried out by international organizations, ECOWAS included. Indeed, while internationalists strove to achieve order in unstable states around the Atlantic and the globe, local individuals and ethnic communities did not necessarily see their own ideals and interests aligned with outer rings of power.[53]

---

[52] U.S. Department of State, Bureau of African Affairs, "Background Note: Sierra Leone," available from www.state.gov/r/pa/ei/bgn/5475.htm, accessed 19 December 2003; and Michael Josiah quoted in Daniel Bergner, *In the Land of Magic Soldiers: A Story of White and Black in West Africa* (New York: Farrar, Straus & Giroux, 2003), 30, 32, 60, 146–7, 178–81.

[53] Adebajo, 250–3, 118; and Department of Foreign Affairs; see also "Economic Development Community of West African States (ECOWAS)," in *New Encyclopedia of Africa*, ed. John Middleton and Joseph C. Miller, vol. 2, 2nd ed. (Detroit, Mich.: Charles Scribner's Sons, Gale, Cengage Learning, 2008), 161–4.

SIGNS OF INTERNATIONAL FEDERATION

The European Union, the North American Free Trade Agreement, and the Economic Community of West African States exemplified the realities and suggested the possibilities of international community. Rising from the smoldering ruins of World War II, the EU reversed hundreds if not thousands of years of conflict between neighboring nations, kingdoms, and empires. Though committed to a competitive capitalist ethic, the EU's member nations rested solidly on the foundation of the welfare state, assuring that all their citizens would benefit from the free trade between the members. Though NAFTA did not go nearly so far in its political and social policies, it too suggested that North America could evolve into a community of nations, trading and migrating freely, while recognizing the autonomy, not only of the dominant cultures, but of regional and immigrant cultures as well. ECO-WAS illustrated the need for strong economies for such supranational conceptions to be effective. Ultimately, loose confederations had to become federations capable of exercising the legitimate power to check states that abused individual and collective human rights.[54]

[54] Lundestad, 155–6; Richard Kearney, "Postnationalist Identities: A New Configuration," in *Empire & Terror: Nationalism/Postnationalism in the New Millenium*, Conference Papers Series, no. 1, ed. Begoña Aretxaga, Dennis Dworkin, Joseba Gabilondo, and Joseba Zulaika (Reno: Univ. of Nevada, Center for Basque Studies, 2004), 29; for questions about the African conditions that seemingly transcend the colonial framework, see Cooper, 130–1, 202–4.

POSTNATIONAL VISIONS — IMAGINED FEDERATIONS

CHANGING WORLD ORDER

In response to migration and conquest, communities and homelands in the North Atlantic World evolved in complex and multiple ways in the modern era. The Micmacs moved from an independent nation to a reservation in a land called Megumaage, then Acadia, then Nova Scotia. Tlaxcalans followed a different path from independence to autonomy, then to statehood within the mestizo nation of Mexico. On the other side of the ocean, the Irish mutated from autonomous earldoms, to colony, to independent state, though incomplete. The Basques straddling a border between two nation-states experienced mostly a fragmented autonomy over the centuries. The Liberians, farther south, followed over 150 years of independence with civil war and the need to reconstruct society. The historic connections between ethnic communities, homelands, and states always bewildering became more so by the turn of the twenty-first century. Writing of his own transnational "community," Tejano Daniel Arreola commented: "If there is a geographical Hispanic/Latino nation, it is a largely fragmented confederation of regional zones and nodes, not a unified area in any real sense." Partially in response to such complexity, supranational states developed. Though decolonization had led to seemingly ubiquitous aspirations for the ethnic self-determination represented by the national state, globalization seemingly demanded the breakdown of borders or at least their reconfiguration. The European Union, like the Iroquois Confederacy and other confederations before it, offered individuals and peoples a model of voluntary incorporation that could create multiethnic cooperation, rather than strife. Unfortunately, implementing the sophisticated federalism necessary was an uncertain process.[1]

Persistent Imperialism

As we have seen, Cuextlan, Ireland, and Granada experienced imperialism at the hands of their neighbors the Aztecs, English, and Moors, hardly evidence of tranquil world systems before transatlantic contact. But imperialism had largely established the modern world order. Gran Canaria became a colony of Castile, Megumage part of New France, and Powhatan's Country part of Virginia in the first great wave of transatlantic empire that ordered the modern world from 1400–1750. These homelands were conquered, colonized, and forcibly tied into vast collections of diverse lands and peoples subordinated to "mother countries" overseas. Between 1750 and 1880 Iroquoia, Santo Domingo, Texas, and the Kru region succumbed to expanding neighbors who, envisioning a republican global order, imitated their former imperial masters in a process of internal colonialism. Formal imperialism repeated itself in a second great wave of empire between 1880–1945, when the great powers, democratic or not, scrambled to acquire the Yalunka country, Morocco, Puerto Rico, and ultimately each other in Europe. (See Figure 2.) Formal colonialism changed form after 1945 as two superpowers, erstwhile empires, struggled for supremacy in a bipolar world with the West based around the North Atlantic. Following a neocolonial system, they acquired satellites, erstwhile colonies, such as Cuba and the Dominican Republic. Starting in 1989, nations such as Latvia, Ukraine, and Armenia began breaking away from the Soviet Union, revealing the Russian Empire beneath, and rearranging the world again though mostly far from the Atlantic. Subsequently, Panama and Iraq experienced invasions by the American empire, as both the political right and left recoined the term for a new age of U.S. hegemony extending far beyond the Atlantic. Spanning the globe, militarily and economically, the remaining superpower persisted in imperialism, frequently intervening in other countries unilaterally and thus losing legitimacy. On the other hand, the

[1] Daniel D. Arreola, ed., *Hispanic Spaces, Latino Places: Community and Cultural Diversity in Contemporary America* (Austin: Univ. of Texas Press, 2004), 33–5; for events behind the development of internal colonial theory, see Ramón Gutiérrez, "Internal Colonialism: The History of a Theory," *DuBois Review: Social Science Research on Race*, 1(Summer 2004): 281–96 – my thanks to the author for providing me a personal copy.

Figure 2. Castillo de San Cristobal (1783), Boulevard Norzagaray, San Juan, Puerto Rico, Historic American Building Survey/Historic American Engineering Record (c. 1934). Courtesy of the Library of Congress, Washington, D.C.

United States could also act with credibility through international organizations, such as the United Nations and the European Union, entities founded on American federalist principles.[2]

HOMELAND, NATION, AND STATE

Resisting imperialism were always independent homelands occupied by bands, clans, tribes, and even nations, related by ancestry or culture. Coahuiltecans, Berbers, the Temne, and the Welsh were peoples in places usually, but not always, independent of outside powers prior to the modern era. Some of these peoples had formed bureaucracies, states to govern their nations and homelands, as did Tlaxcala and Kajoor, states that could

---

[2] Neil Smith, *American Empire: Roosevelt's Geographer and the Prelude to Globalization*, California Studies in Critical Human Geography (Berkeley and Los Angeles: Univ. of California Press, 2003), 454–5; for a brief overview relating conquest and imperialism to colonial, world systems, and other theories, see Kelly F. Himmel, *The Conquest of the Karankawas and the Tonkawas, 1821–1859*, Elma Dill Russell Spencer Series in the West and Southwest, no. 20 (College Station: Texas A&M Univ. Press, 1999), 135–8.

permit them some autonomy within invading European empires. Such indigenous nations survived long periods of subjugation later to reassert their sovereignty, such as the Irish, but homelands were usually much changed by colonialism. For example, rather than Indians, white settlers in New York, black slaves in Haiti, and mestizos in Mexico threw off imperialism in the revolutionary era. Resisting the imperial scramble for Africa, Liberia managed to maintain its independence and Morocco its sultanate, though as protectorates of great powers. After World War II decolonization freed Algeria, Jamaica, and a host of other nations only to be contested between the super powers. In the latest global reorganization, Bretons, Quebecóis, Tejanos, and Chiapanecos unexpectedly called for liberation of their own internally colonized lands, as did many Soviet republics. Despite the wishes of empires and multiethnic states, nations and homelands remained objects of emotional attachment to their particular peoples. Multiethnic states could win national legitimacy and the patriotism of ethnic populations through federalism by providing political and cultural autonomy, rule of law, social welfare, security, and economic development for their regions. Such did Canada hope to provide Nunavut; the United States, Puerto Rico; and Spain, the Basque Country.[3]

CONFEDERATION VS. FEDERATION

As we have seen, prior to contact across the Atlantic, states at times joined together in loose political structures with a weak center. Such a confederacy allowed the Seneca, the Oneida, and the other Iroquois nations the choice of collective or independent action with surrounding peoples. Similar structures could be found among the Temne Kingdoms and between England and Anglo-Ireland. With the spread of transoceanic empires, Aragon, Brittany, and Scotland saw their crowns joined to those of Castile, France, and England, respectively, initially forming confederated states to which they then added the colonized dominions of New Spain, New France, and New England. Successfully rejecting that subordinate status, the American states, the Mexican states, and the Canadian provinces experimented with confederation through the early decades of their development. Though confederation, with its right of secession, proved too loose to hold most countries together, the League of Nations was an example of application of

---

[3]   Desmond King, *The Liberty of Strangers: Making the American Nation* (New York: Oxford Univ. Press, 2005), 174; for the role of class in national integration, see Steve Fraser and Gary Gerstle, eds. *Ruling America: A History of Wealth and Power in a Democracy* (Cambridge, Mass.: Harvard Univ. Press, 2005), 25.

confederate principles to the global stage, with similar consequences given the imperial competition leading to World War II. With postwar decolonization the British Commonwealth of Nations and the French Community attempted to keep their former colonies confederated, commercially or at least symbolically, but the memories of imperialism led Ireland, Senegal, and other states to decline permanent participation. As with military alliances, states generally tolerated confederations only for compelling reasons, so that such unions generally lacked permanence.[4]

A federation, a union of self-governing states with a strong central government, more effectively joined regional units than did a confederation. As we have seen, three neighboring city-states — Tetzcoco, Tlacopan, and Tenochtitlan – formed a federation in 1428, which the latter dominated from the onset. By the time of Charles V, Spain had effectively federated under a single dynasty though Aragon and Castile retained distinct administrations; this contrasted with the unitary structure imposed on Scotland when it lost its parliament on formation of the United Kingdom. The American states discarded the unworkable Articles of Confederation only to have to reassert the federal Constitution at the cost of civil war. Liberia continued imitating American federalism in its own development, in competition with expanding European powers. After World War II, the Allies, confederated as the United Nations, created the Federal Republic of Germany. As we have seen, the West Indian Federation and the Mali Federation were short-lived products of decolonization, ultimately spinning off Jamaica and Senegal, respectively. These latter unions lacked the centripetal force to hold together – federations in name only. By contrast, post-Franco Spain designed perhaps the best model of multiethnic federalism in the North Atlantic World, recognizing all its ethnic regions as autonomous states, ultimately winning over the Basques, even as it integrated into the European Union.[5]

4 Though Canada used "confederation" to describe its union of 1867, its centralized government leaned more toward federation; see D[onald] W[illiam] Meinig, *The Shaping of America: A Geographical Perspective on 500 Years of History*, vol. 2, *Continental America, 1800–1867* (New Haven, Conn.: Yale Univ. Press, 1993), 537; and Ronald L. Watts, "Comparing Forms of Federal Partnerships," in *Theories of Federalism: A Reader*, ed. Dimitrios Karmis and Wayne Norman (New York: St. Martin's Press, Palgrave Macmillan, 2005), 239–42.

5 Mark Kurlansky, *The Basque History of the World* (New York: Walker & Co., 1999), 350–1; for a position in favor of confederation, see Benjamin R. Barber, *Jihad vs. McWorld* (New York: Random House, Time Books, 1995; Ballantine Books, 2001), 288–90.

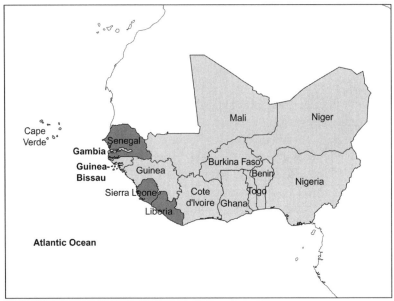

Map C.1. The Economic Community of West African States. Adapted from
www.eia.doe.gov/emeu/cabs/ECOWAS/Background.html, accessed 14 July 2007.
Cartography by Cassingham and Foxworth, courtesy of the Edwin J. Foscue Map
Library, SMU.

Indeed, the major problem with most international organizations
was their poor balance of power, generally with too little at the
center. Because of its confederated structure, the United Nations
had often proven ineffective in its mission to maintain world peace,
especially during the Cold War. Of the postwar confederations the
most promising by far was the European Union, comprised of members voluntarily joining for their mutual economic, rather than military benefits. We have seen that the North American Free Trade
Agreement was a poor imitation of the much more egalitarian European Union because the weight of the United States tilted the balance of power toward the imperial core, subordinating Canada and
Mexico. For the Economic Community of West African States general poverty made financial support for a more centralized organization difficult. (See Map C.1.) Because of its comparative advantages,
the European Union continued evolving from confederation to federation; the central government needed to be more powerful than the
member nations, especially as the number increased. Such federalism

was essential after the Cold War because the order of independent states was too fragmented to maintain peace and regulate economic globalization.[6]

Persistant Ethnic Regions

As we have seen, a major cause of the instability of the postcolonial state and the world order was the reassertion of regional ethnicity. Some of the more cohesive states, such as Senegal, successfully channeled that resurgent pride into a unified multiethnic polity; however, others, such as Sierra Leone, fragmented despite a parliamentary system based on tribal representation. Ethnic nationalism challenged those with multinational and global designs – from the EU to the UN – to understand local histories, if locals were ever to federate into larger wholes. Understanding this, Silvio Torres-Saillant, a professor of Dominican studies and English in New York, argued "that temporarily erecting . . . borders can lead to our self-recognition in our complex diversity. . . . With that goal securely achieved, it will then be realistic for us to aspire to federate our distinct constituencies." Indeed, when Spain, despite Basque terrorism, allowed its own diverse regions to draw borders among themselves, it paradoxically furthered its own integration and that of Europe.[7]

---

[6] Smith, 374–5; Paul Kennedy, *The Parliament of Man: The Past, Present, and Future of the United Nations:* (New York: Random House, 2006), 284–5; examining socioeconomic issues beyond the geopolitical focus of my book, Christopher Chase-Dunn and Thomas D. Hall argue (and I agree) "that overcoming the problems that capitalism has created (danger of terminal warfare, ecological crisis, and huge inequalities) will require the construction of a democratic and socialist world federal state," *Rise and Demise: Comparing World Systems*, New Perspectives in Sociology (Boulder, Colo.: HarperCollins, Westview Press, 1997), 244.

[7] Silvio Torres-Saillant, "Epilogue: Problematic Paradigms: Racial Diversity and Corporate Identity in the Latino Community," in *Latinos: Remaking America*, ed. Marcelo M. Suárez-Orozco and Mariela M. Páez (Berkeley and Los Angeles: Univ. of California Press with the David Rockefeller Center for Latin American Studies, Harvard Univ., 2002), 452–3, 465; Wilma A. Dunaway – "Ethnic Conflict in the Modern World System: The Dialectics of Counter-Hegemonic Resistance in an Age of Transition," *Journal of World-Systems Research* 9 (Winter 2003): 27 – takes a more pessimistic view of movements that "seek to integrate minorities into the failing [capitalist] system."

TRANSNATIONAL MIGRATION

Another major problem confronting the world order was migration, both economic and political; refugees fled their homelands to neighboring countries, to Europe, to the United States. In this movement there were not only millions of Africans, but Asians, and Latin Americans fleeing "underdeveloped" regions for the "modern" world. With quick access by air to London, Paris, or Miami, wealthier immigrants developed overseas communities, their nationalities seemingly unbounded by geography. Many poorer immigrants fled across borders to neighboring states, Sierra Leoneans to Liberia, Moroccans to Granada, Mexicans to Texas. In some cases this created transnational individuals who moved back and forth between countries, as well as traditional immigrants who settled permanently. Improved transportation and communications made the former more common than ever, challenging traditional notions of citizenship and nationalism tied to place of birth and residency. According to Harvard sociologist, Orlando Patterson, a native of Jamaica, "There is no traumatic transfer of national loyalty from the home country to the host polity, since home is readily accessible and national loyalty is a waning sentiment in what is increasingly a post-national world." How could federated lands address men, women, and communities who would not stay in place?[8]

Despite these complexities, every individual man and woman originated in an ethnic group and place; indeed, ethnicity was a marker of place in the world, and the reverse. Though increasingly a global consumer and world citizen, every person had ethnic roots in local communities and homelands even when the larger world appealed more strongly. Regionalism, D. W. Meinig tells us, "tends to be grounded more directly in family and community life, works routinely (and only in part consciously) to sustain local patterns of culture, and thus tends to maintain diversity within the whole. Federalism is a carefully contrived device to balance and harmonize diverse and even conflicting interests, to bring variety into concert with the common good." To the degree that the individual appreciated and then mentally federated local, regional, national, and transnational identities into a whole, an

---

[8]   Eric R. Wolf, *Europe and the People without History* (Berkeley and Los Angeles: Univ. of California Press, 1982), 383; and Orlando Patterson, "Ecumenical America: Global Culture and the American Cosmos," in *The Birth of Caribbean Civilisation: A Century of Ideas about Culture and Identity, Nation and Society*, ed. O. Nigel Bolland (Kingston, Jam.: Ian Randle Publishers, 2004), 632, 643–4, 649.

integrated personality could develop, accommodating conflicting backgrounds for a more integrated world.[9]

However, rather than a tightly hierarchical federalism extending from local neighborhoods to the UN, a more flexible system seemed to be needed. While one might imagine a worldwide federation of concentric communities, the reality of illegal aliens, racial intermixing, permeable borders, global business, and multiethnic homelands argued for more fluid conceptions built around individual choices. Individuals and their families created cultural outliers when they left their original communities, often crossing borders, to settle in foreign lands and cities. There they might create segregated enclaves with their compatriots, intermarry with the local population, possibly assimilate, or create bicultural/multicultural children and communities. Such individuals and communities, common to cities, were difficult to place in a federated framework. This was also true of regions comprised of multiple ethnicities settled over long periods. Quebec served as such an example, including native Algonkians, long settled French and English, with recent immigrant communities from elsewhere in Montreal.[10]

Multiethnic Imagination

To the degree that federalism simply reflected spatial order – circles within circles – it failed to reflect fully the lives and minds of real people. Real people moved in and out of such geometrical figures as departments, provinces, countries, and continents. As business people, farm workers, students, and diplomats, they moved temporarily or permanently from place to place, like arrows and points on a map – from Freetown to London, Washington to Monrovia. People also lived in the intersections of circles, border regions, such as the counties of Northern Ireland between Great

[9] D[onald] W[illiam] Meinig, *The Shaping of America, A Geographical Perspective on 500 Years of History*, vol. 1, *Atlantic America, 1492–1800* (New Haven, Conn.: Yale Univ. Press, 1986), 452–3; although Meinig's comments refer to regionalism in the United States, I find them applicable to homelands around the Atlantic, my focus, and to the rest of the world.

[10] See Nanda R. Shrestha and Wilbur I. Smith, "Epilogue: Geographical Imageries and Race Matters," in *Geographical Identities of Ethnic America: Race, Space, and Place*, ed. Kate A. Berry and Martha L. Henderson, foreword by Dong Ok Lee and Stanley Brunn (Reno: Univ. of Nevada Press, 2002), 279–94; and Moha Ennaji and Fatima Sadiqi, *Migration and Gender in Morocco: The Impact of Migration on the Women Left Behind* (Trenton, N.J.: Red Sea Press, 2008), 92, 96–8.

Britain and the Irish Republic. They could reside in a circle overlapping two circles, as in the Basque Country between Spain and France. They lived in outliers, away from the centers of their nations, in immigrant communities, such as Moroccans in Montreal, or in long-established enclaves, such as Cherokees in Oklahoma. These complex geographical patterns were reflected in the conflicting loyalties of people, yet many successfully accommodated these differences in minds capable of kaleidoscopic imagery, seemingly chaotic, but fundamentally ordered. Studying in Dakar, an American born in South Texas – with paternal lines in Tlaxcala, Granada, and Morocco, with maternal lines in Acadia, Brittany, and Scotland – might see himself as ethnically conflicted, culturally assimilated, or ruggedly individualized, but she might also see herself as a concerned citizen of the world with an ethnic core in San Antonio – circles and tangents of extended loyalty elsewhere. At the beginning of the twenty-first century such a multiethnic imagination was increasingly needed to build reflective political and economic structures, such as dual nationality, joint territorial governance, and common markets. Indeed, confederations and federations were such structures, and they were becoming more sophisticated, but they were not entirely new. As we have seen, early peoples on both sides of the Atlantic had previously imagined and constructed similar human designs.[11]

[11] "Regardless of what definition we apply, it is apparent that federalism is not a concept amenable to an unambiguous descriptive definition" – Mikhail Filippov, Peter C. Ordeshook, and Olga Shvetsova, *Designing Federalism: A Theory of Self-Sustainable Federal Institutions* (New York: Cambridge Univ. Press, 2004), 5; for visions beyond the current global socioeconomic system, see Tony Ballantyne and Antoinette Burton, eds., *Bodies in Contact: Rethinking Colonial Encounters in World History* (Durham, N.C.: Duke Univ. Press, 2005), 419; Immanuel Wallerstein, *World-Systems Analysis: An Introduction* (Durham, N.C.: Duke Univ. Press, 2005), 89–90; and Walter D. Mignolo, *Local Histories/Global Designs: Coloniality, Subaltern Knowledges, and Border Thinking*, Princeton Studies in Culture/Power/History (Princeton, N.J.: Princeton Univ. Press, 2000), 64, 73, 104, 181.

List of Works Cited

Books

Abu-Lughod, Janet L. *Before European Hegemony: The World System A.D. 1250–1350*. New York: Oxford Univ. Press, 1989.

Acosta, Teresa Palomo and Winegarten, Ruthe. *Las Tejanas: 300 Years of History*. Jack and Doris Smothers Series in Texas History, Life, and Culture, no. 10. Austin: Univ. of Texas Press, 2003.

Acuña, Rodolfo. *Occupied America: A History of Chicanos*. 5th ed. New York: Pearson/Longman, 2004.

Adebajo, Adekeye. *Liberia's Civil War: Nigeria, ECOMAG, and Regional Security in West Africa*. Boulder, Colo.: L. Rienner, 2002.

Alie, Joe A.D. *A New History of Sierra Leone*. New York: St. Martin's Press, 1990.

Allen, Paula Gunn. *The Sacred Hoop: Recovering the Feminine in American Indian Traditions*. Boston: Beacon Press, 1986.

Alonzo, Armando C. *Tejano Legacy: Rancheros and Settlers in South Texas, 1734–1900*. Albuquerque: Univ. of New Mexico Press, 1998.

Anderson, Benedict. *Imagined Communities: Reflections on the Origin and Spread of Nationalism*. Rev. ed. New York: Verso, 1991.

Armitage, David. *The Declaration of Independence: A Global History*. Cambridge, Mass.: Harvard Univ. Press, 2007.

——. *The Ideological Origins of the British Empire*. Ideas in Context 59. Cambridge: Cambridge Univ. Press, 2000.

Arreola, Daniel D., ed. *Hispanic Spaces, Latino Places: Community and Cultural Diversity in Contemporary America*. Austin: Univ. of Texas Press, 2004.

——. *Tejano South Texas: A Mexican American Cultural Province*. Jack and Doris Smothers Series in Texas History, Life, and Culture, no. 5. Austin: Univ. of Texas Press, 2002.

[Ashoona], Pitseolak. *Pitseolak: Pictures Out of My Life*. With Dorothy Harley Eber. 2nd ed. Montreal: McGill – Queen's Univ. Press, 2003.

Axtell, James. *Natives and Newcomers: The Cultural Origins of North America*. New York: Oxford Univ. Press, 2001.

Bailyn, Bernard. *Atlantic History: Concept and Contours*. Cambridge, Mass.: Harvard Univ. Press, 2005.

Balfour, Sebastian. *Deadly Embrace: Morocco and the Road to the Spanish Civil War*. New York: Oxford Univ. Press, 2002.

Ballantyne, Tony and Burton, Antoinette, eds. *Bodies in Contact: Rethinking Colonial Encounters in World History*. Durham, N.C.: Duke Univ. Press, 2005.

Banks, Kenneth J. *Chasing Empire across the Sea: Communications and the State in the French Atlantic, 1713–1763*. Montreal: McGill – Queen's Univ. Press, 2002.

Barber, Benjamin R. *Jihad vs. McWorld*. 1995. Reprint, New York: Ballantine Books, 2001.

Barrera, Mario. *Beyond Aztlán: Ethnic Autonomy in Comparative Perspective*. New York: Praeger, 1988.

——. *Race and Class in the Southwest: A Theory of Racial Inequality*. Notre Dame, Ind.: Univ. of Notre Dame Press, 1979.

Barreto, Amílcar A. *Language, Elites, and the State: Nationalism in Puerto Rico and Quebec*. Westport, Conn.: Praeger, 1998.

Barthélemy, Joseph.*The Government of France*, trans. **J. Bayard Morris**. New York: Brentano's Publishers, [1924].

Bartlett, Robert. *The Making of Europe: Conquest, Colonization, and Cultural Change, 950–1350*. Princeton, N.J.: Princeton Univ. Press, 1993.

Beauchamp, William M. *Iroquois Folk Lore: Gathered from the Six Nations of New York*. Empire State Historical Publication, 31. 1922. Reprint, Port Washington, N.Y.: Ira J. Friedman, 1965.

Bellegarde-Smith, Patrick. *Haiti: The Breached Citadel*. Westview Profiles: Nations of Contemporary Latin America. Boulder, Colo.: Westview Press, 1990.

Ben-Ami, Shlomo. *The Origins of the Second Republic in Spain*. New York: Oxford Univ. Press, 1978.

Benjamin, Thomas. *Chiapas: Tierra rica, pueblo pobre – Historia política y social*. Mexico City: Grijalbo, 1995.

Benjamin, Thomas; Hall, Timothy; and Rutherford, David, eds. *The Atlantic World in the Age of Empire*. Problems in World History. Boston: Houghton Mifflin, 2001.

Bergner, Daniel. *In the Land of Magic Soldiers: A Story of White and Black in West Africa*. New York: Farrar, Straus & Giroux, 2003.

Blauner, Robert. *Racial Oppression in America*. New York: Harper & Row, 1972.

Boley, G[eorge] E[utychianus] Saigbe. *Liberia: The Rise and Fall of the First Republic*. New York: St. Martin's Press, 1983.

Bontier, Pierre and Le Verrier, Jean. *The Canarian, or Book of the Conquest and Conversion of the Canarians in the Year 1402, by Messire Jean de Bethencourt, Kt.* Trans. and ed. with notes and an introduction by **Richard Henry Major**. Works Issued by the Hakluyt Society, no. 46. London: Hakluyt Society, 1872.

Branston, Brian. *The Lost Gods of England*. New York: Oxford Univ. Press, 1974.

Brooks, George E. *Eurafricans in Western Africa: Commerce, Social Status, Gender, and Religious Observance from the Sixteenth to the Eighteenth Century*. Western African Studies. Athens: Ohio Univ. Press, 2003.

Burgess, Michael. *Federalism and European Union: The Building of Europe, 1950–2000*. New York: Taylor & Francis Group, Routledge, 2000.

Bush, Barbara. *Imperialism and Colonialism*. History: Concepts, Theory, and Practice. Harlow, UK: Pearson, Longman, 2006.

Caesar, Julius. *C. Iuli Caesaris Commentarii rerum in Gallia gestarum VII; A. Hirti Commentarius VIII*. ed. **T. Rice Holmes**. Oxford: Clarendon Press, 1914.

Cameron, Maxwell A. and **Tomlin, Brian W**. *The Making of NAFTA: How the Deal Was Done*. Ithaca, N.Y.: Cornell Univ. Press, 2000.

Carrasco, Pedro.*The Tenochca Empire of Ancient Mexico: The Triple Alliance of Tenochtilan, Tetzcoco, and Tlacopan*. Civilization of the American Indian Series, vol. 234. Norman: Univ. of Oklahoma Press, 1999.

Carroll, Patrick J. *Blacks in Colonial Veracruz: Race, Ethnicity, and Regional Development*. Austin: Univ. of Texas Press, 1991.

Champaign, Duane. *Social Order and Political Change: Constitutional Governments among the Cherokee, the Choctaw, the Chickasaw, and the Creek*. Stanford, Calif.: Stanford Univ. Press, 1992.

Chase-Dunn, Christopher and **Hall, Thomas D**. *Rise and Demise: Comparing World Systems*. New Perspectives in Sociology. Boulder, Colo.: HarperCollins, Westview Press, 1997.

Chávez, John R. *Eastside Landmark: A History of the East Los Angeles Community Union*. Stanford, Calif.: Stanford Univ. Press, 1998.

——. *The Lost Land: The Chicano Image of the Southwest*. Albuquerque: Univ. of New Mexico Press, 1984.

Chimenti, Elisa. *Tales and Legends of Morocco*. Trans. **Arnon Benamy**. New York: Ivan Obolensky, Astor Books, 1965.

Collins, Roger. *The Arab Conquest of Spain, 710–796*. A History of Spain. Cambridge, Mass.: Basil Blackwell, 1989.

——. *The Basques*. The Peoples of Europe. New York: Basil Blackwell, 1987.

Colvin, Lucie Gallistel. *Historical Dictionary of Senegal*. African Historical Dictionaries, no. 23. Metuchen, N.J.: Scarecrow Press, 1981.

Conley, Robert J. *The Cherokee Nation: A History*. Albuquerque: Univ. of New Mexico Press, 2005.

Connor, Walker. *Ethnonationalism: The Quest for Understanding*. Princeton, N.J.: Princeton Univ. Press, 1994.

Conrad, Margaret R. and **Hiller, James K**. *Atlantic Canada: A Region in the Making*. The Illustrated History of Canada. Toronto: Oxford Univ. Press, 2001.

Cook, Ramsay; **Moore, Christopher**; **Morton, Desmond**; **Ray, Arthur**; **Waite, Peter**; and **Wynn, Graeme**. *Histoire générale du Canada*. Boréal compact, 18.

Trans. from English to French, **Michel Buttiens, Andrée Désilets, Suzanne Mineau, Paule Sainte-Onge,** and **Marcel Trudel.** [Montreal]: Éditions du Boréal, 1990.

Cooper, Frederick. *Africa Since 1940: The Past of the Future.* New Approaches to African History. New York: Cambridge Univ. Press, 2002.

Corbett, Edward M. *Quebec Confronts Canada.* Baltimore, Md.: Johns Hopkins Univ. Press, 1967.

Cornell, Stephen. *The Return of the Native: American Indian Political Resurgence.* New York: Oxford Univ. Press, 1988.

Cornevin, Robert. *Littératures d'Afrique noire de langue française.* Littératures modernes, 10. [Paris]: Presses Universitaires de France, 1976.

Cortés, Hernando. *Hernando Cortés: Five Letters, 1519–1526.* Trans. **J. Bayard Morris.** New York: W. W. Norton, 1969.

Countryman, Edward. *The American Revolution.* Rev. ed. New York: Hill and Wang, 2003.

Crimm, Ana Carolina Castillo. *De León: A Tejano Family History.* Austin: Univ. of Texas Press, 2003.

Curtin, Philip D. *The Atlantic Slave Trade: A Census.* Madison: Univ. of Wisconsin Press, 1969.

Cushman, H. B. *History of the Choctaw, Chickasaw, and Natchez Indians.* 1899. Reprint, Norman: Univ. of Oklahoma Press, 1999.

Darwin, John. *Britain and Decolonisation: The Retreat from Empire in the Post-War World.* Making of the Twentieth Century. New York: St. Martin's Press, 1988.

Davidson, Basil. *Africa in History: Themes and Outlines.* Rev. ed. New York: Macmillan Co., Collier Books, 1991.

Davies, R. R. *The First English Empire: Power and Identities in the British Isles, 1093–1343.* Ford Lectures Delivered in the University of Oxford in Hilary Term 1998. Oxford: Oxford Univ. Press, 2000.

Davies, Wendy. *Small Worlds: The Village Community in Early Medieval Brittany.* Berkeley and Los Angeles: Univ. of California Press, 1988.

De Eguílaz Yanguas, Leopoldo. *Reseña histórica de la conquista del Reino de Granada por los Reyes Católicos, según los cronistas árabes.* Facsimile ed. 1894. Reprint, Granada: Ediciones Albaida, 1986.

Debo, Angie. *A History of the Indians of the United States.* Civilization of the American Indians Series. Norman: Univ. of Oklahoma Press, 1970.

Diamond, Jared. *Guns, Germs, and Steel: The Fates of Human Societies.* New York: W. W. Norton, 1997.

Díaz del Castillo, Bernal. *Historia verdadera de la conquista de la Nueva España.* With an introduction and notes by Joaquín Ramírez Cabañas. 2nd ed. Mexico City: Editorial Porrua, Sepan Cuantos, 1962.

Dickason, Olive Patricia. *Canada's First Nations: A History of Founding Peoples from Earliest Times.* Civilization of the American Indian Series. Norman: Univ. of Oklahoma Press, 1992.

Dickinson, John and Young, Brian. *A Short History of Quebec*. 3rd ed. Montreal: McGill – Queen's Univ. Press, 2003.

Duany, Jorge. *The Puerto Rican Nation on the Move: Identities on the Island and in the United States*. Chapel Hill: Univ. of North Carolina Press, 2002.

Dunaway, Wilma A. *The First American Frontier: Transition to Capitalism in Southern Appalachia, 1700–1860*. Fred W. Morrison Series in Southern Studies. Chapel Hill: Univ. of North Carolina Press, 1996.

Duncan, Barbara R., ed. *Living Stories of the Cherokee*. Chapel Hill: Univ. of North Carolina Press, 1998.

Dunn, D. Elwood and Holsoe, Svend E. *Historical Dictionary of Liberia*. African Historical Dictionaries, no. 38. Metuchen, N.J.: Scarecrow Press, 1985.

El-Ayouty, Yassin. *The United Nations and Decolonization: The Role of Afro-Asia*. The Hague: Martinus Nijhoff, 1971.

Engelbrecht, William. *Iroquoia: The Development of a Native World*. Iroquois and Their Neighbors. Syracuse, N.Y.: Syracuse Univ. Press, 2003.

Ennaji, Moha and Sadiqi, Fatima. *Migration and Gender in Morocco: The Impact of Migration on the Women Left Behind*. Trenton, N.J.: Red Sea Press, 2008.

Erk, Jan. *Explaining Federalism: State, Society, and Congruence in Austria, Belgium, Canada, Germany, and Switzerland*. Routledge Series in Federal Studies. New York: Routledge, Taylor & Francis Group, 2008.

Faiman-Silva, Sandra. *Choctaws at the Crossroads: The Political Economy of Class and Culture in the Oklahoma Timber Region*. Lincoln: Univ. of Nebraska Press, 1997.

Fanon, Frantz. *Les Damnés de la terre*. Paris: François Maspero, 1961.

Fernández-Armesto, Felipe. *The Canary Islands after the Conquest: The Making of a Colonial Society in the Early Sixteenth Century*. Oxford: Clarendon Press, 1982.

Fernández Méndez, Eugenio. *Historia cultural de Puerto Rico, 1493–1968*. San Juan, P.R.: Ediciones "El Cemí," 1970.

Filippov, Mikhail; Ordeshook, Peter C.; and Shvetsova, Olga. *Designing Federalism: A Theory of Self-Sustainable Federal Institutions*. New York: Cambridge Univ. Press, 2004.

First Americans. The American Indians. Alexandria, Va.: Time-Life Books, 1992.

Fischer, David Hackett. *America, a Cultural History*. vol. 1, *Albion's Seed: Four British Folkways in America*. New York: Oxford Univ. Press, 1989.

Foley, Neil and Chávez, John R. *Teaching Mexican American History*. Teaching Diversity: People of Color. Washington, D.C.: American Historical Association, 2002.

Foner, Eric. *Reconstruction: America's Unfinished Revolution, 1863–1877*. New American Nation. New York: Harper & Row, 1988.

Forrest, Alan. *The Revolution in Provincial France: Aquitaine, 1789–1799*. Oxford: Clarendon Press, 1996.

Fraser, Steve and Gerstle, Gary, eds. *Ruling America: A History of Wealth and Power in a Democracy.* Cambridge, Mass.: Harvard Univ. Press, 2005.

Fregosi, Paul. *Dreams of Empire: Napoleon and the First World War, 1792–1815.* London: Hutchinson, 1989.

Furet, François. *The French Revolution, 1770–1814.* Trans. Antonia Nevill. History of France. Malden, Mass.: Blackwell Publishers, 1996.

Gandhi, Leela. *Postcolonial Theory: A Critical Introduction.* New York: Columbia Univ. Press, 1998.

García Venero, Maximiano. *Historia del nacionalismo vasco.* 3rd ed. Madrid: Editora Nacional, 1969.

Geary, Patrick J. *Before France and Germany: The Creation and Transformation of the Merovingian World.* New York: Oxford Univ. Press, 1988.

Gellar, Sheldon. *Senegal: An African Nation Between Islam and the West.* Profiles, Nations of Contemporary Africa. Boulder, Colo.: Westview Press, 1982.

Gibson, Charles. *Tlaxcala in the Sixteenth Century.* Yale Historical Publications, miscellany 56. New Haven, Conn.: Yale Univ. Press, 1952.

González, Gilbert G. and Fernández, Raul A. *A Century of Chicano History: Empire, Nations, and Migration.* New York: Routledge, 2003.

Goodfriend, Joyce D. *Before the Melting Pot: Society and Culture in Colonial New York City, 1664–1730.* Princeton, N.J.: Princeton Univ. Press, 1992.

Grugel, Jean. *Politics and Development in the Caribbean Basin: Central America and the Caribbean in the New World Order.* Bloomington: Indiana Univ. Press, 1995.

Habermas, Jürgen. *The Postnational Constellation: Political Essays.* Trans. and ed., with an introduction by Max Pensky. Studies in Contemporary German Social Thought. 1998. Reprint, Cambridge, Mass.: MIT Press, Polity Press, 2001.

Hall, Thadd E. *France and the Eighteenth-Century Corsican Question.* New York: New York Univ. Press, 1971.

Hall, Thomas D. *Social Change in the Southwest.* Studies in Historical Social Change. Lawrence: Univ. Press of Kansas, 1989.

Harvey, L[eonard] P[atrick]. *Islamic Spain: 1250–1500.* Chicago: Univ. of Chicago Press, 1990.

Hayward, Jack. *Fragmented France: Two Centuries of Disputed Identity.* Oxford: Oxford Univ. Press, 2007.

Hearn, Jonathan. *Claiming Scotland: National Identity and Liberal Culture.* Edinburgh: Polygon at Edinburgh, 2000.

Hechter, Michael. *Containing Nationalism.* Oxford: Oxford Univ. Press, 2000.
——. *Internal Colonialism: The Celtic Fringe in British National Development, 1536–1966.* Berkeley and Los Angeles: Univ. of California Press, 1975.

Heiberg, Marianne. *The Making of the Basque Nation.* Cambridge Studies in Social Anthroplogy, 66. New York: Cambridge Univ. Press, 1989.

Heinl, Robert Debs, Jr. and Heinl, Nancy Gordon. *Written in Blood: The Story of the Haitan People, 1492–1971*. Boston: Houghton Mifflin Co., 1978.

Hillgarth, J. N. *The Spanish Kingdoms, 1250–1560. vol. 1, 1250–1410, Precarious Balance*. Oxford: Clarendon Press, 1976.

Himmel, Kelly F. *The Conquest of the Karankawas and the Tonkawas, 1821–1859*. Elma Dill Russell Spencer Series in the West and Southwest, no. 20. College Station: Texas A&M Univ. Press, 1999.

Hobsbawm, E[ric] J. *Nations and Nationalism since 1780: Programme, Myth, Reality*. 2nd ed. Cambridge: Cambridge Univ. Press, 1992.

Hodges, Tony. *Western Sahara: The Roots of a Desert War*. Westport, Conn.: Lawrence Hill & Co., 1983.

Hoffmann, Eleanor. *Realm of the Evening Star: A History of Morocco and the Lands of the Moors*. Philadelphia: Chilton Books, 1965.

Hogan, Michael J. *The Marshall Plan: America, Britain, and the Reconstruction of Western Europe, 1947–1952*. Studies in Economic History and Policy: The United States in the Twentieth Century. New York: Cambridge Univ. Press, 1987.

Hoig, Stanley W. *The Cherokees and Their Chiefs in the Wake of Empire*. Fayetteville: Univ. of Arkansas Press, 1998.

Hurtado, Albert L. and Iverson, Peter, eds. *Major Problems in American Indian History: Documents and Essays*. Major Problems in American History Series. 2nd ed. Boston: Houghton Mifflin Co., 2001.

Jennings, Francis. *The Founders of America: How Indians Discovered the Land, Pioneered in It, and Created Great Classical Civilizations; How They Were Plunged into a Dark Age by Invasion and Conquest; and How They Are Reviving*. New York: W. W. Norton & Co., 1993.

——. *Empire of Fortune: Crowns, Colonies, and Tribes in the Seven Years War in America*. New York: W. W. Norton & Co., 1988.

——; Fenton, William N.; Druke, Mary A.; and Miller, David R. *The History and Culture of Iroquois Diplomacy: An Interdisciplinary Guide to the Treaties of the Six Nations and Their League*. Syracuse, N.Y.: Syracuse Univ. Press, 1985.

Jones, Michael. *The Creation of Brittany: A Late Medieval State*. London: Hambledon Press, 1988.

Julien, Charles-André. *History of North Africa: Tunisia, Algeria, Morocco from the Arab Conquest to 1830*. Trans. John Petrie, ed. C. C. Stewart. New York: Praeger Publishers, 1970.

July, Robert W. *A History of the African People*. New York: Charles Scribner's Sons, 1970.

Kaplan, Amy. *The Anarchy of Empire in the Making of U.S. Culture*. Cambridge, Mass.: Harvard Univ. Press, 2002.

Karmis, Dimitrios and Norman, Wayne, eds. *Theories of Federalism: A Reader*. New York: St. Martin's Press, Palgrave Macmillan, 2005.

Kearney, Hugh F. *Ireland: Contested Ideas of Nationalism and History.* New York: New York Univ. Press, 2007.

——. *The British Isles: A History of Four Nations.* Cambridge: Cambridge Univ. Press, 1989.

Kehoe, Alice Beck. *America before the European Invasions.* Longman History of The United States. London: Longman, Pearson Education, 2002.

——. *North American Indians: A Comprehensive Account.* Prentice-Hall Series in Anthropology. Englewood Cliffs, N.J.: Prentice-Hall, 1981.

Kennedy, Paul. *The Parliament of Man: The Past, Present, and Future of the United Nations.* New York: Random House, 2006.

——. *The Rise and Fall of the Great Powers: Economic Change and Military Conflict from 1500 to 2000.* New York: Random House, 1987.

King, Desmond. *The Liberty of Strangers: Making the American Nation.* New York: Oxford Univ. Press, 2005.

Kup, A. P. *A History of Sierra Leone, 1400–1787.* London: Cambridge Univ. Press, 1961.

Kurlansky, Mark. *The Basque History of the World.* New York: Walker & Co., 1999.

Laczko, Leslie S. *Pluralism and Inequality in Quebec.* Toronto: Univ. of Toronto Press, 1995.

Langley, Lester D. *The Americas in the Age of Revolution, 1750–1850.* New Haven, Conn.: Yale Univ. Press, 1996.

Laroui, Abdallah. *The History of the Maghrib: An Interpretive Essay.* Trans. Ralph Manheim. Princeton Studies on the Near East. Princeton, N.J.: Princeton Univ. Press, 1977.

Léger, J[acques] N[icholas]. *Haïti: Son histoire et ses détracteurs.* New York: Neale Publishing Co., 1907.

Legey, François. *The Folklore of Morocco.* Trans. Lucy Hotz. London: George Allen & Unwin, 1935.

León Portilla, Miguel, ed. *The Broken Spears: The Aztec Account of the Conquest of Mexico.* Trans. Angel María Garibay K. and Lysander Kemp, with a foreword by J. Jorge Klor de Alva. Rev. ed. Boston: Beacon Press, 1992.

——. *Los antiguos mexicanos a través de sus crónicas y cantares.* Lecturas mexicanas. Mexico City: Fondo de Cultura Económica, Cultura SEP, 1983.

Lewis, Gordon K. *Puerto Rico: Freedom and Power in the Caribbean.* With an introduction by Anthony Maingot. Rev. ed. Kingston, Jam.: Ian Randle Publishers, 2004.

Liss, Peggy K. *Atlantic Empires: The Network of Trade and Revolution, 1713–1826.* Johns Hopkins Studies in Atlantic History and Culture. Baltimore, Md.: Johns Hopkins Univ. Press, 1983.

Lockhart, James. *Nahuas and Spaniards: Postconquest Central Mexican History and Philology.* Nahuatl Studies, no. 3. Stanford, Calif.: Stanford Univ. Press, UCLA Latin American Center, 1991.

Longfellow, Henry Wadsworth. *Evangeline*. Indianapolis, Ind.: Bobbs-Merrill Co., 1905.

Luard, Evan. *A History of the United Nations*. vol. 1, *The Years of Western Domination, 1945–1955*. New York: St. Martin's Press, 1982.

Lundestad, Geir. *"Empire" by Integration: The United States and European Integration, 1945–1997*. New York: Oxford Univ. Press, 1998.

McDaniel, Antonio. *Swing Low, Sweet Chariot: The Mortality Cost of Colonizing Liberia in the Nineteenth Century*. Population and Development. Chicago: Univ. of Chicago Press, 1995.

MacDougall, Hugh A. *Racial Myth in English History: Trojans, Teutons, and Anglo-Saxons*. Hanover, N.H.: Univ. Press of New England, 1982.

MacKillop, James. *Dictionary of Celtic Mythology*. New York: Oxford Univ. Press, 1998.

MacLean, Magnus. *The Literature of the Celts*. Kennikat Series in Irish History and Culture. 1902. Reprint, Port Washington, N.Y.: Kennikat Press, 1970.

McKay, David. *Designing Europe: Comparative Lessons from the Federal Experience*. Oxford: Oxford Univ. Press, 2001.

McNeill, William H. *Polyethnicity and National Unity in World History*. Donald G. Creighton Lectures, 1985. Toronto: Univ. of Toronto Press, 1986.

Maingot, A.P. *A Short History of the West Indies*. Macmillan Caribbean. 4th ed. London: Macmillan, 1987.

Mann, Barbara Alice. *Iroquoian Women: The Gantowisas*. American Indian Studies, vol. 4. New York: Peter Lang, 2000.

Mann, Charles C. *1491: New Revelations of the Americas before Columbus*. New York: Alfred A. Knopf, 2005.

Mann [Trofimenkoff], Susan. *The Dream of Nation: A Social and Intellectual History of Quebec*. Carleton Library Series, 1982. 2nd ed. Montreal: McGill – Queen's Univ. Press,2002.

Medrano, Juan Díez. *Divided Nations: Class, Politics, and Nationalism in the Basque Country and Catalonia*. Wilder House Series in Politics, History, and Culture. Ithaca, N.Y.: Cornell Univ. Press, 1995.

Mees, Ludger. *Nationalism, Violence, and Democracy: The Basque Clash of Identities*. New York: Palgrave Macmillan, 2003.

Meinig, D[onald] W[illiam] Meinig. *The Shaping of America: A Geographical Perspective on 500 Years of History*. vol. 4, *Global America, 1915–2000*. New Haven, Conn.: Yale Univ. Press, 2004.

——. *The Shaping of America*. vol. 3, *Trancontinental America, 1850–1915*. New Haven, Conn.: Yale Univ. Press, 1998.

——. *The Shaping of America*. vol. 2, *Continental America, 1800–1867*. New Haven, Conn.: Yale Univ. Press, 1993.

——. *The Shaping of America*. vol. 1, *Atlantic America, 1492–1800*. New Haven, Conn.: Yale Univ. Press, 1986.

——. *Southwest: Three Peoples in Geographical Change, 1600–1970.* New York: Oxford University Press, 1971.

Memmi, Albert. *Portrait du clonisé précédé du portrait du colonisateur.* Paris: Buchet/Chastel, Correa, 1957.

Menchaca, Martha. *Recovering History, Constructing Race: The Indian, Black, and White Roots of Mexican Americans.* **Joe R.** and **Teresa Lozano Long** Series in Latin American and Latino Art and Culture. Austin: Univ. of Texas Press, 2001.

Mercer, John. *The Canary Islanders: Their Prehistory and Survival.* London: Rex Collings, 1980.

Meyer, Michael C. and Sherman, William L. *The Course of Mexican History.* 5th ed. New York: Oxford Univ. Press, 1995.

Mignolo, Walter D. *Local Histories/Global Designs: Coloniality, Subaltern Knowledges, and Border Thinking.* Princeton Studies in Culture/Power/History. Princeton, N.J.: Princeton Univ. Press, 2000.

Mirandé, Alfredo and Enríquez, Evangelina. *La Chicana: The Mexican–American Woman.* Chicago: Univ. of Chicago Press, 1979.

Mitchell, Marybelle. *From Talking Chiefs to a Native Corporate Elite: The Birth of Class and Nationalism among Canadian Inuit.* McGill – Queen's Native and Northern Series. Montreal: McGill – Queen's Univ. Press, 1996.

Monteiro, Mariana. *Legends and Popular Tales of the Basque People.* 1887. Reprint, New York: Benjamin Blom, 1971.

Montejano, David. *Anglos and Mexican in the Making of Texas, 1836–1986.* Austin: Univ. of Texas Press, 1987.

Mooney, James. *Myths of the Cherokee.* Landmarks in Anthropology. 1900. Reprint, New York: Johnson Reprint Corporation, 1970.

Morales Padrón, Francisco. *Jamaica española.* Seville: Escuela de Estudios Hispano-Americanos de Sevilla, 1952.

Morrissey, Mike and Smyth, Marie. *Northern Ireland after the Good Friday Agreement: Victims, Grievance, and Blame.* London: Pluto Press, 2002.

Muldoon, James. *Identity on the Medieval Irish Frontier: Degenerate Englishmen, Wild Irishmen, Middle Nations.* Gainesville, Fla.: Univ. Press of Florida, 2003.

Murguía, Edward. *Assimilation, Colonialism, and the Mexican American People.* Mexican American Monograph Series, no. 1. Austin: Centre for Mexican American Studies, Univ. of Texas, 1975.

Nieto-Philips, John M. *The Language of Blood: The Making of Spanish-American Identity in New Mexico, 1880s–1930s.* Albuquerque: Univ. of New Mexico Press, 2004.

Nostrand, Richard L. *The Hispano Homeland.* Norman: Univ. of Oklahoma Press, 1992.

O'Neil, Dan. *The Last Giant of Berengia: The Mystery of the Bering Land Bridge.* Boulder, Colo.: Westview Press, 2004.

Olsen, Fred. *On the Trail of the Arawaks*. With a foreword by George Kubler and an introduction by Irving Rouse. Civilization of the American Indian. Norman: Univ. of Oklahoma Press, 1974.

Osterhammel, Jurgen. *Colonialism: A Theoretical Overview*. Trans. **Shelley L. Frisch**. Princeton, N.J.: Markus Weiner Publishers, 1997.

Ott, **Thomas O**. *The Haitian Revolution, 1789–1801*. Knoxville: Univ. of Tennessee Press, 1973.

Parker, **John** and **Rathbone, Richard**. *African History: A Very Short Introduction* Oxford: Oxford Univ. Press, 2007.

Parry, **J. H.**; **Sherlock, P. M.**; and **Maingot, A. P**. *A Short History of the West Indies*. Macmillan Caribbean, 4th ed. London: Macmillan, 1987.

Payne, **Stanley G**. *Spain's First Democracy. The Second Republic, 1931–1936*. Madison: Univ. of Wisconsin Press, 1993.

———. *The Franco Regime, 1936–1975*. Madison: Univ. of Wisconsin Press, 1987.

———. *Basque Nationalism*. The Basque Series. Reno: Univ. of Nevada Press, 1975.

Pennell, **C. R**. *Morocco: From Empire to Independence*. Oxford: Oneworld Publications, 2003.

Perdue, **Theda**. *Cherokee Women: Gender and Culture Change, 1700–1835*. Indians of the Southeast. Lincoln: Univ. of Nebraska Press, 1998.

Pérez, **Emma**. *The Decolonial Imaginary: Writing Chicanas into History, Theories of Representation and Difference*. Bloomington: Indiana Univ. Press, 1999.

Pond, **Elizabeth**. *The Rebirth of Europe*. Washington, D.C.: Brookings Institution Press, 1999.

Price, **Roger**. *A Concise History of France*. 2nd ed. Cambridge Concise Histories. Cambridge: Cambridge Univ. Press, 2005.

Prins, **Harald E. L**. *The Mi'kmaq: Resistance, Accommodation, and Cultural Survival*. Case Studies in Cultural Anthropology. Fort Worth, Tex.: Harcourt Brace College Publishers, 1996.

Reece, **Jack E**. *The Bretons against France: Ethnic Minority Nationalism in Twentieth-Century Brittany*. Chapel Hill: Univ. of North Carolina Press, 1977.

Rees, **Alwyn** and **Rees, Brinley**. *Celtic Heritage: Ancient Tradition in Ireland and Wales*. New York: Grove Press, 1961.

Rendón Garcini, **Ricardo**. *Breve historia de Tlaxcala*. Serie breves historias de los estados de la república mexicana. Mexico City: Fondo de Cultura Económica, 1996.

Reséndez, **Andrés**. *Changing National Identities at the Frontier: Texas and New Mexico, 1800–1850*. Cambridge: Cambridge Univ. Press, 2005.

Richardson, **Bonham C**. *The Caribbean in the Wider World, 1492–1992: A Regional Geography. Geography of the World Economy*. New York: Cambridge Univ. Press, 1992.

Richter, Daniel K. *The Ordeal of the Longhouse: The Peoples of the Iroquois League in the Era of European Colonization.* Chapel Hill: Univ. of North Carolina Press for the Institute of Early American History and Culture, 1992.

Rivas-Rodríguez, Maggie, ed. *Mexican Americans and World War II.* Austin: Univ. of Texas Press, 2005.

Robb, Graham. *The Discovery of France: A Historical Geography from the Revolution to the First World War.* New York: W. W. Norton, 2007.

Rolleston, T[homas W[illiam]. *Myths and Legends of the Celtic Race.* London: G. G. Harrap & Co., 1911.

Rosenbaum, Robert J. *Mexicano Resistance in the Southwest.* With a new foreword by John R. Chávez. 1981. Reprint, Dallas, Tex.: Southern Methodist Univ. Press, 1998.

Rougier, Louis. *La France à la recherche d'une constitution.* Paris: Recueil Sirey, 1952.

Roy-Féquière, Magali. *Women, Creole Identity, and Intellectual Life in Early Twentieth-Century Puerto Rico.* Puerto Rican Studies. Philadelphia: Temple Univ. Press, 2004.

Rozema, Vicki, ed. *Cherokee Voices: Early Accounts of Cherokee Life in the East.* Winston-Salem, N.C.: John F. Blair, 2002.

Running Wolf, Michael B. and Smith, Patricia Clark. *On the Trail of Elder Brother: Glous'gap Stories of Micmac Indians.* Karen and Michael Braziller Books. New York: Persea Books, 2000.

Russell, James W. *After the Fifth Sun: Class and Race in North America.* Englewood Cliffs, N.J.: Prentice Hall, 1994.

Saha, Santosh C. *Culture in Liberia: An Afrocentric View of the Cultural Interaction between the Indigenous Liberians and the Americo-Liberians.* African Studies, vol. 46. Lewiston, N.Y.: Edwin Mellen Press, 1998.

Sahlins, Peter. *Boundaries: The Making of France and Spain in the Pyrenees.* Berkeley and Los Angeles: Univ. of California Press, 1989.

Said, Edward W. *Orientalism.* New York: Random House, Vintage Books, 1978–9.

Sauer, Carl Ortwin. *The Early Spanish Main.* With a new foreword by Anthony Pagden. Centennial Books. 1966. Reprint, Berkeley and Los Angeles: Univ. of California Press, 1992.

Sawyer, Amos. *Beyond Plunder: Toward Democratic Governance in Liberia.* Boulder, Colo.: L. Rienner, 2005.

——. *The Emergence of Autocracy in Liberia: Tragedy and Challenge.* Publication of the Center for Self-Governance. San Francisco: CS Press, Institute for Contemporary Studies, 1992.

Searing, James F. *West African Slavery and Atlantic Commerce: The Senegal River Valley, 1700–1860,* African Studies Series, 77. New York: Cambridge Univ. Press, 1993.

Shatzmiller, Maya. *The Berbers and the Islamic State: The Marīnid Experience in Pre-Protectorate Morocco.* Princeton, N.J.: Markus Wiener Publishers, 2000.

Sheller, Mimi. *Democracy after Slavery: Black Politics and Peasant Radicalism in Haiti and Jamaica.* Warwick Univ. Caribbean Studies. London: Macmillan Education, 2000.

Shick, Tom W. *Behold the Promised Land: A History of Afro-American Settler Society in Nineteenth-Century Liberia.* Johns Hopkins Studies in Atlantic History and Culture. Baltimore, Md.: Johns Hopkins Univ. Press, 1980.

Shillington, Kevin. *History of Africa.* Rev. 2nd ed. New York: Palgrave Macmillan, 2005.

Smith, Anthony D. *The Ethnic Origins of Nations.* New York: Basil Blackwell, 1987.

Smith, Neil. *American Empire: Roosevelt's Geographer and the Prelude to Globalization.* California Studies in Critical Human Geography. Berkeley and Los Angeles: Univ. of California Press, 2003.

Spicer, Edward H. *Cycles of Conquest: The Impact of Spain, Mexico, and the United States on the Indians of the Southwest, 1533–1960.* Tucson: Univ. of Arizona Press, 1962.

Spitzer, Leo. *The Creoles of Sierra Leone: Responses to Colonialism, 1870–1945.* Madison: Univ. of Wisconsin Press, 1974.

Terrasse, Henri. *Histoire du Moroc des origines à l'établissement du Protectorat français.* vol. 2. 1950. Reprint, New York: AMS Press, 1975.

Terrisse, André. *Contes et légendes du Sénégal.* Collection des contes et legends de tous les pays. Paris: Fernand Nathan, Editeur, 1963.

Thompson, Jerry D. *Mexican Texans in the Union Army.* Southwestern Studies, no. 78. El Paso: Texas Western Press, 1986.

Thompson, Virginia and Richard Adloff. *The Western Saharans: Background to Conflict.* Totowa, N.J.: Croom Helm, Barnes & Noble Books, 1980.

Tonge, Jonathan. *Northern Ireland: Conflict and Change.* 2nd ed. London: Pearson Education, Longman, 2002.

Townsend, Richard F. *The Aztecs.* Ancient Peoples and Places. Rev. ed. London: Thames & Hudson, 2000.

Trías Monge, José. *Puerto Rico: The Trials of the Oldest Colony in the World.* New Haven, Conn.: Yale Univ. Press, 1997.

Vale, M.G.A. *English Gascony, 1399–1453: A Study of War, Government, and Politics during the Later Stages of the Hundred Years War.* Oxford Historical Monographs. London: Oxford Univ. Press, Ely House, 1970.

Veyrin, Philippe. *Les Basques de Labourd, de Soule et de Basse Navarre: Leur histoire et leurs traditions.* New ed. N.p.: Arthaud, 1955.

Von Hagen, Victor Wolfgang. *The Aztec: Man and Tribe.* Rev. ed. New York: New American Library, Times Mirror, Mentor Books, 1961.

Vovell, Michel. *La chute de la monarchie, 1787–1792.* vol. 1 of Nouvelle histoire de la France contemporaine. Ed. **Michel Winock**. Collection points, Série histoire. Paris: Editions du Seuil, 1972.

Wallace, Paul A.W. *The White Roots of Peace.* 1946. Reprint, Port Washington, N.Y.: Ira J. Friedman, 1968.

Wallerstein, Immanuel. *World-Systems Analysis: An Introduction.* Durham, N.C.: Duke Univ. Press, 2005.

——. *The Modern World-System.* Studies in Social Discontinuity. vol. 1, *Capitalist Agriculture and the Origins of the European World Economy in the Sixteenth Century.* New York: Harcourt Brace Jovanovich, Academic Press, 1974.

Weber, David J. *The Spanish Frontier in North America.* Yale Western Americana. New Haven, Conn.: Yale Univ. Press, 1992.

——. *The Mexican Frontier, 1821–1846: The American Southwest under Mexico.* Histories of the American Frontier. Albuquerque: Univ. of New Mexico Press, 1982.

Weber, Eugen. *Peasants into Frenchmen: The Modernization of Rural France, 1870–1914.* Stanford, Calif.: Stanford Univ. Press, 1976.

White, Richard. *The Middle Ground: Indians, Empires, and Republics in the Great Lakes Region, 1650–1815.* Cambridge Studies in North American Indian History. New York: Cambridge Univ. Press, 1991.

Widmer, Randolph. *The Evolution of the Calusa: A Nonagricultural Chiefdom on the Southwest Florida Coast.* Tuscaloosa: Univ. of Alabama Press, 1988.

Wolf, Eric R. *Europe and the People without History.* Berkeley and Los Angeles: Univ. of California Press, 1982.

Wood, David M. and **Yeşilada, Birol A**. *The Emerging European Union.* 4th ed. New York: Pearson Longman, 2007.

Wylie, Kenneth C. *The Political Kingdoms of the Temne: Temne Government in Sierra Leone, 1825–1910.* New York: Africana Publishing Co., 1977.

Yacono, Xavier. *Histoire de la colonization française.* Que sais-je? Le point des connaissances actuelles, no. 452. 2nd rev. ed. Paris: Presses universitaires de France, 1973.

Young, Robert A. *The Secession of Quebec and the Future of Canada.* Montreal & Kingston: McGill – Queen's Univ. Press with the Institute of Intergovernmental Relations, 1995.

SELECTIONS FROM COLLECTED WORKS

Abstract from "History of Masimerah Country," comp. **W.T.G. Lawson** (Freetown, 1878). In **Kenneth C. Wylie**, *The Political Kingdoms of the Temne: Temne Government in Sierra Leone, 1825–1910*, pp. 232–3. New York: Africana Publishing Co., 1977.

"Address to the Military, 1801." In *Toussaint L'Ouverture*, ed. **George F. Tyson**. Great Lives Observed, pp. 56–8. Englewood Cliffs, N.J.: Prentice Hall, 1973.

"Austin's Address Explaining Why the Convention Was Called, April 1, 1833." In *Documents of Texas History*, ed. **Ernest Wallace, David M. Vigness**, and **George B. Ward**. Fred H. and Ella Mae Moore Texas History Reprint Series, pp. 74–6. 1963. Reprint, Austin: Texas State Historical Association, 2002.

Ayuntamiento of San Antonio. "Industrious, Honest, North American Settlers." In *Foreigners in Their Native Land: Historical Roots of the Mexican Americans*, ed. **David J. Weber**, pp. 83–4. Foreword by Ramón Eduardo Ruiz. Albuquerque: Univ. of New Mexico Press, 1973.

Barry, Boubacar. "The Subordination of Power and the Mercantile Economy: The Kingdom of Waalo, 1600–1831." In *The Political Economy of Underdevelopment: Dependence in Senegal*, ed. **Rita Cruise O'Brien**. Sage Series on African Modernization and Development, vol. 3, pp. 38–63. Beverly Hills, Calif.: Sage Publications, 1979.

Berger, Peter L. "Introduction: The Cultural Dynamics of Globalization." In *Many Globalizations: Cultural Diversity in the Contemporary World*, ed. **Berger** and **Samuel P. Huntington**, pp. 1–16. New York: Oxford Univ. Press, 2002.

Biard, Pierre. "Relation de la Novvelle France." In *Jesuit Relations and Allied Documents: Travels and Explorations of the Jesuit Missionaries in New France, 1610–1791*, ed. **Reuben Gold Thwaites**. vol. III, Acadia: 1611–1616, pp. 21–283. New York: Pageant Book Co., 1959.

Bock, Philip K. "Micmac." In *Handbook of North American Indians*, gen. ed. **William G. Sturtevant**. vol. 15, Northeast, ed. **Bruce G. Trigger**, pp. 109–22. Washington, D.C.: Smithsonian Institution, 1978.

Canny, Nicholas. "Early Modern Ireland, c. 1500–1700." In *The Oxford Illustrated History of Ireland*, ed. **R[obert] F[itzroy] Foster**, pp. 104–60. New York: Oxford Univ. Press, 1989.

"Charter of the United Nations, June 25, 1945." In *Documents Relating to International Organization*, ed. **Werner Levi**, rev. ed., pp. 10–32. Minneapolis, Minn.: Burgess Publishing Co., 1947.

Chartrand, Jean-Philippe. "Survival and Adaptation of the Inuit Ethnic Identity: The Importance of Inuktitut." In *Native People, Native Lands: Canadian Indians, Inuit, and Meti*, ed. **Bruce Alden Cox**, pp. 241–55. Ottawa: Carleton Univ. Press, 1988.

"Cherokee Editor Elias Boudinot Opposes Removal, 1828." In *Major Problems in American Indian History: Documents and Essays*, ed. **Albert L. Hurtado** and **Peter Iverson**. Major Problems in American History Series, 2nd ed., pp. 204–5. Boston: Houghton Mifflin Co., 2001.

Christopulos, Diane. "Puerto Rico in the Twentieth Century: A Historical Survey." In *Puerto Rico and Puerto Ricans: Studies in History and Society*, ed.

Adalberto López and James Petras, pp. 123–63. New York: Schenkman Publishing Co. John Wiley & Sons, Halsted Press, 1974.

"Columbus on the Indians' 'Discovery' of the Spanish, 1492." In *Major Problems in American Indian History: Documents and Essays*, ed. **Albert L. Hurtado** and **Peter Iverson**. Major Problems in American History Series, 2nd ed., pp. 57–8. Boston: Houghton Mifflin Co., 2001.

"Constitution of Coahuila and Texas, March 11, 1827." In *Documents of Texas History*, ed. **Ernest Wallace**, **David M. Vigness**, and **George B. Ward**. Fred H. and Ella Mae Moore Texas History Reprint Series, pp. 61–2. 1963. Reprint, Austin: Texas State Historical Association, 2002.

"The Constitution of the Republic of Texas, March 17, 1836." In *Documents of Texas History*, ed. **Ernest Wallace**, **David M. Vigness**, and **George B. Ward**. Fred H. and Ella Mae Moore Texas History Reprint Series, pp. 100–106. 1963. Reprint, Austin: Texas State Historical Association, 2002.

"Constitution of the Year XII." In *The Constitutions and Other Select Documents Illustrative of the History of France, 1789–1907*, ed. **Frank Maloy Anderson**, 2nd rev. ed., pp. 342–67. Minneapolis, Minn.: H. W. Wilson Co., 1908.

Cosgrove, Art. "The Gaelic Resurgence and the Geraldine Supremacy (c. 1400–1534)." In *The Course of Irish History*, ed. **T. W. Moody** and **F. X. Martin**, rev. ed., pp. 158–73. Niwot, Colo.: Roberts Rinehart Publishers, 1994.

"Covenant of the League of Nations, January 10, 1920." In *Documents Relating to International Organization*, ed. **Werner Levi**, rev. ed., pp. 1–9. Minneapolis, Minn.: Burgess Publishing Co., 1947.

"A Declaration of the Causes which Impel the State of Texas to Secede from the Federal Union." In *Documents of Texas History*, ed. **Ernest Wallace**, **David M. Vigness**, and **George B. Ward**. Fred H. and Ella Mae Moore Texas History Reprint Series, pp. 194–6. 1963. Reprint, Austin: Texas State Historical Association, 2002.

The Declaration of Independence, April 6, 1813." In *Documents of Texas History*, ed. **Ernest Wallace**, **David M. Vigness**, and **George B. Ward**. Fred H. and Ella Mae Moore Texas History Reprint Series, pp. 39–40. 1963. Reprint, Austin: Texas State Historical Association, 2002.

"Declaration of Independence of the Irish Parliament, 1460." In *Irish Historical Documents, 1172–1922*, ed. **Edmund Curtis** and **R. B. McDowell**, pp. 72–76. 1943. Reprint, New York: Barnes & Noble, 1968.

"Decrees for Reorganizing the Local Government System." In *The Constitutions and Other Select Documents Illustrative of the History of France, 1789–1907*, ed. **Frank Maloy Anderson**, 2nd rev. ed., pp. 24–33. Minneapolis, Minn.: H. W. Wilson Co., 1908.

"Decree upon Slavery." In *The Constitutions and Other Select Documents Illustrative of the History of France, 1789–1907*, ed. **Frank Maloy Anderson**, 2nd rev. ed., p. 204. Minneapolis, Minn.: H. W. Wilson Co., 1908.

"Documents upon the Overthrow of the Spanish Monarchy." In *The Constitutions and Other Select Documents Illustrative of the History of France, 1789–1907*, ed. **Frank Maloy Anderson**, 2nd rev. ed., pp. 418–21. Minneapolis, Minn.: H. W. Wilson Co., 1908.

"Do Not Divulge Cabildo Business! August 8, 1550." In **James Lockhart, Frances Berdan**, and **Arthur J. O. Anderson**. *The Tlaxcalan Actas: A Compendium of the Records of the Cabildo of Tlaxcala (1545–1627)*, pp. 75–7. Salt Lake City: Univ. of Utah Press, 1986.

"Dwallah Zeppie to President Hiliary Richard Wright Johnson, August 1, 1887." In **Tom W, Shick**. *Behold the Promised Land: A History of Afro-American Settler Society in Nineteenth-Century Liberia*. Johns Hopkins Studies in Atlantic History and Culture, p. 91. Baltimore, Md.: Johns Hopkins Univ. Press, 1980.

"Economic Community of West African States (ECOWAS)." *New Encyclopedia of Africa*, ed. **John Middleton** and **Joseph C. Miller**. vol. 2, 2nd ed., pp. 161–4. Detroit, Mich: Charles Scribner's Sons, Gale, Cengage, 2008.

Elliott, John H. "Introduction." In *Colonial Identity in the Atlantic World, 1500–1800*, ed. **Nicholas Canny** and **Anthony Pagden**, pp. 3–13. Princeton, N.J.: Princeton Univ. Press, 1987.

"Excerpts from the Journal of Daniel Claus, from July 26, 1773, to August 10, 1779." In **Vaugeois, Denis**. *The Last French and Indian War: An Inquiry into a Safe-Conduct Issued in 1760 that Acquired the Value of a Treaty in 1990*, trans. **Käthe Roth**, pp. 230–40. Montreal: McGill – Queen's Univ. Press, Septentrion, 2002.

"First Voyage of Columbus." In *Select Letters of Christopher Columbus, with Other Original Documents Relating to His Four Voyages to the New World*, trans. and ed. **R[ichard] H[enry] Major**. Works Issued by the Hakluyt Society [no. 43], 2nd ed., pp. 1–18. London: Hakluyt Society, 1870.

Fitzpatrick, David. "Ireland since 1870." In *The Oxford Illustrated History of Ireland*, ed. **R[obert] F[itzroy] Foster**. pp. 213–74. New York: Oxford Univ. Press, 1989.

Fogelson, Raymond D. "Perspectives on Native American Identity." In *Studying Native America: Problems and Prospects*, ed. **Russell Thorton**, pp. 40–59. Madison: Univ. of Wisconsin Press, 1998.

Foster, R[obert] F[itzroy]. "Ascendancy and Union." In *The Oxford Illustrated History of Ireland*, ed. **Foster**, pp. 161–211. New York: Oxford Univ. Press, 1989.

Gellner, Ernest. "Introduction." In *Arabs and Berbers: From Tribe to Nation in North Africa*, ed. **Gellner** and **Charles Micaud**. Race and Nations, pp. 11–21. Lexington, Mass.: D. C. Heath and Co., Lexington Books, 1972.

Goddard, Ives. "Introduction." In *Handbook of North American Indians*, gen. ed. **William G. Sturtevant**. vol. 17, *Languages*, ed. **Ives Goddard** (1996), pp. 1–16. Washington, D.C.: Smithsonian Institution, 1978.

Gonzales-Berry, Erlinda. "Which Language Will Our Children Speak? The Spanish Language and Public Education Policy in New Mexico, 1890–1930." In *The Contested Homeland: A Chicano History of New Mexico*, ed. **Gonzales-Berry** and **David Maciel**, pp. 169–89. Albuquerque: Univ. of New Mexico Press, 2000.

Grado, Pedro, Rev. "Por la raza y para la raza." In *Foreigners in Their Native Land: Historical Roots of the Mexican Americans*, ed. **David J. Weber**. Foreword by **Ramón Eduardo Ruiz**, pp. 248–51. Albuquerque: Univ. of New Mexico Press, 1973.

"Grænlendinga Saga." In *The Vinland Sagas: The Norse Discovery of America*, trans. with an introduction by **Magnus Magnusson** and **Hermann Pálsson**, pp. 47–72. 1965. Reprint, New York: New York Univ. Press, 1966.

Griffen, William B. "Southern Periphery: East." In *Handbook of North American Indians*, gen. ed. **William G. Sturtevant**. vol. 10, Southwest, ed. **Alfonso Ortiz** (1983), pp. 329–42. Washington, D.C.: Smithsonian Institution, 1978.

Gutiérrez, David G. "Ethnic Mexicans and the Transformation of 'American' Social Space: Reflections on Recent History." In *Crossings: Mexican Immigration in Interdisciplinary Perspectives*, ed. **Marcelo M. Suárez-Orozco**, pp. 309–35. Cambridge, Mass.: Harvard Univ. Press, David Rockefeller Center for Latin American Studies, 1998.

Hall, Loretta. "Cherokee." In *Gale Encyclopedia of Native American Tribes*, ed. **Sharon Malinowski** et al. vol. 1, *Northeast, Southeast, Caribbean*, pp. 380–9. Detroit, Mich.: Gale Publishing, 1998.

Hall, Thomas D. "Ethnic Conflict as a Global Social Problem." In *Handbook of Social Problems: A Comparative International Perspective*, ed. **George Ritzer**, pp. 139–55. Thousand Oaks, Calif.: Sage Publications, 2004.

—— and **Nagel, Joane**. "Indigenous Peoples." In *Encyclopedia of Sociology*, vol. 5, He-Le, ed. **George Ritzer**, pp. 2280–5. Oxford: Blackwell, 2006.

Hanging Maw. "Letter from Hanging Maw to President George Washington, 15 June 1793." In *Cherokee Voices: Early Accounts of Cherokee Life in the East*, ed. **Vicki Rozema**, pp. 93–4. Winston-Salem, N.C.: John F. Blair, 2002.

Hechter, Michael. "Introduction to the Transaction Edition." In *Internal Colonialism: The Celtic Fringe in British National Development, 1536–1966*, pp. xiii–xxiii. Berkeley and Los Angeles: Univ. of California Press, 1975. Reprint, New Brunswick, N.J.: Transaction Publishers, 1999.

Hernández Navarro, Luis. "The Chiapas Uprising," trans. **William Rhett Mariscal**. In *Rebellion in Chiapas*, ed. **Neil Harvey**. Transformation of Rural Mexico Series, no. 5, pp. 51–63. San Diego: Ejido Reform Research Project, Center for U.S.–Mexican Studies, University of California, 1994.

Hinojosa, Gilberto M. and **Fox, Anne A.** "Indians and their Culture in San Fernando de Bexar." In *Tejano Origins in Eighteenth-Century San Antonio*, ed.

Gerald E. Poyo and Gilberto M. Hinojosa, pp. 105–20. Austin: Univ. of Texas Press for the Institute of Texan Cultures, 1991.

Hunter, James Davison and Yates, Joshua. "In the Vanguard of Globalization: The World of American Globalizers." In *Many Globalizations: Cultural Diversity in the Contemporary World*, ed. Peter L. Berger and Samuel P. Huntington, pp. 323–57. New York: Oxford Univ. Press, 2002.

Jennings, N. A. "In Sympathy." In *Foreigners in Their Native Land: Historical Roots of the Mexican Americans*, ed. David J. Weber. Foreword by Ramón Eduardo Ruiz, pp. 238–40. Albuquerque: Univ. of New Mexico Press, 1973.

———. "A Set Policy of Terrorizing Mexicans." In *Foreigners in Their Native Land: Historical Roots of the Mexican Americans*, ed. David J. Weber. Foreword by Ramón Eduardo Ruiz, pp. 187 90. Albuquerque: Univ. of New Mexico Press, 1973.

"John IV to Charles V, Summer 1373." In *Society at War: The Experience of England and France during the Hundred Years War*, ed. C. T. Allmand. Evidence and Commentary, pp. 19–20. New York: Harper & Row Publishers, Barnes & Noble, 1973.

Johnston, Susan. "Epidemics: The Forgotten Factor in Seventeenth Century Native Warfare in the St. Lawrence Region." In *Native Peoples, Native Lands: Canadian Indians, Inuit, and Metis*, ed. Bruce Alden Cox, pp. 14–31. Ottawa, Can.: Carleton Univ. Press, 1988.

Kearney, Richard. "Postnationalist Identities: A New Configuration." In *Empire & Terror: Nationalism/Postnationalism in the New Millenium*, ed. Begoña Aretxaga, Dennis Dworkin, Joseba Gabilondo, and Joseba Zulaika. Conference Papers Series, no. 1, pp. 29–40. Reno: Univ. of Nevada, Center for Basque Studies, 2004.

Keating, Michael. "The United Kingdom: Political Institutions and Territorial Cleavages." In *Federalism and Territorial Cleavages*, ed. Ugo M. Amoretti and Nancy Bermeo, pp. 155–79. Baltimore, Md.: Johns Hopkins Univ. Press, 2004.

King, Duane H. "The Origin of the Eastern Cherokee as a Social and Political Entity." In *The Cherokee Indian Nation: A Troubled History*, ed. King, pp. 164–80. Knoxville: Univ. of Tennessee Press, 1979.

Lack, Paul. "The Córdova Revolt." In *Tejano Journey, 1770–1850*, ed. Gerald E. Poyo, pp. 89–109. Austin: Univ. of Texas Press, 1996.

"Law for Re-establishing Slavery in the French Colonies." In *The Constitutions and Other Select Documents Illustrative of the History of France, 1789–1907*, ed. Frank Maloy Anderson, 2nd rev. ed., pp. 338–9. Minneapolis, Minn.: H. W. Wilson Co., 1908.

Le Clercq, Chrestien. "Nouvelle relation de la Gaspesie." In *Le Clercq: New Relation of Gaspesia*, facsimile ed., pp. 323–443. 1691. Reprint, New York: Greenwood Press, 1968.

Lescarbot, Marc. "La conversion des savvages qui ont esté baptizés en la Nov-velle France cette anne 1610, avec un bref recit du voyage du Sieur de Poutrincout." In *Jesuit Relations and Allied Documents: Travels and Explorations of the Jesuit Missionaries in New France, 1610–1791*, ed. **Reuben Gold Thwaites**. vol. I, *Acadia: 1610–1613*, pp. 51–113. New York: Pageant Book Co., 1959.

"Letter to the Minister of Marine, 13 April 1799." In *Toussaint L'Ouverture. Great Lives Observed*, ed. **George F. Tyson**, pp. 30–1. Englewood Cliffs, N.J.: Prentice Hall, 1973.

"El licenciado Jerónimo de Salazar . . . comunica a Felipe II el ataque de Francis Drake (8 de abril de 1585)." In Antonio Rumeu de Armas, *Piraterías y ataques navales contra las Islas Canarias*. vol. 3, pt. 2, pp. 949–50. Madrid: Consejo Superior de Investgaciones Científicas, Instituto Jerónimo Zurita, [1950].

Lomnitz-Adler, Claudio. "Concepts for the Study of Regional Culture." In *Mexico's Regions: Comparative History and Development*, ed. **Eric Van Young**. U.S.–Mexico Contemporary Perspectives Series, 4, pp. 59–89. San Diego: Center for U.S.–Mexican Studies, Univ. of California, 1992.

Lounsbury, Floyd G. "Iroquoian Languages." In *Handbook of North American Indians*, gen. ed. **William G. Sturtevant**. vol. 15, Northeast, ed. **Bruce G. Trigger**, pp. 334–43. Washington, D.C.: Smithsonian Institution, 1978.

McAlister, Melani. "'One Black Allah': The Middle East in the Cultural Politics of African American Liberation, 1955–1970." In *Bodies in Contact: Rethinking Colonial Encounters in World History*, ed. **Tony Ballantyne** and **Antoinette Burton**, pp. 383–403. Durham, N.C.: Duke Univ. Press, 2005.

Manley, Michael. "Overcoming Insularity in Jamaica." In *The Birth of Caribbean Civilisation: A Century of Ideas about Culture and Identity, Nation and Society*, ed. **O. Nigel Bolland**, pp. 492–503. Kingston, Jam.: Ian Randle Publishers, 2004.

Meillassoux, Claude. "Comment se sont perpétués les Inuit?" In *Population, reproduction, sociétés: Perspectives et enjeux de démographie sociale – Mélanges en l'honneur de Joel W. Gregory*, ed. **Dennis D. Cordell, Danielle Gauvreau, Raymond R. Gervais**, and **Céline Le Bourdais**, pp. 19–45. Montreal: Les Presses de l'Université de Montréal, 1993.

Morley, Morris. "Dependence and Development in Puerto Rico." In *Puerto Rico and Puerto Ricans: Studies in History and Society*, ed. **Adalberto López** and **James Petras**, pp. 214–54. New York: Schenkman Publishing Co., John Wiley & Sons, Halsted Press, 1974.

Ó Corráin, Donnchadh. "Prehistoric and Early Christian Ireland." In *The Oxford Illustrated History of Ireland*, ed. **R[obert] F[itzroy] Foster**, pp. 1–52. New York: Oxford Univ. Press, 1989.

Patterson, Orlando. "Ecumenical America: Global Culture and the American Cosmos." In *The Birth of Caribbean Civilisation: A Century of Ideas about*

Culture and Identity, Nation and Society, ed. **O. Nigel Bolland**, pp. 632–51. Kingston, Jam.: Ian Randle Publishers, 2004.

Pérez Herrero, Pedro. "Regional Conformation in Mexico, 1700–1850: Models and Hypotheses," trans. **Jane Walter**. In *Mexico's Regions: Comparative History and Development*, ed. **Eric Van Young**. U.S.–Mexico Contemporary Perspectives Series, 4, pp. 119–44. San Diego: Center for U.S.–Mexican Studies, Univ. of California, 1992.

Sassen, Saskia. "U.S. Immigration Policy toward Mexico in a Global Economy." In *Between Two Worlds: Mexican Immigrants in the United States*, ed. **David G. Gutiérrez**, Jaguar Books on Latin America, no. 15, pp. 213–27. Wilmington, Del.: Scholarly Resources, SR Books, 1996.

"La segunda relación de lo que se prometió en lo de Canaria. Del hecho que hizieron [sic] los naturales de la Isla de la Gomera . . .." In **Antonio Rumeu de Armas**, *Piraterías y ataques navales contra las Islas Canarias*. vol. 3, pt. 2, pp. 1102–4. Madrid: Consejo Superior de Investgaciones Científicas, Instituto Jerónimo Zurita, [1950].

"Selections from the Testimony of Alhaji Kali Kamara, an Elder of Maforki Chiefdom (Recorded at Port Loko, 21–22 September 1965)." In **Kenneth C, Wylie**. *The Political Kingdoms of the Temne: Temne Government in Sierra Leone, 1825–1910*, pp. 220–1. New York: Africana Publishing Co., 1977.

Shepherd, Kenneth R. "Micmac." In *Gale Encyclopedia of Native American Tribes*, ed. **Sharon Malinowski** et al. vol. 1, *Northeast, Southeast, Caribbean*, pp. 134–41. Detroit, Mich.: Gale Publishing, 1998.

Shrestha, Nanda R. and **Smith, Wilbur I**. "Epilogue: Geographical Imageries and Race Matters." In *Geographical Identities of Ethnic America: Race, Space, and Place*, ed. **Kate A. Berry** and **Martha L. Henderson**. Foreword by **Dong Ok Lee** and **Stanley Brunn**, pp. 279–94. Reno: Univ. of Nevada Press, 2002.

Silver, Philip W. "¡Malditos pueblos!: Apuntes sobre los vascos al final del siglo XX." In *Disremembering the Dictatorship: The Politics of Memory in the Spanish Transition to Democracy*. Portada Hispánica 8, ed. **Joan Ramon Resina**, pp. 43–64. Atlanta, Ga.: Rodopi, 2000.

Simms, Katharine. "The Norman Invasion and the Gaelic Recovery." In *The Oxford Illustrated History of Ireland*, ed. **R[obert] F[itzroy] Foster**, pp. 53–103. New York: Oxford Univ. Press, 1989.

Smith, Erminnie. "Myths of the Iroquois." In *Second Annual Report of the Bureau of Ethnology to the Secretary of the Smithsonian Institution, 1880–81*, dir. J. W. Powell, pp. 51–116. Washington, D.C.: Government Printing Office, 1883.

Smyrl, Marc. "France: Challenging the Unitary State." In *Federalism and Territorial Cleavages*, ed. **Ugo M. Amoretti** and **Nancy Bermeo**, pp. 201–25. Baltimore, Md.: Johns Hopkins Univ. Press, 2004.

Snow, Dean R. "Late Prehistory of the East Coast," In *Handbook of North American Indians*, gen. ed. **William G. Sturtevant**. vol. 15, Northeast, ed.

Bruce G. Trigger, pp. 58–69. Washington, D.C.: Smithsonian Institution, 1978.

"Speckled Snake's (Cherokee) Reply to President Jackson, 1830." In *Major Problems in American Indian History: Documents and Essays*, ed. **Albert L. Hurtado** and **Peter Iverson**. Major Problems in American History Series, 2nd ed., p. 204. Boston: Houghton Mifflin Co., 2001.

Stepan, Alfred. "Federalism and Democracy: Beyond the U.S. Model." In *Federalism and Territorial Cleavages*, ed. **Ugo M. Amoretti** and **Nancy Bermeo**, pp. 441–56. Baltimore, Md.: Johns Hopkins Univ. Press, 2004.

Story, Jonathan. "Spain's External Relations Redefined." In *Democratic Spain: Reshaping External Relations in a Changing World*. European Public Policy Series, ed. **Richard Gillespie, Fernando Rodrigo**, and **Jonathan Story**, pp. 30–49. New York: Routledge, 1995.

"Testimony of Pa Kapr Bundu, a subchief at Rogbongba, in Yoni (Mamela) chiefdom (recorded at Rogbongba, 11 November 1970)." In **Kenneth C. Wylie**, *The Political Kingdoms of the Temne: Temne Government in Sierra Leone, 1825–1910*, pp. 230–1. New York: Africana Publishing Co., 1977.

"The Texas State Constitution of 1845, August 28, 1845." In *Documents of Texas History*, ed. **Ernest Wallace, David M. Vigness**, and **George B. Ward**. Fred H. and Ella Mae Moore Texas History Reprint Series, pp. 149–59. 1963. Reprint, Austin: Texas State Historical Association, 2002.

Tornel y Mendívil, José María. "Relations between Texas, the United States of America, and Mexico." In *The Mexican Side of the Texan Revolution*, trans. with notes by **Carlos E. Castañeda**, pp. 284–378. Dallas, Tex.: P. L. Turner Co., 1928.

Torres-Saillant, Silvio. "Epilogue: Problematic Paradigms: Racial Diversity and Corporate Identity in the Latino Community." In *Latinos: Remaking America*, ed. **Marcelo M. Suárez-Orozco** and **Mariela M. Páez**, pp. 435–55. Berkeley and Los Angeles: Univ. of California Press with the David Rockefeller Center for Latin American Studies, Harvard Univ., 2002.

"A Treaty Held at the Town of Lancaster, in Pennsylvania . . . in June, 1744." In **Cadwallader Colden**, *The History of the Five Indian Nations of Canada, Which Are Dependent on the Province of New York, and Are a Barrier between the English and the French in that Part of the World*. vol. 2, pp. 117–204. New York: Allerton Book Co., 1922.

"The Treaty Held with the Indians of the Six Nations at Philadelphia in July, 1742." In **Cadwallader Colden**, *The History of the Five Indian Nations of Canada, Which Are Dependent on the Province of New York, and Are a Barrier between the English and the French in that Part of the World*. vol. 2, pp. 61–116. New York: Allerton Book Co., 1922.

Trejo, Guillermo. "Mexico: The Indigenous Foundations of Indigenous Mobilization and Ethnoterritorial Conflict (1975–2000)." In *Federalism and*

Territorial Cleavages, ed. **Ugo M. Amoretti** and **Nancy Bermeo**, pp. 355–86. Baltimore, Md.: Johns Hopkins Univ. Press, 2004.

Tuck, James A. "Northern Iroquoian Prehistory." In *Handbook of North American Indians*, gen. ed. **William G. Sturtevant**. vol. 15, *Northeast*, ed. **Bruce G. Trigger**, pp. 322–33. Washington, D.C.: Smithsonian Institution, 1978.

Valderrama Ruoy, Pablo. "The Totonac." In *Native Peoples of the Gulf Coast of Mexico*, ed. **Alan R. Sandstrom** and **E. Hugo García Valencia**. Native Peoples of the Americas, pp. 187–210. Tucson: Univ. of Arizona Press, 2005.

Van Deursen, A. T. "The Dutch Republic, 1588–1780." In *History of the Low Countries*, ed. **J.C.H. Blom** and **E. Lamberts**, trans. **James C. Kennedy**, pp. 142–218. New York: Berghahn Books, 1999.

Watts, Ronald L. "Comparing Forms of Federal Partnerships." In *Theories of Federalism: A Reader*, ed. **Dimitrios Karmis** and **Wayne Norman**, pp. 233–53. New York: St. Martin's Press, Palgrave Macmillan, 2005.

JOURNAL ARTICLES

Bishop, Charles A. "Territoriality among Northeastern Algonquians," *Anthropologica* **28**(spec. issue, nos. 1–2, 1986): 37–63.

Brown, Judith K. "Economic Organization and the Position of Women among the Iroquois." *Ethnohistory* **17**(Summer–Fall 1970): 151–67.

Capdevila, Luc. "Violence et société en Bretagne dans l'aprè-Libération (automne 1944–automne 1945)," *Modern and Contemporary France* **7**(no. 4, 1999): 443–56.

Dunaway, Wilma A. "Ethnic Conflict in the Modern World System: The Dialectics of Counter-Hegemonic Resistance in an Age of Transition." *Journal of World-Systems Research* **9**(Winter 2003): 2–34.

González-Casanova, Pablo. "Internal Colonialism and National Development." *Studies in Comparative International Development* **1**(no. 4, 1965): 27–37.

———. "Sociedad Plural, Colonialismo Interno y Desarrollo." *America Latina* **6**(no. 3, 1963): 15–32.

Grinde, Donald A., Jr. and **Lee, Bruce E.** "Sauce for the Goose: Demand and Definitions for 'Proof' Regarding the Iroquois and Democracy." *William and Mary Quarterly* **53**(July 1996): 621–36.

Gutiérrez, Ramón. "Internal Colonialism: The History of a Theory." *Du Bois Review: Social Science Research on Race* **1**(Summer 2004): 281–96.

Hall, Thomas D. "Ethnic Conflict as a Global Social Problem," in *Handbook of Social Problems: A Comparative International Perspective*, ed. **George Ritzer** (Thousand Oaks, Calif.: Sage Publications, 2004), 141–2.

———. "The Effects of Incorporation into World Systems on Ethnic Processes: Lessons from the Ancient World for the Contemporary World," *International Political Science Review* **19**(no. 3, 1998): 251–62.

Henige, David. "Can a Myth Be Astronomically Dated?" *American Indian Culture and Research Journal* **23**(no. 4, 1999): 127–57.

Hind, Robert J. "The Internal Colonial Concept." *Comparative Studies in Society and History* **26**(July 1984): 543–68.

Hlophe, Stephen. "The Significance of Barth and Geertz' Model of Ethnicity in the Analysis of Nationalism in Liberia." *La Revue canadienne des Études africaines/ Canadian Journal of African Studies* **7**(no. 2, 1973): 237–56.

Hollis, Shirley A. "Crafting Europe's 'Clean Slate' Advantage: World-System Expansion and the Indigenous Mississippians of North America." *American Indian Culture and Research Journal* **28**(no. 3, 2004): 77–101.

Johanson, Bruce E. "Native American Societies and the Evolution of Democracy in America, 1600–1800." *Ethnohistory* **37**(Summer 1990): 279–90.

Laczko, Leslie. "Attitudes towards Aboriginal Issues in Canada: The Changing Role of the Language Cleavage." *Québec Studies* **23**(Spring 1997): 3–12.

Mann, Barbara A. and Fields, Jerry L. "A Sign in the Sky: Dating the League of the Haudenosaune." *American Indian Culture and Research Journal* **21**(no. 2, 1997): 105–63.

Payne, Samuel B. "The Iroquois League, the Articles of Confederation, and the Constitution." *William and Mary Quarterly* **53**(July 1996): 605–20.

Stavenhagen, Rodolfo. "Classes, Colonialism, and Acculturation." *Studies in Comparative International Development* **1**(no. 6, 1965): 53–77.

INTERNET SOURCES

BBC News. "Spain Dig Yields Ancient European."Available from news. bbc.co.uk/1/hi/sci/tech/7313005. stm, accessed **21** December 2008.

———. "Timeline, Sierra Leone: A Chronology of Key Events." Available from news.bbc.co.uk/1/hi/world/Africa/country_profiles/1065898.stm, accessed 30 June 2005.

Central Intelligence Agency. "World Factbook – Liberia." Available from www.cia.gov/cia/publications/factbook/geos/li.html, accessed 28 June 2005.

Department of Foreign Affairs. "Economic Community of West African States." Available from www.dfa.za/for-relations/multilateral/ecowas.htm, accessed 31 December 2003.

———. "Liberia: President Orders Ministers to Oust Corrupt Staff. Available from allafrica.com/stories/200604280505.html, accessed 1 May 2006.

Library of Congress. *The Federalist Papers*, no. 14. Available from Thomas.loc.gov/home/histdox/fed_14.html, accessed 1 July 2008.

U.S. Department of State, Bureau of African Affairs. "Background Note: Senegal." Available from www.state.gov/r/pa/ei/bgn/2862.htm, accessed 21 December 2003.

———. "Background Note: Sierra Leone." Available from www.state.gov/r/pa/ei/bgn/5475.htm, accessed 19 December 2003.

U.S. Institute of Peace, "The United Nations and Western Sahara: A Never-Ending Affair," *Special Report* **166** (July 2006), pp. 18–20. Available from www.usip.org/pubs/specialreports/sr16.pdf, accessed 24 July 2008.

NEWSPAPER ARTICLES

Diouf, Nafi. "Debt Relief Means Electricity for Senegal." *Seattle Post-Intelligencer*, 15 June 2005.

McWilliams, Carey. "A Way Out of the Energy Squeeze?" *Los Angeles Times*, 8 April 1979.

Maharaj, Davan. "Liberian President Is Sought on War Crimes Indictment." *Los Angeles Times*, 5 June 2003.

Ranchero (Corpus Christi), 12 January 1861.

Wade, Nicholas. "Gene Test Shows Spain's Jewish and Muslim Mix." *New York Times*, 5 December 2008.

DISSERTATIONS AND SPEECH

Meschke, Amy. "Women's Lives through Women's Wills in the Spanish and Mexican Borderlands, 1750–1846." Ph.D. diss., Southern Methodist Univ., 2004.

Meyer, Jean. "Historia, nación y región." Keynote address presented at the 25th Coloquio de antropología e historia regionales, Colegio de Michoacán, México, 22 October 2003.

Ramírez, José A. "'To the Line of Fire, Mexican-Texans': The Tejano Community and World War I." Ph.D. diss., Southern Methodist Univ., 2007.

INDEX